American Heathens

Western Histories
William Deverell, series editor
Published for the Huntington-USC Institute on California and the West
by University of California Press and the Huntington Library

American Heathens

Religion, Race, and Reconstruction in California

Joshua Paddison

Published for the Huntington-USC Institute on California and the West
by University of California Press, Berkeley, California, and
the Huntington Library, San Marino, California

Interior design by Doug Davis
Series jacket design by Lia Tjandra
Copyediting by Jean Patterson

Printed in the United States by Thomson-Shore

Library of Congress Cataloging-in-Publication Data

Paddison, Joshua, 1974-
  American heathens : religion, race, and reconstruction in California /
Joshua Paddison.
      p. cm. — (Western histories ; 3)
  Includes bibliographical references and index.
  ISBN 978-0-87328-244-4 (alk. paper)
1. California—Ethnic relations—History—19th century.
2. California—Race relations—History—19th century. 3. Indians of
North America—California—History—19th century. 4. Chinese
Americans—California—History—19th century. 5. California—
History—1850-1950. 6. Reconstruction (U.S. history, 1865-1877)
—California. 7. California—Religion—19th century. I. Title.
  F870.A1P34 2012
  305.8009794—dc23
                          2011029747

CONTENTS

ILLUSTRATIONS

As for ourselves, what shall we say? Let the slaves speak; let the dispossessed Indians speak; let the Chinaman speak. Where is the Christianity of this country?

—Henry Ward Beecher, 1882

Figure 1. The American Missionary Association, formed in 1846 in opposition to slavery, widened its purview to include "the Whites, the Negroes, the Indians, and the Chinese" during the late 1860s. The March 1882 cover of *American Missionary* reflected the association's ambitions for multiracial "uplift." Courtesy of Cornell University Library, Making of America Digital Collection.

Introduction

The title of this book would have puzzled most people living in the United States during the years following the Civil War. The notion of an "American heathen" would have seemed paradoxical. In an era when Americans were debating the contours of national identity more violently than in any period since the formation of the republic, most people agreed that heathens could not be American. The term "heathen," long used in North America as an epithet and a marker of both religious and racial difference, meant (to judge by Noah Webster's *American Dictionary of the English Language*) not simply "pagan" and "unacquainted with the true God" but also "rude, illiterate, wild, uncivilized, barbarous, savage, cruel, [and] rapacious," the very opposite of how most Americans liked to envision themselves. The Fourteenth and Fifteenth Amendments, ratified in 1868 and 1870 respectively, reflected and solidified this attitude when they expanded the circle of citizenship to include largely Christianized African American men but not the nation's mostly unconverted Native American and Asian American men. Along with all women, those men the nation deemed heathens continued to occupy a category of humanity denied suffrage, the right to hold public office, and other benefits of full citizenship.[1]

Yet there were some in the United States, especially in the immediate postwar years, who imagined a wider circle. New England abolitionist Wendell Phillips, for example, when celebrating the passage of the Fifteenth Amendment, reminded his fellow activists that the struggle for human rights in the United States had only just begun. Republicans had finally inserted "the sublime pledge of our fathers, that all men were created equal," into the Constitution, he said, but "it remains for this generation and the next to apply it. With infinite toil, at vast expense, sealing the charter with five hundred thousand graves, we have made it true of the negro. With what toil, at what cost, with what devotion, you will make it true of the Indian and the Chinese, the coming years will tell." For Phillips and those reformers, ministers, and Republicans who shared his views, the ongoing Reconstruction project should not stop with the transformation of the South and the integration of African American men into the body politic. Rather, it should be a nationwide endeavor aimed at purifying the United States not only of the sins of slavery and secession but also of prejudice against Indians and the Chinese. Though generally agreeing with the American majority that these groups did currently deserve to be called heathenish, reformers insisted that they were at least as ready for uplift and as capable to handle the burdens of citizenship as freed slaves.[2]

So was "American heathens" a contradiction in terms or a goal yet to be achieved? For those living in the complex racial and religious cauldron of the trans-Mississippi West, the question was of critical importance. In 1848, the Treaty of Guadalupe Hidalgo had ended the Mexican-American War and extended "all the rights of citizens" to Mexicans living in what was thereafter the American southwest. In this absorption of citizens, Mexicans were legally classified as whites, even though most were viewed otherwise, as mestizos; this policy bent but did not break the nation's commitment to white male suffrage. In addition to these semi-privileged Catholic Mexicans and a small but vocal free black population, the West was home to the vast majority of the nation's Indians and Chinese immigrants, few of whom had adopted Christianity.[3]

These extraordinary demographics, along with the newness of institutions and the propelling force of Manifest Destiny, fostered particularly brutal expressions of discriminatory legislation and violence in the West, carried out by white "pioneers." This brutality reached its height in California in the 1850s, when state and local governments funded genocidal "pacification" campaigns against Indian groups, the state Board of Land Commissioners oversaw the dispossession of Mexican Americans, and legislators denied African Americans, Indians, and Chinese immigrants the right to vote, hold public office, or testify in court against whites. From the perspective of most of the West's white Protestants, Reconstruction looked to threaten their hard-fought control of the region. With African American men voting in 1870, something unthinkable just a decade earlier, would Indian and Chinese men be next?[4]

The postbellum debate over the status of "heathens" in the United States, waged throughout the nation but with particular ferocity in the West, would center on and in California. Profoundly multiethnic, with a Catholic past and a bloody history of war and racial strife, California stood both geographically and imaginatively at the far edge of the nation during the late nineteenth century. The state's Indians, derided as "Diggers," supposedly represented the worst of a degraded and godless race, ranking "lowest among the aborigines." Its Chinese population, far larger than that of any other state, was rapidly growing. Yet this uniqueness was precisely what made California the ultimate testing ground for what could be considered American. Hailed for its promise and feared as a precedent, California—as much as the South—was a central battleground in the national struggle to define citizenship that followed the Civil War.[5]

This is the story of that struggle, in which a wide range of groups contested the proper place of Indians and the Chinese in church, politics, and society. White Protestants—officials, journalists, scientists, women's rights activists, missionaries, and especially clergymen—played central roles, but African American, Mexican American, and Irish Catholic community leaders also shaped the debate. Those Indians and Chinese immigrants who joined Christian churches made use of theological and denominational resources in their own fights for political voice, refuting racist assumptions with their lives, words, and faith. Like the "Negro question," the Indian and Chinese questions carried powerful religious and racial meanings for all Americans.

Lumped together due to their supposedly pagan beliefs, Indians and the Chinese were also linked in the prevailing racial thought of the day. By the 1860s, ethnologists' early confusion over the origins of the two groups had been replaced by a widespread notion that Indians and the Chinese had arisen from the same genetic stock in Asia. In the *Atlantic Monthly* in 1874, for example, journalist Stephen Powers compared the physiognomies, work habits, religious practices, and linguistic patterns of California Indians and immigrants from China, declaring that the two races had a common lineage.[6] Unlike African Americans, Mexican Americans, and Irish immigrants, who all suffered from being considered non- or off-white but who could try to use their Christianity to align themselves with dominant American society, unconverted Indians and Asians were doubly marked as inferior. This bred, at times, conflict between the two groups, as in 1855, when San Francisco merchant Lai Chun-chuen objected to being treated the same as "uncivilized" Indians who "wear neither clothes nor shoes" and "live in wild places and in caves." Firmly located outside both whiteness and Christianity in the public imagination, Indians and the Chinese both tested the limits of national belonging like no other groups.[7]

This is not to overlook significant ways in which perceptions of the two groups differed. Racialization in the United States was always comparative, and nineteenth-century observers constantly juxtaposed Indians and the Chinese with each other and with African Americans, Mexicans, the Irish, and others. In the late nineteenth century, Indians and the Chinese appeared to be on divergent paths: Indians were imagined to be dying out, while the Chinese seemed to be arriving in ever-greater numbers. Both groups were derided as pagan and idolatrous, but Indians seemed to possess no recognizable religion, while the Chinese built conspicuous Buddhist temples. The Chinese were citizens of a foreign nation and were said to carry an allegiance to China impossible to root out, whereas the sovereignty of most Indian nations was no longer recognized by the U.S. government by the late 1860s. This also meant that Indians could benefit from having been born on what was now American soil. A long history of interaction with Euro-American Christianity, accompanied as it was by intermarriage and sexual relations with whites, made Indians appear more culturally and racially mutable than the supposedly stagnant, unassimilable Chinese. These different perceptions shaped governmental policy toward the two groups, leading to divergent "solutions" in the 1880s: exclusion and expulsion for the Chinese and cultural extermination campaigns in the form of allotment and re-education for Indians.[8]

In tracking how the nation arrived at those "solutions" to the heathen question, this book makes two main arguments. The first is that religion was central to formations of race and citizenship in the post–Civil War United States. Historians typically explain racial formation in terms of underlying economic forces—that is, contests over labor, land, resources, and markets—and focus on the maintenance of race through law and science. Following the lead of Alexander Saxton's *The Indispensable Enemy*, published in 1971, scholars who have studied the anti-Chinese movement often emphasize labor competition and the nationwide recession that hit in 1873.[9] Similarly, white–Indian conflict in the West has often been portrayed as driven by Americans' desire for land and natural resources. Though the strength of such economic forces is undeniable, attention to the public and private discourses of the nineteenth century—the way in which Americans talked, wrote, and thought—shows the powerful ways religion shaped the day-to-day expression of those forces.

In recent years, U.S. historians have paid more attention to the interrelationship of religion, race, and citizenship, exploring how those categories were dynamic, contested, and embedded in local social and political contexts.[10] This has long been apparent to historians of African Americans and of the South, who have shown how Christian rhetoric helped naturalize and entrench slavery and Jim Crow, even as black ministers and intellectuals employed Christianity as a tool to combat racism.[11] Scholars of the West, in comparison, have largely ignored how religious ideas shaped racial politics. This book shows that religion in the West was no less implicated in the construction of racial hierarchies, no less available as a tool to racialized groups, and no less central to people's racial beliefs and anxieties.[12]

At the same time, other markers of identity were important, tangling with notions of religion and race. Racial categories were almost always gendered; likewise, Christianity carried specific meanings for how men and women should behave, dress, and work. Missionaries working among both Indians and the Chinese tried to impart and enforce what they viewed as civilized and godly gender roles. At Indian boarding schools, girls learned such domestic skills as cooking, sewing, and ironing while boys learned how to care for livestock and perform manual labor. Christian manhood required a different set of skills and carried a different set of expectations from Christian womanhood. Missionaries also attempted to control the most intimate aspects of converts' lives, encouraging heterosexuality, monogamy, and Christian marriage while reinforcing larger cultural ideas about which sexual practices were natural. Despite the contradiction, Protestant ministers in California who insisted that unrestricted immigration from China was mandated by God actively supported the government's exclusion of Chinese prostitutes, whom they deemed too sinful to deserve access to the United States. Such arguments fed a larger cultural demonization of all Chinese women for their supposed lasciviousness. At the same time, debates about heathens were in some ways also about class: Both Indians and Chinese "coolies" were imagined as outside, and therefore dangerous to, the nation's newfound commitment to free labor and the expansion of industrial capitalism. A group's religious and racial status tended to rise and fall with its economic fortunes, demonstrated by the fluctuating place of Irish and Mexican American Catholics.

This book's second argument is that Reconstruction was a multiracial and multiregional process of national reimagining. It ended not with the removal of federal troops from the South in 1877 but in a knitting together of North, South, and West around a newly robust white Christian identity during the course of the following decade. This claim prompts historians to rethink their deepest assumptions about Reconstruction. Over the past century, few subjects in American political history have received more attention, yet almost none of this scholarship looks west or beyond black and white.[13] Only in the last few years have historians imagined a "Greater Reconstruction"—or, even more broadly, a post–Civil War "Era of Citizenship"—that stretched beyond the period 1865 to 1877 to encompass the Mexican-American War, the Nez Perce War, conflicts over Mormonism, the Wounded Knee massacre, and other western events.[14]

Far more than simply a set of federal policies concerning the remaking of the South, Reconstruction was a reformulation of nationhood that affected Americans of all races, religions, and regions. California in particular acted as a crucible in which diverse groups debated the boundaries of citizenship before reaching a consensus that helped change federal policy. Widening our conception of Reconstruction to include the West highlights interconnections between African American, Native American, Asian American, and Mexican American history and demonstrates that the multiracial, multireligious encounters that made the West a zone of tumultuous cultural contact also indelibly shaped national politics.

Constructing a continental history of Reconstruction also sheds new light on the hoary question: How radical were the Radical Republicans? Since the 1970s, historians of women and gender have emphasized how Republicans re-inserted male privilege into the Constitution, rejecting woman suffrage by defining voters as "male" in the Fourteenth Amendment.[15] Paying attention to religion—especially to Republicans' marginalization of those they viewed as heathens—reveals a different kind of limit to the Republican plan. Considering the postbellum Republicans' insistence that "the negro's hour" had come, historians should have an expansive view of all whose hour had not yet arrived.[16]

The labels heathen and pagan were applied by European colonists first to Indians and later to imported Africans, and from the colonial period onward the terms always carried connotations of both religious and racial inferiority. Along with deadly pathogens, colonists carried with them to the New World inchoate racial ideas forged by Old World conflicts and empire-building. Crude categories of bodily difference—based on perceptions of such attributes as skin color, stature, and hair texture—helped Europeans make sense of the baffling array of Indian cultures they encountered, lived among, and sought to conquer. Religion played an even larger role in this process as colonists drew on the Bible, especially the genealogies given in Genesis, to understand the origins of Indians and whether or not they possessed souls to be saved. The gradual expansion of African chattel slavery in Anglo America after 1619 similarly drew power from a blend of religious and proto-racial explanations of difference. Over time, British colonists grew more pessimistic about evangelizing Indians and Africans, dismissing them as incapable of true conversion. Similar tensions between impulses to include and to exclude —to proselytize or to deny humanity—shaped European colonists' relations with Indians and Africans throughout North America.[17]

During the years between the American Revolution and the Civil War, the varieties of Christianity that proliferated in the expanding United States responded in polarized ways to the increasingly entrenched and scientifically supported idea of race. By the 1830s, southern slaveholders had re-embraced the spreading of Christianity among the enslaved, emphasizing the godliness of obedience and submission as a means of control. Yet slaves' actual Christianity blended African, European, and American elements to produce a set of beliefs and practices that sustained them through oppression and at times encouraged resistance. In the North, free black community leaders and their white allies used Christianity to wage an ever-more-aggressive battle against slavery and racism. Americans similarly debated the issue of Indian removal on religious grounds, with various sides turning to the Bible for evidence to support their own political vision. However, the forced relocation of the Cherokee Nation, carried out in the late 1830s despite its leaders' high-profile embrace of Christianity, along with the persistence of "negro pews" and other forms of institutionalized discrimination throughout the North, showed how religion's potential to promote equality tended to be out-muscled by its potential to sanctify prejudice. The arrival of immigrants from China in the early 1850s further complicated racial and religious hierarchies, fostering new concerns about America's destiny.[18]

This book's first chapter picks up the story in the 1860s, following the Civil War, when the old category of heathen became inscribed with a new political meaning. The passage of the Fifteenth Amendment shifted the basis of suffrage from white to non-heathen manhood as Republican Party and African American leaders successfully elevated the status of freedmen above Indian and Chinese men partly on the basis of their claims to Christianity. In so doing, however, the Republicans inadvertently opened a potential path to citizenship for Indian and Chinese men, who now looked poised to win political rights through religious conversion. In the West, evangelism among Indians and the Chinese became a politically incendiary act, threatening to turn pagan aliens into Christian voters.

"Of One Blood," the middle section of this book, reveals how Protestant reformers attempted to complete the nation's postwar moral cleansing by extending Reconstruction to the Pacific. Led by Methodist, Congregationalist, and Presbyterian ministers and missionaries, these reformers strove to turn California's Indians and Chinese immigrants into educated Christian citizens, thereby furthering God's plan for universal salvation while making the United States more democratic and safer from the threat of heathen voters. Only when the Chinese were converted to Christianity would they "be an element of our population, not to be feared, but to be desired and welcomed," warned the Presbyterian Board of Foreign Missions. Driven by a belief in the superiority of Protestantism over paganism and Catholicism, these reformers challenged the premises of racial hierarchy and ethnology. They struggled, usually unsuccessfully, to eradicate their own racial prejudices, insisting on a doctrine of human universalism while, in subtler ways, employing notions of racial difference. The hundreds of Indian and Chinese Californians who joined Christian churches during the early 1870s found in Protestantism potent weapons to attack xenophobia and discrimination, despite seldom accepting Christianity on the terms demanded by missionaries. This movement triggered fierce resistance from Democrats and other white supremacists, who used everything from mocking cartoons to church burnings to advance their own Christian arguments in support of immigration restriction, the dissolution of Indian reservations, and the essential irredeemability of heathens.[19]

Chapter 2 focuses on contests over the place of the Chinese, which escalated as a result of surging Protestant evangelism and the passage of the Fifteenth Amendment. Chapter 3 looks at debates about California Indians, which came to center on Round Valley Indian Reservation in Mendocino County, site of the nation's largest Christian revival among Indians during the postbellum era. Chapter 4 examines the anti-Catholic dimensions of this development. Considered neither fully white nor fully Christian, Irish American and Mexican American Catholics tried to use the presence of Indians and the Chinese to establish their own credentials as patriotic white Christians, undermining California's interracialist, anti-Catholic Protestant consensus. By 1876, California's Protestant leadership, which had been nearly unanimous in support of racial uplift, open borders, and the reservation system just a few years before, began to splinter.

The final section, "Fly from Evil," chronicles the birth of a new religioracial consensus in California and the United States during the late 1870s and 1880s. Chapter 5 reveals how the frustrations of mission work, coupled with mounting pressure from politicians, newspapers, labor leaders, and the white members of their congregations, led more and more Protestant ministers to publicly question the capacity of Indians and the Chinese to "rise" to the responsibilities of Christian citizenship. Meanwhile, Indian and Chinese churchgoers continued to shape religious and racial debates by insisting on their right to define Christianity, at times abandoning white-led churches for their own autonomous ones. That insistence contributed to a racist public perception that Indians and the Chinese would not and could not convert to Christianity.

Chapter 6 shows how, by the early 1880s, virtually every church leader in California now publicly supported the restriction of immigration from China and the breaking up of Indian reservations into individual allotments, reversing their previous declarations. San Francisco's Chinatown and Round Valley Indian Reservation both became the foci of congressional hearings that helped lead to the passage of Chinese exclusion in 1882 and the General Allotment Act five years later. California ministers' support for those policies aided their realization, bolstering federal lawmakers' attempts to unite North, South, and West around a shared white male Christian identity. The California dream of a multiracial Protestant society, held by these same reformers in earlier years, had been repudiated.

The seeds of Christian anti-racism had not been entirely rooted out, however. This book's conclusion shows how, in the late 1880s and 1890s, a new generation of Chinese American Protestants in California assumed greater responsibility in their churches, using their influence to combat immigration restriction and racial segregation. In the wake of the General Allotment Act's disastrous effects on California Indian groups, new reformers took up the cause of racial justice. California's religious reform movements of the postbellum era ultimately helped lay the groundwork for a shift away from hard-line racial determinism that would continue throughout the twentieth century and into the twenty-first.

The nation's rejection of Indians and Chinese immigrants as citizens in the 1880s came not as a result of race "trumping" religion. Rather, one religio-racial vision—Christian white male supremacy—triumphed over another that emphasized anti-Catholicism and paternalistic racial uplift. In the nineteenth-century United States, religion and race were mutually constitutive systems, at times blending, at times conflicting, each capable of acting as a metalanguage for the other. Americans debated issues of race within the idiom of Christianity, and competing American Christianities strove for supremacy in the settling of racial questions. Both religion and race divided and classified groups into hierarchies. These hierarchies were often mutually reinforcing, marking African Americans, Indians, Asians, and others as inferior in both racial stock and religious beliefs—body and soul. These hierarchies could also clash; in some formulations, Christianity offered equality for all believers, regardless of race or social position.

Conversion could make outsiders into insiders, not over hundreds of years of evolutionary development but immediately. Bound inextricably together, the Negro, Indian, and Chinese questions all hinged on Christianity's potential for both radical egalitarianism and vicious inequality.

CHAPTER ONE

A New Vision of Citizenship, 1861–1870

On January 28, 1870, the final day of debate on the Fifteenth Amendment in California's senate, attorney and future U.S. senator John S. Hager summed up the state Democrats' scornful opposition. Though the amendment's Republican crafters had carefully limited its extension of suffrage to African American men alone, Hager called attention to California's "greater variety" of racial groups: "we not only have the negro, but the Digger Indian, the Kanaka, the New Zealander, the Lascar, and the Chinese." He wished that national Republican leaders guiding the congressional Reconstruction of the South, "who see so much that is sublime and beautiful in the African, could only see our greater variety here—in the full feather—bedizened, painted, tattooed, or *in puris naturalibus,* as we often see them within our borders and in the streets of our commercial city." According to Hager, those who lived among California's astonishing populace, who faced such "variety" every day, fully knew the perils of abandoning the nation's longstanding commitment to white male suffrage.[1]

His words dripping with sarcasm, Hager went on to wonder aloud why Republicans currently favored voting rights for African American men but not for "the poor Indian"—"is there no tear of sympathy for him?"—nor the Chinese, who "have maintained a Government and attained a civilization superior to the negro." Instead of the Republicans' inconsistent and dangerous position, Hager and the Democrats promoted a continuation of the nation's antebellum definition of citizenship based on white manhood. "I believe this country of ours was destined for the Caucasian— our own white race," he declared. To believe in the equality of the races was to ignore both prevailing scientific theory—"ethnologically and physiologically speaking, must we not concede there are distinctions which we can neither conceal or deny?"—and biblical teachings. "In our Father's house, we are instructed, there are many mansions," said Hager, quoting the Gospel of John. "It might also be said in our Father's family there are many races or species of mankind. We cannot change it by legislation. Leave it gentlemen—leave it where God and the immutable laws of the creation have left it, now and forever. For man cannot cover what God has revealed." Both houses of the legislature proceeded to overwhelmingly vote down the Fifteenth Amendment, a repudiation of racial equality that one assemblyman insisted would "endear California to posterity forever."[2]

As Hager's comments indicate, racial thinking was inextricably intertwined with religious belief in California during the 1860s. Political arguments about race were waged within the battleground of Christianity, shaped by the state's demographic diversity. Hager and other Democrats advanced a version of Christianity that sanctified gendered racial hierarchy. Democrats ensured that the issue of African American civil rights could not be separated from that of other racially marked populations, and they used biblical evidence to bolster their claims that African American, Native American, and Chinese American men—along with all women—were undeserving of full citizenship.

At the same time, Republicans and African American leaders in California offered a competing notion of religio-racial citizenship that was equally hierarchical, but with redrawn categories. They argued that it was not "blackness" but "heathenism" that rendered a man unfit for suffrage, opening the door for generally Christianized African American men to become full citizens while continuing to shut out Indian and Chinese men. Debates in California ran parallel to those in the U.S. Congress, where the state's racial makeup complicated Republican efforts to ratify the Fourteenth and Fifteenth Amendments. Out of these debates came a newly federalized definition of citizenship that delivered suffrage for African American men but further marginalized Indians and the Chinese. A man's right to vote in the United States would no longer hinge on his whiteness but on whether he was or was not a heathen.

"This living baptism of fire and blood": California and the Civil War

The Civil War—like all American military engagements so far—was a holy war, seen during and after as a test of Providence and an extension of God's will. The conflict was especially fraught with monumental and confusing religious meaning, as it pit two not-so-different versions of evangelical Protestant Christianity against each other, with both sides laying claim to the same God's favor. "In great contests each party claims to act in accordance with the will of God," Abraham Lincoln noted in 1862. "Both may be, and one must be, wrong. God cannot be for and against the same thing at the same time."[3] For white southerners, triumph would indicate the wickedness of the North, the godliness of secession, and the fundamental virtue of southern ways of life. Northerners hoped for a victory that would reveal God's anger at disunion, with abolitionists trusting that the war would cleanse America of slavery and perhaps trigger the dawning of the millennium. African Americans throughout the split nation viewed the conflict as the linchpin of God's plan to bring his people out of bondage, as he had done for the ancient Israelites.[4]

The outbreak of war divided California as it did the United States as a whole. An unusual mix of southerners, midwesterners, and New Englanders populated the state, along with Mexican Americans, Native Americans, and immigrants from every continent on earth. Both southern and northern branches of the Methodist and Baptist churches operated in California, and ministers of all denominations used their pulpits to defend their cause, although pro-Union speakers enjoyed increasing support as the war raged on.[5] At state meetings in 1861, for example, the northern Methodists declared that the "moral judgment of the world has never justified a revolution so causeless as this," while the southern Methodists cautiously urged "peace with all men." California's pro-southern voices generally urged Christian pacifism, as when Democratic U.S. senator Milton S. Latham averred, "The Christian religion is one of peace, not of strife and contention."[6]

On the other extreme, Unitarian minister Thomas Starr King toured California, preaching of the war's holiness to packed houses. According to one observer, King's visit to Weaverville in 1861 left the crowd "in ecstasies. . . . Even the men from Virginia and Texas admired him although he lashed the Secessionists without mercy." King portrayed the conflict as "the cause of wrong against right," condemning the South's secession as "a geographical wrong, an economical wrong, a moral wrong, a religious wrong, a war against the American Constitution, against the laws of the globe, against the New Testament, against God."[7] King's constant touring and absolutist rhetoric earned him the reputation of having "saved" California for the Union, a notion he believed held only "one percent of truth," but by September 1861 he could rejoice that San Francisco was "as thoroughly clamped to the government and as warlike as Boston." That same month, a crowd hung William Anderson Scott, a pro-southern Presbyterian minister, in effigy in front of his San Francisco church and banished him from the pulpit after he declared Jefferson Davis "no more a traitor than George Washington" at a meeting of the Presbytery of California.[8]

Although King was a devoted abolitionist, California's loyalty to the Union did not immediately translate into civil rights for the state's small African American population, who had been barred by early state legislatures from voting, testifying against whites in court, serving in the militia, buying public lands, sending their children to public schools, and marrying whites. In 1860, the state's Republican Party opposed only the extension of slavery into new territories, not its continued existence in the South, nor did it support increased political rights for African Americans in California. In the late 1850s, Democrats and Republicans had both claimed to champion free white men, denouncing each other as the "nigger party."[9] Democrats called Republicans "abolitionists" and "fanatics," and each party assailed the other as "nigger worshippers," mixing charges of racial treason with religious heresy. In 1857, Republican gubernatorial candidate Edward Stanly, a slave owner from North Carolina, bizarrely found himself attacked by his opponent for alleged antislavery religious radicalism. Stanly countered that he had "never contended that Slavery was contrary to the teachings of the Bible." State Republicans' religious conservatism, white supremacy, and tolerance for the continuation of slavery in the South merely mirrored the national party's positions; Lincoln himself repeated at his 1861 inauguration what he had promised on the campaign trail: "I have no purpose, directly or indirectly, to interfere with the institution of slavery in the States where it exists."[10]

As the war dragged on, however, California's Republicans followed the national party toward an uneasy support of African American political rights. After using cries of "niggerism" to elect a Republican governor and three congressmen and to assume control of the state legislature in 1861, the party gradually embraced abolition after being forced to by Lincoln's Emancipation Proclamation of January 1, 1863. In addition to being a military necessity, emancipation began to appeal to white Californians who hoped that the end of slavery would curb further black migration to the state. "Give the black man liberty at his own home in the sunny South, and he will surely not seek the cold climate of the North to better his condition," one Republican told a San Francisco audience in 1864. State Republicans, who christened themselves "Unionists" from 1863 to 1867 to attract anti-secession Democrats, also discovered in abolition a way to gain the moral high ground on Democrats. After generally ignoring the issue of slavery in earlier years, the 1864 Unionist–

Republican platform declared slavery "an institution condemned by God and abhorrent to humanity, a stain upon the nation's honor and a clog to its material progress." In this spirit, the Unionist–Republican controlled state legislature repealed a restriction on African American legal testimony against whites in March 1863 and ensured that California ratified the Thirteenth Amendment abolishing slavery in 1865.[11]

After years of ignored petitions and unanswered prayers, California's leading African Americans celebrated the swift changes brought by the Civil War as outpourings of God's blessings to the faithful. In August 1863, Rev. Thomas Myers Decatur Ward rejoiced with his congregation at San Francisco African Methodist Episcopal Church. Born free in southern Pennsylvania not far from Gettysburg, with a "voice full-toned and sonorous, its intonations at times almost musical," T. M. D. Ward proclaimed the Civil War a divine mechanism of deliverance for America's "dark-browed, outcast sons and daughters." He insisted, "The nation shall emerge from this conflict regenerated and redeemed. This living baptism of fire and blood, will purge us from the tin and dross of inhumanity and wrong." Missionary Elder of the Pacific Coast since the gold rush and a tireless founder of churches up and down California, Ward had guided a decade of activism and spiritual development in the state, and now, through war, God appeared to be finally rewarding that faithful work. "The terrible black laws which, one year ago, disgraced our State code, thanks to God, no longer crimson the cheek of the State with shame," he said. "To the eternal God belongs all the praise."[12] Rallying support for a war they viewed as God's punishment for "the national sin of Slavery," Ward and other African American spokesmen regarded their political victories as "so many steps forward in the right direction, which God, justice, humanity, and the progress and safety of this nation alike demanded."[13]

In addition to expressing what were no doubt deeply felt private religious convictions, such wartime proclamations of holy deliverance and divine favor served public, political functions. To members of his San Francisco congregation, Ward's themes of optimism, redemption, and rescue echoed familiar tropes long used by black ministers to encourage solidarity and activism. By ascribing emancipation, the progress of the war, and political victories to Providence, California's leading African Americans continued an antebellum strategy of positioning themselves as pious, patriotic Christians deserving full citizenship. They wanted to lend a "hard, horny hand of toil" to the Christian regeneration of the state, if white Californians would only accept it.[14]

"Negro for breakfast, Chinese for dinner, and Digger Indian for supper": Postwar Politics

By 1864 it was clear that, however far they had come, the journey ahead for African Americans in California would still be arduous. Lecturer Emma Hardings acknowledged that, like the Israelites after escaping bondage in Egypt, African Americans now faced their own path through the desert: "the way ahead is open to us, but it lays through a wilderness where we must suffer and endure; over which we must fight our way, midst hardships and difficulties, until we convince the American people that we are as capable of enjoying all the rights of citizenship as themselves." Indeed, convincing Californians that African Americans deserved "all the rights of citizenship" as promised by the Civil Rights Act of 1866 and the Fourteenth and Fifteenth Amendments occupied the state's African American leadership for the second half of the 1860s. Through a flurry of conferences, parades, petitions, speeches, sermons, letters, and editorials, California's black activists strove to push California in line with the Radical Republican agenda of the Northeast.[15]

California's African Americans continued to rest their arguments for civil rights on their ennobling Christianity, which they insisted would make them responsible citizens. Privately, at such events as the State Convention of Colored Citizens in 1865, leaders urged each other to "maintain temperance," "discountenance licentiousness," and "develope the highest state of Christian morals." They challenged whites to live up to their professed Christian ideals, appealing to "the Legislature of a Christian people for our right of suffrage, upon the broad principle of human justice, as taught by the great rule, 'Do unto others as you would they should do unto you.'"[16]

Such arguments increasingly fell on deaf ears, however. Political developments in the postwar years revealed the year 1865 to be not the beginning of popular support for African American civil rights in California but in fact the zenith of the movement's popularity. After the war, California's Democratic Party reunited in opposition to congressional Reconstruction. It waged a renewed campaign of Christian white supremacy in 1867 and stormed back into power, retaking the governorship, the assembly, and nearly the senate, as part of a national backlash against Republicans.[17] At the local level, San Francisco officials re-excluded African Americans from the city's Fourth of July parade in 1866 after inviting them to participate for the first time the previous year. Outgoing Unionist–Republican governor Frederick Low urged the legislature to ratify the Fourteenth Amendment but, supported by new Democratic governor Henry H. Haight, legislators refused to bring the ratification resolution to a vote. In January 1870, after the Democrats had gained even more power in the 1869 election, John S. Hager and other legislators rejected the Fifteenth Amendment outright, making California one of only six states—along with New Jersey, Delaware, Kentucky, Maryland, and Tennessee—to vote down the amendment.[18]

The Democratic Party re-ascended to power in the late 1860s by linking African American civil rights to two larger and more troublesome populations in California: Indians and especially the Chinese. There were, after all, fewer than 5,000 African Americans in the state in 1870 (.7 percent of the population), according to the federal census, while the Chinese numbered almost 50,000 (8 percent) and Indians about 30,000 (5 percent).[19] Whereas Mexican Americans were legally considered white under the terms of the Treaty of Guadalupe Hidalgo, African Americans, Indians, and the Chinese had been legally lumped together since the 1854 state supreme court case *People v. Hall*. In that decision, the court had ruled that Chinese residents could not provide testimony in court against whites because they, like Indians, fell into the category "black," which "must be taken as contradistinguished from white, and necessarily excludes all races other than the Caucasian."[20]

Extending this logic, postwar Democrats insisted that suffrage for African American men would inevitably lead to the granting of those rights to Indians and the Chinese, and they forecasted a future for California in which whites would be outnumbered and oppressed. The 1867 Democratic platform held that Republicans' supposed hopes for "the suffrages of negroes, Chinese, and Indians . . . if carried into practice, would end in the degradation of the white race and the speedy destruction of the government." The Democrats summarized their message in a cartoon—widely distributed as a letter sheet—depicting George C. Gorham, the Republican gubernatorial candidate in 1867, holding an Indian man, a Chinese man, and an African American man on his shoulders, while Brother Jonathan—a precursor to Uncle Sam—warns him, "The load you are carrying will sink you to perdition, where you belong." Meanwhile, a Republican Party operative leads an ape to be added to the stack, posing the ethnologically vexing question: Where exactly is the dividing line between human and animal, once you get this far down the racial hierarchy?[21]

Democrats fought against African American civil rights by creating a powerful set of rhetorical oppositions pitting whites against African Americans, Indians, and the Chinese: light versus dark, piety versus sinfulness, holiness versus beastliness, individuality versus aggregation, marriage and

Figure 2. Distributed as a letter sheet by Democrats in 1867, "The Reconstruction Policy of Congress, as Illustrated in California" portrayed Republican gubernatorial candidate George C. Gorham as a radical who would upend the nation's doctrine of white male suffrage. Courtesy of the Bancroft Library, University of California, Berkeley.

family versus polygamy and solitude. Senator Eugene Casserly argued that the Fifteenth Amendment would mean "suffrage to the Chinaman in this and every other State," and he contrasted "the Chinaman"—who was "tainted" by a "leprosy of sin not fit to be named among men"—with the "intelligent, progressive working man of California": "at his side is the partner of his life, linked to him in the golden round of Christian marriage, and about them rise up sons and daughters." The Democratic San Francisco *Examiner* denounced the Civil Rights Act of 1866 as "an infamous, blasphemous and beastly attempt to break down the barriers which God Almighty has erected, and to mongrelize, debase and degrade distinct natural species, which, in His wisdom, He has made separate." Universal manhood suffrage, Democrats maintained, ran counter to natural law and God's law.[22]

This onslaught put state Republicans on the defensive. They de-emphasized African American civil rights—going so far as to announce in their 1869 platform that "the negro question has ceased to be an element in American politics"—and took great pains to reassure voters that, Democratic claims to the contrary, they did not favor extending suffrage to either Indians or the Chinese. Some Republicans rejected African American suffrage as well, especially when campaigning in more conservative areas of the state. "This is not an issue in this campaign," complained Frank M. Pixley from gold country in 1867. "It has not been made so by the State Convention; and though Haight says we are in favor of giving to the Mongolian and negro the right of elective franchise, as well as to the Digger Indian, I deny the charge in toto." Lacking a war to unite them, the Unionist coalition of Radical Republicans, moderates, and pro-war Democrats splintered in 1867, hastened by the explosive issue of racial suffrage. Radicals reassumed the Republican name and, at their July 1867 convention, declared themselves both in favor of black male voting rights and "unqualifiedly opposed to coolie labor."[23]

To explain the contradiction of favoring suffrage for African American men but not Indian and Chinese men, Republicans pointed to African Americans' service to the Union during the Civil War, their English-language skills, their American nativity, and especially their Christianity, which supposedly equipped them for citizenship and elevated them above pagans.[24] Questioned in Congress by Democrat William Ellis Niblack as to why the Chinese should not also benefit from the Fourteenth Amendment, California's Representative William Higby replied, "The Chinese are nothing but a pagan race. . . . They bring their clay and wooden gods with them to this country, and as we are a free and tolerant people, we permit them to bow down and worship them." When Niblack protested that "the negro is of a pagan race, and is a pagan before he came here," Higby replied, "But he is not a pagan now. The negro is as much a native of this country as the gentleman or myself." Republicans had originated this strategy during earlier debates in the California legislature over the state's testimony restrictions. William H. Sears had argued in 1862 that African Americans, unlike the Chinese, "speak the same language and profess the same religion that we do," and therefore deserved full testimony rights.[25]

George C. Gorham's doomed run for governor in 1867 demonstrated the difficult tightrope Republicans walked. Gorham supported African American suffrage and, early in the campaign, declared himself sympathetic to the plight of Chinese "Coolies" because, "I believe in the christian religion, and that rests upon the universal fatherhood of God and the universal brotherhood of man. The same God created both Europeans and Asiatics." Gorham's religious liberalism—perhaps bolstered by his close ties to the Central Pacific Railroad, which relied on Chinese labor—opened him to a barrage of vituperation from Democrats, who quipped that he favored voting rights for "Chinese, Niggers and Diggers."[26]

As the campaign wore on, Gorham increasingly emphasized his opposition to Indian and Chinese suffrage. He tried to carve out a middle position on Chinese immigration by denouncing the importation of "slaves" but supporting the right of free Chinese migrants to come. In reference to the cartoon depicting him with "Sambo," "John Chinaman," and "Lo, the poor Indian" on his shoulders, Gorham declared that he "could go through the campaign with the weights they had placed upon me if they wouldn't place a Copperhead upon the top of the whole." The election results showed that he could not, in fact, bear the weight. After Haight beat Gorham by ten percentage points, Gorham's supporters acknowledged that it was his "outspoken advocacy of *the brotherhood of man*" that had cost him the election.[27] No major candidate from either party in California would display as much support for the Chinese for the remainder of the nineteenth century. Gorham's notion of "the universal fatherhood of God and the universal brotherhood of man" would be mocked in California political circles for two decades.[28]

Facing Democratic assaults, African American leaders hastened to separate their plight from that of Indians and the Chinese. "In their speeches they have given us Negro for breakfast, Chinese for dinner, and Digger Indian for supper, until such miserable twaddle have become sickening to all sensible men," complained newspaper editor Peter Anderson.

African American leaders aggressively cooperated with the Republican strategy of using Christian rhetoric to advance their cause. This tack was a continuation of their earlier arguments for civil rights, which had emphasized their moral superiority to Indians and the Chinese even while in theory condemning all forms of prejudice. In 1862, Anderson, after declaring the lack of full testimony rights given to Indians and the Chinese "inhuman, barbarous and unjust," had offered a "more plausible excuse" than race for why those groups should be deprived: "they being heathens and not comprehending the nature and obligation of our oath." In contrast, Anderson asserted, "The Negro is a Christian: there is a strong religious sentiment in his nature, a feeling of awe and reverence for the sanctity of an oath which renders his judicial testimony sacred to him." Similarly, an African American visitor to Hoopa Valley Indian Reservation reported in 1863 that, despite the "thousands of dollars issued to alleviate the wants of this species of humanity," the Indians were "sinking lower in the scale of moral, physical and intellectual degradation." African Americans, on the other hand, "without these thousands of dollars ... have plodded on slowly, yet steadily in the pathway of Christian civilization and improvements." In the early 1860s, African American spokesmen had displayed an ambivalent attitude toward Indians and the Chinese, combining Christian sympathy with Christian disdain for their backwardness and pagan beliefs.[29]

This ambivalence curdled during the postwar period, when the desperate political climate pushed African American leaders to intensify their attacks on especially the Chinese. Many African American newspapers throughout the country demonized the Chinese during these years, but the pages of the *Elevator* and the *Pacific Appeal,* San Francisco's two black papers, became particularly filled with anti-Chinese diatribes. Writers assailed the Chinese for being "alien to our customs, habits and language, heathen in their worship, and naturally licentious." They complained that they, "native Christian Americans," were lumped with "foreign heathens." Bombarded by Democratic rhetoric, California's African American leaders turned Indians and the Chinese into foils against which they asserted their own superior Christianity, patriotism, and modernity. Whatever their differences, Democrats, Republicans, and African American spokesmen agreed that Indians and the Chinese were unfit for citizenship.[30]

As was typical throughout the North, California's white Protestant leaders generally supported Reconstruction and the Republican Party. State Methodists and Congregationalists both established committees to raise money for freed southern slaves following the Civil War. During the pivotal political campaign of 1867, many Protestant church leaders tried to put the weight of Christianity behind Gorham and the Republicans. Methodist minister Henry Cox campaigned alongside Gorham, declaring it his duty as a Christian to support "that party which advocated the widest liberty and broadest freedom" and insisting that he "could not talk religion without politics, nor politics without religion." Cox's activism earned him scorn from Democrats, who denounced him for worshipping at the "idolatrous political altar of Mongrelism." One writer for the San Francisco *Examiner* lambasted Cox for foolishly trying to convince voters that "Gorham is the real Moses to lead the sluggish and idle Canaanites, Asiatics and Diggers to a treasury overflowing with milk and honey." Despite the efforts of Cox and other Protestant ministers, Californians rejected the Republicans' plans, pushing the party further and further away from issues of racial justice.[31]

"A pagan and heathenish class": California, Federal Reconstruction, and Gender

These debates in California echoed debates *about* California occurring at the national level, as lawmakers strove to replace the hazy antebellum definition of citizenship, which had varied from state to state, with a new set of uniform federal parameters.[32] Between 1865 and 1870, congressional deliberations of Reconstruction returned repeatedly to the prospect of extending political rights to California's Indians and the Chinese. Considering the Fourteenth Amendment, Pennsylvania's Edgar Cowan wondered, "What is its length and breadth? . . . Is the child of the Chinese immigrant in California a citizen?" sparking a discussion of the advisability of Chinese American citizenship. The debate soon turned to the status of Indians, with Wisconsin's James Rood Doolittle warning that the amendment "would bring in all the Digger Indians of California." Discussion of the Fifteenth Amendment became similarly embroiled by debate over differences between "the white race and the black race and the yellow race and the red race." Ultimately, the wordings of the amendments that went forward to the states were compromises hammered out by various factions of the Republican Party with an eye toward securing ratification. Like their counterparts in California, national Republicans were willing—when not eager—to limit the benefits of Reconstruction to African American men.[33]

    An exchange in 1869 between Frederick T. Frelinghuysen, a Republican senator from New Jersey, and Thomas A. Hendricks, a Democrat from Indiana, illustrates the competing religio-racial visions of the two parties. Debating the Fifteenth Amendment, Frelinghuysen explained, "I am not in favor of giving the rights of citizenship or the right of suffrage to either pagans or heathens. . . . I am not in favor of taking steps backward into the slough of ignorance and of vice, even under the cry of progress." Hendricks attacked this line of reasoning, wondering why Republicans refused to include the Chinese: "I believe they said they were pagans; but they are not such pagans as we find in Africa. . . . Is it the business of this Government to prescribe what God or in what form men shall worship?" Hendricks went on to point out that "the Jew" and "the infidel, who recognizes no God at all," were both allowed to vote. Frelinghuysen then clarified the Republicans' argument: "not that a man must be a Christian to be a voter, but that it was not our duty to extend the rights of naturalization and citizenship to a pagan and heathenish class." Hendricks replied that his party's formulation of citizenship was much simpler: "Sir, I am in favor of men voting in this country who belong to the white race, and conduct themselves properly."[34]

In this exchange, Hendricks and Frelinghuysen vocalized the two parties' competing definitions of citizenship. Democrats continued to put forward the "old and well-tried" notion of a "white man's Government" that rested on biblical authority as well as scientific theories. In contrast, Republicans espoused a new form of political hierarchy that dropped the insistence on whiteness while reinforcing the importance of Christian manhood. In other words, Republicans were willing to allow racialized American men to become citizens only if they were Christians. Explaining why "the Chinaman" should never be offered the right to naturalize, Nevada's William Stewart summarized the Republican position: "I should be willing to allow him to become a citizen as much as anybody else if he would renounce his pagan religion and his attachment to his own Government, which bind him irrevocably, which bind him for all time and in all countries and in all places. . . . Until they have republicanized or christianized, do not talk about incorporating them into our body politic." The "colored man," on the other hand, Stewart called "an American and a Christian, as much so as any of the rest of the people of the country. He loved the American flag." A shared Christianity made extending political rights to African American men safe and even virtuous, according to Republicans, while the pagan beliefs of Indians and the Chinese marked them as both racially and spiritually dangerous.[35]

Although the Republicans' rhetoric was decidedly Protestant, they did not object to suffrage for all non-Protestants; as Hendricks pointed out, Catholics, Jews, and even atheists could vote under the Republican plan. Republicans singled out "pagan" and "heathen" men—categories that encompassed much of the world's population but in the United States meant Indians and Asian immigrants—for exclusion from full citizenship. Republicans might not be able to transform the United States into an entirely Protestant nation, as some openly desired to do, but they could marginalize those groups they considered the most depraved, uncivilized, and godless. In this sense, congressional Reconstruction, though bitterly divisive, carried within it an opportunity for sectional, religious, and racial reconciliation through the construction of a new kind of national identity. Republicans invited men of different types—northerners, southerners, and westerners; Protestants, Catholics, and Jews; whites and African Americans—to unite around what they were not: heathens.

Of course, Republicans also invited American men to unite around something else they were not: women. Shrugging off longstanding connections between women's rights and antislavery, Republicans resisted calls from women's organizations to include them in Reconstruction's expansion of political rights.[36] In California, most Republicans ignored appeals issued by a nascent women's rights movement led by Laura de Force Gordon, who delivered the state's first public lecture for woman suffrage in 1868 and who helped organize a statewide women's rights convention in January 1870. A few state Republican politicians publicly supported woman suffrage, but their party held to a traditionally paternalist ideology of separate spheres.[37]

Predictably, Democrats pointed to their rivals' acceptance of limited political rights for white women as one more inconsistency. Noting that Republicans did not "propose to extend suffrage to women," Democrat John S. Hager approvingly reiterated their justification that, "as it is argued, laws are general, and for certain social reasons women as a class should be excluded." Following this line of reasoning, he asked, "How much more imperatively do certain social reasons demand that the negro, as a race, should also be excluded?" Here, Hager cited the legal and, in his view, biblically decreed subjugation of woman to man as precedent for the subjugation of inferior races to whites. For Democrats, godly hierarchy of gender echoed and justified godly hierarchy of race.[38]

Given the boldly inclusive rhetoric of California's early women's rights activists, it was not surprising that most politicians—along with mainstream newspapers—rejected their claims. "All prejudice should be thrown aside against both color and sex," Gordon said in the state assembly chamber in 1868. "Let the Constitutions of the several States be amended so that white and black, red and yellow, of both sexes can exercise their civil rights." Writing for the San Francisco *Pioneer*, the first women's rights newspaper in the American West, Kitty Clover issued a broad call for religious and racial tolerance, complaining that "we despise our Catholic friends, and ridicule his superstitious observances of saint's days; we scoff at the peculiarities of our Jewish neighbor and think time should have changed his ideas; we scorn the poor colored man who plods on to his daily labor, and throw stones at the industrious Chinaman." Inspired by their backgrounds in Quakerism, spiritualism, and antislavery, California reformers issued calls for human rights that were among the most radical of any made in the postbellum United States.[39]

At other times, however, women's rights activists in California found it impossible to resist the temptation of invoking white Protestant solidarity rather than human universalism. During her popular speaking tour of California in 1869, New England reformer Anna Dickinson initially excoriated Californians for their harsh treatment of the Chinese. Within a few weeks, however, Dickinson was presenting white Protestant women as a potential help to white Republican men in their fights against Democrats who, according to Dickinson, depended on votes from Irish Catholics, African Americans, and—someday soon—the Chinese. "But I as an American woman put intelligence, culture and Christianity against heathens, barbarians and ignorant foreigners," she declared. "I put American women as an offset to all this deluge of foreign civilization."[40]

By insisting that white Protestant women had as much or more right to the ballot as African Americans, Irish Catholics, and the Chinese, Dickinson portrayed white Protestant women as crucial allies to white Protestant men in a struggle over national identity. This tactic, also embraced at times by national women's rights leaders, helped activists win suffrage for women in Wyoming Territory in 1869, but in California, Democrats and most Republicans dismissed such claims. Democrats, back in control of state politics after 1867, had no reason to relinquish their vision of a California led by godly white men, and the Republicans refused to add women's rights to an agenda already under fire for radicalism.[41]

At both the state and national levels, that Republican agenda sprang from a combination of political necessity and genuine religious conviction. On one hand, the national Republican Party's postbellum embrace of African American male voters but rejection of "heathen" men provided a way for it to achieve its reconstruction of the South without alienating the party's western and conservative wings. To ensure that the focus of Reconstruction remained on African American men, Republicans needed a plausible way to exclude Indian and Chinese men just as they excluded white women. Demonizing heathens served concrete political ends. At the same time, the idea of establishing and protecting the United States as an explicitly Christian nation appealed to many Americans following the chaos of the Civil War. Republican Congressmen attempted to curb immorality by criminalizing the mailing of "vulgar and indecent" materials in 1865 (later expanded into the Comstock Act of 1873) and attacking "lustful" Mormon polygamy. Republicans' notion of political rights based on non-heathen manhood was an extension of this larger postwar movement concerned with reinforcing the nation's holiness and sense of divine approval. If the war had cleansed the United States of the sin of slavery, Republicans hoped to use its momentum to further purify their broken nation.[42]

Not all national Republicans endorsed their party's vision of a United States in need of protection against pagan forces. Some Radical Republicans, descendants of the moral absolutist wing of the antebellum antislavery movement, instead espoused a Christianity of universalism, toleration, and benevolent uplift.[43] They sympathized with such human rights activists as Wendell Phillips, who was calling for a more sweeping constitutional amendment guaranteeing full citizenship for every man, "be he Indian, negro or Chinaman." When Massachusetts senator Charles Sumner tried to remove the word "white" from federal naturalization requirements in July 1870, he triggered a showdown over the limits of Reconstruction between these Republicans and their more conservative colleagues, with both sides laying claim to the mantle of Christianity. Sumner based his argument on his reading of the Declaration of Independence: "According to this vow *all men* are created equal and endowed with inalienable rights. But the statutes of the land assert the contrary; they declaring that only all white men are created equal." He went on to read the story of Peter's three denials of Jesus from the Gospel of Matthew, comparing William Stewart, who led the Republican opposition to his plan, to Peter.[44]

Stewart and other moderate Republicans countered with incredulity and indignation. "Because I am opposed to pagan imperialists, Chinese who do not understand the obligation of a Christian oath being incorporated into the body politic, the Senator from Massachusetts reads from a Christian book, from the Bible, to prove that I have denied my faith!" fumed Stewart. "I say that any Christian gentleman, any Christian man who will trust our institutions to the hands of pagans, has denied the faith of his fathers." Oregon's George Williams agreed: "Does the Declaration of Independence mean that Chinese coolies, that the Bushmen of South Africa, that the Hottentots, the Digger Indians, heathen, pagan, and cannibal, shall have equal political rights under this Government with citizens of the United States? Sir, that is the absurd and foolish interpretation." Even Henry Wilson, Sumner's fellow Radical senator from Massachusetts, opposed the change because he said it would further encourage "Coolie" labor, violating "the sublime doctrines of the New Testament" on which the Constitution rested.[45]

Sumner and his allies tried to counter with their own religious vision. Samuel C. Pomeroy from Kansas complained that "the gospel that is preached and revered here is twisted into a system to protect caste and prejudice and slavery. I say, Mr. President, that when the gospel is distorted in that manner, commend me to paganism. Let me be a pagan if I have got to give adherence to a gospel that does not believe in the brotherhood of mankind." Sumner insisted: "Worse than any pagan or heathen abroad are those in our midst who are false to our institutions." In the end, Sumner's plan lost, thirty votes to fourteen. The emergent Republican notion of nonheathen male citizenship held. Later that year, the Senate confirmed that the Fourteenth Amendment had "no effect whatever" on the status of Indians, the vast majority of whom remained non-citizens.[46]

More conservative than the national party, California's Republicans never had counterparts to Sumner or Pomeroy, and Gorham's 1867 gubernatorial defeat drained the party of what radicalism it did possess. During debates over the Fifteenth Amendment in California's legislature, only one Republican, Assemblyman Seldon J. Finney from San Mateo County, actively defended African Americans, and he did so by granting their natural inferiority while insisting that a lack of suffrage rights would make them "still more degraded." Democrats nevertheless denounced Finney as an "apostate to his race." Whereas Unionist–Republican governor Frederick Low, a self-described radical, had consistently denounced the ill treatment the Chinese encountered in California and called for laws to protect them, in 1868 Republicans in the state legislature banded together with Democrats to ask Congress for a suspension of immigration from China. "The Chinese in our midst are Pagans," complained their memorial. "In their social relations they are below the most degraded specimen of the American Indian, and but very little above the beast.... It is utterly impossible that they should ever become citizens." The California legislature would continue to send similar memorials to Congress throughout the 1870s.[47]

"A melancholy record of neglect and cruelty":
Implications for Chinese Americans and Indians

Barred from naturalizing by the federal government, Chinese immigrants faced a spate of discriminatory laws in California that denied them the right to testify against whites in court and to attend public schools; in addition, officials imposed special mining and head taxes and repeatedly attempted to ban all Chinese from the state.[48] In the 1850s, Chinese Californians had found a champion in Presbyterian missionary William Speer, who had viewed the political and spiritual needs of his Chinese parishioners as inseparable. In a series of lectures, editorials, tracts, and petitions, Speer had urged the legislature to support Chinese immigration, lower the foreign miners tax targeting the Chinese, protect their civil liberties, and grant them full testimony rights.[49]

With Speer's help, affluent Chinese Californians had managed to insert their voices into the public sphere, where they tried to harness the power of Christian rhetoric for themselves. "You reproach us that we are idolatrous, that we do not practice the precepts of Christ, but if we are not deceived, Christ orders his disciples to look upon all men as brothers, and to treat them as brothers," a group of San Francisco merchants wrote in an open letter to white Californians in 1855. "Is it then consistent with the Christian religion—the religion of humility and love—to deny the humanity of an entire race of men, and to treat them as a species inferior and unworthy of pity?" Pun Chi, another merchant, enlisted Speer's help to translate a petition to U.S. Congress on behalf of the Chinese in California following *People v. Hall.* Pun Chi asked, "if the religion of Jesus really teaches the fear of Heaven, how does it come that the people of your honorable country on the contrary trample upon and hate the race which Heaven most loves, that is, the Chinese? Should this not be called rebellion against Heaven? And how is it possible to receive this as of the religion of Heaven?" These merchants used Christian precepts to defiantly reproach California from outside the religion, secure in the belief that their own religiosity surpassed white American hypocrisy.[50]

Speer left California in 1857, and his replacement, Augustus Ward Loomis, was initially more interested in the intellectual and spiritual development of his Chinese pupils than their political status. When a group of Chinese businessmen asked him to step into Speer's role as their advocate in securing the full testimony rights and repealing the foreign miners tax, Loomis helped them hire a lawyer but did little else, vowing, "I do not intend to get mixed up in any political matters (unless I slip in by accident)." He believed they had "dim prospects" for success, noting, "too many in the churches here seem very lukewarm—would rather see the Chinaman back across the waters—many in the churches too, I fancy, think less of them than of the *niggers*." The Congregationalists, Episcopalians, Southern Baptists, and Catholics, who had all sent missionaries to labor among California's Chinese during the 1850s, had given up by the end of the Civil War, discouraged by what one Episcopalian termed the "insurmountable difficulties of *reaching* our Chinese population." Church leaders issued a few scattered calls for tolerance, continuing to insist as they had in the 1850s that Providence brought the Chinese to California to be saved from damnation.[51] Increasingly common were Christian white supremacist treatises such as Arthur B. Stout's *Chinese Immigration and the Physiological Causes of the Decay of a Nation,* an early entry into what was becoming a booming genre of anti-Chinese books and pamphlets. According to Stout, God had blessed "the great Caucasian Race of men" with "supremacy in elevation of mind and beauty of form over all mankind." Chinese immigration threatened "the purity of the race," because "it is vain for man to seek to unite that which the Creator has so distinctly divided."[52]

As public sentiment turned more and more against the Chinese in California, Indians in contrast began to seem increasingly tragic figures. This was a far cry from their image during the 1850s, when state officials had appropriated millions of dollars to fund genocidal "pacification" campaigns against California Indian groups, a local arm of a national effort aimed at opening the West to white settlement and economic incorporation. After considering banishing all "wild" Indians from California, the government established five reservations and two "farms" in the mid-1850s on which about ten thousand Indians were forcibly gathered. The remainder of California's dwindling Indian population hid out or found work as wage laborers at ranches or towns, unprotected by laws and frequently targeted by violence. Although outright extermination was generally considered "too revolting to all sense of justice and common humanity to be entertained by a virtuous and Christian public," according to one San Francisco newspaper, the dominant public discourse had marked "Digger" Indians as godless and racially inferior, destined to be swept away by progress and Christian civilization.[53]

In the 1860s, however, a new image of California Indians as demoralized victims of white aggression and political corruption emerged alongside older ideas of Indian savagery. J. Ross Browne, hired by the U.S. Treasury Department to investigate Indian reservations on the Pacific,

wrote a series of reports, letters, and exposés detailing government corruption and the California Indians' pitiful living conditions. "All they ask
is the privilege of breathing the air that God gave to us all, and living in
peace wherever it may be convenient to remove them," he wrote in
Harper's Magazine in 1861. "Their history in California is a melancholy
record of neglect and cruelty." This trend toward seeing Indians as victims
was part of a national attitude shift that prompted President Ulysses S.
Grant's peace policy in 1869.[54] However, the idea that Indians were destined by God to disappear soon remained dominant in the 1860s. "They are
beyond the reach of teachers and preachers," insisted the *Daily Alta California*. "They will die and 'make no sign.'" Excluded from the benefits of
Reconstruction, Indians joined the Chinese as political and religious outsiders, unprotected and scorned by Republicans and Democrats alike.[55]

The Fifteenth Amendment, ratified in February 1870 despite California's rejection of it, brought a new political order to the state and
nation. The loose antebellum definition of citizenship based on white
Christian manhood had given way to a new federalized definition that divided Christian men, black and white, from women and heathens. Republicans and leading African Americans throughout the state celebrated
the change. "We have now fully attained to our majority; the perfect
stature of citizenship," noted activist Jeremiah B. Sanderson. "We must
now put on the garments and assume the responsibilities of political
manhood."[56] Democrats and other enemies of African American suffrage decried the amendment, questioned its legitimacy, obstructed its
implementation, and warned that a terrifying precedent had been set.
"The car of mongrelism rolls on," reported the Sonoma *Democrat*. "Let
its drivers beware, lest they get crushed beneath its wheels." Suffrage
based on white Christian manhood, though those categories were far
from stable as criteria for limiting citizenship rights, had successfully
maintained social hierarchy in California for twenty years. Citizenship
based on non-heathenism looked to prove more volatile, given many
churches' stated goal of converting the globe to Christianity. Always politically subversive, evangelism—the collapsing of barriers between
Christians and heathens—had become exponentially more dangerous.
A new question now loomed: If religion rather than whiteness was to be
the yardstick of citizenship, what would happen if heathen men started
becoming Christians?[57]

California would be the testing ground for that question. On May 10,
1869, the driving of the golden spike completed the transcontinental railroad and connected California to the United States more securely than

ever. That same year, President Grant began the implementation of his peace policy, soon placing church groups in control of Indian reservations, including those in California. A diverse group of missionaries—some with experience in China, others on Indian reservations, others among freed slaves in the South—aggressively targeted California's Indians and Chinese residents, intent on extending Radical Reconstruction to the West and fulfilling California's spiritual destiny. Charles Loring Brace, Methodist director of the Children's Aid Society of New York, visited California in 1868 and foresaw the religio-political fight brewing in the state. "The old battle of humanity fought out on our [East] coast, of justice to the negro, is going on here in different form—of justice to the pagan," he wrote. "The same weapons are used, the same appeals to low and ignorant prejudices of race, and the same assertion of the universal rights of humanity." In California, the "old battle of humanity" had entered a new stage, with new stakes.[58]

OF ONE BLOOD, 1870–1876

God hath made of one blood all nations of men for to dwell on all the face of the earth, and hath determined the times before appointed, and the bounds of their habitation; that they should seek the Lord ...

—Acts 17:26–27

CHAPTER TWO

THE POLITICS OF CHINESE EVANGELISM

A certain kind of popularity has been growing up for China and the Chinese recently," noted A. W. Loomis in September 1868. After a flurry of failed missionary attempts by various denominations in the 1850s, only the Presbyterian Board of Foreign Missions had managed to maintain a Chinese mission in California into the mid-1860s. For several years, Loomis's mission in San Francisco's Chinatown, operating in the modest building his predecessor William Speer had erected in 1853, represented the only missionary outpost dedicated to Chinese evangelism in the Western Hemisphere.[1]

Between 1868 and 1872, however, Loomis witnessed an onslaught of missions, chapels, schools, boarding houses, and Sunday school classes targeting the Chinese of California. The most prominent of the new arrivals was the Methodist Episcopal Church, which opened Chinese Sunday schools throughout California, and a three-story Mission Institute in the heart of San Francisco's Chinatown, operated by Otis Gibson, an outspoken missionary who had spent several years in Fuzhou, China. The American Missionary Association, working with local Congregationalist churches, established a string of language schools for Chinese pupils up and down the state, modeled after their schools for former slaves in the South. The American Tract Society hired agents to distribute Chinese-language pamphlets throughout California, the American Baptists launched an aggressive missionary campaign, and the Southern Baptists and Episcopalians restarted their efforts. Protestant missionaries simultaneously targeted the Chinese of New York City and Portland, Oregon, but by far the majority headed for California, home to 87 percent of the nation's 56,000 Chinese residents in 1870.[2]

Several developments came together in the late 1860s to trigger this wave of evangelism. The completion of the transcontinental railroad in May 1869 focused national attention on California and facilitated an intracontinental flow of goods, ideas, and people. Once a remote out-post, California was now securely integrated into national economics and affairs. In July 1868, the United States and China agreed on a new treaty, shepherded by diplomat Anson Burlingame, aimed at increasing commercial ties between the two countries. The Burlingame Treaty pro-tected "free migration and emigration" in both directions and gave Chi-nese migrants living in the United States the "same privileges, immunities, and exemptions in respect to travel or residence" as enjoyed by immi-grants from most-favored nations. Burlingame's treaty and mission to Washington, D.C., received enormous publicity and turned churches' at-tention to Chinese immigrants. Soon after, in June 1870, the importation of seventy-five Chinese workers by a shoe-factory owner in North Adams, Massachusetts, generated headlines and debate throughout the North-east. The "Chinese question" was increasingly a national one.[3]

Running parallel to these events, the ongoing Reconstruction of the South provided a precedent, training ground, and institutional model for the missionization of the Chinese of California. "Shall not this Associa-tion join the Chinese to the Freedmen in its labors?" urged the *American Missionary*, organ of the American Missionary Association, in 1869, not-ing that the two groups were "already united in sharing the hatred and prejudice attached so unjustly to color." The American Missionary As-sociation began diverting a portion of its laborers from the South to Cal-ifornia, including John Kimball, Bureau Superintendent of the District of Columbia, who became the association's first California state superin-tendent.[4] The American Baptists, Presbyterians, and Methodists sent missionaries to the Chinese of California and to southern freed slaves. To many northern Protestants, the remaking of the South seemed a first step toward global conversion; California, with its access to the Pacific, seemed a perfect next step.[5]

Building on their pre-war opposition to slavery and Indian removal, this diverse group of Protestant reformers strove to extend Reconstruc-tion's political victories for African Americans to the nation's Chinese and Indians while converting those groups to Christianity. These re-formers took up the implicit challenge of the turn away from white male citizenship represented by the Fifteenth Amendment—if Chinese and Indian men were denied suffrage not because of their race but because of their pagan beliefs, then conversion to Christianity would prepare them for full citizenship just as African American men had been pre-pared. By saving souls, missionaries believed they could make the United States purer, freer, and more democratic. Accordingly, during the early

1870s, California's missionaries and almost all of its Protestant leaders enthusiastically embraced unrestricted immigration from China and the federal government's Indian "peace policy" (discussed in the next chapter) as parts of God's plan for universal salvation.

Missionaries' beliefs in racial justice and Protestant superiority were inseparable. Reformers understood evangelism as a way of assimilating heathen groups into Protestant America, turning outsiders into insiders by reshaping their lives. This discourse positioned missionaries and ministers as godly guardians of American democracy, protecting the nation against an infiltration of dangerous pagan influences. Missionaries' ever-optimistic accounts of conversion and revival among the Chinese reflected their constant need for attention and financial donations as well as their postbellum zeal.

For those Chinese men and women who joined Protestant churches, adoption of Christianity was part of a larger process of ethnic reformation and self-identification, as they came to terms with living in a country that marginalized and largely despised them. Like other California groups, Chinese converts used Christianity in political struggles over the parameters of American citizenship.

California's white reformers and Chinese churchgoers encountered local, sometimes violent resistance, ranging from mocking editorials to church burnings, from political attacks to physical assaults. For many white Christian Californians, the Fifteenth Amendment represented a horrifying precedent, and they used their own Christian arguments to combat evangelism and the extension of suffrage to Indians and the Chinese. The Democratic Party continued to try to mobilize white Californians with a doctrine of Christian white male supremacy, while the Republicans advanced a more gradated racial vision, increasing their attacks on the Chinese while supporting political rights for African Americans and the long-term assimilation of Indians. California's African American leaders, having based their claims to suffrage largely on their Christian manhood, continued to distance themselves from "heathens" in their fight against racial segregation in education. As during the 1860s, Christianity provided the language with which competing groups defined and contested race.

Although generally united in their dedication to racial uplift, Protestant missionaries and ministers in California espoused a wide range of racial attitudes. Some advocated radical egalitarianism and universal human equality, using biblical evidence to challenge scientific racism. Most viewed the Chinese as "degraded" and "childlike," theoretically not because of innate racial inferiority but because of their heathen beliefs, which retarded their ability to advance in education and civilization. Considering themselves benevolent patriarchs and matriarchs overseeing spiritual children, these missionaries attempted, with varying degrees of success, to refashion converts' gender roles, sexual practices, dress, language, and work habits in accordance with a Protestant model. A small number of Protestant ministers publicly questioned the godliness of racial equality, marking the smoldering beginning of a debate among California church leaders that would not ignite until later in the decade.

The Fifteenth Amendment cast a long shadow over this Chinese evangelism and the way Californians perceived it. Suffrage based on non-heathen manhood opened a potential door for Christian men of any race to become voters. This possibility infused evangelism with powerful political meanings that emboldened both missionaries and their critics. In the 1870s, debates about racial citizenship would hinge on the conversion experience: who was eligible, how to measure it, and what it revealed about God's plans for the United States.

"Rejoice that they are coming here": Protestant Support for Chinese Immigration

Like most Protestant leaders in California during the decade following the Civil War, John Todd saw the hand of Providence in the arrival of the Chinese. A Congregationalist minister from Massachusetts who visited California during the late 1860s, Todd envisioned the newly linked corridor of New York, California, China, and Europe as a "highway of commerce and of learning, of brotherly kindness, of the messengers of peace, and of the Gospel of Christ." He believed that "a road which goes into the far west of the Pacific, does not stop there. In ways that we do not know, it reaches into the spiritual world, and is the bearer of spiritual good to our race. It already melts away our prejudices, and brings us into brotherhood with all the nations." For Todd and like-minded missionaries, a moment of tremendous promise seemed at hand; the United States, having rooted out slavery just as technology united the globe, stood poised to usher in God's kingdom on earth.[6]

This shared vision of impending global conversion notwithstanding, the arrival of so many missionary organizations sparked a degree of interdenominational jostling. In his letters to the Presbyterian Board of Foreign Missions, A. W. Loomis expressed dismay at the competition that had suddenly risen over Chinese scholars, resources, and attention. "Other denominations are *firing up* on the California Chinese question—

and they will steal away all my boys if they possibly can and they have no conscience about it," he complained in 1870. Each denomination offered English-language classes for Chinese pupils, but a major philosophical difference divided the Presbyterians from other groups in California: Loomis and his fellow Presbyterian missionaries conducted their religious services in Cantonese, while the others held theirs in English, holding to the prevailing belief that English was uniquely and divinely fitted for Christian truths. The Presbyterians, considering themselves "foreign" missionaries rather than domestic ones, operated in California as they did in China and elsewhere, preaching the gospel in the native language while separately teaching English.[7]

Despite these differences and squabbles, the missionaries who targeted California's Chinese residents during the first half of the 1870s shared an overriding optimism about the spiritual and intellectual potential of the Chinese. In their initial reports and public writings, missionaries presented the Chinese as enthusiastic pupils quickly absorbing the English language and Christian truths. "The universal report concerning these pupils is encouraging," announced Congregationalist George Mooar in 1871, a pronouncement echoed by missionaries throughout the state during these years. Missionaries publicized baptisms in local and national publications and held frequent public celebrations at which Chinese pupils recited Bible verses, sang hymns, and preached. This rhetoric of rapid progress was in no small degree a function of missionaries' need for constant fundraising and attention-getting; in California as in other parts of the world, missionaries had financial incentives to portray their missions as thriving. At the same time, this particular postbellum momentum encouraged missionaries in California to view themselves as poised to effect great change for God.[8]

Their optimism spread to local churches. One by one, state denominational conferences endorsed Chinese missionization, local ministers opened their pulpits to missionaries, and dozens of churches began their own Sunday school classes for the Chinese. To greater or lesser degrees, the state's major Protestant newspapers—the Congregational *Pacific,* Presbyterian *Occident,* Methodist *California Christian Advocate,* and Episcopalian *Pacific Churchman*—all supported evangelism to the state's Chinese and gave space to missionaries' reports and pleas. A tentative consensus formed among missionaries, ministers, and editors about how the Chinese should be treated, the meanings and import of their immigration, and God's desire for them to come to the United States.[9]

Even more emphatically than their counterparts had done in the 1850s and 1860s, most Protestant leaders in the early 1870s embraced Chinese immigration as a splendid part of God's plan for the spiritual conquest of the earth. The Methodist Episcopal annual conference scolded politicians who sought to ban the Chinese, insisting that "any attempt to repel Chinese immigration by means of intimidation and discriminating exaction, is unstatesmanlike, impolitic and anti-Christian." Far from seeing Chinese immigration as a necessary evil, leaders called on Christians to "rejoice that they are coming here where we can teach them at a saving of seventy-five per cent and at least a generation earlier" than in China.[10]

In addition to the desire to convert the Chinese to Christianity, this embrace of Chinese immigration sprang from at least three sources: a belief in the universal human right of mobility, a self-interested desire to continue sending missionaries to China, and the notion that the United States would benefit from accommodating Chinese workers and settlers. "We must 'go' ourselves 'to every creature,' and as long as we must go we do not see how we can refuse other men the same right to go and come anywhere on this free planet," surmised the *Pacific*, quoting the Gospel of Mark. From missionaries' perspectives, spreading the good news to the entire globe took precedent over maintaining impermeable national borders. The *American Missionary* condemned any limits on immigration, noting, "We have broad lands yet unpeopled, great resources yet undeveloped, free institutions that have only been strengthened by the strains upon them, and a religion that is commissioned to conquer the world."[11]

To California's Protestant leaders, proper treatment of the Chinese was essential to winning their trust and saving their souls. As William Speer had done in the 1850s, some missionaries worked for an expansion of Chinese residents' political rights, including the right to provide legal testimony against whites, protection from violence, and escape from the discriminatory measures targeting Chinatown that were passed by the San Francisco Board of Supervisors in the wake of the Burlingame Treaty. Citing that treaty and the Fourteenth Amendment as well as the Bible, religious spokesmen called for fair treatment and equal protection under the law, reminding Californians that "every outrage committed upon a Chinaman is so much added to the barrier which they are only too willing to throw up between themselves and us—between their religion and ours." Methodist Otis Gibson was an especially public proponent of Chinese political rights and soon became notorious for his pugnacious demeanor, at one point warning anti-Chinese rabble-rousers

Figure 3. Methodist missionary Otis Gibson was San Francisco's most outspoken defender of Chinese immigration and evangelism during the early 1870s. From N. R. Johnston, *Looking Back from the Sunset Land* (Oakland, Calif., 1898). Courtesy of the Huntington Library, San Marino.

that he would protect the Chinese "as long as his powder lasted" and praying that "the Lord would assist him to shoot straight." In 1873, while the Board of Supervisors was considering a round of anti-Chinese ordinances, Gibson appeared on behalf of a group of Chinese merchants to protest the laws and later translated and secured publication of their plea for equality. Even Loomis, who claimed to want no involvement in politics, corresponded with the San Francisco mayor and chief of police to request proper protection for the city's Chinese residents and preached sermons of tolerance in English from street corners to "the crowd of whites . . . though *ostensibly* for the Chinese."[12]

By 1872, religious reformers could point to two political victories. In 1871, a U.S. circuit court voided California's foreign miners tax; a year later, the state legislature granted Chinese residents the right to testify against whites in court, nearly a decade after the state's African Americans had won that right. Church leaders could celebrate the granting of full testimony rights as a victory for Christian compassion, but the largest reason for the change was a massive anti-Chinese riot in Los Angeles in October 1871, during which a mob of white men burned, shot, or lynched at least eighteen Chinese residents. Newspapers blamed the "Los Angeles horror" on the state legislature for its refusal to protect the Chinese by giving them the right to testify against whites. The legislature's granting of full testimony rights to the Chinese was, however, not evidence of politicians' increasing sympathy for Chinese residents, but a naked attempt to ensure social order, confirmed by anti-Chinese ordinances passed throughout the state during the early 1870s. However, churches' moral suasion campaigns helped create a climate in which granting full testimony rights to a largely despised group was more possible.[13]

In an era when some Protestant thinkers in the Northeast were employing biblical evidence to refute polygenesis and racial science, a few members of California's religious leadership advanced similar arguments in a considerably more hostile political climate.[14] "The assertion that the Chinese are an inferior race of men is not a new cry to raise against a people held in subjection," noted H. C. Bennett from the floor of the San Francisco Mechanics' Institute. Bennett was secretary of the San Francisco Chinese Protection Society, a group that hired policemen to patrol city streets, thwarting anti-Chinese harassment. In the same speech, he called the "heathen . . . barbarians" more holy than many Christians and quoted Acts 17:26—"[God] hath made of one blood all nations of men"— to defend their continued immigration. By invoking Acts 17:26, Bennett joined a long rhetorical tradition in the United States—one that ran from

Olaudah Equiano to Frederick Douglass to Wendell Phillips—of employing the verse in defense of human rights. Just as missionaries borrowed techniques from their denominations' work in the American South, Bennett and other Protestants drew on a longstanding trope of the antislavery movement in defense of the Chinese and the unity of humankind.[15]

Missionaries tried to view the Chinese Californians they labored among not as racially inferior but as spiritually misguided. This religious chauvinism could take either of two forms. Some missionaries, displaying little interest in or knowledge of Chinese religions, simply condemned the beliefs Chinese immigrants brought with them as "superstitions" and "idolatrous worship." These Protestants described the unconverted Chinese as "poor, self-righteous, unprincipled, opium-eating heathen" and "an army of heathen, selfish, cruel, corrupt and corrupting." Such rhetoric heightened the importance of missionaries' own evangelistic efforts by portraying Chinese beliefs as foreign, repugnant, and irrational, in desperate need of transformation for the safety of the nation.[16]

In contrast, others praised Chinese Buddhism and Confucianism for the morality and intellectual rigor they imparted, even as these missionaries maintained the ultimate limitations of any non-Christian faith. "We call these people pagans, and they are, but they are not barbarians," wrote one Congregationalist minister, "they have a literature, some of which, for purity and elevation, will compare not unfavorably even with christian thought and utterance; their theoretical and practical morality is higher than that of any other heathen people." Loomis thought so highly of the classic Chinese texts that he edited a volume of James Legge's translation of them, published in San Francisco in 1867, in which Loomis compared them to Christian scripture before noting that "they fall short of the high standard of morality which we find in the Bible." By praising and even circulating Chinese religious ideas, these missionaries aimed to counter prevailing notions of the Chinese as corrupt and irreligious. In its review of Loomis's edition of the Chinese classics, *The Nation* correctly surmised that his motive was the "enlightenment" of the California public so that it might "treat its Chinese fellow-citizens as men, rather than as brutes." These ministers' unshakeable belief in the superiority of their own Protestantism led them to promote Chinese religious ideas as a political act, portraying the Chinese as a moral, intelligent people lacking only the "regenerating influence" of Christianity.[17]

Such advocacy carried intense political meaning in the aftermath of the passage of the Fifteenth Amendment, when the question of Chinese citizenship and suffrage loomed over all discussions of Chinese missions. White reformers disagreed on whether Chinese men should be granted full citizenship rights before or after conversion to Christianity. Echoing the logic of congressional Reconstruction, some Protestants called for full citizenship for only Christianized Chinese men. According to the Presbyterian Board of Foreign Missions, the Chinese "cannot be safely entrusted with the rights of citizenship . . . unless they are brought out of the darkness of their natural state and the bondage of their pagan religion into the light and liberty of the gospel." The *California Christian Advocate* opposed suffrage for pagan Chinese "not because they are copper-colored, but because they lack the necessary qualifications for self-government." These arguments promoted Chinese evangelism as a way to allow the nation to live up to its newfound commitment to citizenship for all non-heathen men.[18]

Others advocated full citizenship for all Chinese men, regardless of religion. This argument also worked as self-promotion because it presented evangelism as a crucial protection against dangerous heathen voters. The American Baptist Foreign Mission Society observed that "the Chinese are destined to become before long a large and worthy portion of our adopted American citizenship"; therefore, mission work was "one of the most imperative duties of the hour." According to this line of thinking, the "principles of justice" demanded that Chinese men be turned into citizens, just as African American men had been. American Missionary Association state superintendent William Pond declared, "It is not the first time,—it may not be the last time—that God has linked our own national safety, with our care for men oppressed, out-cast and darkened."[19]

"Idolatry is not our God": Opposition to Chinese Evangelism

Despite framing their evangelism in terms of "national safety," mission workers in California encountered violent opposition that they likened to what northern missionaries found in the South during these years. Missionaries complained that anti-Chinese "hoodlums"—a word apparently coined in San Francisco in the early 1870s—harassed their scholars, throwing rocks and spitting on them as they attempted to attend church, forcing missionaries to hire policemen to guard church doors. In 1869, arsonists burned down a Methodist Episcopal church in San Jose that had recently begun holding Sunday school classes for the Chinese. Otis Gibson reported that the pastor had received an anonymous letter warning that "he will see his church again only in ashes, and threatens his life if he continues to teach the Chinamen."[20] Religious leaders likened the anti-

Chinese forces in California to "that which hung negroes to lamp-posts in New York in 1863," re-enacting "the same thing over again that opposed the abolition of slavery." In fact, by 1868 a California branch of the Ku Klux Klan was attacking and robbing Chinese men in gold country, hanging them from trees by their heels. Missionaries could not help but use the American South and the larger ongoing struggle for African American rights as a framework for understanding their work in California. Not incidentally, they designed their comparisons to elicit support from a national and local audience they knew to be sympathetic to the long antislavery movement.[21]

In the early 1870s, widespread popular antipathy to the Chinese was echoed by only a few voices within California's Protestant power structure. The most visible anti-immigration minister was Milton B. Starr, a Congregationalist in rural Placer County, who in 1873 agreed to become "grand lecturer" of the People's Protective Alliance of California, a coalition of local nativist organizations. "Prohibit the further immigration and importation of heathen into your chosen inheritance," he urged in his screed *The Coming Struggle.* "Remove the last plague-spot of paganism, with its ignorance, vice, and oppression, from your shores. Idolatry is not our God." He excoriated missionaries to California's Chinese for being too lazy to go to China, where proper mission work should be conducted. During one speech in San Francisco, Starr held up a pro-immigration sermon written by Otis Gibson and declared that "the time would come when the author, and those who indorsed it, would be ashamed of it."[22]

A small number of other religious leaders broke rank to question the doctrine of racial equality. William Lobscheid, a pastor of a United German Evangelical Lutheran church in San Francisco, called for a revision of the Burlingame Treaty to protect California's white working men from debased labor competition. "The Mongolian is physically and intellectually inferior to the European," he insisted. The *California Christian Advocate,* though energetically in support of mission work among California Indians, ran an editorial in 1873 insisting that "different races ... cannot amicably, beneficially and wisely dwell together. If a remedy can be found for preventing a further influx of a pagan people to our shores we shall rejoice in it."[23]

Furthermore, lay members of many congregations resisted opening their church doors to the Chinese. "There has been some strong feeling and talk on the part of some of the pew holders against such use of their churches," observed one visitor to San Francisco in 1872, "but Dr. [A. L.] Stone and the other pastors have stood square up and carried the day so far." William Pond resigned his pastorate at San Francisco's Third Congregational Church after white members balked at allowing seven Chinese men to be baptized and received into the church. Pond's resignation chastised the objectors enough that they granted admission to the Chinese converts, and Pond's last act as pastor was to conduct their baptisms.[24]

In the early 1870s, committed leaders such as A. L. Stone and William Pond managed to overcome the opposition to the Chinese they encountered in their churches from laypeople and in their profession from the likes of Milton B. Starr. One minister assured the American Missionary Association that Starr, though attracting attention with the People's Protective Alliance of California, "is old, weak and his course is not approved." Religious leaders had a more ambivalent relationship with the state's politicians, both Democratic and Republican, who intensified their attacks on the Chinese in the wake of the Fifteenth Amendment.[25]

"We are a Christian civilization": Racial Politics in California, 1870–1876

As it had been since *People v. Hall*, the question of political rights for the Chinese remained intertwined with those for African Americans and Indians, even as the ratification of the Fifteenth Amendment ushered in a new era of racial politics in California. State Democrats, having re-ascended to power in the late 1860s based on their opposition to African American, Indian, and Chinese suffrage, found themselves lacking a pressing issue to motivate voters in the same way. Democratic politicians and newspaper editors nonetheless continued to espouse a doctrine of Christian white male supremacy, arguing that the notion of racial equality was nothing more than unholy "fanaticism." Democratic U.S. senator Eugene Casserly declared in 1870 that the Chinese presence in California "threatens to supplant the entire Christian forces of our civilization by forces which are not merely Asiatic but pagan." He urged the government to halt immigration from China, a call that became an annual plank in Democratic state platforms.[26]

Stubbornly recycling their arguments from earlier eras, California's Democrats refused to acknowledge the significance of the Fourteenth and Fifteenth Amendments. In 1871, they lost the governorship and control of the state assembly to Republicans, who advanced a more nuanced view of race.[27] The party's lukewarm support for African American political rights continued, based on a limited vision of equality that largely excluded Indians and the Chinese. "There are classes for whom we have a stronger repugnance than negroes," observed the Republican San Francisco *Chronicle* while considering the Civil Rights Act of 1875. State Republicans grudgingly accepted African American men into the body politic.[28]

Having largely based their claims to suffrage on their Christian manhood, African American community leaders felt compelled to maintain proper dignity and piety. "We deem morality, religion, intellectual culture, industry and patriotism indispensable in view of our changed condition as American citizens," asserted the California Conference of the African Methodist Episcopal Church in 1870. Armed with suffrage and Christian respectability, leading African Americans turned their attention to a longstanding source of inequality: segregation in education.[29]

An informal separate school system for African American children had formed in California in the 1850s, and in 1860 racial segregation became written into state law when the legislature forbade "Negroes, Mongolians, and Indians" from attending public schools with white children, permitting but not compelling local districts to maintain separate schools. In 1870, the legislature reorganized state education, requiring that "children of African descent, and Indian children" be educated in segregated schools; districts were not obligated to educate Chinese children at all. African American activists, who had protested substandard segregated schools since the 1850s, escalated their efforts in the early 1870s, vowing to make politicians "show who they serve, God or Mammon."[30] Encouraged by new Republican governor Newton Booth's opposition to segregated education, activists brought legal action against a San Francisco principal who refused to admit eleven-year-old Mary Frances Ward into his all-white school. To their disappointment, the state supreme court upheld segregation in the 1874 decision *Ward v. Flood*, maintaining that separate-but-equal schools did not violate the Fourteenth Amendment. Democrats and other opponents of desegregation celebrated the ruling as upholding God's natural order; the San Francisco *Examiner* deemed it "a most sacrilegious and suicidal act to permit the children of white men, whom God has made in His own image, to be forced into the public schools attended by the children of mulattoes and negroes."[31]

The issue of segregation in education may have especially galled California's African American leadership because it lumped them once again with Indians and the Chinese, a vestige of the pre-1870 era they had hoped to put behind them. After winning suffrage, some African Americans had felt they could afford to soften their attitude toward the Chinese. After denouncing the Chinese throughout the late 1860s, Philip A. Bell's *Elevator* announced in July 1870 that "the excitement about Chinese immigration is needless. We fear no deluge of Chinamen." In 1873, African Methodist Episcopal minister W. H. Hillery condemned anti-Chinese demagoguery while, in the *Elevator*, a writer defended the Chinese against charges of "inferiority and unfitness; mental and physical incapacity; we have become too accustomed to such clamour to be moved by it." In his 1873 autobiography, published in San Francisco, former slave James Williams asked, "Didn't God create the Chinaman as well as the American?" Such sentiments were virtually indistinguishable from those expressed by California's missionaries to the Chinese. Suffrage allowed African American leaders to express a broader range of attitudes about the Chinese than had been possible in the 1860s.[32]

However, the fight over school segregation—along with continuing competition for employment in the increasingly harsh economic climate that set in after 1873—encouraged leading African Americans to renew their efforts to distance themselves from Indians and the Chinese. Working with Republican allies, African American activists sought access for their children to white schools without including Indians and the Chinese in their efforts. The *Pacific Appeal* explained their strategy in 1872: "Heretofore it has been the policy of our opponents to couple the claims of colored American citizens with the most objectionable classes, such as Mongolians, etc., which would make any just measure obnoxious enough to insure its defeat." While noting that "the Indian has been badly treated—sometimes shamefully," the *Elevator* tended to portray Indians as subhuman pagans, calling them "dastardly red skins," "devils," and "half-naked, ignorant savages." Similarly, both of San Francisco's black newspapers spoke out against Chinese immigration in 1873 even as they condemned anti-Chinese violence and San Francisco's discriminatory ordinances. According to the *Elevator*, protecting Christian America from pagan invaders would earn more of God's approval than trying to save those invaders' souls.[33]

This conflicted, ultimately practical approach paid dividends in their fight against school segregation at the local level; despite the setback of *Ward v. Flood*, Republicans and African American reformers managed to desegregate San Francisco, Oakland, and several other municipal school districts by 1875. Indian children continued to be educated in separate schools when they were educated at all; Chinese children had no public school options after the San Francisco Board of Education closed the nation's sole public school for Chinese children in 1871.[34]

California's Republicans, who had generally opposed only the immigration of Chinese "coolies" in the late 1860s, counterbalanced their continuing support of African American political rights by matching Democratic anti-Chinese xenophobia in the early 1870s. The Republicans' state party platform in 1871 decried the Chinese for being a people "incapable of assimilation with our own race." Although such pronouncements approached the racism employed by the Democrats, Republicans usually maintained that it was not whiteness but Christian manhood that Chinese men lacked. Ex-state attorney general Frank M. Pixley declared that "he did not oppose Chinese immigration because he regarded the Chinese as an inferior race, for in some things they were a superior race to ours."[35]

On the contrary, Republicans explained that they opposed Chinese immigration and citizenship because the Chinese were hopelessly pagan coolies, without families or morals, the diametrical opposite of the free, Christian, wage-laboring, married men—black and white—championed by the party. U.S. Representative Aaron A. Sargent complained that the Chinese's "pagan customs" made it impossible for them to assimilate, noting, "By their religion or their superstition their bones, even, are returned to China after their death." He continued, "We are a Christian civilization. A pagan civilization is necessarily inconsistent with it." The San Francisco *Chronicle* similarly condemned Chinese immigrants for failing to "adopt our manners, our customs, our clothing, our food, our language, or our religion," while praising African Americans for being "with us still, in sympathy, in interest, in habit, in language, in religion."[36] By characterizing all Chinese men as pagan coolies, Republicans rhetorically stripped them of their self-sufficiency, morality, and manliness. This discourse, which emphasized intractable cultural differences rather than racial ones, allowed Republicans to engage in anti-Chinese race-baiting without espousing blatant white supremacy, which they still denounced as un-Christian and Democratic.[37]

However, this logic dictated that those Chinese men who converted to Christianity should be eligible for suffrage rights. During the early 1870s, California's Republican politicians neither endorsed nor attacked evangelism to the state's Chinese, indicating ambivalence about the desirability of Christian Chinese citizens. The federal government did not directly support Chinese evangelism the way it subsidized Indian missions, but neither did politicians oppose it. However, other anti-Chinese agitators rushed to denigrate white missionaries as traitors to their race and to insist that the Chinese could not adopt Christianity. The sensationalistic San Francisco tabloid *Thistleton's Jolly Giant* excoriated "all corporated shoddy societies who go about teaching filthy and abominable heathens Christianity, instead of first looking after the white children." The paper

Figure 4. *Thistleton's Illustrated Jolly Giant* made frequent attacks on both Roman Catholic priests and Protestant missionaries to the Chinese. The July 18, 1876, issue showed Otis Gibson playing "horsee" with former prostitutes, an unmanly activity supposedly glimpsed through a window of the Methodist Chinese Mission Institute. Courtesy of the Huntington Library, San Marino.

repeatedly mocked missionaries to the Chinese, especially "Rev. China-man Gibson"; artists caricatured him as possessing a Chinese-style queue and showed him on all fours playing "horsee" with his "harem" of Chinese prostitutes. San Francisco writer Henry George, several years before his *Progress and Poverty* would bring him fame as an economic theorist, wrote in the New York *Tribune* that "the Chinese among us will, as a rule, remain the heathens they are." He continued, "The Chinese seem incapable of understanding our religion; but still less are they capable of understanding our political institutions." By linking the religious and political incapacities of the Chinese, George acknowledged the politically dangerous ramifications of Chinese evangelism that fueled opposition to missionaries, from editorials to church burnings.[38]

"Those painted-faced brazen little women": Protestant Responses to Chinese Prostitution

Given that Chinese men outnumbered Chinese women twelve to one in California in 1870, and that women of all races continued to pose no threat as potential voters under the Fifteenth Amendment, it is not surprising that politicians focused most of their scorn on Chinese men. However,

Chinese women occupied an increasingly prominent place in the political imagination in the early 1870s, when an emerging discourse portrayed all Chinese women as prostitutes, disease-ridden and depraved.[39] One visitor to San Francisco described glimpsing Chinese prostitutes in a flophouse suffering from a "loathsome disease with which the vengeance of God has cursed sinful humanity." According to white observers, God had written prostitutes' sins onto their bodies in the form of disease. In 1870, the San Francisco Board of Health reorganized and began attacking prostitution in Chinatown, adding the weight of medical authority to widespread concerns about Chinese women's innate sinfulness.[40]

Just as they made use of the stereotype of the Chinese coolie, politicians seized on the figure of the Chinese prostitute to urge the necessity of immigration restriction. In March 1870, the California legislature passed a pair of laws barring Chinese coolies and prostitutes from entering the state, forcing all would-be immigrants from China to prove they possessed "correct habits and good moral character." In 1875, Representative Horace F. Page, promoting a federal bill modeled on California's 1870 statutes, urged the U.S. Congress to "send the brazen harlot who openly flaunts her wickedness in the faces of our wives and daughters back to her native country." Passed in 1875, the Page Act—the federal government's first substantial restriction of immigration—ultimately curbed the arrival of Chinese women far more than men, creating further gender imbalance among the Chinese and strengthening the perception that Chinese men were perpetually and unnaturally bachelors.[41]

California's Protestant leaders chalked up politicians' nativist rhetoric to campaign opportunism, noting that it tended to rise and fall with the election cycle, and they refuted the notion that all Chinese men were enslaved coolies.[42] Yet, on the question of prostitution, missionaries reinforced prevailing ideas that equated Chinese women with sexual sin. During the antebellum period, American missionaries in China had often sent back reports of Chinese sexual depravity, especially prostitution, to emphasize the wantonness of pagan ways. Missionaries in California brought these preconceptions with them. "Nearly all the Chinese women in California are a disgrace to their nation," Loomis wrote in the *Overland Monthly* in 1869, calling for the founding of a "house of refuge . . . into which some of these poor creatures may be gathered." By 1874, the Presbyterians and Methodists had both created mission homes for Chinese women in San Francisco aimed at "rescuing" prostitutes "from a life of sin," training them to be "useful Christian women," and placing them in church members' homes or marrying them to Christianized Chinese men.

Ministers' wives and other church women carried out the work, erecting a parallel mission structure that they controlled. Although dozens of women missionaries labored in California's Chinese Sunday schools and missions, men dominated positions of power within churches, conferences, and mission societies. Work among Chinese prostitutes gave women missionaries a sphere of influence wherein their gender was an undeniable asset in carrying out God's work.[43]

Their efforts rested on the assumption that virtually all Chinese women in California were "secondary wives" (also described as "concubines") or prostitutes, both classes constituting nothing more than "articles of traffic." This assumption enlarged missionaries' sphere of influence while making them allies of the police, Board of Health, and public officials eager to stamp out perceived Chinese immorality. The police department was happy to turn suspected Chinese prostitutes over to the two mission homes, where the women would be off its hands and off the streets. In November 1874, Otis Gibson and two other California ministers, Presbyterian Ira Condit and Baptist E. L. Simmons, sent Horace F. Page affidavits in support of the representative's efforts to restrict the entry of coolies and prostitutes. A few months before, Gibson and Condit had served as expert witnesses for the state of California after immigration officials had refused to allow twenty-two Chinese women to enter the state under suspicion of being "lewd and debached." Gibson's and Condit's affidavits to Page repeated what they had testified that summer: "certainly nine-tenths" of the Chinese women in San Francisco were "enslaved prostitutes," bought and sold in an extensive underground economy.[44]

Protestant ministers chose to cooperate with officials because they viewed Chinese prostitution as a blight on the nation. Representing an unholy mix of lust, commerce, disease, and slavery, the specter of prostitution was especially appalling for Protestant leaders. However, rather than condemning the prostitutes as "brazen harlots," as such politicians as Horace F. Page did, missionaries usually viewed them as exploited victims, sinful but, like all sinners, capable of redemption. "Those painted-faced brazen little women were not always thus," one Methodist minister reminded his congregation in 1871. "They are ignorant, as almost all the *women* of China are, but they are not destitute of affection and of virtue." Located at the extreme edge of society, Chinese prostitutes nonetheless remained, in the eyes of missionaries, part of God's family. Even as missionaries' conflation of Chinese women and prostitutes reinforced a politically powerful stereotype, their insistence on racial uplift carried a radical potential for breaking down barriers between society's insiders and outsiders. "What maketh us to differ from them?" asked Presbyterian missionary Samantha D. Condit. "God's grace alone."[45]

The cooperation between California's Protestant ministers and the government in 1874 heralded a change in the relationship between missionaries and officialdom. Politicians had found, in prostitution, a soft spot in ministers' opposition to immigration restriction. At the same time, with their cultural authority and unmatched knowledge of the Chinese, missionaries had proved ideal expert witnesses and legitimators of government policy. When federal attention increasingly turned to California's Chinese population in the second half of the 1870s, ministers would play a central role in the events to come.

"One universal God": Chinese American Christian Activism

In the minds of most white missionaries, California's Chinese converted to Christianity for one obvious reason: the religion's superior spiritual truths. When describing their own adoption of Christianity to white evangelical observers, some Chinese churchgoers spoke in similar terms. Episcopalian Dang Gong explained, "Formerly I was very ignorant and stupid. I served images and false gods." Aside from the relative theological merits of Christianity they may have perceived, Chinese Californians who joined Protestant churches gained access to a potentially powerful political and cultural discourse.[46]

Although the subject attracted considerable attention in the 1870s, the number of Chinese Californians who converted to Christianity during those years remains impossible to estimate, not least because "conversion" was a process rather than an act, and its meaning varied from person to person.[47] Chinese Californians' interaction with Christianity might have included any, some, or all of the following activities: learning English from a Christian teacher, listening to street preachers' sermons, talking with door-to-door missionaries, going to Sunday school services or Bible classes, boarding in a mission house, joining the Chinese Young Men's Christian Association, undergoing baptism and formally joining a church, becoming a colporteur or "native helper," or attending seminary to become a minister. Most Chinese residents had had some exposure to Christianity in China, thanks to missionary campaigns that dated back to the early nineteenth century, and many of the most active members of California's missions had been members of Protestant churches in China.[48]

While the number of Chinese men and women who underwent baptism in California was small—Otis Gibson counted 371 Chinese baptisms in the United States by May 1876—thousands more interacted in one way or another with Christianity, accepting and rejecting particular elements. "Sometimes when they tell you that they love and worship Jesus, closer inquiry will show that they also worship 'Josh,'" warned the New York *Christian Union,* reporting on California's Chinese missions. Indeed, Chinese Californians' response to Christianity ranged widely, with some such as Dang Gong explicitly rejecting their past beliefs as idolatry and others adding aspects of Christianity to their pre-existing religious worldview. As in any congregation, Chinese church groups waxed and waned over time in enthusiasm, dedication, and orthodoxy.[49]

Chinese Californians discovered that significant costs accompanied joining a Christian church, most especially separation from family, including ancestors. Jee Gam, who joined a Congregationalist church in 1870 and became a missionary and eventually an ordained minister, described a Chinese member of his mission in Oakland who had "given up every thing to serve Christ except one thing, and that was the worship of ancestors; for he said that he was the only child of his mother, and it would surely break her heart if she knew that he had forsaken the worship of his forefathers." Chinese Christians reported feeling pulled between old and new friends, old and new countries. In his memoirs, Presbyterian Huie Kin recalled a debate between Chinese Christians and Confucianists in Jee Gam's Oakland mission in the early 1870s that caused "many an emotional upset" for the Chinese Christians, "for we were torn between appeals for our loyalty to the Word of God on the one side and on the other to the age-old wisdom of our national sage." Already persecuted by whites, Chinese Christians could find themselves rejected by their countrymen, separated from sources of ethnic pride and identity.[50]

On a practical level, churches provided Chinese Californians with access to English-language skills, help with travel arrangements back to China, places to lodge, and sometimes jobs, although Kwan Loy and other colporteurs reported that they took pay cuts to serve God. Chinese scholars took advantage of California's interdenominational competition by moving from mission to mission in pursuit of better accommodations and treatment. "They see that there is a rivalry as to which school shall get them," complained A. W. Loomis in 1871, "—they begin to set a price on themselves, and to go from one school to another according as they imagine they will receive more petting and attention in one school or the other."[51]

By adopting Christianity, Chinese Californians also gained a voice in the religio-political debates of the era. As they had since the 1850s, non-

Christian Chinese sometimes tried to harness Christian rhetoric, as when a group of San Francisco merchants protested the city's anti-Chinese ordinances "in the name of our country, in the name of justice and humanity, in the name of Christianity, (as we understand it)," but those who joined churches spoke with the support and authority of California's Protestant structures. At an anniversary celebration of the Methodist Episcopal Chinese Mission Institute in 1875, Ma See gave an original address defending unrestricted immigration. "If this world was created by the one universal God; if it belongs to God; if men are all created equal; if all men come from one family; if these things be so, *and they are so,* then the Chinese, of course, have the same right to come to this land, and to occupy the land, that the people of any other nation have," he said. That same evening, Chan Pak Kwai's address rebuked the United States for failing to live up to its professed values: "I like the laws of this country because they give equal rights to all men, great and small, rich and poor, white or black. I like these laws if only they were executed according to their true meaning."[52]

Even when their speeches did not directly address politics, Chinese Christians promoted Chinese immigration by framing their travels as part of God's plan. "Our country is 8,000 miles away from yours, yet He has brought us over here to learn to worship Him," said Episcopalian Fong Doon. "He had something better than gold to show us here." Christian language and theology gave Chinese converts weapons to attack xenophobia, legal discrimination, and racial science; California's churches gave them an audience, and the religious press disseminated their arguments.[53]

The annual anniversary programs that included speeches by such Chinese Christians as Ma See, Chan Pak Kwai, and Fong Doon also advanced political messages in quieter ways. Typically featuring hymns, musical performances, prayers, skits, and original addresses, anniversary programs displayed Chinese Christians' English proficiency, intelligence, decorum, and piety to a public audience. By participating, Chinese Christians rebutted notions of Chinese racial inferiority and essential irreligiosity.

In the 1873 Methodist Episcopal anniversary program, three Chinese Christians acted out a "dialogue" titled "American Civilization" written by Eliza Chamberlain Gibson, Otis Gibson's wife and fellow missionary. Cheng Game and Dane Shun portrayed men troubled by differences they perceived between the United States and China. "I think the American people have a higher civilization than the Chinese people, and are richer," Cheng Game said, "and can do many things which the Chinese people cannot do," such as build railroads, steamships, and telegraph lines. Bar Kui, portraying a Christian convert in the skit, happily informed them of the reason for the differences: "It is because the American people worship God, and the Chinese people worship idols." By the scene's end, Cheng Game told Bar Kui, "What you say seems to be good doctrine. We will think about it. If the idols are truth, we ought to worship the idols; but if God is truth, we ought to worship God. We want to find the truth." While unsubtly glorifying American technological and religious progress, the play presented the Chinese as rational decision-makers in search of metaphysical truth, a far cry from the pictures painted by politicians and anti-Chinese agitators.[54]

It is impossible to know how the script might have been different if it had been written by the Chinese actors themselves. An act of collaboration between unequal partners, the performance resembled broader relations between white missionaries and Chinese churchgoers during the early 1870s. Chinese church members participated in denominational structures controlled by white missionaries and ministers, weighing the advantages and disadvantages of Christianity as offered. Unable to escape their own racial assumptions, missionaries continually scrutinized Chinese pupils for signs of "true" belief, refusing to baptize them until they had demonstrated piety, sincerity, and evangelical zeal for months or years, notwithstanding incentives to boost their missions' numbers. Later in the decade, Chinese Christians would try to assume greater responsibility within California's missions when they did not reject those structures altogether.

In the early 1870s, the momentum of Reconstruction had moved westward, giving most Protestant leaders in California confidence in the nation's ability to absorb, transform, and be strengthened by Chinese immigration. Full citizenship—including the right to naturalize, testify, hold public office, and vote—seemed around the corner for Christianizing Chinese men, notwithstanding the hostility of both Democratic and Republican lawmakers. After all, the "best Christian people" in California already viewed the Chinese as "men and brothers," and if missionary reports were to be believed, progress was being made daily in Chinese missions, Sunday school classes, and schools. Miraculously, reports from missionaries working among Indians, California's other "heathen" population, were even brighter. The unfolding of Providence seemed at hand.[55]

CHAPTER THREE

THE PLACE OF CALIFORNIA INDIANS

In May 1874, Mary K. Colburn wrote to the American Missionary Association to share news of an astonishing religious revival she was witnessing at Round Valley Indian Reservation in Mendocino County, California. Eight hundred Indians at Round Valley had converted to Christianity in the previous few weeks, she said, including all seven "chiefs" of the reservation's main tribal groups. "Meetings are thronged, and nightly songs of praise and prayer ascend from the lips of these new-born souls," Colburn wrote. "They speak with deep emotion of the love of Jesus. . . . One evening fifty Indians spoke, and the language of all was a yearning desire for clean hearts and pure lives for themselves and their people." For Colburn, who, along with fellow missionary Mary A. Burnett, had arrived at Round Valley the previous year, the scene surpassed anything she had seen in her nine years of labor for the American Missionary Association, which had included stints among African Americans in Virginia, South Carolina, and Georgia and among the Chinese in Stockton, California. "My experiences among the Freedmen of the South and the Chinese of California were rich and varied," she noted, "but never have I witnessed such an outpouring of the Holy Spirit and such an ingathering of souls as now; and these trophies are plucked from the lowest class of humanity—the *California Digger Indians*."[1]

Colburn's travels from the American South to Stockton to Round Valley illustrate the interconnected Protestant movements for African American, Chinese, and Indian uplift that blossomed in the ten years following the Civil War. Propelled by the promise of Reconstruction, postbellum reformers looked west. With its tens of thousands of Indians and Chinese residents, not to mention its long-foretold future as a Christian utopia, California represented a prime mission field in this nationwide endeavor. Missionary men and women, supported by national organizations, state conferences, and local churches, endeavored to turn Chinese and Indians in California into educated Protestant citizens.

Round Valley was the largest of California's Indian reservations, and its Christian revival the largest in the nation during Ulysses S. Grant's peace policy era. These factors pushed it into the center of controversies that raged in California and the nation over the place of Indians in church and society. Overseen by the Methodist Episcopal Church under the terms of the peace policy, Round Valley and its minister-agent J. L. Burchard became lightning rods for abundant praise and harsh criticism. For Protestant leaders and missionaries, Round Valley came to symbolize Indian men's ability to quickly "rise" to civilized status and claim a place in the body politic alongside African American men and, they hoped, Chinese American men. Protestant leaders insisted that the Round Valley story proved that Indians could move toward civilization and Christianity while retaining certain aspects of their Indian identities—living under tribal structures, on commonly held land. They could be both Indians and Christian citizens; those categories were not mutually exclusive. For opponents of Indian suffrage and assimilation, Round Valley represented fraud, mismanagement, and, above all, proof of Indians' inability to change, to become true Christians, and to prove themselves worthy of citizenship. As with the case of proselytism among the Chinese, evangelism among Indians threatened the political status quo in the wake of the Fifteenth Amendment and the nation's shift away from strict white male suffrage. Round Valley became a central battleground in the fight over Indians' redeemability and their prospects as Christians and citizens.

"Humane, civilizing, and Christianizing influences": The Peace Policy in California

Unlike missionaries to the Chinese, whose efforts were financed by their denominations, missionaries working among California Indians received funds from the federal government under the terms of President Grant's peace policy. Convinced that federal Indian policy was a revolting failure, Grant instituted a series of reforms between 1869 and 1872 aimed at promoting "civilization and ultimate citizenship" for Indians, now treated as "wards of the nation" rather than as fully sovereign powers.[2] Grant's reforms included the appointment of wealthy philanthropists to a Board of Indian Commissioners to oversee Indian affairs and increased efforts at Indian missionization and education. Beginning with the Quakers and expanding to other churches, Grant turned each reservation in the country over to a Christian denomination, which appointed its ministers to be

Indian agents. The new agents were expected to hire godly men and women who would work closely with missionaries sent by the denomination. The U.S. government had a long history of subsidizing Indian missions, but the peace policy represented an unprecedented commitment to evangelism inspired by the government's ongoing reconstruction of the South. Grant intended to transform reservations from loci of poverty and corruption into centers of Christian learning where Indians would be protected from white settlers' vices and their own "savage" past. As for "wild" Indians not on reservations, they were to be cajoled—or coerced, if necessary—to move to one. The peace policy had teeth.[3]

In 1871, the Department of the Interior granted the Methodist Episcopal Church control of California's reservations, which had been consolidated into three locations: Round Valley, Hoopa Valley, and Tule River. Like most evangelicals and Indian reformers throughout the country, California's Protestant press immediately lauded Grant's plan for its focus on Christian uplift. "The Peace Policy is humane, fraternal and Christian," reported the *California Christian Advocate*. "It recognizes the degraded and savage tribes and clans of Indians as human beings who are capable of intellectual and moral improvement." The *Pacific* enthused that "for the first time since the beginning of this country, our Indians, so far as the government is concerned, are under really humane, civilizing, and Christianizing influences." Due to this unique collaboration between church and state, California's Indians, long neglected by state conferences and national missionary societies, seemed poised for Christian transformation in accordance with God's postbellum plan for global conversion. Church leaders' support for the new policy sprang from their belief that Indians, like the Chinese, were human beings who could be turned from pagan ways and granted full inclusion in Christian brotherhood.[4]

As the issue of Chinese immigration soon would, Grant's plan for Indians divided eastern congressmen from their western counterparts, with western politicians more often denouncing the peace policy as naïve, sentimental, and dangerous for white settlers. However, California's congressmen, both Republicans and Democrats, initially supported the peace policy as a superior alternative to the deplorable system J. Ross Browne had exposed during the 1860s. Aaron A. Sargent extolled the advantages of approaching Indians "with the Bible" rather than "with the rifle in hand and treating them like wild beasts." Democratic senator Eugene Casserly agreed: "Let us try a new policy; let us give it a fair try." Compared to many of their western colleagues, California's politicians had few conflicts between whites and Indians to worry about by 1870; the violent campaigns of the 1850s had killed, scattered, or driven into hiding most of those Indian groups not placed on reservations. Non-reservation Indians had become such a valuable laboring class in southern California that Democratic representative Samuel Beach Axtell protested the notion of creating a reservation for them. "We have no wars with our Indians," he boasted, calling them "peaceful, hard-working, and tolerably intelligent" and "very useful to the ranchero." Because a previous generation of Californians had decimated and marginalized the state's Indian population, officials at first welcomed the peace policy as a way to better integrate Indians into California's economy and society.[5]

Politicians' initial support for the peace policy revealed a persistent and growing split between the issues of Indian and Chinese political rights in California. Though both groups were excluded from the benefits of Reconstruction due to their pagan beliefs, they occupied increasingly different spaces in the religio-political landscape. By 1870, Republicans and Democrats agreed that Chinese immigration posed a threat to the state's economic and moral well being. As their attitudes toward the Chinese hardened, their attitudes toward Indians in some ways softened. Some politicians actively supported evangelism to California Indians and were able to imagine one day conferring full citizenship rights to Christianized Indian men. That day may have been far in the future, but it was at least imaginable, while Chinese citizenship was becoming harder and harder for them to conceive. For missionaries, both groups were equally redeemable through the power of God, but for political leaders, Indians represented less of a threat to the social order and were therefore more easily imagined as full members of the body politic.

The so-called Modoc War of 1872 and 1873, however, alerted politicians and church leaders alike to the submerged tensions lurking in rural California while striking a blow to the popularity of the peace policy. In 1864, the Office of Indian Affairs had pressured a group of Modoc Indians from the California-Oregon border region into moving to a reservation in southern Oregon. Disgusted by the harassment they received from nearby Klamath Indians, about 180 Modocs led by Kintpuash (known to whites as Captain Jack) returned to northern California in 1870, clashing with white settlers who now occupied their lands. The government sent in the Army to relocate the Modocs in 1872, but the Indians managed to hold the soldiers off for several months. After agreeing to talk with government commissioners, on April 11, 1873, the Modocs killed unarmed negotiators General Edward Canby and Eleazer Thomas, a Methodist minister from Petaluma who had volunteered to help end the

Figure 5. The Modocs' murder of unarmed negotiators Edward Canby and Eleazer Thomas seemed, to many whites, confirmation of Indians' unalterable savagery. "They thirsted for their blood like tigers," reported *Harper's Weekly* alongside this image from the issue of May 3, 1873. Courtesy of the Huntington Library, San Marino.

standoff. For observers around the country already suspicious of the peace policy, the murders crystallized fears about what resulted from "placating" Indians. Although the Board of Indian Commissioners quickly blamed the situation on the misjudgment of previous administrators, the conflict seemed to many Americans a test that the peace policy had decidedly failed, even after Captain Jack and three other Modocs were hanged in October 1873.[6]

In California, the response to the murders of Canby and Thomas was thunderous, with hatred of Indians soaring to heights not seen since the early 1850s. The *Chronicle* insisted that the murders proved Indians to be a "bloody, merciless, savage race ... incapable of Christianity and civilization, and to whom the arts of peace and pursuits of industry are impossible." The *Examiner* insisted, "There is only one way to treat Indians, and that is to send them all, individually and collectively, to see the Great Spirit, where they will occupy more congenial quarters than this world can afford them." In this spirit, several San Francisco business owners put on display what they claimed were Indian scalps, while a local rat poison salesman began advertising himself as a "Modoc exterminator."[7] With few exceptions, secular newspaper editors—Democratic and Republican, black and white—agreed that the peace policy was "a complete failure and disgrace," the Modocs must "expiate their offense with their blood, even unto the last man," and Indians were forever destined to be nothing more than "blood-thirsty savages."[8]

The San Francisco *Chronicle* predicted that "religious enthusiasm" for Grant's policy would be "silenced around the dead body of Dr. Thomas," and in fact some clergy members were sufficiently horrified by the murders as to demonize Indians and condemn the peace policy. At Thomas's enormous public funeral in San Francisco, a memorialist attributed his death to the "treachery" of "savage barbarians" in their "fierce though futile struggle" against the forces of "civilization and progress." Soon after, Presbyterian minister Robert Patterson, a longtime friend of Thomas, wrote an article for the *Overland Monthly* in which he called Indians "hunters and butchers of humanity, who would devastate a continent to preserve it for their hunting-ground." Disputing Indians' right to ownership of their lands, Patterson called for the immediate breaking up of all reservations and the application of "divinely instituted" violence to "enforce obedience" to Protestant American ways. "There is no law of heaven more absolute than that which decrees the extermination of tribes which persist in savage habits and vices," he wrote.[9]

However, like Indian reformers and peace policy supporters around the country, most of California's church leaders mourned the deaths of Canby and Thomas while advocating caution about judging Grant's policy—or the Modocs—too harshly.[10] The *Pacific, Occident, California Christian Advocate,* and *Pacific Churchman* all called for the execution of the specific Indians who had committed the murders but denounced the notion of a widespread extermination of the Modocs or all Indians, insisting on the continuing efficacy of the peace policy. One writer in the *California Christian Advocate* noted, "It is quite popular with a certain class to style the murder of Canby and Thomas 'an act of unparalleled treachery, etc.;' while everybody who knows anything of our country knows that it has been paralleled repeatedly by individuals and by men in authority." This writer also charged that Canby had moved his troops closer and closer to the Modocs during negotiations, a violation of the "rules of war" that was typical of the government's dealings with Indians: "With what grace can we utter a word of vengeance and denunciation against the 'red fiends,' while

our tongues are silent concerning, and our hands slack to punish, the mis-
deeds of our own people, by which these wars are fomented?"[11]

California's Protestant leadership defended the humanity of Indians
in a time of virulent public antipathy, hoping to buy more time for a peace
policy that had barely begun. It did not help that the Methodist Episcopal Church's initial appointments of agents in California fared poorly.
David H. Lowry resigned from the Hoopa Valley reservation in 1872 amid
charges that he had contracted syphilis from a "*digger squaw*" under his
care, and Hugh Gibson lasted only fifteen months at Round Valley before
quitting due to severe illness.[12] Observers who visited California's reservations in the early years of the peace policy found little to praise. In the
Overland Monthly, journalist Stephen Powers called them "lazarettos,
pest-houses, which are finishing well the work that was initiated twenty
years ago with the bayonet and bullet," and he reported that a missionary at Hoopa Valley could only entice Indians to attend Sunday school "by
the promise of a lickerish luncheon." According to Powers, after months
of instruction, the missionary still "dared not withdraw the post-Biblical
dough-nuts." Travel writer Charles Nordhoff visited Round Valley for
Harper's Magazine and declared the reservation "an injury to the morals
of the community in whose midst it is placed" and "an injury to the Indian, whom it demoralizes."[13]

A few months after the Canby and Thomas murders, the Methodist
California Conference was forced to request funds from the national
Methodist Episcopal Missionary Society to help establish permanent
mission stations on its three reservations. "Politicians and military officers have no sympathy for the President's Indian policy," the Conference
complained. "They watch us closely, report our lack of success, and pre-
dict the abandonment of the policy. Without some aid and co-operation
on the part of the Church we cannot hope to command the confidence
of the public, or to accomplish much in civilizing and Christianizing the
Indian tribes of this continent." California's religious leaders felt they
needed a miracle to dispel the bad press and skepticism that had surrounded Indian evangelism in the wake of the Modoc War. A year later,
at Round Valley, an apparent miracle arrived.[14]

"The best fruit of the Peace Policy": Revival at Round Valley

When Methodist minister John Luther Burchard arrived in Round Valley
in October 1872, he found the reservation "in much disorder." The illness
of former agent Hugh Gibson had left him incapable of overseeing daily
operations, and the Army's relocation of more than a thousand Indians

from nearby Little Lake Valley to the reservation—more than doubling the number of people there—had taxed food supplies to the point that a local paper reported that the Indians were "literally starving to death."[15]

In fact, living conditions had been frequently harsh on the reservation since its creation in 1856 as the Nome Cult Farm, one of seven such Indian detention centers established in California by the federal government in the mid-1850s. Renamed Round Valley Indian Reservation in 1860 after the valley in which it was located, it housed an ever-fluctuating population of local Yuki and relocated Nomlaki, Wailaki, Concow Maidu, Little Lake Pomo, Pit River, Redwood Valley, Potter Valley, and other Indian groups from northern California and the Central Valley, lumped together as "Round Valley Indians." Initially, all 25,000 acres of Round Valley were allocated for the reservation, but a steady in-migration of white settlers left the Indians with the use of only about 4,800 acres by 1872. Soldiers from Camp Wright, a U.S. Army post constructed nearby during the 1860s, generally protected the interests of whites when conflicts arose with Indians. Many of the settlers hoped to see the reservation entirely broken up, thereby legitimating their land claims; others were content with the status quo because they relied on reservation Indians as a source of cheap agricultural labor. The reservation's inexact boundaries and uncertain future bred frustration and fatalism among government agents and employees. Though forbidden to leave, Indian groups managed to come and go, remaining on the reservation until a better option presented itself.[16]

J. L. Burchard quickly initiated a series of reforms aimed at improving conditions on the reservation and Christianizing the Indians. Born in Delaware but ordained in Missouri into the southern wing of the Methodist Episcopal Church, Burchard had transferred to the church's northern branch in California in 1870 and become a firm believer in Indians' potential to become Christians and citizens. Accordingly, he hired only Christian employees with "good moral character." He organized Indians into work crews to construct several buildings and cultivate almost a thousand acres of reservation lands. He gave each Indian family a plot of ground to plant a personal garden if they wished. He started a second day school for Indian children and maintained Sunday services, and he requested musical instruments from the government to thwart "melancholy and gloom." American Missionary Association agents Mary K. Colburn and Mary A. Burnett arrived in mid-1873, giving up their work with the Chinese in Stockton in hope of "bringing these Indians out of darkness, into the glorious light and liberty of the Gospel."[17]

Compared to urban missionaries among the Chinese, Burchard held much more power to shape Indians' daily lives. Supported by employees, nearby Army soldiers, and the federal government, Burchard controlled Indians' access to food and medical care, determined where on the reservation they could live, and compelled their labor. This power allowed him to attempt to restructure Indians' gender roles, sexuality, dress, comportment, living arrangements, and work in accordance with Anglo-Protestant ideals. Burchard removed all sweathouses from the reservation, believing them to foster disease and paganism; he also began replacing Indians' grass huts with whitewashed wood houses and encouraged Indians to sleep in beds rather than on the ground. He forbade Indians from burning their dead, instead establishing a cemetery for each tribal group. He encouraged Indian men and women to practice monogamy and formally marry in a Christian ceremony, and in October 1873, he officiated at the wedding of Poney Stone and Lou Townend, the "first lawful Christian marriage celebrated between two full-blooded Indians on this Reservation." Journalist Stephen Powers reported that, during a visit to Round Valley, he glimpsed a *"i-wa-mūsp* (man-woman)" among the Yuki wearing a dress and possessing a deep voice and "whisker." At Powers's suggestion, Burchard "exerted his authority and caused this being to be brought to headquarters and submitted to a medical examination," revealing the Yuki to be "a human male without malformation, but apparently destitute of desire and virility." Emboldened by his steadfast belief in the superiority of Protestantism, Burchard wielded sufficient power to intrude into every aspect of the Indians' lives, no matter how intimate.[18]

For Indians who disobeyed, told lies, or acted violently, Burchard enforced discipline by locking them up alone overnight or, if necessary, having them whipped. In 1874 he reported that he had ordered employees to whip Indian men on six occasions during his first two years at Round Valley, insisting that the punishments were "not excessive; *never* cruel, but always with good results." When Indians left the reservation, which they frequently did, Burchard employed the Army to try to bring them back. Nonetheless, the number of Indians at Round Valley dropped from 1,700 when he arrived in 1872 to 1,112 in 1873 and 976 in 1874, suggesting that some Indians protested Burchard's policies with their feet.[19]

Among white Californians, at least, Burchard's efforts initially earned praise. Eager for a success story, the Methodist *California Christian Advocate* ran a series of articles touting the improvements at Round Valley, reporting that the Indians "are all well fed and clothed, enjoy good health, seem to be well contented and comparatively happy." Even the Mendocino

Democrat, generally hostile toward the peace policy and the reservation, printed a glowing report of Burchard's administration, predicting "much greater success in the way of products and general improvement of the Reservation and benefit to the Indians than has ever been attained at any former time in the history of this Reservation."[20]

One dissenting voice came from the San Francisco *Daily Alta California,* a consistent opponent of the peace policy, which in early 1874 reported that Burchard was secretly planning to turn most of Round Valley over to a local sheep rancher, thereby evicting "a large number of settlers." Burchard denied the charges, and H. C. Benson's *California Christian Advocate* sprang to his defense, insisting that the reports had been concocted by settlers—whom the paper called "trespassers"—looking to poison Burchard's reputation. "It is surely the duty of Christian men, who are friends of the Indians, to come to the rescue—to rebuke evil-doers and to expose falsehood," wrote Benson.[21] With this rhetoric, the *California Christian Advocate* turned the rumors about Burchard into a test for Christians as to which newspaper they believed. True Christians, the paper argued, supported Burchard as well as the reservation system he represented. The *Daily Alta California* responded that it was Benson who was being ungodly for repeating Burchard's supposed lies and failing to act "the part of a Christian and mediator." The dispute between the two newspapers, which raged on for several months and spilled over into other papers, demonstrated the continuing split between California's religious and secular press over Grant's Indian policy. Benson's spirited defense had turned Burchard into an emblem of the peace policy even before the revival began capturing headlines.[22]

In the middle of this quarrel, a different kind of report began to issue from Round Valley that focused much more public attention on the reservation. Beginning in January 1874, Burchard began holding seven-evenings-a-week prayer services for the Indians in the two schools. One month later, Burchard informed the Commissioner of Indian Affairs that 490 Indians had joined the church, and "very many of them give bright evidence of genuine conversion, praying and talking with an intelligence that astonishes and confounds us all, beyond measure." Burchard, Colburn, Burnett, and other reservation employees kept up the revival services for forty-six straight nights, and the number of reported converts rose steadily throughout the year: 800 by the end of March and 974 by the end of December, comprising the entirety of the reservation.[23]

To Burchard and his employees, the mass conversions seemed sincere in that they brought immediate changes to the Indians' behavior and appearance. Burchard reported that "all dancing, swearing, drinking, gambling, Sabbath-breaking, and all the pagan practices and habits, have been abandoned; citizens' dress universally adopted." According to an employee, several zealous Indians had begun "very earnestly and efficiently preaching Jesus to their respective tribes in their own tongues." By September, six Indian men had been licensed as Methodist preachers. Dozens of newly Christianized Indian couples were legally married in accordance with the Protestant model.[24]

As word of the revival spread, outsiders began heading to Round Valley to witness the phenomenon for themselves. Methodist visitors confirmed that the Indians' conversions were genuine and would be long-lasting. After watching an Independence Day program featuring music and recitations by Indian children, one minister reflected, "The more I see of the fruits of the revival, the more and *more* I am convinced that it is of God. There seems to be a permanent and steady work going on here." He predicted that full citizenship was only a few years away: "If these Indians continue to improve in the next five years as they have in the last year, the work of this Reservation will be well-nigh completed, and these wards of the Government will be educated to be useful, orderly and industrious citizens." Benson himself traveled up from San Francisco in late September, at one point awkwardly sharing a coach with two settlers who—not realizing Benson's identity—denounced his *California Christian Advocate* for its insults to Round Valley "trespassers." Benson happily announced to his readers, "There has not been a single case of apostasy.... The pentecostal baptism of last winter was genuine, or we are utterly unable to judge of the fruits of the Spirit."[25]

Even military officers were impressed by the Indians' religious zeal. Samuel Breck, sent by the Army to investigate the revival, praised the missionaries' efforts and the Indians' rapid improvement in morality and education. While noting that nearby white settlers "seemed very doubtful about the permanency of this change, and genuineness of the professions of the Indians," Breck expressed optimism about the Indians' future: "I am convinced that great good has already been accomplished." Similarly, A. G. Tassin, a lieutenant at Camp Wright, declared Round Valley "very probably, the best conducted Indian reservation in the United States." Under Burchard, the Indians were "well fed and clothed and their progress in christianity and civilization is truly wonderful." Tassin described watching a young Indian man "with a stick on a sand bar" explaining Euclidean geometry to a group of his friends, leaving Tassin "astonished."[26]

For observers and reservation employees alike, the revival at Round Valley demonstrated Christianity's potential to uplift all human beings, even "Diggers." Benson noted, "Like children, the converts will be liable to stumble and fall. We have confidence, however, in the grace and mercy of the Lord; the appliances of the gospel are suited to all possible conditions of humanity." J. L. Broaddus agreed that the revival revealed the "power of our holy religion to purify and elevate even the most degraded of our race." Broaddus's use of "our" race rather than "their" race demonstrated his rejection of rigid racial categories. For these missionaries and ministers, Indians were "degraded" and "like children" not because of their race but because of their pagan beliefs, now transformed through the workings of the Holy Spirit.[27]

To be sure, the Methodists' perceptions of events at Round Valley were colored by their desire for good news for the peace policy in a time of crisis and their hopes for global conversion. They seized on the revival as a vindication of the reservation system. "This is the best fruit of the Peace Policy of President U. S. Grant," Burchard informed the Commissioner of Indian Affairs. The stream of articles about the revival printed by the *California Christian Advocate* strengthened the paper's position in its ongoing debates with the *Daily Alta California* and other skeptics. In fact, Burchard's evangelical success served the needs of peace policy proponents throughout the country. The American Missionary Association, the national Missionary Society of the Methodist Episcopal Church, the New York *Christian Advocate,* and the New York *Independent* all publicized the Round Valley revival. Isaac Mast, a Methodist minister from Pennsylvania who visited California in 1874, touted the progress of Round Valley Indians in his travel memoir. "They have left off their heathen practices, have formed civilized habits," he wrote. Their lives constituted "abundant proof of the wisdom of President Grant's policy toward these unfortunate wards of the nation." Round Valley had become a symbol of humanitarianism toward Indians, the efficacy of the reservation system, and the peace policy's potential to solve the Indian question once and for all.[28]

"No negro in the South was ever treated worse": *Opposition to the Peace Policy*

At the same time, Round Valley's new prominence made it an even larger target for enemies of Indian assimilation. Just as opponents of Chinese immigration questioned the sincerity of Chinese Christians, opponents of Indian citizenship mocked the notion that more than 900 Indians had suddenly become true believers. The *Daily Alta California* echoed the skepticism of Round Valley settlers about the permanency of the change. The paper accused Burchard of "bribing, cajoling or driving" the "unfortunate savages, who cannot read, who do not understand English.... True religion is not something that can be given to red men in breech-cloths like a dose of medicine." Another writer mocked Burchard's reports of Indians "crowding to the church. They would do the same thing to a circus, if one came along the next day.... The stories are all nonsense." On another occasion, the newspaper warned, "Educate a full-blooded Indian, give him all the advantages of our academies, colleges, universities, and the probable result will be that he returns to his tribe, perhaps as a missionary, very soon relapses into his old Indian habits, and, instead of his graduating clothes, his dress-parade suit will be a breech-cloth." In these attacks, the newspaper tried to have it both ways, arguing that the Indians' conversions could not be genuine because of their racial inferiority *and* because of the poor treatment they had received from whites. Alternating between crocodile tears and racist dismissals, the paper combated the peace policy by ridiculing the very idea that Indians—especially Round Valley Indians—could ever become true Christians.[29]

An even stronger assault came from Democratic U.S. representative J. K. Luttrell, who inspected Round Valley in November 1874. Luttrell gave a speech to the Indians praising the reservation's administration, and Burchard believed that the congressman had left with the impression that Round Valley had "no parallel," but two months later Luttrell excoriated Burchard from the floor of Congress during a debate on the peace policy. Luttrell recommended turning Round Valley over to a private entrepreneur who offered to run it as a business, cover all expenses, and reap the profits from the sale of agricultural goods. When a Republican asked if this plan would "reduce these Indians to a state of peonage," Luttrell responded that under Burchard the Round Valley Indians "are worked just like peons" and are "stripped, tied up, and whipped like dogs, just as was done in days gone by in the Southern States with the negroes. No negro in the South was ever treated worse than some of these Indians have been treated." In his report to the Office of Indian Affairs that he filed the next day, Luttrell claimed that the Round Valley Indians lived in "grass huts, with scarcely any covering and with but little clothing," were "poorly fed," "maltreated and badly used," and showed "but little aptitude" for their educational studies. He admitted that "many Indians gave evidence of Christianity" but complained that Burchard devoted "much attention to their spiritual wants, to the neglect of their physical." For these problems and for "adhering to a system of punishment both brutal and barbarous," Luttrell recommended Burchard's removal.[30]

By his own admission, Luttrell's attack dovetailed with his desire to end the peace policy and privatize the reservation system. Like the *Daily Alta California,* Luttrell used a show of sympathy for Indians to denigrate Republican Indian policy. His likening of Round Valley Indians to southern slaves was an attempt to use Republicans' own antislavery rhetoric against them, just as California's politicians—including Luttrell himself—called Chinese men "slaves" and cited the Thirteenth Amendment as grounds to halt the immigration of Chinese "coolies." Luttrell's criticism that Burchard was misguided in focusing on converting Indians to Christianity, together with his plan to turn Round Valley into a privately run agricultural factory, showed that he viewed Indians first and foremost as a labor source to be exploited.[31]

Luttrell's charges stirred up a new round of controversy about Round Valley, with advocates of the peace policy once again portraying the Indians as true Christians and the attacks on Burchard as ungodly. Round Valley employees, local military officers, and pro-Burchard settlers wrote a volley of letters to various government officials assuring them that Luttrell's allegations were "a pack of contemptible falsehoods and lies." A group of more than thirty Round Valley settlers cosigned an open letter to the Commissioner of Indian Affairs praising Burchard's "kind treatment and superior teaching" and insisting that "the Indians have been taught to read and write, and to observe the Sabbath; what *more* can be asked?" In a letter to the Mendocino *Democrat,* Burchard invited skeptics to "visit this reservation . . . , meet with them in their places of worship, hear them sing, and talk, and pray; compare their present 'civilization' with their former condition." Burchard also requested that the government make an immediate full investigation of Round Valley, and he chalked up Luttrell's attack to political motivations.[32]

As for corporal punishment, Burchard admitted that he ordered whippings for several Indians but said he was merely following the disciplinary standards of "other reservations in this State." The state and national Methodist press sprang to Burchard's defense, insisting that the whippings were "only what would be necessary in any family government," and that "nine-tenths of the citizens of this valley do not regard the punishment as unreasonable." According to Burchard and his supporters, an attack on the reservation was an attack on Christianity, the Republican Party, and the redeemability of Indians. Their support of whipping—a

practice the Commissioner of Indian Affairs called "demoralizing and de-
testable" in a letter reprimanding Burchard—as a form of discipline typical to any "family" was in line with most Protestants' view of Indians as
spiritual children and missionaries as stern Christian parents.[33]

As expected, California's secular press seized on Luttrell's charges to
further refute the Round Valley revival and discredit the peace policy.
The *Daily Alta California* reported that Burchard's boast of having "converted the red people suddenly" was "improbable and in bad taste," given
Luttrell's findings. A writer for the Mendocino *Independent Dispatch*,
another newspaper in favor of breaking up the reservation, belittled the
settlers who had cosigned a letter of support for Burchard, describing
them as a group of mostly newcomers to the valley that included a "half
breed Spaniard," a "poor old man" who wanted a job on the reservation, a
"poor half-witted fellow [who] dances in bar rooms for whiskey," two
members of the "Indian church," several "strangers," a "very dark Spaniard,
[who] belongs to the Indian church and sleeps in the Indian lodges when
in the valley," and likely one or two Indians. This writer's characterizations relied on stereotypes of race, class, age, and religion to damn Burchard's supporters, mingling notions of racial inferiority, poverty, dotage,
and paganism.[34]

Burchard's supporters received a chance to explicate their defense
when the Office of Indian Affairs sent inspector William Vandever to
Round Valley in April 1875. Vandever—a devout Presbyterian, longtime
Republican, and employee of the Grant administration—likely arrived
predisposed to favor Burchard, and he uncovered nothing in his investigation that made him change that view. Employees, Army officers, and
settlers exclaimed the changes the Indians had recently undergone: They
no longer practiced "promiscuous sexual intercourse," they had made
"great progress in religious instruction," and their children were now
"raised as among white people." Vandever also met with the captains of
the seven largest tribal groups at Round Valley, accompanied by H. C.
Benson, who had traveled up from San Francisco to represent the Missionary Society of the Methodist Episcopal Church. According to Vandever's and Benson's reports, all of the captains praised Burchard for
doing "more for the Indians than all the Agents who had preceded him."
Peter Hudson, captain of the Redwood Valley tribe, declared that he
"liked Agent Burchard, who had led them out of darkness into the light."[35]

Vandever told the Office of Indian Affairs that his investigation had
disproved Luttrell's charges, and that the Indians were a "devout, orderly,
church-going people. I spent three Sabbaths with them, and can say from

actual observation that I have seldom been among a people that seemed to enjoy church privileges, and religious exercises as much as they do." The *California Christian Advocate* and New York *Christian Advocate* trumpeted the news of Burchard's vindication, urging "Christian voters" in Luttrell's district to vote him out of office on the basis of "Christian principle."[36]

Burchard and the peace policy had survived another assault, and for the moment, their mutual prospects looked bright. In June 1875, the Army closed Camp Wright, an action Burchard had long advocated as a symbol of the government's new approach to Indians. In October, the Methodist California Conference happily renewed his appointment while the denomination's Lay Electoral Conference affirmed its support for the peace policy, expressing faith that—"judging from the experience on the Round Valley Reservation"—Grant's policy would "in a decade of years . . . save the Government from all expense in the support of Indians, and result in their entire Christianization." More than a year into the revival, Burchard noted that all 985 Round Valley Indians remained steadfast Christians. "A more thoroughly reformed, changed people, I have never known," he reported. "We now have a church membership in respect to numbers and consistent piety equaled by few churches of our land; and, for the first time within the knowledge of the white man, the increase of the Indians here exceeds the decrease." California's Protestant leaders looked forward to a near future when Indians—far from being a race of savages doomed to die out—would join their fellow black, white, and Chinese Americans as Christian citizens in a new nation.[37]

"This is our home": Christianity and Native American Cultural Transformation

Whereas Chinese Californians had the option of moving from church to church in search of more favorable treatment, reservation Indians in California had, per government dictate, only the Methodist Episcopal Church officially serving them. Round Valley Indians could leave—and some did under Burchard—but those who remained had to accommodate to the Methodist Church and the ramifications of Burchard's beliefs. The fact that so many Indians at Round Valley joined the church is attributable to several factors: the enthusiasm of the reservation's employees and missionaries, the emotionalism and contagious nature of revivalism, pre-existing intertribal conflicts and intratribal power structures, and the possibilities Christianity offered for cultural survival and transformation.

In fact, the revival of 1874 was not the first religious movement to sweep Round Valley in the early 1870s. A pan-Indian religious revival, later called the "1870 Ghost Dance" by anthropologists, moved from the Great Basin into northern California and Oregon after 1870, spreading the idea that a certain form of round dancing would trigger the end of this world and the arrival of a utopian new one populated by all Indians, living and dead.[38] One reason the Army relocated more than a thousand Indians from Little Lake Valley onto the Round Valley reservation in May 1872 was because the Indians were alarming white settlers by holding "grand dances" due to a "prophetic report" that the "ocean is going to rise and roll in upon the land very soon, or that a comet or some other destructive element is to visit the earth and scatter desolation and ruin." Immediately after that relocation, agent Hugh Gibson recorded that all the Indians at Round Valley refused to plant crops because "they have all become convinced that the world is to end during the month of August next."[39]

Disappointment that the new world did not arrive as hoped might have contributed to the Indians' subsequent turn toward Christianity. In the midst of the Methodist revival, Burchard reported that the Indians "now see they have been twice deceived by false prophets" and are no longer interested in having any "scare, excitement, and religious dances." Of course, Protestantism offered its own paradisiacal future, complete with apocalypse and resurrections. Riley Elliott, a Christian convert who died at Round Valley in 1874, said from his deathbed, "I am going home to die no more. I am close to that last river; Jesus is on the other side, and will stretch out his hand to help me over." The theology of the Ghost Dance, with its elements borrowed from Christianity, paved the way for the Methodist revival.[40]

As with the Ghost Dance, Christianity carried the potential to unite Round Valley's various tribal groups around a shared cosmological vision. During the revival, Burchard marveled that all feuding between and within Indian groups had ceased. Christianity allowed each group to retain their older sense of tribal identity while encouraging a shared pan-Indian consciousness. Just as Chinese Christians worried about the eternal souls of their heathen countrymen, Christian Indians began to worry about the fate of unsaved Indians throughout the region. According to one visitor, the Round Valley Indians planned to hold a "camp-meeting some time in October [1874] the Lord willing, to which they think of inviting Indians from abroad to attend with the hopes of doing them good. These Indians have the missionary spirit burning in them."[41]

The Round Valley revival services followed an evangelical Protestant model well honed by the 1870s.[42] Nighttime meetings, crowded rooms, public testimonies, singing, and baptisms contributed to a highly charged emotional atmosphere. Observers described Indians "weeping" in rooms stuffed with people "almost to suffocation," encouraging an uncontainable excitement of body and emotions. "I so happy I can't sit still; I don't know what to do; seem like Jesus lift me right up," exclaimed one Indian. Said another, "I feel changed. Something has got into my heart, into my bones, into my brains, and the brain must take charge of it."[43]

Round Valley missionaries made use of pre-existing tribal hierarchies to spread the effects of the revival. By targeting tribal captains, who had traditionally been spiritual as well as political leaders, missionaries took advantage of these men's influence. "The chiefs and leaders are actively working for their new Master, and urging their tribes to come to Jesus," noted Mary K. Colburn. Captains John Brown (Yuki) and Charles Munsell (Concow Maidu) became licensed Methodist preachers, adding the authority of the church to their already substantial standing on the reservation.[44]

Despite the breadth of the revival, adoption of Christianity carried with it the danger of separation from non-Christian friends and family for Round Valley Indians. Marriage and kinship ties connected Indians on the reservation to Indians throughout California and Oregon, some of whom were hostile to Christianity. "I feel very sorry sometimes; my wife is not a Christian, and does not help me in the good way," complained one man. "She often laughs at me for being a Christian, and says things that make me feel very bad. But I pray to our Father to help me to bear it, and not abuse her for it." As in the case with Chinese church members, Indians jeopardized existing relationships when they adopted Christianity.[45]

However, Christianity gave Indians, like Chinese churchgoers, an avenue to engage in politics. One visitor described watching the Round Valley Indians praying "earnestly for the President, and those who were making our laws at Washington, that they might be given wisdom to make good laws, seemingly, under the conviction that they greatly needed it." Ostensibly directed to God, such public pleas were ways of criticizing governmental policy.

On another occasion, the Round Valley captains called a meeting with the reservation's employees to inform them that local white settlers had been telling the Indians that Burchard was stealing from them. During the meeting, however, the captains defended Burchard as a godly influence. Munsell said that Burchard "is the first man that is not ashamed to shake our dirty hands, and speak to us the good kind word." Ukiah captain Mike Hunter asserted, "We want to have our land, and live in peace like educated white people." Harry Wood agreed: "We want all this territory to hunt and fish in. This is our home. We will live and die here. Here we will stand. We must not listen to outsiders, but stick to our Agent and pray for him." These pronouncements aligned Christianity with egalitarian treatment of Indians and support for their claims on reservation lands. They said they supported Burchard because he offered Christianity, treated them as "brothers," and forwarded their interests in a wider political arena in which they also interacted, as demonstrated by white settlers' attempts to turn them against Burchard.[46]

Burchard's willingness to shake the Indians' "dirty hands" symbolized, for Munsell, the minister's egalitarian spirit, his use of corporal punishment notwithstanding. In an era when most white Californians viewed Indians and the Chinese as racially inferior and irredeemably pagan, Burchard and other like-minded Protestants offered an alternative explanation of cultural difference that emphasized spiritual progress and Christianity's redemptive powers. Attacked by politicians, newspapers, "hoodlums," and a few fellow ministers, these white missionaries and their Indian and Chinese church members threatened to dissolve divisions between Christian and heathen, outcast and citizen. Meanwhile, Munsell and other Indian and Chinese church members attempted to harness Christianity's political and cultural power for themselves, positioning themselves to best advantage in California's shifting religio-political order.

Of course, Round Valley Indians had encountered Christianity before the advent of the peace policy, just as most of California's Chinese residents had been exposed to the religion before leaving China. Decades of interaction with Spaniards, Mexicans, and Americans had given Round Valley Indians at the very least an understanding of the basics of the religion. A Roman Catholic priest named Luciano Osuna had been preaching to Indians throughout Mendocino County since 1864, and he reported that older Indians at Round Valley remembered Catholic doctrine from their time on Franciscan missions in the early nineteenth century. Osuna's stubborn dedication to Round Valley's "Catholic" Indians would soon lead to a violent clash with Burchard, part of a broader escalation of conflict between California's Catholics and Protestants that occurred in the 1870s over questions of race.

ANTI-CATHOLICISM AND THE LIMITS OF
PROTESTANT CONSENSUS

T he announcement that James Buchard, California's most popular
Roman Catholic orator, would address the question "White Man
or Chinaman—Which?" ensured a packed house, but the turnout
for his talk on February 25, 1873, exceeded all expectations. So many people crowded into St. Francis of Assisi Church, one of the biggest in San
Francisco, that all sitting and standing room filled, and many were turned
away at the door. Ordained into the Society of Jesus in Missouri, Buchard
had served in California since 1861, becoming known as a stirring speaker
and forceful defender of Catholicism. His lecture on the Chinese question
only furthered this reputation. He denounced emigration from China as
an "influx of thousands of ignorant idolators" that was degrading the lives
of white American laborers. He disputed the notion, advanced by "phil-
anthropic citizens" and Protestant "religious zealots," that Chinese immigrants were becoming Christians, insisting, "They are as great pagans
to-day as they were in the beginning. . . . I have very little confidence that
any considerable number, if any one at all, of all the Chinese population
will ever be converted to Christianity here." Rather than filling California with "this inferior race; these pagan, these vicious, these immoral
creatures, that are incapable of rising to the virtue that is inculcated by
the religion of Jesus Christ," Buchard advocated limiting immigration to
"European immigrants—these hard-working, economical, intelligent white
people. . . . 'Tis the white race we want."[1]

Few if any of the audience members that evening knew two secrets
from Buchard's past that no doubt would have influenced their reaction
to his speech. The first was that, as a young man, Buchard had studied for
several years to be a Presbyterian minister before experiencing a change of
heart that led him instead to Jesuit training. The second secret would have
been far more shocking: Buchard had been born and raised on a Delaware
Indian reserve in present-day Kansas. The son of a Delaware father and a

French mother who had been adopted by Comanches as a girl, Buchard was known as Watomika until his baptism in 1847. Although some of Buchard's fellow Jesuits knew of his religious and racial background, he kept it hidden from the California audiences who turned out for his sermons and speeches. As a one-time member of a racially marked group who had found acceptance among whites through religious conversion and migration to California, Buchard was a beneficiary of the same type of mission work he condemned when extended to the Chinese. In an era of surging anti-Catholicism, Buchard used the specter of the Chinese to align himself and the Catholic Church's European immigrant membership more firmly with Christian whiteness.[2]

Buchard's anti-Chinese agitation and hidden Indian past demonstrate the unexpected and complex intersections of Catholicism, anti-Catholicism, and race that emerged in California during the early 1870s. Conflicts over public schools, immigration, and Indian policy exacerbated long-simmering tensions between Protestants and Catholics, giving rise to a vigorous anti-Catholic movement that marked "Romanists" as both racially and religiously inferior. Irish and Mexican Catholics in particular inhabited ambiguous religio-racial spaces, considered neither fully white nor fully Christian. Anti-Catholic discourse was a powerful component of the Protestant consensus in the early 1870s that supported unrestricted immigration and the peace policy as divinely inspired tools in the incorporation of Chinese immigrants and Indians into American society.

By 1876, however, that consensus would start to break down. In San Francisco, Irish Catholics increasingly staked their claim to Christian whiteness on their opposition to Chinese immigration, successfully portraying themselves as potential allies to white Protestants in a common struggle against debasing pagan outsiders. At Round Valley Indian Reservation, a dispute between Catholics and Protestants revealed the limits of Protestant missionaries' universalism and racial tolerance. Meanwhile, Catholic Church leaders were pulled between a desire to convert Indians and the Chinese in accordance with the Church's longstanding commitment to universal evangelism, on one hand, and a temptation to demonize them to elevate the status of their "off-white" membership, on the other. While theoretically uniting Protestants, anti-Catholicism was at times leveraged by competing Protestant groups for opposite political purposes. Anti-Catholicism in California carried shifting, contradictory racial meanings for Irish and Chinese immigrants as well as for Indians, African Americans, and Mexican Americans, at times dovetailing with white supremacy, at times with racial egalitarianism.

"Public school soup":
The School Question and Race in San Francisco

Anti-Catholicism in the United States, which traced its deep roots to the Reformation and colonial conflicts with Spain and France, had surged during the 1830s, 1840s, and 1850s in response to the annexation of northern Mexico and increased immigration from Ireland and Germany. The nativist American Party—better known as the Know Nothings— won stunning victories throughout the country in the mid-1850s by offering in anti-Catholicism a fleeting distraction from sectional conflict.[3] In California, the Know Nothings elected their entire slate of candidates in 1855, capturing the governorship and both houses of the legislature. Fear of Catholic dominion in California spurred Protestant missionary efforts, while ministers called Californios' Catholic burial rites "a grade above paganism" and vandals desecrated Junípero Serra's grave. However, compared to the Northeast, anti-Catholicism remained relatively weak in California during the 1850s as chaotic social conditions encouraged Protestants to embrace Catholics as co-civilizers of an untamed land. The state's Know Nothings were markedly less anti-Catholic than the national party; the first state governor, Peter Burnett, was a Catholic convert; and a number of Irish Catholics rose to prominence in state government.[4]

After a lull during the war-torn 1860s, anti-Catholicism in the United States re-emerged in the 1870s as a major political issue and preoccupation of Protestant thinkers. Bolstered by continuing emigration from Ireland, Germany, Italy, and eastern Europe, Catholics now constituted about 15 percent of the U.S. population in 1870 and more than half of some urban centers. The Church's increasing numbers encouraged a new flexing of political muscle. Throughout the country, Catholics strove to reform public school systems, which they viewed as unabashedly Protestant. Asserting that the King James Bible, Lord's Prayer, and hymns used in public schools were sectarian, activists called on local governments to abolish those practices or to grant parochial schools a portion of tax funds or exemption from taxation. In 1869, Cincinnati's school board prohibited the reading of all religious books in its public schools, and over the next few years, school boards in New York City, Chicago, Buffalo, and Rochester did the same. The "school question" became a divisive issue in local and national politics. Republicans, under fire for their Reconstruction policies, seized on anti-Catholicism as a way to cast themselves as protectors of American institutions rather than as the extremists Democrats portrayed them as. Recycling rhetoric from the antebellum period and earlier, Republican politicians and Protestant church leaders decried Catholicism as incompatible with American values of individualism and democracy. They pointed to the Vatican Council of 1869, which defined the dogma of papal infallibility, and American Catholics' support of Pope Pius IX in his conflict with the Kingdom of Italy, as evidence of Catholics' mindless allegiance to a foreign power. On the school question, most Republicans promoted a continuation of the Protestant-dominated status quo while a few went further, urging a complete separation of church and state to protect schools from Catholic influence.[5]

In California, the muted anti-Catholicism of the 1850s and 1860s gave way to a vigorous movement in the early 1870s centered in San Francisco. In 1870, more than 40 percent of the city's residents were foreign-born European immigrants, with Irish Catholics by far comprising the largest group.[6] As Catholics rose in power and prominence, Protestant leaders began issuing warnings about the creeping threat they posed. "The Roman Catholic element in our population is certainly an element of trouble and danger," reported the Congregationalist *Pacific* in 1867. "A class of people largely ignorant, degraded, and vicious is a burdensome class, and demands care, patience, and watching." George Thistleton's *Jolly Giant,* a tabloid largely devoted to sensationalistic exposés of alleged Catholic conspiracies, began publication in 1873 and soon claimed to be outselling all other weeklies on the Pacific coast. By 1874, San Franciscans supported five American Protestant Association lodges and a branch of the Orange Order, organizations dedicated to combating the spread of Catholicism. Local Protestant ministers denounced Catholicism as a perversion of Christianity; in the words of Congregationalist Samuel V. Blakeslee, "Romanism" was nothing more than "idolatry . . . clearly in violation of the Gospel of Jesus Christ."[7]

Because of these deep animosities, the school question erupted in San Francisco with as much force as almost anywhere in the nation. Struggles between Protestants and Catholics over education in California had occurred intermittently since 1855, when the legislature outlawed the teaching of all "sectarian and denominational doctrines" in publicly funded schools. In 1861, Zachariah Montgomery, a Catholic state senator, had unsuccessfully tried to extend public funding to religious schools; his proposal had split California's Protestant ministers, with some viewing it as a way to promote Christianity among schoolchildren and others decrying it as a Catholic plot to usurp funds for nefarious purposes. As Catholics' numbers grew in California during the 1860s and 1870s, they intensified their efforts at winning funding or tax exemption for parochial schools and at ending Protestant practices in the supposedly nonsectarian public schools. The state's two Catholic newspapers, the *Monitor* and *Catholic Guardian,* complained that parochial schools suffered while "godless" Protestant public schools received state support. In response to Catholic pressure, Democratic state superintendents established several "cosmopolitan" public schools in San Francisco with instruction in French, German, or Spanish. Catholics and their allies in the Democratic Party took control of the San Francisco school board in the early 1870s and in 1874 ruled that the Lord's Prayer was too sectarian for use in public schools.[8]

As their counterparts did in other states, Republicans in California used the school question to present themselves as traditionalists preserving old-fashioned morality against Catholic corruption. In their 1871 and 1875 state platforms, Republicans declared their opposition to any division of school funds to include parochial schools. This move served as a distraction from the party's support for the integration of African Americans students into all-white schools, which failed at the state level due to *Ward v. Flood* but succeeded in San Francisco in 1875. However, California's Republican U.S. senator, Aaron A. Sargent, broke with his party to oppose racially integrated schools, and during congressional debates, he cited the Catholic menace as a bigger threat than segregation to American schoolchildren. He described the Catholic Church as a "powerful, far-reaching influence," wielding "great wealth" and the "fanaticism" of its devotees, "working day by day to strike down your common-school system." According to Sargent, in this time of crisis, the integration of African American students would "re-inforce that adverse influence." Anti-Catholicism proved useful to both sides of the racial integration debate in California.[9]

San Francisco's Protestant leadership responded to the school question with disgust and dismay. They viewed public schools as the bedrock of American Protestantism and citizenship, and they insisted that the Catholic Church's true aim was not the removal of sectarian materials but the "destruction of our common school system, as the one formal and potential antagonism of the Roman Papal Hierarchy." At the same time, they scoffed at the notion that the Lord's Prayer was offensively sectarian. In an 1875 sermon, Presbyterian minister John Hemphill explained that the prayer was "an address to the universal Father which may be used with good conscience by Pagan, Jew, or Christian."[10] Born in Ireland into a Presbyterian family, Hemphill had brought to California an intense hatred of Catholicism forged by decades of Anglo-Irish conflict, and he had found plenty of incentives in San Francisco to differentiate himself as "Scotch Irish" from Irish Catholics. Hemphill rose to prominence in the early 1870s on the basis of his virulently anti-Catholic sermons, speeches, and writings. He drew cheers with his outraged denunciations of Catholic "vampires" and grabbed attention with a series of attacks on the outspoken Jesuit James Buchard. George Thistleton's *Jolly Giant*, which usually chided Protestant ministers for not being sufficiently anti-Catholic, deemed Hemphill "the greatest man in California."[11]

In his enthusiasm for decrying "Popery," Hemphill drew heavily on racialized language. After Buchard gave a speech calling Catholics the "elite of Christendom," Hemphill retorted that he "might with equal justice pronounce the lazy Mexicans 'the elite of Christendom.'" He said that outlawing the Lord's Prayer because it offended Catholics was akin to removing books that offended Chinese Confucianists. "Come, gentlemen of the Board of Education, be consistent," he said sarcastically. "Bring down your system of education to suit the requirements of the Chinaman." The *Jolly Giant* foresaw a similarly slippery slope: "The Chinaman will by and by want to instruct the pig-tailed children of his tribe in the doctrine of Confucius, and should we be fortunate enough to bag a few of the red-skinned savages into our schools they too will demand equal rights with the Irish priest." The paper also published a cartoon that portrayed the school board as a group of chefs cooking "public school soup"; a snake instructs an Irish Catholic chef to poison the soup while a German and Frenchman add their spices and an apelike African American and ratlike Chinese man look on. In these instances, anti-Catholicism merged with a generalized antipathy toward racially marked groups: Catholics, Mexicans, Indians, African Americans, and the Chinese were all lumped together as debasing outsiders.[12]

In particular, many Protestant observers emphasized similarities between Catholic and Chinese worship practices. Extending an older discourse that partly sprang from competition between Catholic and Protestant missionaries in China, many Protestants in California drew attention to the robed priests, bowing, candles, incense, rituals, "idols," and mysterious "sensuality" they equated with Catholicism and Chinese Buddhism. "Go right from St. Mary's [Cathedral] to the Chinese Temple where they worship 'Josh' and you can't tell the difference," wrote one Protestant in 1869. "St. Mary has the best music but the priests of Josh beat Rome on skirts and magnificent dresses and idols." The fact that San Francisco's Chinatown had grown up around the cathedral encouraged such equations. This writer's reference to "skirts and magnificent dresses"

Figure 6. *Thistleton's Jolly Giant* remained ever vigilant for possible Catholic threats. This cartoon from March 28, 1874, portrays M. J. Donovan, an Irish Catholic member of the San Francisco school board, as a would-be poisoner of the city's public schools. Courtesy of the Huntington Library, San Marino.

reflected the way in which Chinese men and Catholic priests were both depicted as inhabiting an ambiguous gender, simultaneously effeminate and sexually threatening. In California, old ideas about lecherous, decadent priests mingled with fears of miscegenation and cultural contamination. Pushed to its extreme, as it was in the pages of the *Jolly Giant,* this discourse labeled Catholics and the Chinese as equally inassimilable, unchangeable, and beholden to foreign allegiances.[13]

"Christianity or Paganism": Irish Catholics and the Chinese

Protestant leaders in San Francisco directed special animus toward the city's Irish Catholic population. Protestant writers presented Irish Catholics as violent, lawless, and drunken, stereotypes borrowed from antebellum nativist rhetoric as well as from the English press. Mounting public concern about "hoodlumism" in San Francisco focused mostly on Irish Catholic youths, who were thought to be responsible for most of the city's street crime. While missionaries and ministers usually emphasized the degrading effects of Catholicism, more secular voices portrayed the Irish as

JO H N THE HEATHEN CHINEE.   R OM CATHOLIC MIKE.

WHERE IS THE DIFFERENCE?

Figure 7. On its cover for July 13, 1878, *Thistleton's Illustrated Giant* equated "John the Heathen Chinee" and "Roman Catholic Mike," portraying both Chinese and Irish Catholic immigrants as undesirable and subhuman. Courtesy of the Huntington Library, San Marino.

racially inferior. Illustrators for *Jolly Giant* and its competitor, the *Wasp*, depicted Irish Catholics as simian, a caricature commonly employed by such national publications as *Harper's Weekly* and *Puck*. In a much-discussed 1873 speech decrying hoodlumism, Republican ex-Attorney General Frank M. Pixley orientalized Irish Catholic youths by dubbing them "street Arabs." In the same lecture, he partly blamed their "demoralization" on the presence of the Chinese, further linking the two groups. Religious and racial prejudices combined to mark San Francisco's Irish Catholics as less than white.[14]

San Francisco Catholics and their Democratic allies responded to these slurs by defending the racial and religious reputation of Irish Catholics. The *Monitor* blamed hoodlumism not on the racial inferiority of the Irish but on the absence of proper Catholic morality in the public schools. By acknowledging the horrors of street crime while disputing its causes, this line of attack placed Catholics on the side of law and order while shifting the blame to Republican Protestants. The Democratic *Examiner* complained that many ignorant Californians "look upon the Irishman in his raw state as inferior to the Modoc and classify him with the untutored African, in his native wilds." In reality, reported the paper, the Irish were "probably the purest blooded of all the peoples of Europe." Like Irish immigrants elsewhere in the United States, California's pro-Irish voices did not refute the idea that the Irish were racially distinct from other groups, merely that they were racially inferior. In his 1878 celebratory treatise *The Irish Race in California, and on the Pacific Coast,* Irish Catholic priest Hugh Quigley outlined the various ethnological branches of humanity, calling the Celtic race the "most remarkable, and powerful, and durable known to history."[15]

Given this acceptance of the notion of racial difference, San Francisco's Chinese population presented an irresistible religious and racial other against which Irish Catholics could contrast their own Christian whiteness. African Americans, longstanding targets of Irish antipathy in the Northeast, constituted less than 1 percent of the city's population in 1870, representing too small of a presence to draw much ire. The Chinese, on the other hand, represented about 5 percent of the city. Like the Irish, the Chinese were largely confined to low-paying blue-collar jobs, fueling an intense labor competition that heightened racial and religious animosities.[16] The *Monitor* and *Catholic Guardian,* vying with each other and with secular papers for readers, decried Chinese immigration as ruinous even while insisting, "The white man has, in reality, nothing to fear from the competition of other races." The Catholic papers called for greater solidarity among white workers "of all creeds and of all political parties" in the face of the Chinese threat: "All other issues but that of the great one—Christianity or Paganism—must be set aside, and minor differences be forgotten in the presence of a common danger." The construction of the Chinese as a "common danger" put Irish Catholics on the side of white Christian patriotism. Such rhetoric mixed racial assumptions about the inferiority of the Chinese with religious constructions of degraded paganism, wielded by Irish Catholics in the service of announcing their own claims to racial and religious citizenship.[17]

Such sentiments clashed with the Catholic Church's ongoing mission work in China and its tentative attempts to evangelize the Chinese of California. Archbishop Joseph Alemany had tried intermittently since the 1850s to recruit Catholic missionaries in China to relocate to California, but a failed experiment with Thomas Cian—a Chinese-born priest who came to San Francisco in 1855 but who could not communicate with Chinese immigrants due to his ignorance of Cantonese—epitomized his frustrations. When the onrush of Protestant missionaries to the Chinese arrived in the late 1860s, the Catholic Church opened a small Chinese chapel and several parishes began Sunday school classes aimed at the Chinese, but they attracted few worshippers. Reverend John Valentini explained in 1877 that he had given up on the Chinese in 1870 because, "As soon as they saw there was nothing material to be gained they left off." In an 1874 letter to a superior, Archbishop Alemany bemoaned his continual inability to attract missionaries and Chinese parishioners. "Must I abandon all hope?" he asked. "Must I leave the large number of Chinese here and through the diocese without any efficient provision for them, and without any missionaries to work for them? . . . I cannot give up the affair." Like most of California's Protestant church leaders, Alemany focused on evangelism and extending his denominational reach. For Catholic Church leadership, the Chinese population was another niche among the panoply of California groups served by the Church.[18]

Considering these conflicted Catholic attitudes, it is little wonder that James Buchard's speech addressing the question "White Man or Chinaman—Which?" filled St. Francis of Assisi Church on February 25, 1873. The speech was also a direct outgrowth of school controversies. The lecture was a fundraiser for the Catholic schools attached to Presentation Convent, which were struggling to pay the property taxes they owed. A few months earlier, Buchard had lectured on another controversial topic—woman suffrage, which he condemned—to raise money for Catholic Sunday schools. At the start of his speech on the Chinese question, he said that he "almost wished" he had not chosen the topic but did so to best aid the Presentation Convent schools. His anti-Chinese diatribe that night represented many things at once: publicity for the Catholic side of the school question; a reflection of harsh labor competition between Irish Catholics and the Chinese; a rebuttal of Protestant rhetoric that lumped Irish Catholics with pagan and racially inferior groups; and part of an internal debate among Catholics about the meanings of Chinese immigration. Speaking just six days after Pixley had denounced the city's "street Arabs," Buchard tried to harness mounting anti-Chinese xenophobia in service of Catholics. As a Jesuit, Buchard enjoyed a degree of autonomy within the diocese that afforded him opportunities to serve the Lord as he saw fit. Like his other public defenses of Catholicism, his anti-Chinese speech bolstered his own prominence while giving Church approval to the animosities felt by many working-class Catholics in San Francisco.[19]

Buchard's former identity as a Delaware Indian further complicates the meanings of the speech. Given prevailing ideas in California about the savagery of Indians, it is not surprising that Buchard did not advertise his Indian past in San Francisco. Denouncing the Chinese in the name of promoting the "white race" was part of Buchard's process of distancing himself from his own past. There was, in fact, a minor tradition of Indians in California objecting to the presence of the Chinese, just as Chinese community leaders tried to elevate themselves above Indians; this tradition dated from the 1850s, when conflicts between the two groups were common in mining areas. Weimah, leader of a band of Nisenan Indians in Nevada County, balked in 1854 at moving to a reservation while the Chinese remained free. "The Indians are better than the Chinese, and you allow them to remain among you," he reportedly said. "Remove the Chinese first—then we will go." Buchard was silently part of that tradition. His physiognomy, education, and status as a Jesuit priest afforded him the option of living as white, which he exercised to the point of appointing himself a protector of whiteness itself.[20]

Designed to attract attention, Buchard's speech prompted a strong response from Protestant church leaders. The Presbyterian *Occident* took issue with the notion that no Chinese Californians had been converted, insisting that if Buchard had as much "grace of Christ in his heart" as some Chinese Christians, he would not be "inciting the hatred of race among his bigoted adherents." The San Francisco Methodist Preachers' Meeting asked missionary Otis Gibson to deliver a rebuttal to Buchard, which he did with gusto on March 14 in Platt's Hall. Gibson redirected Buchard's attacks on the Chinese onto Catholics. America's great institutions—its free press, *"free schools,* with an open Bible," and civil liberties—were indeed under attack by "a class of foreigners, [but] not Chinese." "Popery," he declared, "is more dangerous to Republican institutions than Paganism." He insisted that, while China's civilization and religion were inferior to the Christian United States, "that does not prove in the least the inferiority of the race." He suspected that Buchard's real complaint with Chinese workers was that they did not tithe to the Catholic Church and were not "the subjects of his Holiness, the Infallible Pope, or under control of the Catholic priesthood." As to the notion that the Chinese were incapable of conversion to Christianity, Gibson called it "blasphemous." Converting, educating, and elevating Chinese men and women: "This is the Protestant, the American way of solving the Chinese question."[21]

In these responses, Protestant church leaders made use of Buchard's prominence to promote their own racial vision. Gibson's speech, which was covered by San Francisco papers and published as a pamphlet underwritten by local Chinese businessmen, put anti-Catholicism to use in defense of Chinese immigration and Protestant evangelism. Truly directed to his fellow Protestants rather than to Catholics, Gibson's remarks expressed an evangelical Protestant conception of social difference that emphasized religion rather than race. Instead of using Christian logic to cast the Chinese as pagan outsiders, as both Democratic and Republican politicians were doing in the 1870s, Gibson advanced an interpretation of Christianity that embraced the Chinese as potential allies against a global Catholic menace. As Gibson well knew, exactly what the "American way of solving the Chinese question" would be was very much in dispute in 1873. Anti-Catholicism strengthened the position of California's evangelical leaders in the settling of that dispute. Yet at other times, Protestants promoted their mission work by warning that the pope was working to "cunningly and perseveringly instil the dogmas of his church" among the Chinese of California. Whether portraying the Catholic Church as coveting or denouncing the Chinese, Protestant leaders bolstered their cause.[22]

"An insult to our blood": The 1876 Federal Hearing on Chinese Immigration

The tangled issues of Catholicism, the Irish, and the Chinese entered a new phase in the fall of 1876 when a joint special committee of the U.S. Congress conducted a month-long hearing in San Francisco investigating the effects of Chinese immigration. The federal hearing was prompted in part by the findings of a California state senate investigation in April of that year, during which dozens of businessmen, policemen, officials, and ministers had testified as to whether Chinese immigration advanced or hindered "Christian civilization." During the state hearing, the openly anti-Chinese state senators had led witnesses to support their foregone conclusions. The only uncooperative witnesses were Protestant ministers and most of the eighteen Chinese men interviewed. Otis Gibson and Presbyterian minister H. H. Rice insisted that Chinese immigration was beneficial to the United States, while the Chinese witnesses generally denied knowledge of the subjects—prostitution, gambling, disease, violence—lingered over by state senators. Only one mention of the Irish was made during the state hearing, by a Chinese man from Sacramento who noted, "No Chinaman can take a walk up and down the street unless you find an Irishman or a Dutchman strike them down." The witnesses' surprising inattention to Catholicism was probably due to the fact that five of the seven senators asking the questions were Democrats.[23]

The federal hearing that fall was twice as long and, although the joint committee included several Democrats, the questioning was presided over by its Republican chairman, Oliver Morton. Morton ran the hearing almost like a criminal trial, with Aaron A. Sargent and Frank M. Pixley acting the part of prosecutors of the Chinese and local attorneys Benjamin Sherman Brooks and Frederick A. Bee acting as the defense, with both sides allowed to call and question witnesses.[24] This format opened space for anti-Catholicism, employed by several defenders of the Chinese. During his opening remarks, Brooks insisted that the anti-Chinese sentiment in California was confined chiefly to "the foreign population— to the Irish." Otis Gibson extolled the economic benefits of a "healthy and much-needed competition between the Chinaman and the Irishman," and he said that European immigrants were as guilty as the Chinese in perpetrating crimes and vice. A. W. Loomis testified that Chinese immigrants posed no danger to American institutions because, unlike Catholics, "they do not purpose to intermeddle with our religious rights; they have no hierarchy; they are not sworn to support any religious system; they are mixed up at home; they have no one religion." Believing that the best defense is a good offense, these proponents of the Chinese attempted to redirect focus onto a Catholic menace that, in their opinion, dwarfed the negligible ills of Chinese immigration.[25]

Such responses frustrated Sargent and Pixley, who strove to separate Chinese immigration from the larger issue of U.S. immigration policy. Although both men had used anti-Catholic rhetoric in the past, in this context it only muddied waters they wanted to keep clear. Just two years after denouncing dangerous Catholic "fanaticism" in Congress, Sargent here presented himself as a champion of Irish Catholics, enfolding them into the category of white European-American Christians debased by Chinese competition and immorality. He and Pixley badgered and mocked uncooperative witnesses, barraging them with round after round of questions until they contradicted their earlier testimony. This animus turned into physical violence on November 17 when, during a recess, Pixley scuffled with Presbyterian minister William W. Brier after arguing about the Chinese question. According to Gibson's account, Pixley "seized Mr. Brier by the beard and shook him . . . and immediately struck Mr. Brier a severe blow in the face."[26]

Congregationalist minister Samuel V. Blakeslee presented testimony that frustrated Sargent and Pixley in a different way. In the 1850s, Blakeslee had come to San Francisco as an agent for the American Missionary Association with the intention of evangelizing the state's Chinese population, among other groups. His letters to the association had praised the Chinese's intellectual and spiritual promise. "The day I believe will come when the Chinaman, as the right hand companion of the American, will stand shoulder to shoulder with him in every good cause," he wrote in 1853. Blakeslee soon gave up on evangelizing the Chinese due to his inability to communicate with them, focusing instead on saving Mexican Californians from the "blinding" effects of "Romanism." By the time of the 1876 hearing, he had split from most of his Protestant colleagues, believing that it was "false Christianity and false common sense" to ignore the "immense evils" of Chinese immigration, but he retained his antipathy for Catholicism.[27]

As the only stridently anti-Chinese minister who testified, Blakeslee was a potentially useful witness for Sargent and Pixley, who steered clear of any mention of Catholicism during their questioning. Morton and Brooks, however, asked for Blakeslee's opinions on Irish Catholics, whereupon the minister declared them "inferior in intelligence, inferior in morality" to Protestant Americans and stated that their immigration had the "same general effect" as that from China, differing only "in degree." He further observed that Irish Catholics did not assimilate into society because priests "mean to keep them separate" and "under their control." Despite his denunciations of Chinese immigration, Blakeslee's testimony was only partially useful to Sargent and Pixley because his anti-Catholicism disrupted the duo's attempts to build a broad-based white Christian coalition.[28]

During the hearing, San Francisco's secular press lambasted pro-immigration ministers as hypocrites who cared only for lining their pockets with the money they supposedly earned from evangelizing the Chinese. The *Chronicle* excoriated Brier for looking "upon God and religion as the convenient ministers to his own fleshly comforts" and declared that California's white "boys and girls" would not be "driven either by missionary rant, Christian cant, or the hunger and thirst of capital, into habits of enforced idleness, vice and crime." These sorts of charges aligned missionaries with such capitalists as railroad magnate Charles Crocker, who supported Chinese immigration and acknowledged before the committee that he had donated money to Chinese missions in California. Missionaries and capitalists were both presented as betraying white laborers for their own financial gain. In fact, nearly half of the witnesses who testified supported Chinese immigration, a group that included not just ministers and large-scale employers but also lawyers, doctors, farmers, merchants, and laborers. Ostensibly the leading men of California, ministers and capitalists received special scorn because they commanded a degree of cultural influence that required refutation.[29]

Another line of attack positioned pro-immigration ministers as dangerous to the sexual purity of California's white women. The *Wasp*

"THEY ARE PEACABLE",

"THEY ARE CLEAN",

GIBSON'S & LOOMIS
THEORY EXAMPLIFIED.

"THEY ARE HONEST",

FACTS AND FIGURES MAKE LIARS OF THOSE TWO CHARLATANICAL DIVINES.

Figure 8. Local media ridiculed Protestant ministers Otis Gibson and Augustus W. Loomis following their pro-Chinese testimony at the 1876 U.S. congressional hearings on Chinese immigration in San Francisco. In this cartoon for November 18, 1876, the *Wasp* suggested that their advocacy for the Chinese paved the way to interracial mixing. Courtesy of the California Historical Society, San Francisco.

published a cartoon mocking "those two charlatanical divines," Gibson and Loomis, showing the Chinese as filthy thieves and murderers; one panel, titled "Gibson's and Loomis theory examplified," depicts a white woman with a Chinese husband and monstrous children. Not to be outdone, the *Jolly Giant* put a drawing of a Chinese man and white woman embracing on its cover with the label, "The Rev. Otis Gibson says 'Chinamen would make good husbands for our daughters!'" In fact, neither Loomis's nor Gibson's testimony touched on the subject of intermarriage; Brier, when asked about it, had stated that it would not be "very good taste in a white woman to marry a Chinaman." Nevertheless, the specter of miscegenation was so powerful that the editors of the *Wasp* and *Jolly Giant* invoked it to damn those they considered traitors to their own race.[30]

The anti-Catholic content of the Protestant ministers' testimony opened them to rebuke from expected and unexpected places. The *Monitor and Guardian,* now merged into one paper, criticized those who represented the Chinese question as a "purely Irish quarrel, in which

Americans must take up a position of impartiality and secure justice for both sides." In a lengthy dissection of the hearing transcript, the New York *Catholic World* rebuked the "Vatinian hatred" and "deadly venom" displayed by Protestant ministers, scoffing at the idea that a "glorious cohort" of Catholic "martyrs and confessors" could be more dangerous than "Ah Sin and Fan Chow!" Furthermore, "only persons of the third sex" could "pretend to believe" that devout Catholics cannot also be patriotic Americans. This last insult turned Protestants' depictions of "unmanly" priests back on them, questioning the masculinity of California's Protestant ministers as well as their dedication to God and the white race. Surprisingly, the *Jolly Giant* also took offense at ministers' characterizations of Irish immigrants, even though the paper had previously declared Irish Catholics more "objectionable" than the Chinese. In this new climate, the *Jolly Giant* sided with whiteness, calling Gibson's testimony "an outrage on our race. It is an insult to our blood." Just as Sargent and Pixley rejected anti-Catholicism to better make their case against the Chinese, California's noisiest anti-Catholic newspaper momentarily embraced its avowed enemies in the name of racial solidarity.[31]

On November 15, with the hearing still underway, this anticlerical sentiment extended into the realm of street protest during a mass anti-Chinese meeting in San Francisco's Mechanics' Pavilion. During a procession of anti-coolie clubs (including the Woman's Anti-Coolie Association), one group carried a mock gallows, from which they hung Otis Gibson in effigy. Once at the pavilion, the crowd set fire to the effigy. During the meeting, at which San Francisco mayor A. J. Bryant and other prominent politicians spoke, local judge J. J. Tobin attacked the ministers who had cast aspersions against the Irish, asking, "if the country's flag was to be defended, to whom would Chinese admirers look—to Chinamen or Irish?," raising cheers from the crowd of several thousand. Writers for local papers soon after suggested that, next time, the lynchings would not be done in effigy. The *Pacific* and the San Francisco Methodist Preachers Meeting objected to the anti-Gibson demonstration and its "spirit of violence and threatened assassination," but both declined to offer an opinion on the question of Chinese immigration for the time being. California's evangelical Protestant consensus of the early 1870s, with its simultaneous denunciation of Catholicism and embrace of Chinese immigration, had begun to show cracks. By the end of 1876, Irish Catholics had carved a place for themselves within the increasingly powerful and broad-based anti-Chinese movement. The unstable lines dividing insider and outsider in California were being redrawn.[32]

"I asked him if he was not a white man":
Luciano Osuna, Catholics, and the Peace Policy

At about the same time as the public dispute between Gibson and Buchard, another conflict between a Methodist minister and a Catholic priest was brewing in California. A clash at Round Valley Indian Reservation between Methodist agent J. L. Burchard (not to be confused with the Jesuit James Buchard) and a Franciscan priest named Luciano Osuna drew wide attention and was interpreted in wildly different manners by Protestant and Catholic observers.[33]

Born in Guadalajara, Luciano Osuna had been training to be a priest in Culiacán when the War of the Reform engulfed Mexico in the late 1850s. Following the reestablishment of the anticlerical regime of Benito Juárez in 1861, Osuna fled to San Francisco, where he was ordained and sent by Archbishop Joseph Alemany to minister to Catholics in rural Lake and Mendocino counties. Osuna devoted special attention to local Indians, traveling between various groups and serving as their advocate to the Catholic Church. "I have been with the indians most of the time; they are sick and hongry and so I am hongry with them; we have no place where to live, nothing to do to work our living," he informed a bishop in 1872. "The indians are starving in both respects, in the body and in the soul and with good desires and words we will not relieve them; we must do something, otherwise our charity will not reach them." Such comments indicate the extent to which Osuna identified with the Indians he ministered to; he slept in their camps, ate what they ate, and rejected fine clothes the Indians could not afford. This commitment to poverty and humility, springing from a Franciscan tradition of apostolic living and service, likely helped Osuna gain Indians' trust, as did his knowledge of Spanish.[34]

Osuna routinely visited Round Valley during the 1860s without opposition from Indian agents, but that free access ended with the arrival of Burchard in 1872. As a Methodist minister and government agent, Burchard viewed himself as wholly responsible for the spiritual and physical care of the reservation Indians. Hostile to Catholicism as well as to challenges to his authority, Burchard vehemently opposed Osuna's presence on the reservation. Burchard's right to do so was unclear under the terms of Grant's peace policy. Each reservation was placed under the control of a single denomination, but the government did not explicitly forbid other churches from carrying on activities there.

Banned by Burchard, Osuna nonetheless continued to visit the reservation, telling Alemany, "we cannot leave these little brothers into the hands of these wolves." One day in the fall of 1873, reservation employees discovered Osuna in an Indian camp and brought him into Burchard's office. According to Burchard's later account, he showed Osuna the governmental regulations outlawing all white men from the reservation other than those approved by the agent. "I asked him if he was not a white man," recalled Burchard. "He said he was, but that he was a Catholic priest, and had a right to go where he pleased to teach the people." The two argued until Burchard struck Osuna with a cane. According to Burchard, it amounted to two gentle strikes: "no bone broken, or blood drawn, or any injury resulted from the blows." Osuna, on the other hand, claimed in a deposition that Burchard "struck him with his cane several times, beat and threw him down and offered other violence to him." Burchard's employees threw the priest off the reservation several more times over the next few months, during which time the Methodist revival began and increasing numbers of Indians joined the church. Finally, on April 18, 1874, Burchard had Osuna arrested by local Army soldiers and charged with insanity in nearby Covelo. Burchard claimed that Osuna was mentally unstable, but the judge and board of physicians disagreed, setting him free.[35]

The conflict between Burchard and Osuna became a source of contention between Catholics and Protestants in Mendocino County and throughout California. Catholics rushed to Osuna's defense: Catholic soldiers gave him especially gentle treatment while in custody, Catholic settlers offered to help defray the costs of his trial, Church leaders collected evidence to "prove Burchard an infamous slanderer," and Charles Ewing, the Church's advocate in matters of Indian policy in Washington, D.C., lobbied the Office of Indian Affairs to allow Osuna access to Round Valley.[36] According to Catholics, the Church's longstanding mission work among California Indians, dating to 1769, coupled with Osuna's more recent ministrations, justified his presence on the reservation. Osuna insisted that the "great majority" of the Round Valley Indians were Catholics, but that the Methodist missionaries used lies and bribery to sway them toward Protestantism. "For like the wolf who does not stop until he has finished off the sheep, neither will these Methodists stop until they infiltrate the Indians with their erroneous beliefs," he wrote.[37]

For Alemany and other Catholics, the injustice at Round Valley was symbolic of the peace policy's rampant anti-Catholicism. Catholics in California joined with others throughout the United States in complaining about the lack of Catholics on the Board of Indian Commissioners and the fact that only seven of the country's seventy-two reservations had been turned over to the Catholic Church. Priests in Washington, Oregon, Minnesota, New Mexico, and Arizona clashed, like Osuna, with Protestant agents over access to "Catholic" Indians. The Church established the Catholic Bureau of Indian Missions in Washington, D.C., in January 1874 to protest these policies and to lobby for increased "religious liberty" on reservations.[38] In San Francisco, the *Monitor, Catholic Guardian,* and *Examiner* all lambasted the peace policy as unfair to the Catholic Church and dire for the Indians. The *Catholic Guardian* even insisted that the Modoc War could have been avoided if Catholics rather than Methodists had been in charge of Pacific coast reservations. A professor at Santa Clara College, writing in the college magazine, reported that the government had taken "so many Indian agencies out of Catholic hands (the only hands that can manage them with anything like success) merely to promote the interests of a set of blundering fanatics."[39]

In these complaints, Catholics portrayed themselves as heroic protectors of helpless Indians, a new cycle of a rhetoric as old as the Spanish mission system in the Americas. Unlike the Chinese, indigenous North Americans had been included as at least nominal members of the Catholic Church for centuries while being comparatively ignored by Protestant groups. This long history of Indian participation in the Catholic Church made the anti-Catholicism of the peace policy seem especially galling. The issue also allowed Catholics to cast themselves as simultaneously persecuted and morally courageous, the only true champions of what the *Monitor and Guardian* termed the "oppressed and despised red men." Whereas the Chinese proved useful to Catholics as a counterpoint to their own whiteness and Christianity, Indians served as a vehicle for expressing Catholic bravery and compassion.[40]

There were strict limits to this Catholic advocacy of Indians, however. Unlike Protestant reformers during this period, Catholic Californians did not issue calls for citizenship or suffrage rights for Indians. Osuna's egalitarian attitude notwithstanding, most Catholics were content to include Indians only on the bottom rung of church and society. A few would not grant them even that place, such as a Santa Clara College student who insisted in the college magazine that Indians "deserved the sentence of extirpation" for their "inhuman" savagery. A priest laboring among Indians along the northern California coast complained that local white settlers, even those declaring themselves "staunch" Catholics, questioned whether Indians truly had souls. "Why they ought all to shoot down these beasts," one of his parishioners told him. As with the question of the Chinese, Catholics in California disagreed about the place and character of Indians. Catholics could alternate between seeing them as subhuman savages and seeing them as long-suffering victims, an oscillation that characterized general American attitudes toward Indians in the late nineteenth century.[41]

"Ragged, filthy, bare-footed, unwashed and uncombed": The Place of Mexican American Catholics

Just as Irish Catholics had compelling motivations to elevate themselves above Chinese immigrants, Mexican American Catholics in California had reasons to distance themselves culturally and racially from Indians. As the once-powerful generation of land-owning Californios died or were dispossessed, Mexican Americans dropped in racial status, social standing, and wealth. In 1870, state officials attempted to bar Mexican Americans from holding public office due to their mestizo heritage. Although the state supreme court upheld their legal whiteness in *People v. de la Guerra*, Mexican Americans had been pushed to the edges of the public arena, their cultural privilege evaporating in increasingly anti-Catholic California.[42]

In their *testimonios*, speeches, and writings from the 1870s, Californios often demonized Indians as savage marauders who had brought only violence and disorder into Mexican California life. "When the Americans came to this country, they found it already oriented on the path of civilization," Theresa de la Guerra told an interviewer in 1875. "But the Reverend missionary Fathers found it filled with hundreds of thousands of Indians thirsty for the blood of Christians." Similarly, Mariano Guadalupe Vallejo described how Californios had made "countless sacrifices to redeem [northern California] from the hands of the barbarous heathen."[43] Such remarks portrayed Mexicans as the original Christian civilizers of California, undeserving of the shabby treatment they were receiving under Protestant American rule. Californios insisted on a racial and religious difference between themselves and Indians, an extension of the Spanish colonial hierarchy that had placed self-styled *gente de razón* at the top. Luciano Osuna, a much more recent immigrant to California who had not seen his power erode, possessed an atypical Mexican outlook on Indians.[44]

Not linked to the Chinese historically or ethnographically, as they were to Indians, many Californios nonetheless viewed them with hostility. In the 1870s, Californios claimed that the Chinese, "like the locusts of Egypt, [had] invaded our state," harming "the spread of the white race." Romualdo Pacheco, California's first Mexican American representative to the U.S. Congress, joined other California politicians in opposing Chinese immigration. In an 1882 speech, he contrasted the Chinese, a "mongrel race," with Americans, who "are composed chiefly of the best of European immigrants and their descendants. Our language is the same, our forms of worship are similar, and we are governed by the same laws." Such remarks, while virtually indistinguishable from other politicians' speeches, took on different meaning coming from a Californio. Pacheco's use of the epithet "mongrel" suggests a transference of anti-Mexican rhetoric onto the Chinese. He cast himself, and his fellow "Spaniards," as members of one more Christian European immigrant group imperiled by pagan outsiders. Pacheco, it should be noted, was an unusual Mexican Californian. He spent most of his childhood in Hawaii, left the Democratic Party for the Republican, and reportedly barely spoke Spanish. His anti-Chinese sentiments were, like those of the priest James Buchard, part of his personal accommodation to the costs and benefits of claiming whiteness.[45]

In the Osuna conflict, Protestants drew on anti-Mexican and anti-Catholic rhetoric to portray him as an obsessive lunatic, racially debased and sexually depraved. Burchard emphasized that Osuna was "bare-footed, unwashed, uncombed, torn robe, cow manure and mud between his toes and on his feet." The *California Christian Advocate* dismissed Osuna as a "ragged, filthy, bare-footed, unwashed and uncombed Mexican." The fact that Osuna slept in the Indian camps, sometimes among Indian women, prompted "insults and hooting and scoffing" from reservation employees, including jokes that some of whom he termed his Indian "children" were literally such. The *California Christian Advocate* asserted that Osuna "was in the habit of going upon the Reservation in the night and creeping into the Indian rancherias to sleep with the natives"; by throwing the "filthy creature (who called himself a priest)" out, Burchard had protected the sexual and moral purity of "his" Indian women.[46]

Just as Burchard asked Osuna whether he was a white man on the night of the caning, this attention to the priest's unkempt appearance was a way of questioning his racial manhood. White men, Protestants suggested, did not dress like Indians. The notion that Osuna, as a Mexican, was a "half-breed" gave special power to the charges that he was having sex with Indian women. Considered mixed-race himself, Osuna was seen as simply continuing that legacy of miscegenation in Round Valley. The charges also resonated with Protestant fears of priestly licentiousness and misuse of power, as expressed in the *Jolly Giant* and other anti-Catholic publications. They framed Osuna's actions as merely another example of the fanatical intensity with which Catholics supposedly threatened American society, adding Indian reservations to the list of American institutions imperiled by Catholic aggressors.

At the same time that it damned him as less than white, Osuna's perceived sexual exploitation of Indian women threatened Burchard's status as patriarchal Christian protector. During the period of his conflicts with Osuna, the agent expressed dismay several times to the Office of Indian Affairs that local white men were "stealing" Round Valley "squaws" or visiting them at night for the purposes of prostitution. During the Methodist revival, one of the reasons Burchard encouraged Indian couples to marry was to "protect them from the evil and seductive influences of degraded and low white men, as well as the intimate relations with each other." Osuna, then, was one more challenge to Burchard's authority and status as self-appointed guardian of female sexual virtue. Burchard and his allies perceived the conflict with Osuna as a power struggle over who had access to Indian bodies, minds, and souls. In a letter to a local newspaper, a supporter of Burchard insisted that Indians "must be taught to look up to one man alone, and learn that he for the time being is in supreme authority over them." Osuna's presence on the reservation challenged Burchard's "supreme authority," undermined his power, and called into question his manly command of the reservation. Belittling Osuna's race, class, and masculinity was one way to reassert that authority; striking him with a cane was another. The caning was consistent with Burchard's policy of corporal punishment for Indians on the reservation. When words failed to ensure his authority, Burchard turned to the cane or the whip.[47]

"Entirely satisfied with the Methodist church": Round Valley Indians and Catholicism

After proving his sanity in April 1874, Osuna abandoned the reservation, focusing instead on founding an Indian mission in a nearby valley.[48] Archbishop Alemany, however, refused to give up. In February 1875 he sent a petition, cosigned by Grass Valley bishop Eugene O'Connell, to the Office of Indian Affairs requesting permission to build a chapel at their own expense at Round Valley "for the purpose of teaching the Catholic Indians and administering to their spiritual wants." In a letter to Alemany assessing their chances for success, Charles Ewing emphasized that the question would turn on the Church's ability to prove that there were indeed Catholic Indians on the reservation—a difficult feat, given the ongoing Methodist revival.[49] The Office of Indian Affairs, directed by the Secretary of the Interior to look into whether granting the petition would create "dissensions and strife," turned to its investigator William Vandever, who had recently visited Round Valley in response to the charges levied against Burchard by Congressman J. K. Luttrell. Vandever elected not to revisit the reservation but merely asked Burchard to furnish affidavits by employees giving their side of the story. Having just vindicated Burchard in the Luttrell controversy, Vandever had no intention of even considering the Catholic side of the matter, informing the Office of Indian Affairs that he judged Osuna an "enthusiast or lunatic, acting without authority of the church," well before he had received the affidavits.[50]

In addition to sending statements from himself and his employees, Burchard gave Vandever the minutes of a meeting he had held on June 12, 1875, with twenty Round Valley Indian leaders regarding the petition. According to the document, the tribal leaders

> spoke freely, and very decidedly. Their unanimous voice was strongly opposed to the admission of the Catholics. Several of them said that if the Catholics wanted to teach them why did they not do so when they had the opportunity. They said that they were entirely satisfied with the Methodist church, and expected to remain in, and stand by this church as long as they live. One Indian said that if the Catholics were allowed to come, he did not think an Indian would remain on the reservation, and was sure that he would not.

Though offered by Burchard as definitive proof that there were no Catholic Indians at Round Valley, the meeting minutes suggest a more complex situation. For one thing, only tribal leaders were invited. They were the same men who had been specifically targeted for conversion by Burchard and reservation missionaries during the revival of the previous year; at least two of the meeting participants, John Brown and Charles Munsell, were licensed Methodist preachers. Of all the Indians on the reservation, these twenty were among the least likely to welcome a competing denomination. Furthermore, Burchard and most of the reservation employees were anti-Catholic Methodists; their influence, direct and indirect, surely shaped the Indians' response. In fact, the threat advanced by "one Indian" that they would all leave if Alemany's petition were granted echoed Burchard's own statement to Vandever that "myself and each one of my employees would resign, and go off the reservation" if a Catholic chapel were built.[51]

Other evidence demonstrates that many Round Valley Indians, whatever religious body they considered themselves a part of, did support the presence of Catholicism on the reservation. Burchard's own complaints against Osuna acknowledged that Indians attended the priest's ceremonies, harbored him at night against Burchard's wishes, and left the reservation to attend mass at nearby sweathouses. This all occurred concurrently with the Methodist revival. For at least some Round Valley Indians, joining the Methodist church clearly did not erase all pre-existing religious attitudes, suggesting a simultaneous acceptance of elements of Protestantism, Catholicism, and, likely, the Ghost Dance and older belief systems. The presence of Osuna on the reservation benefited Indians by placing them in a position to choose between religious bodies competing for their attention, giving them a modicum of power.[52]

Whatever their thoughts about Catholicism as a religion, more than a few Round Valley Indians seem to have recognized Osuna as a potential ally, one whose poverty and humble demeanor differed markedly from Burchard's patriarchal authoritarianism. Given his comparative lack of power on the reservation, Osuna may have cultivated those personal qualities precisely because they endeared him to the Indians, just as he likely chose to hold mass in off-reservation sweathouses—outlawed by Burchard for their connections to pagan dancing and rituals—due to their spiritual connotations and forbidden status. According to Burchard, Osuna informed Round Valley Indians that they should have the right to "have sweat-houses, gamble, and dance," a toleration of syncretism and folk practices that generally (though decreasingly) characterized the Catholic Church in the American southwest and Latin America. If Osuna was in fact having sex with one or more Indian women, as Protestants suspected, those relationships might have further cemented his ties to the Indians; if he was not, the mere fact that he slept alongside Indians in their huts shows an intimacy that contrasted sharply with the Indians' relations with stern, parental Burchard.[53]

Vandever, however, was satisfied that the Round Valley Indians with "entire unanimity" opposed the construction of a Catholic chapel. In his report to the Office of Indian Affairs, he furthermore declared that Osuna's "fanatical and mischievous character" had brought on himself any violence he had received. Unsurprisingly, the *California Christian Advocate* also opposed the petition, considering its "effrontery" another machination of the "papal priesthood" to undermine the peace policy and the American way of life.[54]

On July 17, the Department of the Interior rejected the petition. Three days later, Vandever informed Burchard of the good news, ending his letter, "The Lord be with you and bless you. May he preserve Round Valley Reservation from the power of its enemies." This display of Vandever's biases symbolized the ways in which the process had disfavored Catholics at every step. From Commissioner of Indian Affairs Edward P. Smith, a Congregational clergyman, to William Vandever, a devout Presbyterian, to J. L. Burchard, a Methodist minister, Protestants controlled the process that resulted in the petition's denial. Catholics were left only to complain of the peace policy's "Sectarian fanaticism, Protestant bigotry, and anti-Christian hatred," in the words of the New York *Catholic World,* which in 1877 included an inflammatory version of Osuna's story—"thrown into prison, brutally beaten, and expelled from his flock"—in its list of anti-Catholic effronteries. Beginning in 1878, Democratic U.S. congressmen began lobbying for the extension of full religious freedom to Indian reservations, but Republicans killed the bills. Catholics and their Democratic allies had far better luck chipping away at Protestant hegemony in local school districts than on federal Indian reservations, though in both instances they portrayed themselves as agents of a broad religious liberty threatened by Protestant sectarianism.[55]

Ultimately, the Catholic Church's failed defense of Osuna demonstrated the strength of the Protestant grip on Indian reservations as well as the marginalized position of Catholics in postbellum California. However, the Osuna controversy also revealed weaknesses within the Protestant consensus. Burchard and his supporters degraded Osuna's racial manhood, displaying an anti-Mexican bigotry that belied their stated support for Christian universalism. Osuna's radical humility made Burchard's arrogant paternalism toward Indians especially apparent, and the Round Valley Indians' encouragement of Osuna—during the height of the Methodist revival—showed their dissatisfaction with aspects of the Protestant plan. Meanwhile, Catholic complaints about Burchard further fanned flames of public skepticism about the long-term efficacy of the peace policy. Protestant leaders protected Round Valley from Catholic intrusion but would find it increasingly difficult to defend the reservation system and the idea that Indians were on the cusp of becoming Christian citizens.

In California in the 1870s, anti-Catholicism and white supremacy often bled together, marking Irish and Mexican Catholics in particular as racially and spiritually inferior. Protestants portrayed Catholics as lunatic, debased, lascivious, and foreign, the opposite of how white Protestants generally imagined themselves: reserved, self-controlled, moderate, respectable, and patriotic. In this regard, anti-Catholicism in California resembled the national movement. The complex ethnic dynamics of the state, however, created a unique series of intersections of anti-Catholicism and racial thought. In the face of intensifying anti-Catholicism, some members of California's heterogeneous Catholic Church used the presence of heathen Indians and Chinese to improve their own religious and racial reputation, even as other Catholics struggled to create space for those groups within the Church. While promising to unite, anti-Catholicism exposed splits within Protestant California as it became used by opposing sides in debates over the place of racially marked groups in church and society.

By 1876, mounting public opposition to Chinese immigration and the peace policy threatened to create new coalitions around Christian whiteness rather than broad-based interracial Protestantism. In the late 1870s, murmurs of conflict within Protestant California would grow to become a din of controversy as the Chinese and Indian questions pitted Protestant clergymen against one another, destroying their anti-Catholic, pro-immigration, pro–peace policy consensus.

FLY FROM EVIL, 1877–1887

Son, observe the time and fly from evil.

—Ecclesiasticus 4:23

CHAPTER FIVE

THE FRACTURING OF PROTESTANT CALIFORNIA

B etween resolutions lauding the importance of Christian women and condemning the evils of tobacco, delegates to the Methodist Episcopal Church's California Lay Electoral Conference for 1879 paused to mark an "event of significance in the progress of the Church." A Chinese Christian named Chan Pak Kwai was present on behalf of the church's mission in San Francisco's Chinatown, while Charles Munsell, captain of the Concow Maidu, represented the mission at Round Valley Indian Reservation. The delegates agreed that the two men's presence at the conference pointed to "the time when the Methodist Church shall gather in one the children of all nations." Although the conference likely marked the first and only time their lives intersected, Chan Pak Kwai and Charles Munsell had much in common. Both men had joined Protestant churches in California in the early 1870s. Both were licensed Methodist preachers, confident public speakers, and dedicated political activists. Chan Pak Kwai had recently returned from a lecture tour throughout the Midwest, during which he had defended the doctrine of free immigration and excoriated California's anti-Chinese "bummers, demagogues, and politicians." At Round Valley, Charles Munsell was known for his earnest sermons as well as his outspoken calls for political self-determination for Indians.[1]

There is no suggestion in the proceedings that Chan Pak Kwai and Charles Munsell were invited to address the 1879 Methodist Lay Elec- toral Conference. The delegates passed no resolutions addressing the questions of Chinese immigration, Indian policy, or the boundaries of U.S. citizenship. This was a marked change from the Lay Electoral Con- ference of 1875, at which delegates had predicted that the peace policy would "in a decade of years" bring about the "entire Christianization" of America's Indians and had praised Chinese immigrants for their "will- ingness to be taught our language, to live under our laws, to adopt our civilization, and to be come converts to our Christianity." By 1879, consensus among California's Methodists about the Chinese and Indian questions no longer existed. Silent but impossible to ignore, Chan Pak Kwai and Charles Munsell's presence at the conference begged a question that was fracturing Protestant California during the late 1870s: How desirable were heathens as Christians and citizens after all?[2]

California's few Protestant leaders who had questioned the doctrines of universal human equality, unrestricted immigration, and inclusive citizenship in the early 1870s grew in number during the second half of the decade, sparking conflicts within and between churches, denominations, and conferences. Growing pessimism about the efficacy of mission work prompted more and more Protestant ministers, newspaper editors, and writers to rethink previously agreed-upon evangelical goals. They increasingly questioned the fitness of Indian and Chinese men and women to "rise" anytime soon to the level of white Christian civilization. Evermore-intense public pressure from politicians, mainstream newspapers, and labor groups also encouraged this shift, as did the rewards of attention, money, and power that some ministers discovered awaited them for denouncing, in particular, the Chinese. In San Francisco, the widening anti-Chinese movement of the late 1870s offered a way for Protestants and Catholics to unite around Christian white supremacy, even while new fissures emerged around issues of class. At Round Valley, still the focus of intense scrutiny by proponents and critics of the peace policy, the arrival of a new minister-agent with pessimistic views of Indian "character" paralleled and encouraged increasing public frustration with the prospects of integrating Indians into church and society.

Struggles between Christian factions continued to be shaped by the efforts of Indian and Chinese churchgoers. As more and more white ministers rejected the notion of racial uplift, some Indians and Chinese Christians repudiated white church bodies in favor of their own, autonomous structures. In so doing, they insisted on their ability to define Christianity in terms of their own needs and beliefs, sometimes including a mix of older and newer ideas and practices. Indian and Chinese church members joined other California groups in using Christianity to promote their racial and political visions.

"Plundering the poor Indians": The Fall of J. L. Burchard

On July 4, 1876, Round Valley Indian Reservation marked the nation's centennial in spectacular style. First came a procession, with thirteen Indian girls dressed in white, with red and blue sashes to represent the thirteen colonies, followed by thirty-eight more girls representing the current states, bearing a banner labeled "President Grant's Peace Policy." Then was a series of speeches and exercises, including a twelve-year-old Indian boy's reading of the Declaration of Independence and a sermon by Methodist missionary Franklin Kellogg emphasizing how "Indians are in a better condition to-day than they were before the white man discovered this land." Finally, there was a grand feast, followed by fireworks. One observer concluded that Round Valley agent J. L. Burchard had "succeeded in implanting in the breasts of these Indians" a fierce "devotion to the government that protects them and provides for them." The centennial celebration was surely "the climax of this teaching."[3]

The day's events, carefully orchestrated by Burchard and reservation employees with the consent of the Indian participants, celebrated at once the health of Round Valley Indians, the reservation system, the peace policy, and the stewardship of Burchard. Though mocked by the *Daily Alta California* and other papers, attacked by J. K. Luttrell from the floor of the U.S. House of Representatives, and maligned by Catholics for his rude treatment of Luciano Osuna, Burchard was still standing, still insisting that Indians could become full and faithful Christians. "I have never known as great a stability with any race of people in their Christian faith," the agent wrote in his 1876 annual report. "I have not heard an oath or seen an intoxicated Indian on this reservation within the last two years." The peace policy that had given the Methodists control of California's Indian reservations was likewise still in place in July 1876; like Burchard, it continued in the face of relentless criticism. The Independence Day festivities proclaimed that both Burchard and the peace policy were here to stay, a message intended for white onlookers in Mendocino County and elsewhere, for a delegation of visiting Indians from Hoopa Valley Reservation who Burchard hoped would choose to relocate to his reservation, and for the Round Valley Indians themselves.[4]

In fact, the celebration did turn out to be the "climax" of the peace policy in California. Just a few days later came the shocking news that the Lakota and Northern Cheyenne had defeated George Armstrong Custer's battalion near the Little Bighorn River in the Montana Territory. In California as throughout the nation, newspaper editors already hostile to the peace policy seized on the "massacre" to further discredit an Indian policy they considered naïvely optimistic about true "Indian character." The San Francisco *Chronicle* called for "no treating or temporizing hereafter with the red brutes.... Destitute of every humane and merciful instinct, proficient only in the lessons of cruelty and torture, let the heavy hand of speedy retribution hasten them to their doom." Though directed at the Lakota and Northern Cheyenne, such pronouncements fed into a wider anti-Indian discourse in California that periodically escalated following episodes of violence, such as what had followed the Modoc War.[5]

Following Custer's defeat, opponents of the peace policy in California and across the United States redoubled their efforts to strip oversight of reservations from the Department of the Interior, with its minister-agents appointed by churches, and give it to the Department of War. Only the firm hand of the Army, asserted the *Daily Alta California* and other papers, could put a stop to the waste, corruption, and misguided philanthropy of the "shameful" peace policy. These voices usually couched their criticism in terms of their sympathy for "poor" Indians swindled by corrupt agents or left to starve by religious zealots who cared only for their souls. A few newspapers, especially in rural areas, expressed open hostility toward Indians, whom they viewed as incapable of ever "advancing" in civilization. Rejecting Indians' fitness for suffrage, the Mendocino *Beacon* suggested that those who "sympathize with the poor red man and say he is so terribly abused and all that . . . [should] try life on the border for a few years and they will soon change their minds as to the redeeming qualities of the noble red man." Whether or not they claimed to have the Indians' best interests in mind, opponents of the peace policy agreed that its central assumption—the notion that, with guidance, Indians could one day soon assimilate into Christian America—was sentimental bunk.[6]

Just as they did during the Modoc War, Protestant newspapers in California urged readers not to overreact to Custer's defeat by giving up on the peace policy and the redeemability of Indians. H. C. Benson's Methodist *California Christian Advocate* continued its tenacious defense of the peace policy in the face of the "vindictive spirit" it detected following the battle at Little Bighorn. The paper blamed opposition to the peace policy on two familiar targets: "Romish Jesuits" and corrupt politicians. Turning reservations over to the Department of War would be disastrous. "No sane man believes that the army will civilize or Christianize any barbarous people," the paper opined; "soldiers as a rule are destitute of Christian morality."[7]

At Round Valley, Burchard reported to the Office of Indian Affairs that the talk of transfer to military control "has had a bad influence on the Indians, they have been dispirited, do not plant and cultivate their gardens to that extent and degree as they otherwise would, their hopes seem crushed, blasted." At the end of July 1876, the rumors had made them so "uneasy" that the agent asked the Indians to turn in their firearms—which he had always permitted on the reservation—an order *"they have submitted* to." Acutely aware of national political trends, Round Valley Indians exerted their political will in ways they could—complaining, refusing to spend their leisure time cultivating reservation property, and evidently seeming capable of violence. By taking away the guns of the reservation's "peaceable, quiet, inoffensive, Christian Indians," Burchard again asserted his patriarchal control over the reservation. For all his optimism about Indians' potential as Christian citizens, Burchard did not believe that they were yet as rational and capable of restraint as his white employees.[8]

Burchard maintained this attitude despite the near-constant troubles he encountered with those employees. Other than Burchard's wife and son, almost every prominent reservation employee eventually caused a problem in one way or another. Mary Colburn and Mary Burnett, the two missionaries who had presided over the beginning of the Methodist revival of 1874, left after offending Indians and other employees for "never mingling with whites or Indians out of school and seeming to have no interest in common with other people." In 1875, Burchard fired reservation physician E. B. Bateman, his friend for more than fifteen years, for illegally selling government medicine and for suspicion of adultery with a local married woman. Then, in early 1876, a group of discharged employees launched what he termed an "iniquitous and malicious persecution" against Burchard.[9] Following their allegations, the Office of Indian Affairs began an investigation of irregularities in the agent's finances that would drag on for ten years before the U.S. Attorney finally cleared him of all dishonesty in 1885.[10]

Newspapers in Mendocino County and San Francisco gleefully covered these embarrassments as part of their assault on the peace policy. Burchard's old foe J. K. Luttrell then cited those articles in the House of Representatives to oppose further money for reservations run by minister-agents. "That is the way your Christian ministers have been managing affairs in my district; that is the way they have been plundering the poor Indians," he thundered.[11] Burchard and the *California Christian Advocate* continued to wage a counter-campaign throughout 1876 and early 1877, but the government's investigation of reservation finances undermined their ability to defend the agent's reputation as they had done in earlier years. Although Luttrell was a Democrat, attacks on Burchard—and, by extension, the Republican peace policy—came from papers from all parts of the political spectrum, including the Republican San Francisco *Chronicle.* By mid-1877, Burchard had become a public symbol of mismanagement, if not outright corruption. The ongoing Christian revival at Round Valley was simply proof, according to the press, that Methodist agents "subserved justice and duty to religious promptings." Focusing on religious uplift for Indians was a mistake, these critics insisted, because they could never become true Christians, missionary reports notwithstanding.[12]

On June 17, 1877, Burchard tendered his resignation to the Office of Indian Affairs. He gave no reason for quitting, but the constant attacks he had faced in the press, along with the government's investigation of his bookkeeping, must have exacted a toll on him. Before he left Round Valley, he filed a report contrasting reservation Indians' present-day burial practices with those existing when he had arrived in 1872. Whereas before they had "gathered around the grave wailing most pitifully, tearing their faces with their nails till the blood would run down their cheeks, pull[ing] out their hair and such other heathenish conduct," now, as Christians, they "look upon their dead as not annihilated and lost to them, forever, or some other undefined superstitious idea, but that the good, as having a home in Heaven, where they will see and be with them again." Burchard felt proud of this "wonderful change," an indication to him that Round Valley Indians had internalized Christian theology and codes of conduct. Having presided over the largest Native American revival of the peace policy era, he left Round Valley believing that the effects of his administration had vindicated Grant's policy and the notion that Indians were well on their way to Christian civilization.[13]

After Burchard decided not to organize an Independence Day celebration in 1877, Round Valley Indians held a meeting and elected to "honor the day at their own expense." The "wholly . . . Indian affair" resembled the previous year's, with orations, a feast, and fireworks—supplemented, however, by a dance conducted by a dozen Indians "grotesquely dressed as growlers." According to the *California Christian Advocate*, which rarely missed a chance to defend the peace policy, the independently produced celebration proved that "they love the government and very highly appreciate the Christian policy in Indian management which is accomplishing so much for them." Burchard, who had resigned but was still on the reservation, no doubt took heart from the day, although the "growler" dance likely gave him pause, given his efforts to eradicate traditional dancing on the reservation. By including the dance in the day's festivities, the Indian organizers demonstrated an easygoing mixing of American and native ceremonial traditions. Recasting a traditional dance as a form of patriotism, the Indian organizers asserted their desire for both autonomy and inclusion, continuity and change. Being Christians or Americans did not necessarily mean giving up all older ways. The names of the organizers were never recorded, but they were likely the tribal captains, men who were most closely aligned with Methodism and Burchard; their inclusion of the dance might also have been a way to capture the sympathies of reservation Indians less inclined toward Christianity and U.S. nationalism.[14]

"Dirty on the inside of their clothes":
The End of the Peace Policy

The minister whom the Methodist Episcopal California Conference put in charge of Round Valley after Burchard's departure brought a starkly different attitude to the job. Henry Bradley Sheldon, who hailed from Ohio but who had been in California since 1852, was a former "pioneer" minister who had spent most of his time in the ministry working among white settlers in rural northern California. For all his paternalism, Burchard had consistently championed the Indians' spiritual and intellectual potential. Sheldon, who informed the Office of Indian Affairs that he was at Round Valley "not by my own seeking or choice, but in *obedience* to the earnest call of the Church," took a much dimmer view. From the first, Sheldon's letters to the Office of Indian Affairs were filled with displays of disgust and disapproval. He insisted that Round Valley Indians "have not the intelligence and judgment of those east, or north, indeed I know of none in the United States, so low in the scale as human beings." He remarked, "Our Indians are improvident, I allow, but what Indians are not?"[15]

When assessing the religiosity of reservation Indians, Sheldon saw not a marvelous revival but a group of opportunistic heathens who had misled previous missionaries. In his first annual report, he wrote:

> Four years ago a "wonderful revival" took place on this reservation and nearly all the Indians "joined the church" and were baptized; but I fear that by far the larger proportion had not an intelligent idea as to what those ceremonies meant. On taking charge here I found a few (about twenty) who seemed really desirous of being Christians; some of these have and some have not experienced a radical change of heart. Some are as intelligent, earnest, growing Christians (for their advantages) as I have ever known. Of 798 [church] members reported last year, 20 are all that the missionary thinks

are worthy of the name. This wonderful falling off is sad, and yet why should they be carried and reported, when they are devoid even of the *form* of godliness? . . . One of our Indians described the defection in this way: "Indians all good Christians long as sugar-barrel not empty; but bimeby sugar all gone, mos' all slide back."

Burchard's much-ballyhooed revival, according to Sheldon, was a farce. Virtually no Round Valley Indians were advanced enough to truly embrace Christianity; they had gone along with the revival simply out of materialistic gain.[16]

Sheldon echoed skepticism about the revival that had been voiced earlier by white settlers and newspapers looking to delegitimize Burchard's administration. Sheldon's perspective was shaped not by political animus or a self-interested desire to see the reservation dismantled but by his pessimism about Indian "character." He arrived during a low point in religious enthusiasm on the reservation, born from the rumors of transfer to the Department of War and the change of agents, and he projected backward to assume the revival had always been such. Furthermore, Sheldon did not recognize the form of Christianity practiced by Round Valley Indians, with its mixing of various elements and traditions, as genuine. His dismissal of the revival reflected his definitions of what Christians looked like and how they acted—what he termed the "*form* of godliness." At the same time, it is probable that Sheldon perceived something that Burchard had missed or had chosen to deemphasize: Some Indians had multiple motives for joining the Methodist Church, ones that included calculated self-interest. However, Sheldon's characterization of the four-year revival as nothing more than a ploy was surely misguided, given its longevity and the detailed reports written not just by Methodist ministers—who, after all, had an interest in promoting the efficacy of the peace policy—but also by military officers.

Whatever the nature of the religious phenomena that had taken place under Burchard, it did not continue under Sheldon. A steady exodus of Indians occurred during Sheldon's tenure, reducing the reservation's population from about 1,000 when he arrived in 1877 to half that two years later. In 1885, a Calpella Indian named Charlie Brown who left during Sheldon's tenure told the U.S. Senate's Committee on Indian Affairs why he did so: "We were worked there too hard, and didn't give us enough to eat." He continued,

Up at the reservation they told us about the Democrat and Republican. They said the Republican would show us what to do; how to get a home, how to work; and how to live, how to raise vegetables of all kinds; and they said we could have our own land, 6, 7, 8, or 50 acres for ourselves. Every agent said so, but we didn't get anything; . . . but I can read and write and find out things through the newspapers; and so I said to my people they have promised us everything and we have got nothing, so we better leave.

Asked about polygamy among his group, Brown reported that the Calpellas were serial monogamists: "We don't marry by license like the whites. We did that way when we were at the reservation and were Christians. We married then by license, but that didn't do us any good, so we let it go." For Brown and the Calpellas, forced labor, insufficient food, unfulfilled promises from the government, and pressure to conform to unfamiliar religious and sexual rules made living on the reservation under Sheldon intolerable.[17]

The single largest contingent that departed was a group of about two hundred Potter Valley Pomos, led by a man known variously as Napoleon Bonaparte, Captain Jack, and Che-Na-Ta-Da-La. In 1878, they bought a plot of land near the town of Ukiah City under a "communistic plan," hired a lawyer, and threatened to have Sheldon arrested for kidnapping if he tried to bring any Indians back to Round Valley. Sheldon blamed their departure on Bonaparte's megalomaniacal control and the Indians' desire for family land plots—a spurious explanation, given their decision to pool their money and buy land in common, an arrangement favored by the Calpellas as well. Charlie Bourne, a member of the Potter Valley contingent that left the reservation, told the Senate Committee that their land near Ukiah City "belongs to all our folks, and nobody can take it." He reported that he had fled the reservation because, after only two months of schooling, he had been forced to work full time. "I wanted to understand something, but they would not let me stay at school," he said. "After I had been at school they put me to work like a dog."[18]

The Potter Valley Pomos left in protest of Sheldon's administration and to gain greater autonomy, including religious autonomy. In 1880, the Methodist Episcopal California Conference reported that, at the Indian community near Ukiah City, "a Sunday-school is taught, and occasional religious meetings are conducted. The captain or chief was a church member while at Round Valley." Unlike the Calpellas, who seem to have left much of Christianity behind when they left the reservation, the Potter Valley Pomos chose to practice Christianity—in whatever form—on their own terms, in their own services, rather than participate in Sheldon's church. Leaving the reservation did not necessarily mean leaving Christianity behind, notwithstanding Sheldon's protests that off-reservation Indian children were "being brought up in idleness and shame."[19]

Beginning in 1879, even those Indians who remained at Round Valley rejected Sheldon's authority. In April, tribal leaders met to adopt resolutions they sent to the Department of the Interior demanding Sheldon's removal. By 1882, open conflict had engulfed the reservation, with Round Valley Indians sending multiple letters to the federal government and the California Methodist Episcopal Conference complaining about Sheldon. John Brown, licensed Methodist minister and captain of the Yuki, asked Sheldon's district elder to remove the agent because "whenever the Indian man and woman come to church he [Sheldon] preach about them. And called them dirty on the inside of their clothes. And it sound very bad in their ears." Two groups of Round Valley Indians wrote to President Chester A. Arthur to ask for Sheldon's removal, with the Yuki complaining that the agent "says we come to church with clean clothes outside and dirty clothes inside and we don't want to go to church any more when he talks that way and we don't want him for preacher, we want our preacher that's all. If we have one preacher then we go to church and try to be good."[20]

In their petitions, these Indians portrayed themselves as pious Christians striving to follow church precepts but being thwarted by Sheldon's un-Christian behavior. Their complaints focused as much on Sheldon's racial attitudes as on his policies. Unlike Burchard, whom Munsell had praised for being "not ashamed to shake our dirty hands," Sheldon told Indians that they possessed perpetually "dirty" bodies. As with the Potter Valley Pomos who left the reservation altogether, the Yukis preferred "our preacher" to Sheldon. The fact that he treated them like second-class citizens in church, where all believers were supposed to be brothers and sisters in Christ, was especially galling.[21]

Indians were not the only ones who objected to Sheldon; like Burchard, Sheldon faced intense criticism from local settlers, newspaper editors, and disgruntled employees, who predictably charged him with mismanaging the reservation.[22] California's Methodist leadership, which had tirelessly supported Burchard through all his travails, reappointed

Sheldon to Round Valley each year but, as time passed, became disenchanted with his administration. George O. Ash, Sheldon's district elder in 1879, expressed shock at how much recidivism he saw among the reservation Indians, recommending that the church "abandon at once this field of labor" unless sufficient attention was given to spiritual concerns. A few months later, Methodist minister J. L. Broaddus, former agent at Hoopa Valley, joined several other Round Valley settlers in sending a letter to their U.S. representative complaining that Sheldon only "pretends to christianize and civilize" the Indians: "We assert that with possibly a few exceptions there is no such thing as Christianity amongst them but on the contrary they form an immense place of prostitution sufficient to degrade and destroy our young men and to be a blot and curse on one of the fairest vallies in this state." Other ministers reported in 1880 that the "morals of the Indians are low. Drinking, gambling and licentiousness are constantly encouraged by bad and beastly white men." They concluded that the earlier "reports of extensive revival . . . we are satisfied, were widely overdrawn."[23]

In a few years, Methodist leadership had gone from trumpeting Round Valley as a site of God's burgeoning global revival to condemning it as a locus of prostitution, sin, and fraud. This remarkable reversal was part of a larger rethinking of the peace policy that occurred among Protestants in California and the nation during these years. Throughout the late 1870s, Protestant newspapers and journals in the East debated the policy, the reservation system, and the challenges of Indian missionization.[24] California's religious press was likewise consumed by the question, with more and more ministers expressing frustration with missionaries' inability to maintain the promising results of the early 1870s, even as the *California Christian Advocate, Pacific,* and *Occident* officially continued to support the peace policy through 1879. Another solution to the Indian question, discussed in California since the 1850s, began to grow in popularity: the allotment of reservation lands in severalty.[25]

Noisy champion of the peace policy though it had been, the *California Christian Advocate* began warming to the notion of allotment in 1878. Individual family plots, followed eventually by full citizenship rights, might assimilate Indians more quickly into Christian American society than perpetual segregation on remote reservations. In 1880, with Round Valley appearing more and more mired in sin and heathenism, the paper called for a "new departure" in Indian policy. Individual homesteads would allow Indians to cultivate their own farms, making use of God's bounty while learning the value of hard work, thrift, and responsibility. The Congregationalist

Pacific announced its support of allotment a year later. Even departed agent Burchard, for so long the public face of the peace policy in California, was convinced by 1878 that the state's reservations should be broken up into individual land plots. He informed Secretary of the Interior Carl Schurz, "The Indians want land. Homes of their own. . . . If we can really greatly better the condition of the Indians, and save so much to the government, and prove to the world that political reform can be effected, why not do it."[26]

The details of how allotment would work were fuzzy in these proposals; what they agreed on was that the reservation system had run its course. Allotment began to appeal to different Protestants in different ways in the late 1870s. For those still committed to racial egalitarianism, the plan promised a neo-Jeffersonian future of agrarian equality and full citizenship for all. For those exasperated by the constant controversies and allegations of mismanagement that dogged minister-agents in California, allotment shifted the burden of evangelism to local churches rather than the state conference. For such white supremacist ministers as Baptist T. P. Crawford, who condemned the "amalgamation and assimilation" of different races as contrary to God's plan, allotment gave Indians the self-sufficiency to maintain racial purity and fulfill their own separate destiny.[27]

In the midst of this change of public opinion, Sarah Winnemucca arrived in San Francisco to deliver a series of lectures in late 1879 on behalf of her tribe, the Northern Piute of western Nevada. Relocated by the government to reservations in Oregon and then Washington, the Northern Piute had splintered and suffered attacks from competing Indian groups. Winnemucca, a Christian and former translator for the Army, was traveling across the country to raise sympathy for her people and draw attention to the "peace policy hypocrites" she blamed for their plight. She directed most of her scorn at a particularly abusive agent at the Malheur Reservation in Oregon, but in her final lecture in San Francisco she widened her attack to all white Christians who permitted such abuses to continue. "The preachers get up in their pulpits and fairly dance before their congregations, and talk about preaching us the Gospel, and convert us," she announced in Platt's Hall. "Do they do it? They don't do no such thing. I want homes for my people, but no one will help us. I call upon white people in their private homes. They will not touch my fingers for fear of getting soiled. That's the Christianity of white people."[28]

Winnemucca's skillful use of Christian rhetoric, mixed with her moral indignation and sarcastic sense of humor, won her frequent applause from

San Francisco audiences. Covered extensively by local newspapers, Winnemucca's lectures contributed to a climate increasingly suspicious of the
aims and results of the peace policy.[29] Although Winnemucca did not en-
dorse allotment and in fact praised some Methodist agents, she directed
such wrath at corrupt agents and hypocritical missionaries that audiences
could not help but conclude that a radical new Indian policy was needed.
The newspapers that covered her talks were uniformly opposed to the
peace policy; they folded her story into a larger narrative about the
"wretched" policy's record of abuse and failure, conducted in the name of
winning conversions to Christianity. "Surely none have been made yet,"
observed the *Daily Alta California*, "and how can any sensible person an-
ticipate that any will or can be civilized?"[30]

Such notions echoed throughout the country in 1880, at which
point public criticism of the peace policy reached fever pitch. That year,
Commissioner of Indian Affairs Ezra Hayt resigned amid charges of
corruption, while a high-profile lecture tour by Ponca leader Standing
Bear directed even more attention to the inequities of the peace policy,
especially Indian removal practices. In Boston, Philadelphia, and other
eastern cities, Protestant reformers created the Boston Indian Citizenship Association, the Women's National Indian Association, the Indian
Rights Association, and other organizations dedicated to forging a new
path for U.S.–Indian relations. Protestant reformers and church leaders had been the strongest supporters of the peace policy during the
1870s, and their abandonment of it in the early 1880s sealed its fate. By
1882, the Office of the Interior had ended church control of all Indian
reservations.[31]

The peace policy was over, and few people mourned its passing. At
Round Valley, complaints from Indians and employees had reached such
a level in 1882 that the California Methodist Episcopal Conference finally
decided that agent H. B. Sheldon had to be removed. However, the end
of the peace policy meant that the decision was no longer theirs to make,
as Sheldon was now wholly in the employ of the Department of the Interior, which informed the Methodist Conference that "there was no
other Reservation in the nation more satisfactorily managed, in the opinion of the Government at Washington, than was that at Round Valley."
From here forward, all personnel decisions would be made not on religious grounds but "in reference to business qualifications *only*." Against
the wishes of his conference, his employees, and the Round Valley Indians, Sheldon remained agent. This, in a way, was fitting. His dim view of
Indians' potential matched the new era beginning to dawn.[32]

"Either the cross or the dragon": Chinese Question Controversies

In an 1876 letter on the topic of Indian missions, Nicholas Congiato, Jesuit priest at Saint Joseph's Church in San Jose, paused to remark, "There is nothing now in this part of the world, except the Chinese question." Indeed, the controversies over Indian policy paled in comparison to the violent disagreements over Chinese immigration and evangelism that arose in California during the second half of the 1870s. The 1876 state and federal hearings on Chinese immigration had placed ministers in the public spotlight, where they would remain throughout the developments leading to Chinese exclusion in 1882. Following the hearings and the effigy lynching of Methodist Otis Gibson, many California ministers continued to argue for free immigration and civil rights for the Chinese, but they did so in an increasingly hostile public climate. More and more ministers joined politicians and secular newspaper editors in denouncing the presence of the Chinese, sparking bitter debates within and between conferences and congregations.[33]

During the 1877 annual meeting of the General Association of Congregational Churches and Ministers in California, debate on the Chinese question overshadowed other matters. Samuel V. Blakeslee, the one-time missionary to the Chinese who had denounced them during the federal hearings the previous fall, articulated the anti-Chinese position in a lengthy address. He described a not-too-distant future in which the Chinese would be voters, lawmakers, and judges. "Then must the sons and daughters of Christians in our land be brought before heathen tribunals, by heathen marshals, to be tried as to their lives, liberty, and property, by heathen juries, influenced by heathen prejudices," he warned. He insisted that it was "false Christianity, false benevolence, false patriotism, false confidence, false love of the world, false estimate of the gifts of God" to continue to open "immatured" America to the "corruptions" of Asia.[34]

Extended debate followed Blakeslee's remarks, with several ministers rebuking Blakeslee's arguments as "caste prejudices" and pointing out, "The Chinese are not the worst people in San Francisco," presumably thinking of Irish Catholics. However, these voices were outnumbered by anti-Chinese Congregationalists, who drafted a series of resolutions that, after further debate and revision, were passed unanimously. After condemning mob violence and supporting the continuation of mission work among the Chinese of California, the Congregationalists passed a third resolution:

That we express it as our conviction that the Burlingame treaty ought to be so modified, and other such measures be adopted by the General Government, as shall restrict Chinese immigration, and shall especially prevent the importation of Chinese prostitutes, and so relieve us from impending peril to our republican and Christian institutions.[35]

Before this moment, individual clergymen in California such as Milton B. Starr and Samuel V. Blakeslee had condemned Chinese immigration, but the Congregationalists' 1877 resolution marked the first time an entire state conference declared its opposition. The public response was noisy. Gibson promptly denounced the third resolution as "cowardly demagogism," calling it "a remarkable instance of the effect of a perverted public sentiment upon good men." Congregationalist William Pond, superintendent of the American Missionary Association's campaign among the Chinese of California, reported, "I am not prepared to defend [the third resolution], and do not believe that it is defensible."[36]

California's politicians and secular newspapers, on the other hand, seized on the resolution as evidence that immigration restriction was consistent with biblical teachings, no matter what such activists as Gibson insisted. Aaron A. Sargent, Republican U.S. senator from California, read the Congregationalist resolutions from the floor of Congress, and the California state senate printed the resolutions and Blakeslee's speech as appendices in the official transcript of the 1876 state hearing. In a much-discussed letter to the New York *Tribune*, James G. Blaine, a Republican senator from Maine who hoped the anti-Chinese movement would propel him into the White House, cited the resolution as evidence that the "enlightened religious sentiment of the Pacific Coast" now favored immigration restriction. The anti-Chinese San Francisco *Argonaut* went so far as to claim that there was no longer "a single respectable clergyman of any denomination—Catholic, Protestant, Jew, or Gentile—who does not oppose Chinese immigration, excepting, of course, those missionaries who live upon their presence."[37]

The *Argonaut's* statement was grossly untrue, but increasing numbers of California ministers did join the Congregationalists in calling for immigration restriction or outright exclusion in the late 1870s. In a sign of the changing times, Methodist Henry Cox, who in 1867 had been called a traitor to the white race by Democrats for his support of Republican

gubernatorial candidate George C. Gorham, now threw his weight behind the anti-Chinese movement. At an immense anti-Chinese mass
meeting in San Francisco in April 1876, Cox acknowledged that his opposition to the Chinese seemed "something very strange," but "in the Chinese we find a people who can never better us nor elevate themselves,
who are serfs and who bring to us their prostitutes, their dirt and pollu-
tion and their heathen rites." Prominent Baptist minister O. C. Wheeler
told state legislators that the Chinese would, if not thwarted, "permeate
every portion of our whole country, undermine and control every prof-
itable industry, subvert and destroy all our free institutions, replace our
sanctuaries with the temples of idolatry, and transform our land into the
generator and hot-bed of every foul and unclean thing." Delegates to the
San Francisco Sunday School convention of 1879 listened politely to a
pro-immigration lecture but greeted an anti-immigration speech with "a
storm of applause." By 1879, the Congregational *Pacific*, Methodist *California Christian Advocate,* and Baptist *Evangel* now opposed unrestricted
immigration from China.[38]

The tide was clearly turning. These ministers' denunciations of the
Chinese contributed to a wider intensification of anti-Chinese sentiment
in California that occurred in the late 1870s. Testimony at the 1876 federal hearing had been split roughly in half between pro- and anti-Chinese
immigration speakers, but as the decade wore on, pro-immigration voices
became scarcer and scarcer. State Democrats continued their relentless
campaign of Christian white supremacy, while state Republicans, finally
freed from the onus of defending southern Reconstruction after 1877, tried
to outdo the Democrats in denouncing the Chinese, part of the Republican party's retreat from racial justice struggles nationwide.[39] In October 1877, a new state political movement emerged—the Workingmen's
Party of California—rising to power with a populist message blaming the
recession and unemployment on corrupt capitalists and Chinese coolies.
The Workingmen, led by Irish Catholic drayman Denis Kearney, employed
an anti-Chinese rhetoric even more aggressive than that of the Democrats and Republicans, openly threatening arson and murder if the Chinese
were not expelled. The new party won major victories in the 1878 elections and commandeered about one third of the seats at that year's second California constitutional convention. The new constitution, which
the Workingmen largely wrote and helped ratify, forbade all corporations
and government agencies from employing "any Chinese or Mongolian."[40]

Along with emphasizing the supposed economic ruin and unfair job
competition Chinese immigration wrought, anti-Chinese activists depicted

it as the harbinger of a holy war between Christianity and heathenism, with California as the battleground. "Never before was christianity brought face to face with paganism in a death struggle," announced the president of a San Francisco Anti-Coolie Club, "for I tell you that either the cross or the dragon must go down in this present conflict, and the question of supremacy is to be decided on these shores." Central to this notion was the idea that the Chinese would and could not adopt Christianity, missionary reports notwithstanding. In yet another memorial protesting Chinese immigration, the California state senate insisted that, despite decades of evangelism, "we have not evidence of a single genuine conversion to Christianity, or of a single instance of an assimilation with our manners, or habits of thought or life." Even if a few Chinese immigrants have adopted Christianity, these arguments went, the cost in terms of American morality was too steep: "Where we have converted one Chinaman to Christianity, their influence has degraded ten white men to practical heathenism." Such arguments blended racial and religious bigotry, portraying the Chinese as a "degraded and pagan race" forever physically and morally inferior.[41]

Anti-Chinese agitators had many reasons to insist that few if any Chinese immigrants had truly converted to Christianity. This allowed them to continue to lump all Chinese together as "uneducated, ignorant, servile, brutish pagans"—in the words of the San Francisco *Examiner*—undeserving of political rights. This also refuted the idea, repeated so often by Protestant missionaries, that Providence was guiding the Chinese to America to be saved. If they were not, in fact, being converted, then it was clearly not God's plan that was bringing them to California. Praising the Congregationalists' 1877 resolutions, the San Francisco *Morning Call* agreed that Chinese immigration "was not providential with a view to their conversion, as more favorable results would necessarily follow from the Divine interposition." Edward P. Baker, a Congregationalist minister who joined the chorus of anti-Chinese voices in 1877, scoffed at the notion of Providence guiding the Chinese to California. "Not everything that *is*, is Providential, in the sense of being just what it *should* be," he told his congregation. "Bad things take place in a general way under the Divine Providence, but they are still bad for all that." Chinese immigrants' supposed failure to convert to Christianity proved that it was not contrary to God's will to ban them from coming.[42]

Extending the anticlerical atmosphere that had surrounded the 1876 federal hearing, newspapers and politicians mocked and decried ministers who continued to insist that the Chinese were fully capable of Christianity. These ministers, they declared, were nothing more than a "small band of zealots, fanatics, and demagogues" who dishonored their race and calling. Several anti-Chinese plays and novels published in San Francisco in the late 1870s included villainous ministers who cloak in holy platitudes their desires to profit financially from the Chinese. In Henry Grimm's play *The Chinese Must Go,* Rev. Howard Sneaker is presented as a "pious fog-producer" who "never earned a day's wages in his life" but is content to "go around and blow about the brotherhood of man as long as he can fool the fools out of sixty dollars a day."[43] Such characters were clearly modeled on the public perception of Otis Gibson, one of the most hated men in California, who received a barrage of venom for his allegedly hypocritical promotion of the "universal brotherhood of man." The *Chronicle* declared Gibson's book *The Chinese in America* "slovenly" and puerile; Gibson reported being accosted on the streets of San Francisco by "white heathens" demanding that "the Chinese have got to go, *and you will go with them.*" When Gibson paid a visit to the state legislature in early 1880, a Democratic assemblyman tried to pass a motion having him expelled.[44]

During debates over the Chinese problem in the state's second constitutional convention in 1878 and 1879, delegates from all three parties mocked pro-immigration ministers as misguided race-traitors who misinterpreted the word of God. "They would Mongolize this land in a vain missionary effort to bring the Chinaman to a knowledge of the true God," declared Republican John F. Miller. "He has his gods whom he will not destroy." Miller dismissed the idea that Acts 17:26—"God hath made of one blood all nations of men"—necessitated sympathy for the Chinese. "It is the economy of Providence that man shall exist in nationalities, and that they shall be divided by the antipathies of race," he said. "Why this should be is not for us to inquire." Other delegates agreed: "What has these long-faced preachers done? They have driven our poor white men, our white boys, and white girls into hoodlumism. They have made our poor white girls what? Prostitutes!"[45] As with the 1876 federal hearing, anti-Chinese agitators insisted that the sexual purity of California's white women was endangered by Chinese immigration and by the ministers who supported it. In 1876, the specter had been miscegenation; now, it was prostitution. Delegates' economic and political arguments repeatedly returned to discussions of Chinese immorality, heathenism, and sin, resting as often on the Bible as on economic evidence or political theory.

Only one delegate spoke out against the anti-Chinese statutes: Charles V. Stuart, a farmer from Sonoma County who admitted that he relied on Chinese labor. Stuart urged his fellow delegates to "act like civilized, just, and Christian men; not to do an act that would shock all humane men throughout the world, both Christian and Pagan." Following the lead of Gibson and other pro-Chinese Protestant ministers, Stuart attempted to shift the focus onto Irish immigrants and other Catholics. "Who form our rioters and hoodlums?" he asked. "Who fill our almshouses? Who are plotting to overthrow our public schools? Who stuff our ballot boxes? Who are conspiring to overthrow and destroy our Government, and to utterly stamp out liberty, that despotism over conscience, mind, and muscle, may rise upon the ruins? . . . Not Chinamen." During the 1876 federal hearing, such comments had been common, but in the 1879 convention Stuart was alone in these sentiments and earned only scorn from his fellow delegates, many of whom were Catholics themselves. The anti-Chinese movement had, for the moment, subsumed Protestant–Catholic tensions in San Francisco.[46]

Using arguments that echoed those being employed against the assimilability of California Indians, delegates insisted that the Chinese could never become Christians. "The Mongol will never kneel at your altars nor worship the living God," declared delegate Charles C. O'Donnell. "Paganism, like a black pall, still shrouds the heathen in impenetrable night, where the sun of Christianity can never penetrate." Clitus Barbour, a high-ranking member of the Workingmen's Party, made the comparison with Indians explicit. "The American Indian and the Chinaman possess different kinds of civilization to our civilization," he said. "They differ in the methods in which they resist it, but it is none the less resistance." Barbour noted that "the best scholars" believed that "Asiatics are probably an Indian race," a reference to ethnologists' general acceptance of a common origin for the two groups. This notion bolstered the idea that both Indians and the Chinese were racially and spiritually unassimilable, similarly stagnant and debased. "Like the North American Indian . . . ," surmised the *Argonaut*, "the Chinaman must *die*."[47]

Unsurprisingly in such a climate, ministers discovered that their white congregations increasingly objected to Chinese evangelism. This had been true to a certain extent in the early 1870s, but ministers, largely united in support of immigration, had managed to convince laypeople of the importance of Chinese mission work. After 1876, white congregations grew more hostile. In 1877, A. W. Loomis complained that anti-Chinese prejudice among lay Presbyterians had grown to such an extent that "pastors have deemed it expedient not to be too demonstrative in favor of the Chinese." Chinese Sunday school classes, begun with such enthusiasm, languished for lack of teachers. One white woman in San

Francisco quit teaching after a year, complaining that the opium fumes emanating from her students "so nauseated her that she could not eat." William Pond, hoping to add a Chinese Sunday school at a Congregationalist church in rural Oroville, was informed that "the Christian people in Oroville would be loth to render any active assistance.... Such is the general prejudice against the Chinese now existing, they fear that the cause of Christ amongst the whites of the community would be more injured than would be compensated for by good dun to the Chinese." Feeling themselves outnumbered by Catholics and godless settlers, white Protestants in Oroville refused to lower their status by racially integrating their churches.[48]

Ministers encountered increasing incentives to de-emphasize Chinese evangelism in the face of lay opposition. William Pond complained in 1878 that, between the deepening economic depression and rising anti-Chinese sentiment, donors to the American Missionary Association were harder and harder to find: "men who subscribed a year ago and did it pleasantly, answer you with a scornful denial to-day." M. H. Savage, an American Missionary Association worker who had moved to Los Angeles after laboring among freed slaves in the American South, reported, "It certainly requires as complete consecration to give one's self to the Chinese work as to the work among the colored people—To be sure here there is not the *bitter ostracism* some experience South, but there is a growing opposition to anything being done for them and many professed Christians oppose anything that tends to elevate the Chinaman." More and more church leaders lacked the "complete consecration" necessary to go on championing the Chinese.[49]

"The Chinese must go":
Isaac S. Kalloch and the New Anti-Chinese Movement

Church leaders who, on the other hand, denounced the Chinese discovered newfound opportunities for personal and political advancement. The meteoric rise of Baptist minister Isaac S. Kalloch demonstrates how much could be gained. Kalloch, a former "boy preacher" whose career as a Boston abolitionist had been cut short by a much-publicized adultery trial, arrived in San Francisco in 1875. With help from local Baptists, he constructed Metropolitan Temple, the largest Baptist church in the United States, which he routinely filled to capacity with his bombastic, often political sermons. For a time, Kalloch's church boasted of maintaining the biggest Chinese Sunday school in the world, and its pastors chided those who would "drive the heathen away from our shores, thus depriving them of perhaps their only chance of salvation." Throughout 1877, however, Kalloch made headlines with a series of fiery anti-Chinese sermons. He contrasted his style of Christianity—"the religion of common life, the light of poor men's homes, the comfort of poor men's hearts" —with the Christianity of Gibson and other defenders of the Chinese, which he called "the religion of cant—a Pecksniffien piety—very proper and very pious, but always leaving the wounded sufferer on the side of the road." The only "wounded sufferers" he saw, of course, were white laborers. Kalloch insisted that Chinese evangelism should occur in China, not California, and soon after terminated the Metropolitan Temple's Chinese mission work.[50]

As the Workingmen's Party of California began to grow, Kalloch initially condemned it as a band of "incendiaries" and "blatherskites," but in July 1878 he reversed his position, declaring Denis Kearney "an agent in the hands of Providence." Thereafter, Kalloch served as the semi-official chaplain of the Workingmen, lending institutional and rhetorical support to Kearney's white labor movement. The Workingmen had been generally hostile to ministers, declaring Christianity a "cloak" used by thieves, even while some of its leaders used biblical quotations to defend the party's militarism and unabashedly compared Kearney to Jesus Christ.[51] Kalloch lent the movement legitimacy and a meeting place, as Metropolitan Temple became overflowed with white laborers thrilled by Kalloch's denunciations of "this monopoly ridden and Chinese cursed city." He escalated his attacks on the Chinese, renouncing the notion that they could ever be converted to Christianity under any circumstances. "They are utterly and hopelessly foreign, alien and unassimilating," he thundered. In June 1879, Kalloch accepted the Workingmen's nomination to be their candidate in that fall's San Francisco mayoral race, his reward for service to the party and an acknowledgment of the power he already wielded.[52]

The ascension of Kalloch, Kearney, and the Workingmen challenged existing political and religious structures in San Francisco. Nearly every newspaper in the city—religious or secular—attacked the party, sometimes for opposite reasons. The Protestant press, which had long linked "hoodlumism" with Catholicism, portrayed the Workingmen as godless "white heathen" immigrants who "hate civil and religious liberty." Protestant newspapers and ministers directed special animus at Kalloch, whom Gibson condemned for urging the "mad European ignorant mob on in their work of intimidation and ruin." Whether or not they supported continued immigration from China, Protestant leaders objected to the Workingmen's bloodthirsty rhetoric and Kalloch's pandering oratories. The fact that Kearney and many of the Workingmen were Irish predisposed Protestants to view their movement as part of a larger Catholic threat to American institutions they decried throughout the 1870s.[53]

Already under attack over the public school question and other issues, San Francisco's Catholic Church worked hard to distance itself from the Workingmen's rabble-rousing. In 1877 and 1878, Archbishop Joseph Alemany issued three pastoral letters in response to the rise of the Workingmen, urging Catholics to "stand by authority" and to "stay away from such seditious, anti social and anti-Christian meetings." The *Monitor*, longtime champion of San Francisco's Irish working class, denounced Kearney's incendiary brand of populism as akin to that of the "*sansculottes* of Paris."[54]

When attacking the Workingmen, Catholic leaders made it clear that they too opposed the "flood" of "Chinese incubus," but insisted that the "remedy lies not in the mad torch of Anarchy." The "right way" for Irish Catholics to oppose the coming of the Chinese was to do it "quietly, legally and constitutionally," as when Alemany signed his name to a public petition supporting immigration restriction in 1879; the "wrong way" was through mob violence, which would feed anti-Catholic hysteria by giving "unfriendly and designing politicians" enough "political capital … to last them in their Know-Nothing diatribes for twenty years to come." Alemany and the *Monitor* condemned both the Workingmen and the Chinese to bolster Irish Catholics' claims to whiteness, Christianity, and patriotism. Workingmen Party leaders retorted that they were "willing to obey priests and bishops in all church affairs," but that Alemany had no business commenting on "temporal affairs."[55]

Leading African Americans in San Francisco similarly denounced the Workingmen. Peter Anderson's *Pacific Appeal*, which had grown more accepting of the Chinese throughout the 1870s but still opposed Chinese immigration, initially called Kearney "novel and interesting" and printed Kalloch's anti-Chinese sermons verbatim. By 1879, however, the paper had aligned itself with "intelligent native-born Americans" in opposing the "foreign" Workingmen and their new state constitution. "I am satisfied that if every Chinamen were now out of the State and city of San Francisco, the same complaint would be made against [negroes]—that they were interfering with the work of the laboring men, and that the 'negro must go also,'" warned one writer.[56]

Though not exactly making common cause with the Chinese, these writers decided that it was not in African Americans' best interests to encourage the proliferation of racist mobs. With suffrage attained and

San Francisco's schools now opened to their children, leading African Americans had fewer reasons to separate their plight from that of the Chinese, as had been deemed necessary in earlier years. Drawing on their knowledge of conflict with Irish immigrants in the Northeast, most African Americans decided that the Workingmen posed a greater threat.[57]

San Francisco's officials and mainstream press likewise criticized the Workingmen for their coarse, violent rhetoric and class-based radicalism. The Board of Supervisors attacked the movement as it rose in power, collaborating with local police and judges to repeatedly arrest the Workingmen's leadership to thwart the party's growth. Republican and Democratic newspapers alike condemned the party as dangerous, inadvertently heightening the movement's mystique among disaffected Irish Catholic and German voters. The only exception was the *Chronicle*, which provided relatively positive coverage until its publishers, Charles and Michael de Young, tried to create their own third party to compete with the Workingmen in 1879. A war of words broke out between Kalloch and the de Youngs, with Kalloch using his pulpit to denounce the brothers—according to one account—as the "spawn of the brothel, conceived in infamy, dandled in the lap of a prostitute, bastard progeny of a whore, hybrid monster from hell." In a remarkable series of events, Charles de Young shot Kalloch days before the mayoral election, propelling the minister to victory from his sickbed. A year later, Kalloch's son—like his father, a Baptist minister—shot and killed Charles de Young in retaliation.[58]

The rise of the Workingmen's Party of California—though denounced by virtually all authorities—had the effect of broadening the anti-Chinese movement. The party's violent attitudes allowed more restrained voices to portray their own anti-Chinese rhetoric as comparatively benign, even compassionate. Chinese exclusion—as opposed to expulsion or outright extermination—could be presented as a commonsensical, moderate position. Exclusion brought together Catholics and Protestants, Democrats and Republicans, ministers and politicians as a middle way between the new extremes of unrestricted immigration and mob violence.

Kalloch's two years as mayor of San Francisco were marked by constant battles with the Republican-dominated Board of Supervisors, which impeached him for malfeasance in 1880 but was unable to remove him from office. Kalloch used his power as mayor to launch an investigation into the health "nuisance" posed by Chinatown, producing a block-by-block itemization of "filthy and unhealthy" structures. Announcing his findings, Kalloch insisted, "We have to overcome the prejudice of piety and the criticisms of cant. We have to resist the sentimentalism and become indifferent to the anathemas of the East.... We have to beat back the barbaric hordes of paganism." Kalloch marked race by mixing the languages of science and theology, interweaving concerns about sanitation and public health with warnings about the effects of paganism.[59]

Kalloch's urging of Californians to "become indifferent to the anathemas of the East" acknowledged a conflict over Chinese immigration between westerners and easterners that intensified as more and more Californians embraced exclusion in the late 1870s. President Hayes's veto of an 1879 bill revising the Burlingame Treaty to limit immigration from China triggered another wave of mass meetings in California and encouraged the perception that naïve "easterners" did not understand the true nature of the Chinese threat. In fact, the national Republican and Democratic parties both supported exclusion by 1880, swayed by the vehemence of their western wings and, in the Republicans' case, by an eagerness to abandon "race issues" after the end of southern Reconstruction. Yet California newspapers insisted that the "ponderous thinkers of the East" dismissed the Chinese threat with nothing but "disdain."[60]

Eastern Protestant church leaders, not politicians, were the ones expressing disdain at the notion of immigration restriction. East Coast Protestant newspapers dismissed California's growing anti-Chinese movement as nothing more than "deep race prejudice" against a "frugal, honest, and willing" workforce.[61] At times, eastern Protestant leaders drew on popular conceptions of westerners as uncouth and violent to contrast them with the supposedly peaceable Chinese—not to mention easterners. "Judging by the character of the saints in the Senate of the State of California, who protest so bitterly against these men because they *do not become Christians,* one is compelled to believe that, with them, to become a Christian is to carry a revolver, drink bad whiskey, and chew tobacco," observed the New York *Christian Advocate.* Henry Ward Beecher and Joseph Cook, two of the nation's most prominent ministers, both visited California in the late 1870s to rally Protestant support for Chinese immigration and evangelism. In a much-publicized sermon in San Francisco's Union Hall in 1879, Cook urged California's "men and women of intelligence" to speak out against the anti-Chinese "Romish Church" and opportunistic "ward politicians" who dominated the debate. After touring Chinatown with Gibson as guide, Cook declared it no more crowded, dirty, or sinful than white neighborhoods in San Francisco, New York, Boston, and Glasgow.[62]

Few in California looked kindly on such campaigns by "Eastern busybodies." California's secular press mocked their pronouncements as that of the "sentimental schoolboy," and protestors disrupted Cook's speech in Union Hall with jeers and rocks. Eastern ministers' condescending attitudes toward westerners offended the regional pride of California's Protestant leaders, if anything encouraging them to stiffen their opposition to Chinese immigration. The *Pacific* insisted that "the opinion of the average Californian is worth very much more than Mr. Beecher's" and objected to Cook's joke that "only those already spoiled" were being ruined by Chinese opium and prostitution. In response to the Boston *Congregationalist*'s dismissals of the Chinese threat, Samuel V. Blakeslee wrote a letter to the paper in 1879 explaining that while "you at the East regard the priest-ridden Irish alone as an element of vast possibilities of evil to our country," Californians were witnessing the explosive results of "intermingled" Irish and Chinese threats. Only federal immigration restriction could thwart the "mobs, fires, devastations" that were certain to engulf not just California but the entire nation.[63]

The changing tenor of the times became apparent when the U.S. Congress returned for a second hearing on Chinese immigration in San Francisco in August 1879, part of the House of Representatives' inquiry into the causes of the ongoing depression. Unlike the balanced testimony at the 1876 hearing, nearly every witness at the 1879 hearing decried the effects of Chinese labor and immorality. Although ostensibly there to discuss the economic effects of Chinese immigration, witnesses repeatedly mentioned the Chinese's supposed unwillingness to convert to Christianity as a sign of their debased, unassimilable natures. "A Chinaman once said to me, 'If you give me four bit I will play to Jesus, and for four bit more I will take it all back,'" said one manufacturer. "It is so in regard to Americanizing them." The anti-Irish and anti-Catholic comments that had been so prominent at the 1876 hearing were almost entirely absent from the 1879 session—excepting the testimony of Otis Gibson.[64]

As before, Gibson insisted that Chinese immigration "only stimulated and benefited the industries of California," and he now chalked up the depression to "laziness and liquor." Pestered at length by the congressmen, Gibson said that he supported limiting immigration from all foreign countries—"not from China alone"—because European Catholics represented "more of a curse to this land than the Chinese are." Asked his opinion of a potential "cross between Americans and Chinese," Gibson replied, "I think that a cross between the American and Mexican Indian is worse, and I think that a cross with the colored people is a little further removed."

If anti-Catholicism failed to convince the congressmen, Gibson was willing to demonize other racialized groups to improve the reputation of the Chinese, a common tactic in California's unstable social order.[65]

The hearing's only other pro-immigration testimony came from an Irish-born shoemaker and law student named Patrick J. Healy. Healy offered what he acknowledged was a "radical and visionary" economic plan, blaming the depression on a "stagnation in trade" and calling for absolute free trade, land redistribution, and universal suffrage. Queried if he thought it "healthy . . . for paganism to become the order of the day in California," Healy responded, "Yes, sir; essentially so. Paganism is just as moral a religion as the religion which is now practiced in California, where the ministers of the gospel are stock-sharps and land-thieves, as the records of the city will prove." When asked if he approved of a "cross between Irish and Mongolians," Healy said he did: "It would produce a race of human beings that would be the terror of the world."[66] Healy's unusual testimony demonstrated that at least some Irish San Franciscans refused to be pitted against the Chinese. His embrace of an Irish-Chinese "cross" turned popular stereotypes on their heads, celebrating the notion of the two marginalized and oft-compared groups intermarrying to "terrorize" the world.

Healy's dissenting views on Chinese immigration represented part of a counter-discourse advanced by a small number of white Californians who supported political rights for the Chinese more out of secular humanitarianism than Christian universalism. A San Francisco educator named Augustus Layres advanced this line of argument most forcefully in a series of sometimes-anonymous pamphlets he published in the late 1870s. In 1876, he founded the *Chinese Record,* an intermittently published newspaper that presented pro-Chinese arguments in both Chinese and English. Though Layres, a Protestant, occasionally engaged in anti-Catholic scapegoating, he tended to invoke liberal themes of "truth, right, and justice" to defend the presence of the Chinese rather than the opportunity to convert them to Christianity.[67]

Poet Joaquin Miller was another prominent secular pro-Chinese spokesman who argued that Chinese migrants brought American "art, civilization, freedom or truth" back to China with them, thereby improving the entire world. Christianity was notably missing from his list. Miller was also a well-known proponent of political rights for California Indians; his 1873 memoir *Life Amongst the Modocs: Unwritten History* had championed the much-despised Modoc Indians during the Modoc War. In the book, Miller mocks missionaries as self-satisfied and arrogant, especially two "sour, selfish, and ungrateful wretches" he guided to the top of a mountain with a stunning view of northern California. "They did not even lift their eyes to the glory that lay to the right or to the left," he wrote. "Hastily, indeed, they muttered something, hurriedly drew some tracts from their pockets, brought far away into this wilderness by these wise, good men, for the benighted heathen, then turned as if afraid to stay, and retraced their steps." Miller, Layres, and Healy represented the tiny beginning of an anti-racist movement in California that was not affiliated with churches and that based its arguments on liberal ideas of individual freedom and equality rather than biblical evidence.[68]

"Can every man have this faith?": Chinese American Responses

Already cut off from many family members and friends, Chinese Protestants in California found themselves losing their white allies as racial animosities intensified in the late 1870s. This helped propel some Chinese churchgoers out of white-led churches. At about the same time that two hundred Potter Valley Pomos left Round Valley Indian Reservation for their own Indian-led community and church, a group of Chinese Christians left the Presbyterian mission in San Francisco. The conflict that led to their secession centered on the Youxue Zhengdaohui, known in English as the Chinese Young Men's Christian Association, an organization for Chinese Christian men founded in San Francisco in the early 1870s. Originally interdenominational, the organization had splintered by 1875 into a parallel set of auxiliaries associated with the Presbyterian, Congregationalist, Baptist, and Methodist missions. Chinese YMCAs acted as gateways to the mission, providing a meeting place where Chinese men curious about Christianity studied, worshipped, talked, and sometimes lived with those who had already joined the church. Members agreed to "forsake idolatry and all bad habits" and to "love one another, and to watch over, care for, and help one another."[69]

A. W. Loomis's Presbyterian mission maintained a Chinese YMCA branch in its basement, serving as an independent social club, boarding house, and worship space for Chinese men connected to the mission. In 1877, however, Loomis left for Europe to improve his wife's health, and the Presbyterian mission in San Francisco fell into the administration of John Glasgow Kerr, a physician and missionary who had recently returned from China. Although an outspoken advocate of political rights for the Chinese, Kerr brought to the job rigid ideas of how a mission should be run, forged by his experiences in Canton.[70] Finding "confusion and a want of system efficiency" in the mission, Kerr came to resent the "secret power" he believed the Chinese YMCA exerted over mission affairs.

In May 1878, judging the Chinese YMCA to be an "incubus on the work of the mission," Kerr notified the association that he was dissolving its charter because it had become "controlled in a great measure by those of its members who are not Christians." Faced with the choice of leaving or staying under Kerr's rules, twenty-nine of the mission's forty-two Chinese members left on July 10, renting a room a block away on Stockton Street and holding their own English lessons and religious services. The leader of the renegade mission was Fong Noy, whom Otis Gibson in his book *The Chinese in America* had singled out as the most "advanced... Chinese scholar of the Pacific Coast." Fong Noy told the *Chronicle* that the offshoot mission's purpose was to bring the Chinese "out of darkness into light."[71]

This schism in the mission divided California's Presbyterian leadership, with former missionaries to China generally siding with Kerr and local Presbyterians supporting the offshoot Chinese YMCA. Like H. B. Sheldon at Round Valley, Kerr and his supporters refused to recognize the unorthodox religious practices of the Chinese YMCA as true Christianity. J. C. Nevin, the missionary in charge of the Presbyterian Chinese mission in Los Angeles, followed Kerr's lead in dissolving the local Chinese YMCA, which he considered a "guild." "I found them here going through all sorts of forms in regard to Christianity but without any of the power, and I put my foot on the thing as I would on a viper," Nevin explained. "Men too ignorant to read their own language intelligently were explaining the Scriptures! Non professing men were appointed to *preach*!" Not only were the Chinese YMCA members practicing an unrecognizable lay version of Christianity, but their autonomy challenged white missionaries' ability to govern.[72]

Presbyterians who had been in California longer than newcomers like Kerr and Nevin tended to be broader in their definition of Christianity, viewing the efforts of the Chinese YMCA as genuine or, at the very least, a step in the right direction. Albert Williams, a pastor in San Francisco since 1849, sided with Fong Noy and the Chinese YMCA. He informed the Presbyterian Board of Foreign Missions that it should support the seceders rather than Kerr's mission because the Chinese YMCA had more Chinese Christians as well as the "most intelligent" and "exemplary too." Mrs. M. A. Knox, who worked among Chinese women in San Francisco, believed that Kerr and other returned missionaries failed to "realize that the partially enlightened Chinese on this Coast, have been educated to a spirit of freedom and independence of thought, in this land of liberty, the like of which they have never seen in China." Whether or not it was because American values were rubbing off on them, the majority of the Chinese mission chose autonomy over accommodation, independence over subjection to Kerr's rule. Like the Potter Valley Pomos, they preferred their own version of Christianity to that offered by an autocratic missionary.[73]

Those Chinese Christians who remained with Kerr said they did so on religious grounds. In a letter to the Presbyterian Board of Foreign Missions, they explained, "Those who worship idols, and their ancestors have seized authority in the Association and this has given rise to disorder. They do not love to study the Bible and care nothing for the church of our Lord, often making light of those who have joined the church, and esteeming the gospel as of much less importance than the things of the world." Whatever their true reasons for remaining in the mission, they explained their decision to the board in terms of religious sincerity, a way of framing the split that portrayed themselves as genuine Christians. Rejecting the Christianity of Fong Noy and other Chinese YMCA leaders as insincere, these Chinese Christians cast their lot with Kerr, one indication of the many fault lines that ran through Chinese Christian communities.[74]

After word reached Loomis in Edinburgh of the split in the mission, he decided to return to San Francisco, and the board sent Kerr back to China over his objections. Loomis approached the members of the offshoot Chinese YMCA and found them "all willing and ready to return to the Mission as formerly, but they did not urge it, and they signified that if it was not agreeable to us, or to the Board that they should return they could continue as they were." Only after Loomis promised that the Chinese YMCA could occupy the basement "*as before*," operating their own set of services and activities, did the members agree to return to the mission, which they did on December 23. Having spent more than $250 of their own money to rent and outfit their independent mission, the members of the Chinese YMCA were no doubt tempted by the free rent offered by Loomis. When treated with respect and generally left to their own devices by someone like Loomis, they were content to remain in white-led church bodies, with their willingness to leave a constant reminder of the power they wielded. No doubt aware of the claims made by Kalloch and other anti-Chinese voices about the alleged failures of Chinese missions, Chinese Christians knew that missionaries could scarcely afford to lose their converts.[75]

Chinese Christians wielded another sort of power as well: the rhetorical power of Christianity, which they continued to use to combat the rising tide of anti-Chinese sentiment in the United States. At the 1877 anniversary celebration of the Methodist mission in San Francisco, Lee Tong Hay gave an indignant speech describing the unfair laws and constant street violence that Chinese Californians suffered under. "There are so many vicious white ruffians, who stone and beat Chinamen without cause," he said. "In no country is there a record of such cruel and bloody outrages as from part of the history of California." Methodist Chan Pak Kwai and Congregationalist Jee Gam both took trips east during the late 1870s in support of Chinese immigration and suffrage. Jee Gam told the Chicago *Times* that if Chinese immigrants "were allowed to vote there would be much less of the clannishness now exhibited among them, and they would adopt civilized ways much more freely than they do at present."[76]

During Chan Pak Kwai's tour of Methodist churches in the Midwest, he countered claims that Chinese immigrants refused to assimilate or convert to Christianity, blaming their perceived "clannishness" on American racism. "In San Francisco the mission-work has been wonderful, when it is considered that it is with a people who are isolated from all social, political, or civil position," he declared. As the struggle over Chinese exclusion became a national one, Chan Pak Kwai used Methodist networks to insert his voice into the debate. Anti-Chinese forces perceived him as enough of a threat in the battle to shape eastern public opinion that California's press attempted to discredit the tour, claiming that Chan Pak Kwai merely recited speeches he barely understood that had been written by a white journalist, and that the whole "humbug" was nothing more than an attempt to reap a profit from the "maudlin sentimentalists of the pro-Chinese type."[77]

In their speeches and writings, some Chinese church members offered a radically inclusive vision of Christianity and citizenship. "Can every man have this faith, be he white, black, red or yellow?" Jee Gam asked. "Yes. The beggar can have it as well as the king. The poor can have it as well as the rich; and the negro, the Indian and the Chinaman." Similarly, Congregationalist lay preacher Lem Chung embraced a Christianity that united racial groups. "Some may say: he may be a Christian, but he is not my countryman, not near to me," he wrote. "I am a white man, he is black, or he is a yellow man, he does not belong to my family or friends. I will not love him. It can be no sin to hate him. Not so, my friends." Such pleas for broad, cross-racial acceptance represented a call for Christian universalism that was issued less and less in the late 1870s. Speaking to white Protestants who were increasingly wooed by appeals to white Christian solidarity rather than interracial Protestantism,

Figure 9. Jee Gam, a longtime lay preacher and Chinese immigrants' rights activist, became an ordained Congregationalist minister in 1895. From N. R. Johnston, *Looking Back from the Sunset Land* (Oakland, Calif., 1898).

Jee Gam and Lem Chung emphasized Christianity's potential to transcend racial differences.[78]

Other Chinese Christians did not hesitate to employ divisive rhetoric to better their own position. At an anniversary celebration for the Oakland Methodist mission, Chan Pak Kwai warned that "probably far greater dangers to American society and civilization lie in the direction of the godless, Sabbath-breaking European immigrants...than in the presence of a few peaceable and industrious Chinese." Suffrage for the Chinese was therefore necessary to thwart the rising Catholic menace. In an interview with a San Francisco newspaper, he marveled at how the United States extended citizenship to "ignorant, indigent, and indolent" European immigrants but not to the "industrious, intelligent, and progressive" Chinese. Echoing arguments made by Gibson and other Protestants, Chan Pak Kwai offered the Chinese as an immigrant group more in line with American values than Catholic Europeans. With white Protestant support for the Chinese dwindling, Chan Pak Kwai attempted to resuscitate Protestant–Catholic divisions in the service of Chinese political rights.[79]

Not all Chinese churchgoers agreed that immigration restriction would be undesirable. During the state senate's hearing on the Chinese question in 1876, Lem Schaum, a geologist and longtime member of a Congregationalist church in Sacramento, urged legislators to halt immigration from China because it drove down wages, heightened racial animosities, and hindered evangelism. "It must be stopped in some way, and then we can look after those [Chinese] Christians educated in this country," he said. "Looking at this thing from a Christian viewpoint, I think that christianity is not advanced by this immigration, and I would give anything in the world to have it stopped." Probably strategically pandering to the biases of the anti-Chinese legislators interviewing him, Lem Schaum invoked the language of Christianity to effect political change on behalf of those Chinese migrants already in the United States. Similarly, Moy Jin Kee, a Methodist lay preacher in New York City, complained in 1879 that most immigrants coming from China were "not Chinese in the proper sense of the term," but Tartars (Manchus who had invaded China beginning in the seventeenth century) and "half-breeds arising from intermarriage between the low-class Chinese and the Tartars." Employing a racial logic that resonated in 1870s America, Moy Jin Kee advocated restricting the immigration of racially impure and lower-class migrants. His comments to the New York *Times* were carried by the *Daily Alta California* as one more piece of evidence in support of exclusion.[80]

By the end of the 1870s, those Californians who remained support-
ive of Chinese immigration and evangelism mourned the changes they observed among Protestant leaders in California. In his 1879 autobiography,
Albert Williams lamented the "new attitude on the Chinese question"
that had taken root, one that was "only a palpable contrast and contradiction to former professions and commitments—a dissent, amounting
to a denial, of convictions once held unimpaired. One is led to inquire,
Have principles once regarded sound and established become obsolete
and void?" As for himself, Williams could see "no reason for the abandonment of the ground heretofore confided in as holding eternal principles
of right." Older certainties about both the Indian and Chinese questions
had given way to new confusion and debate. Frustration with the slow
gains of mission work, coupled with rising racial animosities that accompanied economic depression, had called into question the Christian
potential of Indians and the Chinese. In the 1880s, this confusion would
give way to a new consensus. The dream of a racially diverse Protestant
America held by reformers in the decade following the Civil War would
be relinquished in favor of a less "sentimental" view that afforded little or
no room to African Americans, Indians, or the Chinese. A new order
was on the rise.[81]

CHAPTER SIX

California and the Consolidation of
White Christian Nationalism

In February 1879, the U.S. Congress passed a bill restricting the number of Chinese immigrants on any vessel bound for the United States to fifteen. During debate over the bill, congressmen who favored immigration restriction frequently situated the Chinese question within the broader history of American race relations. "Mr. Speaker, twice in our history we have been called upon to determine questions arising from the difference of races," explained Albert S. Willis, Democratic representative from Kentucky. "Our first experience was with the red race .... He is to-day the same sullen, unconquered alien savage that he was in the earliest colonial history of our country.... Our next experience was with the black race. Need I recall the bitter animosities, the section strife, the political and religious dissensions which marked its progress?" Willis wondered, "If our experience has been a failure, or at best a doubtful success, with the African and the Indian, what can we expect from the Mongolian." The presence of Indians and African Americans in the United States, Willis and other congressmen argued, had bred only conflict and vexation, and the "third experiment with an alien race"—the Chinese— was already bringing more of the same. Ignoring the many differences of religion, class, gender, ethnicity, politics, and region that divided white Americans, these congressmen portrayed "alien" African Americans, Indians, and Chinese immigrants as the source of the nation's problems.[1]

Chinese immigrants' pagan beliefs were an integral part of their supposed racial inferiority. Republican and Democratic congressmen who supported the bill couched their arguments in terms of spiritual contamination nearly as often as they did in terms of economic ruin and political threat. According to congressmen, the Chinese were "guilty of hideous immoralities." In their wake, "Christian churches are turned into heathen temples and homes for idols." Missionaries' efforts amounted to a "fearful failure," while the "demoralization of the white is much more

UNCLE SAM'S TROUBLESOME BED FELLOWS

Figure 10. "Uncle Sam's Troublesome Bed Fellows," published in the *Wasp* on February 8, 1879, illustrates the precarious positions of religious and racial minorities in post-Reconstruction America. Uncle Sam has kicked the Chinese immigrant and the Mormon from his bed, while the Native American and African American figures look close to earning expulsion. The once-troublesome Irish Catholic, on the other hand, can sleep easy. Courtesy of the Huntington Library, San Marino.

rapid by reason of the contact than the salvation of the Chinese race." Supporters of the bill, who came from the Republican, Democratic, and Greenbacker parties and from the North, South, and West, mixed biblical and ethnological evidence to present the Chinese as a threat to "our own Christian race."[2]

Coming less than two years after the removal of federal troops from the South, the fifteen-passenger bill represented part of the Republican and Democratic parties' efforts to heal the still-raw wounds of the Civil War by emphasizing a common white Christian heritage that linked the North, South, and West. Between 1877 and 1887, the federal government drastically altered its policies pertaining to racialized groups in the United States, ending southern Reconstruction (1877), terminating the peace policy (by 1882), excluding Chinese immigrants (1882), and breaking up reservation lands through allotment in severalty (1887). During these same years, Utah's Mormons faced increasing governmental pressure to abandon polygamy and come into greater alignment with dominant Christianity. In an era of economic recession, unprecedented labor strife, and lingering sectional animosities, white Christian nationalism allowed northerners, southerners, and westerners to find common ground.[3]

In California, politicians and newspapers representing both parties had long called for the end of the reservation system and a stop to Chinese immigration. These positions had once pitted them against Protestant church leaders, who had most strongly supported the notion that Indians and the Chinese could become—and indeed were becoming—patriotic Christian citizens. During the late 1870s, Protestant ministers had become divided on racial questions, with more and more questioning the notion that Indians and the Chinese had any proper place in American churches or society. In the early 1880s, new accord on the Chinese and Indian questions emerged, with California's church leaders almost universally supporting exclusion and allotment, albeit sometimes for different reasons than did politicians. Only after church leaders came to support exclusion and allotment did those policies become enacted into federal law. With Christianity the language of American politics, ministers wielded unique power to sway public opinion, even as they responded to the shifting opinions of their laities. Their embrace of immigration restriction and allotment played a critical role in the enacting of those policies, as they joined politicians in support of a pair of solutions that promised to finally resolve the Chinese and Indian questions, not through uplift and inclusion but through marginalization and erasure.

"Lay aside the queue and Chinese dress": Paving the Path to Exclusion

The fifteen-passenger bill of 1879, although vetoed by Republican president Hayes, represented a step in the Republican Party's retreat from racial justice issues in the late 1870s. At their national convention in June 1876, the Republicans had adopted a resolution calling on Congress to investigate the effects of Chinese immigration on the "moral and material interests of the country." At that convention, the minority of Republicans who opposed the resolution often did so on religious grounds. "I denounce it as contrary to that great law of Christian love which proclaims that there is no difference between men, no matter of what race they be," proclaimed Edward L. Pierce from Massachusetts. Similarly, during debate over the fifteen-passenger bill three years later, Ohio's Stanley Matthews objected that the bill violated "the Christian rule, the law of divine benevolence and of human brotherhood." However, as during Charles Sumner's failed effort to remove the word "white" from the nation's naturalization statute in 1870, such arguments failed to convince the majority of Republicans, who joined with Democrats in offering a competing interpretation of biblical evidence. Attacking the Chinese allowed Republicans to further shield themselves from the charges of racial radicalism they had faced since before the Civil War while appeasing their western colleagues.[4]

The passage of the fifteen-passenger bill made Chinese immigration again a topic of national debate, with the large majority of eastern Protestant churches and newspapers—along with many in the South and Midwest—opposing the bill.[5] Those ministers in California who remained committed to free immigration from China sent a petition to President Hayes, urging him to veto the bill. California's anti-Chinese religious leaders—Protestants, Catholics, and Jews—sent their own petitions to Hayes; one from Isaac S. Kalloch's Metropolitan Temple insisted that the bill was "vital to our civil peace, our business prosperity and our Christian civilization." The San Francisco *Chronicle* interviewed six clergymen about the bill, and all six hoped it would become law.[6]

Such petitions and statements allowed anti-Chinese congressmen to argue that "Christian testimony from the Pacific Coast" favored immigration restriction. "I say it is not simply the ignorant who hold these opinions," declared California's Republican senator, Aaron A. Sargent. He cited the state Congregationalists' 1877 resolution urging immigration restriction, noting, "They are the ministers of a large, respectable, and conservative denomination.... From the pulpit and the bench and the work-shop alike, and all alike, comes the same testimony and the same strong objection." J. K. Luttrell, Democratic representative from Mendocino County and old foe of the peace policy, similarly cited the Congregationalists' resolution during one of his party's annual attempts to introduce a bill prohibiting Chinese immigration. He added that "ministers of every denomination" opposed the coming of the Chinese, listing several Methodists, Episcopalians, and Catholics.[7]

Hayes's veto of the fifteen-passenger bill, although explicitly done for economic rather than humanitarian reasons, predictably provoked another round of anti-Chinese mass meetings in California. Anti-immigration congressmen lacked sufficient votes to override the veto and so had to postpone the effort, but the Chinese question simmered throughout the 1880 election season. National Republicans joined the Democrats and Greenbackers in declaring their opposition to Chinese immigration in their 1880 platforms, with each party questioning the others' commitment to the issue. On the eve of the election, a letter surfaced supposedly written by Republican presidential candidate James Garfield expressing his support for the existing Burlingame Treaty with China. The controversy over the letter encouraged all sides to stiffen their anti-Chinese stances.[8]

In California, support for Chinese immigration continued to dwindle. In the same 1879 election in which Baptist minister Isaac S. Kalloch became mayor of San Francisco, Californians voted on a referendum asking whether they were for or against immigration from China. Fewer than 900 voters—about .6 percent—indicated they were for it. Pro-immigration activists pointed out that the ballots were all marked "against" in tiny type, putting the burden on those who supported immigration to write in "pro" and causing many to vote against immigration without being aware they had done so. Nevertheless, it was harder and harder for ministers in California to insist that the "christian element" supported the Chinese while "their oppressors and persecutors are anti-christians," as Congregationalist A. L. Stone had argued in 1869. In its 1879 annual report, the best the Methodist committee on Chinese missions could offer was that "good men honestly differ" on the subject.[9]

After 1880, even that "differing" became scarce. The closest thing to a controversy involved San Francisco's most famous anti-Chinese clergyman, Mayor Kalloch. After the San Francisco Board of Supervisors tried to oust him from office for inciting mobs and engaging in other "unscrupulous and unprincipled" behavior, delegates at the California Baptist Convention considered a resolution in May 1880 distancing themselves from Kalloch and his son, currently in prison for the murder of *Chronicle* publisher Charles de Young. Kalloch and his supporters managed to vote down the resolution, but the anti-Kalloch animus was so strong that, a year later, fourteen of the state's Baptist churches seceded from the California Baptist Convention and organized their own association. Unsurprisingly, San Francisco's Chinese Baptist Church, organized in 1880 by the Southern Baptist Home Mission Board, joined the new association, and it sent three Chinese church members as delegates to the first convention. In Metropolitan Temple the following Sunday, Kalloch dubbed the seceders the "Chinese Convention . . . because all their hatred of me and war upon me are solely because of my hostility to the Chinese invasion of this coast." Spokesmen for the offshoot convention bristled at the label and denied that it was Kalloch's views on Chinese immigration that had prompted their secession, even while proudly asserting that they were "the only Baptist pastors to-day committed to Chinese evangelization." As did Kalloch's other enemies, the new Baptist conference made it clear that it objected to his outrageous personality, his sensationalistic sermons, and his aggressive power-grabbing, not his opposition to Chinese immigration.[10]

The rising anti-Chinese sentiment continued to subsume tensions between Catholics and Protestants in San Francisco. The school question ceased to spark much controversy, as both sides, for the moment, found common ground in opposition to the Chinese.[11] California's Catholic leadership had mostly suspended the Church's mission work in Chinatown by the late 1870s, and the decline of the Workingmen's Party after 1879 freed them to condemn Chinese immigration without danger of being associated with Kearney's radicalism. In 1880, a San Francisco priest wrote to an eastern Catholic leader to explain that "99 out of every hundred" San Franciscans opposed Chinese immigration. "There is no distinction of religion, race or politics in this matter," he wrote. "The unanimous voice of the whole state is against the Chinese." The *Monitor* continued to condemn the Chinese in the name of "white labor" and "Christian society." Catholics added their voices to the anti-Chinese din, counting themselves among the white Christians imperiled by pagan outsiders.[12]

Since the construction of St. Mary's Cathedral in San Francisco in 1854, an exterior wall had borne the words, "Son, observe the time and fly from evil," from the Book of Ecclesiasticus. As Chinatown grew up around the cathedral, these words seemed to enjoin those seeking opium, sex, or other vices available in the neighborhood. Soon after Kalloch's San Francisco Board of Health declared Chinatown a health nuisance in 1880, with the cathedral abutting the condemned quarter, Archbishop Joseph Alemany took the building's advice to heart. He hatched a plan to relocate the cathedral "from its present objectionable location to some more respectable and more suitable part of the city," eventually constructing a new edifice on Van Ness Avenue about a mile farther west. The *Daily Alta California* explained that a new cathedral had become necessary because "unsightly and obtrusive immorality... flaunts itself right at the very doors" of St. Mary's, such that "respectable people can scarcely overcome their repugnance at visiting the place." The move demonstrated Catholic leaders' eagerness to associate their church with white Christian respectability, further physically segregating the Chinese while marking them as hopelessly depraved. By 1882, two Protestant congregations had similarly fled Chinatown. First Presbyterian Church had been sold to the Presbyterian Board of Foreign Missions for the purpose of Chinese evangelism, and First Baptist Church was sold to Chinese businessmen and converted into a "tenement house." White congregations' flight out of Chinatown encouraged the complaint that "Joss houses have taken the place of our churches," used as further evidence for the necessity of exclusion.[13]

Figure 11. In the 1880s, Archbishop Joseph Sadoc Alemany sought a more "respectable" location for San Francisco's cathedral outside of Chinatown. A new Cathedral of Saint Mary of the Assumption opened in 1891 one-and-a-half miles west of the original. Portrait by Henry Steinegger. Courtesy of the Bancroft Library, University of California, Berkeley.

As the U.S. Congress inched closer and closer to Chinese exclusion, ratifying a new treaty with China in 1881 that allowed the United States to regulate immigration, virtually no one in California continued to publicly defend the doctrine of unrestricted immigration. Even Otis Gibson, so long vilified as the state's most outspoken champion of the Chinese, had gradually shifted his stance to the point that he too supported restriction. In 1873, in his response to the Jesuit priest James Buchard, Gibson had insisted that it was a "God-taught principle" that "opens wide the doors of our great country on the East and on the West . . . *equally* to all mankind, without *distinction of race, color, or previous condition of servitude.*" The following year, however, Gibson provided crucial support for the Page Act restricting the immigration of Chinese coolies and prostitutes on moral grounds. By the time he published *The Chinese in America* in 1877, which on the whole was a bold defense of the Chinese, Gibson advocated limiting the number of immigrants from all countries to two hundred per vessel. Here, and in his testimony in the 1876 and 1879 federal hearings in San Francisco, Gibson sought a compromise position that acknowledged the supposed dangers of massive Chinese immigration while insisting that European Catholics be similarly regulated.[14]

In April 1880, Gibson went a step further, sending a letter to San Francisco's U.S. representative Horace Davis outlining a plan to restrict immigration from China. Citing their "dissimilarity in dress and general social customs, and their slowness to assimilate to the forms and customs of our civilization," Gibson for the first time accepted the idea that immigrants from China posed a more serious risk than those from other countries. Rather than revising the Burlingame Treaty, Gibson advocated asking the Chinese government to issue a proclamation requiring immigrants to the United States to "lay aside the queue and Chinese dress." Such a proclamation would not only aid the assimilation of the Chinese in America but would "lessen the rate of immigration more than fifty percent." A year later, Gibson published a modified version of his plan in the New York *Christian Advocate*. He now called on the U.S. government, rather than China, to criminalize the wearing of the queue and native dress. "If it is objected, that it is beneath the dignity of this great nation to legislate about the cut of a man's coat or the length of his hair," he wrote, "the answer is, That the purpose and intent of the proposed legislation is to limit Chinese immigration, and to secure, as far as possible, a homogenous people in all our land."[15]

Gibson's plan flew in the face of his prior activism and publicly stated beliefs. In 1873, he had appeared before the San Francisco Board of Supervisors on behalf of the city's Chinese residents to protest a proposed ordinance requiring the county jailers to cut off all Chinese prisoners' queues, along with other discriminatory measures. Eight years later, Gibson was calling for federal legislation requiring that all Chinese men in America be forced to cut their hair and abandon their native dress. He now supported the popular notion that the Chinese were wholly different from other immigrant groups and deserved special attention as unassimilable aliens. At the same time, however, Gibson's plan resisted the idea that either racial inferiority or intractable religious beliefs made the Chinese different. Only their dress and hair, not their race or supposed paganism, made the Chinese a special threat. In this regard, his plan resembled those advanced by reformers who sought to remake Indians' physical appearance as an outer sign of inner civilization. Although discriminatory, Gibson's plan did envision a path to assimilation for the Chinese without violating the country's commitment to free immigration from China.[16]

The *California Christian Advocate* praised Gibson's plan, and Gibson published a revised version a year later in the Boston *Zion's Herald*, now insisting such a law "would check 75 per cent of the immigration" from China. Perhaps best seen as a last-ditch effort to avert total exclusion, Gibson's plan nonetheless reinforced the idea that every non-Chinese resident of California supported immigration restriction of one kind or another. Asked "directly" at the San Francisco Methodist Preachers' Meeting in March 1882 if he was in favor of the restriction of Chinese immigration, Gibson answered, "I am." With the line between restriction and exclusion increasingly meaningless, California's most stalwart defender of the Chinese, with those two words, joined virtually every other public figure in the state in opposition to Chinese immigration.[17]

For Gibson and many Protestant ministers, embracing immigration restriction did not mean abandoning hopes for evangelizing the Chinese or protecting their basic human rights. The *Pacific* opined, "since they are here (no matter by what supposed wisdom or folly) it is our privilege and our duty to treat them with kindness, with honor, with justice." In fact, some church leaders argued that exclusion would actually aid evangelism because anti-Chinese hostility would diminish, and those Chinese men and women in California would be more likely to convert to Christianity once cut off from pagan influences from China. The *California Christian Advocate* insisted that exclusion "cannot injure the Chinese who are already here. We have no doubt but it will be to their advantage." The paper also stated that it disagreed with "those who think the Chinaman never can become Americanized. It will take a long time, but it can and will be done. Because we need time to do this work, we believe in limiting immigration." Taking a different approach, a writer for the *Pacific* argued that exclusion would help mission work in China because "a migrating generation deteriorates. Their transition hurts them.... Accordingly, Chinamen are not so impressible here as in China." Such arguments cast exclusion as beneficial not just for white Americans but for the Chinese as well. These ministers had come to see exclusion as a way to aid their longstanding efforts to convert the Chinese both in the United States and in China.[18]

With a few notable exceptions, Protestant leaders in California made it clear that their support for exclusion was not support for violence or harassment, and most continued to frown on politicians' constant anti-Chinese agitation. Gibson excoriated the "mad roar of race prejudice and political demagogism" that emanated from yet another anti-Chinese rally, held in San Francisco in March 1882. He accused the clergymen who spoke at the rally, most prominently Congregationalist Charles D. Barrows, of pandering to the basest instincts of the mob. "If the popular clamor had been on the other side of the Chinese question, it is quite possible that these ... reverend gentlemen would have been willing to immolate themselves upon that altar also," wrote Gibson.[19]

Most ministers did not speak at such rallies or use their pulpits to praise the Workingmen's Party of California, as Kalloch did. However, by supporting immigration restriction, church leaders aided the anti-Chinese movement, which since the 1860s had made exclusion its primary goal. By speaking of the unique perils of Chinese immigration, they helped further demonize Chinese men and women in California. When ministers and Protestant newspapers called the Chinese "crude and intractable material," "inhuman," or "punishment" sent by God, they used their cultural and religious authority in support of a larger discourse stamping the Chinese as dangerous, diseased, and inferior. In 1882, differences of opinion between clergymen who favored restriction and those who favored full exclusion, or between those who supported Chinese evangelism and those who scorned it, mattered less than their agreement that Chinese immigration was a threat to Christian America that must be stopped.[20]

As ministers arrived at a new consensus on the question of Chinese immigration in the early 1880s, Chinese church members in California chose to mute their pro-immigration activism, instead expressing their political views in subtler ways. In an article for the New York *Christian*

Union in 1880, Congregationalist lay preacher Jee Gam refrained from directly declaring his opposition to exclusion. He instead focused on refuting the common idea that Chinese immigrants had no desire to permanently settle in the United States, and he blamed the scarcity of Chinese women on anti-Chinese sentiment. Chinese men "say they like California, but it is almost in the hands of the hoodlums," he wrote, "and so, they say, we don't bring our wives." Jee Gam explained that he retained Chinese dress and a queue to better evangelize among his countrymen, noting, "I have more influence over my people than if I were dressed like an American." This was no doubt a response to those such as Gibson, who viewed native dress and hair as markers of foreignness that needed to be eradicated.[21]

One week after Gibson's restriction plan appeared in the New York *Christian Advocate,* the San Francisco Methodist Chinese Mission Institute held a celebration to honor him for being chosen as a delegate to the first Ecumenical Methodist Conference in London. Church member Chan Hon Fan offered a tribute to Gibson that pointedly thanked him for championing the Chinese against hoodlums and agitators. "Once he was burned in effigy, and many times his precious life has been threatened by the unprincipled rabble of this city, because he preached the gospel to the Chinamen," he said. "We thank God for Dr. Gibson's virtue and integrity. He has always stood firm for the right, without regard to nationality or race, and has cheerfully lent a hand to the needy and helpless." Whether or not Chan Hon Fan knew of Gibson's changing opinion of immigration restriction, his remarks expressed both gratitude and an expectation that Gibson would not swerve from standing up "for the right" now in their hour of greatest need.[22]

Gone, though, for the moment, were the forceful expressions of support for Chinese immigration that had been present in Chinese church members' speeches and writings in the 1870s. Having lost their strongest supporters, Chinese Christians perhaps recognized that such activism would only further alienate their dwindling ranks of white allies. With exclusion looking more and more certain, Chinese Christians picked their battles with care.

The reversals made by Gibson and other ministers that made California's new consensus possible also did not go unnoticed in the East. A month after Gibson's plan to criminalize Chinese queues and native dress appeared in the New York *Christian Advocate,* S. L. Baldwin, a former missionary to China, replied with an article expressing "great surprise" at Gibson's recommendation. "At first I could only look upon it as a joke—

an attempt on his part to get the anti-Chinese people to commit themselves to an egregious absurdity," Baldwin wrote. "But the article has all the appearance of sincerity, and I am obliged to think that the author . . . has been so far affected by the moral (or immoral) atmosphere of California, as to contemplate seriously this absurd interference with a man's right to dress as he pleases." In Baldwin's view, Gibson had been infected by the same immoral prejudice that drove Denis Kearney, whose crude ways and violent rhetoric had made him a laughingstock throughout the East after an 1878 lecture tour.[23]

The rift between eastern and western clergy that had developed in the late 1870s deepened in the early 1880s, leading to clashes at national conferences. At the 1882 annual meeting of the American Baptist Home Mission Society, the committee on Chinese missions declared that it judged exclusion as "opposed to the spirit of the Christian religion . . . brought about by an unchristian race prejudice and the rivalry of political parties ambitious for power." Feeling that he "could not sit still and let the east wind blow like that without a protest," Granville Abbott, pastor of Oakland First Baptist Church and a leader of the anti-Kalloch faction of California Baptists, rose to protest the report. Abbott said that in fact the Chinese comprised a "helot class, and in a moral condition which threatens all in this country most to be valued in family and social life." He insisted that he represented not the "sand-lot view" but "the best thought of the best men on the Pacific Coast." Extended debate ensued, with ministers from California and Oregon almost alone in supporting exclusion.[24]

When Congress again took up the question of Chinese immigration in March 1882, Protestant church leaders and newspapers in the East renewed their objections to restriction. Blaming the bill on the "timid people of California and the other Pacific states," the New York *Independent* proclaimed that the enactment of exclusion "would furnish a suitable occasion for proclaiming a day of fasting and prayer, that God would save the people from their own delusions." The New York *Christian Advocate* agreed: "This bill is saturated with race prejudice and caste exclusiveness." In an impassioned sermon, Henry Ward Beecher berated "our Fool-Congress" for shutting "the door of Christianity, of liberty and of hope" to the Chinese. "I tell you that this is an outrage, and God writes down 'asses' against the men who voted for it," he thundered.[25]

For these eastern Protestant leaders, some of whom were former abolitionists, the Chinese question unavoidably paralleled the Negro question. In their view, both groups were unjustly despised out of ignorance and racial bigotry, and they compared the Chinese exclusion bill to the Fugitive Slave Act. "Four millions of blacks were made free on the basis of the truth that 'all men are free and have inalienable rights to life, liberty and pursuit of happiness,'" recalled the Philadelphia *Presbyterian*. "But we shall have to fight it over again if the Chinaman is to be excluded." A form of waving the bloody flag, such arguments attempted to reinvigorate antislavery sentiment on behalf of another oppressed racial group. In particular, these ministers lamented the fact that the Republican Party supported exclusion because it lent further credence to the notion that the party's support for African American political rights—now largely a thing of the past—had been based on crass politics, not humanitarianism or religious commitment. Western Republicans' embrace of the anti-Chinese movement supported white southerners' argument that conflict was inevitable when racial groups mixed, a justification for the oppression and disenfranchisement of southern African Americans occurring in the early 1880s.[26]

A decade earlier, California's clergy had seen similar parallels between African Americans and the Chinese, but by the 1880s, the comparison had flipped in meaning. Now, they joined the larger anti-Chinese movement in portraying Chinese "coolies" as the equivalent of African slaves. The *California Christian Advocate* objected to easterners' use of the old spirit of abolitionism to condemn exclusion, when in fact "hatred of slavery is one cause of opposition to the importation of coolies." Anti-Chinese agitators had made similar comparisons between Chinese coolies and African slaves since the 1860s, language that appealed to both Democrats (by suggesting that both groups were inferior) and Republicans (by using moralistic anti-slavery rhetoric and the Thirteenth Amendment). By 1882, such arguments had reached fever pitch. "It is slavery in another form," insisted the *Daily Alta California*. "Will you men of the East and West and Northwest, who paved your way to victory over the slave-power upon a road macadamized with the skulls of freedmen, now shirk your duty or belie your professions, or undo your noble work?"[27]

"Aliens in blood, aliens in faith": The 1882 Federal Exclusion Debates

The 1882 congressional debates over Chinese immigration resembled the 1879 ones, in that both the anti-immigration majority and the pro-immigration minority consistently cast their arguments in terms of Christianity. Republican, Democratic, and Greenbacker proponents of exclusion mixed racial and religious discourses to demonize the Chinese. They warned that unchecked immigration would turn Americans into "a mongrel race, half Chinese and half Caucasian, as to produce a civilization half pagan, half Christian, semi-oriental, altogether mixed and very bad." They called the Chinese "aliens to our civilization, aliens in blood, aliens in faith, and clogs to the free movement of the wheels of Christian civilization and enlightened progress." Congressmen insisted the Chinese had "low, groveling ideas of virtue and religion" commensurate with their emaciated, leprous bodies. Again and again, congressmen claimed that the Chinese were hopelessly pagan and learned only English, not Christianity, from mission schools. "Sir, as a Christian citizen, I protest against the desecration of this Christian land by the erection of any building dedicated to the profane orgies of heathenism," declared New York's J. Hyatt Smith, "or the toleration of a people with no faith or interest in common with our Republic, and ignorant of even the name of the living God."[28]

Anti-Chinese congressmen's doomsday talk was so strong that Senator Wilkinson Call from Florida felt compelled to declare that he opposed the entry of Chinese immigrants because they cheapened labor and not because they endangered American Christianity, which he deemed too hearty to be under any threat from paganism. Rejecting the idea that "Christianity totters and quakes with dread at the advance of the Mongolian," Call said he put his faith in "the old Bible and the principles of our Constitution." Although Call too supported exclusion, his comments pointed to contradictions in the dominant anti-Chinese position. If Christianity was inherently superior to paganism, how could paganism be a true menace? If "the Caucasian race is superior in metal force, intellectual vigor, and morals to any other branch of the human family," as Henry Moore Teller, Republican senator from Colorado, insisted, what did it have to fear from the Chinese? Such paradoxes revealed a religious and racial anxiety central to the anti-immigration movement. By simultaneously praising the superiority of white Christian America and bemoaning its fragility, congressmen appealed to American chauvinisms while emphasizing a need for continual vigilance in defense of religious, racial, and national purity.[29]

In 1882, as in earlier debates over the Reconstruction amendments, congressmen compared the Negro, Chinese, and Indian questions at length. During the late 1860s, Republicans had won political rights for African American men while excluding Indians and the Chinese partly on the basis of their supposedly pagan beliefs. In the post-1877 political climate, however, many Republicans joined with Democrats in lamenting the troublesome presence of all three "alien" races. Oregon's Demo-

cratic senator, La Fayette Grover, insisted that the "all men" of the Declaration of Independence could not have truly meant *all* men, given that
the nation's founders had displayed no interest in the "elevation of the
colored races of mankind," Indians or Africans. "On what ground, then,
can it be claimed that the hereditary policy of this Government requires
us to open our ports to the admission of all races of mankind without
discrimination?" he asked. Republican John P. Jones said he wished that
"some one" in the seventeenth century had outlawed the importation of
Africans to North America because, like the Chinese, "it was the immigration of an incongruous race, of a race that could not assimilate or
amalgamate with us." Talk of African Americans' embrace of Christianity, so prominent in the Reconstruction-era debates, was quieter, as the
majority of Republicans continued to distance themselves from any taint
of racial or religious radicalism.[30]

George Frisbie Hoar from Massachusetts led the counterattack of
those congressmen who denounced exclusion as a new form of "the old
race prejudice." Hoar announced, "I believe that the immortal truths of
the Declaration of Independence came from the same source with the
Golden Rule and the Sermon on the Mount. We can trust Him who
promulgated these laws to keep the country safe that obeys them." In
response to the news that California's clergy now unanimously favored
immigration restriction, Ezra Taylor, a Republican from Ohio, declared,
"What a comment on the religion of the nineteenth century! There was
a time when the cross conquered . . . but to-day it cowers and shrinks
and begs to be helped in the shadow of a Chinese joss-house in California, surrounded by lepers such as our Saviour cured. If that be so I
recommend a reorganization of the Christian churches of California."
These congressmen, decidedly in the minority, put forward their own vision of a muscular Christianity that drew its strength from universalism, inclusion, and uplift. They pointed to Christianity's transformation
of African slaves—"far more pagan than the Chinese"—into today's
pious freedmen as evidence of the religion's power to "elevate the bar-
barian to our standard."[31]

Anti-immigration congressmen dismissed such talk as "sentimentalism" and offered their own biblical counter-evidence. Greenbacker Charles
Brumm read a string of Bible verses—including Matthew 5:29, "if thy right
eye offend thee, pluck it out and cast it from thee"—to suggest that Jesus
Christ would have voted for Chinese exclusion. Brumm informed his pro-
immigration colleagues, "gentlemen, you are wrong, and for you I can only
say, 'Lord, forgive them, for they know not what they do.'"[32]

After weeks of debate, first the Senate and then the House voted overwhelmingly to send the innocuously titled "act to execute certain treaty stipulations relating to Chinese" to President Chester A. Arthur. Democrats and Greenbackers were nearly unanimous in their support; Republicans split roughly in half, with westerners strongly in favor and New Englanders the most opposed. After Arthur vetoed the bill because he judged its length of twenty years too long to be in accord with the 1881 treaty with China, Congress rushed through a revised version halting immigration for only ten. This bill received even more yes votes, and President Arthur signed it into law on May 6, 1882. The United States had banned the immigration of all "Chinese laborers . . . both skilled and unskilled" for ten years.[33]

The California press closely followed the daily twists and turns of this process. Recycling tactics they had used against California's pro-Chinese clergymen in years gone by, mainstream newspapers lambasted pro-immigration congressmen for their "sentimental" Christian rhetoric, which they assumed covered up selfish economic motives. The *Chronicle* called New England Republicans "hypocrites in morals, aristocrats in disguise" who secretly worked for "the corporations and land monopolists." The press directed special animus toward George Frisbie Hoar in a manner reminiscent of their earlier treatment of Gibson. The *Daily Alta California* labeled Hoar "a synonym of shame and a moral traitor. . . . He has lived too long for his fame and should go forth like Judas and hang himself." With California's politicians and now clergy more or less united on the question of Chinese immigration, newspapers targeted New England Republicans as the greatest remaining enemies of white Christian solidarity.[34]

California's religious press expressed few worries that New England would come around to the West's perspective. "It took ten years to make this coast so nearly unanimous in sentiment as it now is, and it may take more years to render the entire national sentiment as strong," noted a writer for the Congregational *Pacific*. He predicted that the country, once united, would not stop with the Chinese; it will soon "restrict the too rapid coming of undesirable populations from whatever quarter," including "the vicious classes, the off-scourings of cities, the out-pourings of alms-houses, and all the debased and diseased wretches of the earth." Chinese exclusion was an important first step in ensuring America's religious and racial purity, but the Chinese were not the only "undesirable" group polluting the nation. Further safeguarding was required.[35]

"The Indian must go down*": Toward Allotment*

With the Chinese question seemingly settled, the federal government's attention shifted to Indians in the mid-1880s. The Office of Indian Affairs had officially terminated the peace policy in 1882, resuming full control of reservations, but the Indian question seemed as befuddling as ever. Indians, of course, were not an immigrant group that could be excluded, and with "frontier" areas becoming scarcer and scarcer, they could not easily be relocated or pushed any farther west. Outright extermination was politically—if not morally—untenable, and by the late 1870s, the government officially acknowledged that Indians were not going to be "dying out" on their own anytime soon. By 1882, almost everyone now agreed that the reservation system was a failure, breeding corruption and permanent dependence, but what would be better?[36]

If Indians could not be excluded, further relocated, or exterminated, perhaps they could be made to simply disappear. The idea of allotting reservation lands in severalty to Indians became dominant in the 1880s primarily because it seemed a way to eliminate Indians altogether, not physically but culturally. Allotment, together with boarding schools, promised to strip Indians of everything that made them outsiders—their native languages, their traditional cultural practices, their tribal affiliations, and especially their pagan beliefs. To be sure, under the peace policy, J. L. Burchard and other agents had striven to convert Indians to Christianity and had suppressed Indian dancing and other forms of cultural expression. However, the peace policy had not demanded that Indians renounce their tribal affiliations and in fact had relied on pre-existing tribal structures, capitalizing on Indian leaders' cultural authority to enforce discipline and encourage conversions to Christianity. Peace policy agents had accepted the idea that Indians would continue to live communally and retain tribal identities, at least for the present. Allotment, on the other hand, was designed to break up Indian communities, end communalism, and destroy tribal affiliation. Willing or not, Indians would be "absorbed" into the nation, culturally exterminated for their own good and for the good of white Christian America.

The drive for allotment shared much with the movement for Chinese exclusion. Like exclusion, allotment was predicated on the idea that there was no more room in white Christian America for racialized heathens. Proponents of both movements assumed that Christian evangelism among Indians and the Chinese was a failure up to this point but might succeed if individuals were cut off from family and community ties. Both exclusion and allotment appealed to different groups of Americans in different ways, gaining the support of unabashed white supremacists as well as self-styled "friends" of Indians and the Chinese. Both movements were a mix of assimilation and expulsion, theoretically offering Indians and those Chinese already in the United States paths to citizenship while marking them as dangerous and inferior. As with the end of southern Reconstruction, exclusion and allotment reflected the government's new treatment of African Americans, Indians, and the Chinese as threats to the nation's religious and racial homogeneity.

A major difference separated allotment from Chinese exclusion, however. Even if their cultures and religious beliefs needed to be eradicated, Indians were not imagined as racially unassimilable in the same way that the Chinese were. Allotment and boarding school campaigns sprang from the idea that Indian bodies might be erased of their Indianness, made white—or something close to it—through education and Christianity. Most proponents of exclusion did not imagine that Chinese bodies could be similarly erased of that which made them Chinese—"it is in the blood," insisted California's U.S. senator John F. Miller—despite increasing scientific certainty that Indians were genetically from Asia.[37]

Race, though, was never simply scientific, and attitudes toward Indians were shaped by centuries of interaction and intermarriage with various North American groups. In 1880, the California legislature widened an 1850 antimiscegenation statute to include the Chinese, now outlawing "the marriage of a white person with a negro, mulatto, or Mongolian." As in the 1850 law, Indians were missing from the list, a reflection of the still-common if not socially acceptable mixing of Indians, Mexicans, and whites in California. This history of intermarriage and interracial sex in the West made Indians seem less racially fixed than the Chinese.[38] With xenophobia on the rise in the 1880s, Indians also benefited more and more from their North American nativity. "We are partial to the Indians," reported the *Pacific* in 1882, noting, "They are native Americans. They come to us from no foreign land, with no questionable aim." These factors, coupled with still-strong postcolonial nostalgia and the fact that neither physical expulsion nor extermination were possibilities, created greater space in the body politic for Indians—if they could be divested of all signs of Indianness.[39]

Allotment and education promised to do just that. Members of the Women's National Indian Association, the Indian Rights Association, and other organizations that sprang up as support for the peace policy declined overwhelmingly advocated the breaking up of reservation lands and the administration of allotments to Indians in severalty. Striving to "secure the disintegration of all tribal organizations," these reformers argued that private property and land ownership would destroy tribal affiliation while "Christian education"—ideally in boarding schools—would prepare a new generation of Indians for citizenship.[40] Richard Henry Pratt's Carlisle Indian Industrial School, established in Pennsylvania in 1879, served as the model for removing Indians from their communities at a young age to give them religious and industrial training. Although the Indian reformers of the 1880s generally operated independently of churches, their vision was one of Christian assimilation no less than that espoused by missionary organizations. In the view of the American Missionary Association's Charles W. Shelton, "the Indian *must go down*. Extermination or annihilation is the only possible solution of the question. ...You can send to the Indian the rifle and exterminate him in this way...or we can send to the Indian the gospel of Christ, this great power of civilization, and through its influence exterminate the *savage*, but *save the man*." Reformers sought to exterminate everything that was "savage" about Indians to save their souls, purifying the nation in the process.[41]

In the 1880s, California's Protestant leaders embraced allotment for the same reasons they had supported reservations and the peace policy a decade earlier: it seemed to promote "civilization, citizenship, and religion" for Indians. Like Chinese exclusion, allotment seemed a new tool for achieving old goals. Private property and family farms would cultivate American Protestant values of virtue, hard work, and autonomy. "The Indians have a right to the soil—so much as they are willing and able to cultivate," offered the *California Christian Advocate* in 1880. Indians should be "forced to labor for a living or left to starve." Allotment, then, amounted to tough love for Indians—no more special treaties or government handouts. Meanwhile, the government's expenses would be reduced, "surplus" lands could be sold off to white settlers, and—with tribalism destroyed—Indians' "lawlessness and restlessness" would diminish. In showing "justice and generosity to the small remnant of this persecuted and sad race" through the distribution of allotments, everyone would benefit.[42]

California's secular newspapers likewise embraced allotment, but for a different mix of reasons. Remaining skeptical of Indians' ability to convert to Christianity, the *Daily Alta California* favored allotment because it emphasized manual labor over missionization, properly teaching Indians "firstly, habits of industry and then their prayers." The *Chronicle* supported allotment because it would "leave a vast area [of reservation lands] that might be opened to white settlers" while forcing Indians "to take the chances of existence the same as any other member of the community." According to this line of thinking, Indians—rather than being subjugated and oppressed—actually received special benefits from living on reservations, squandering good land and government resources while learning nothing of civilization. "The holding of lands in common not only prevents personal pride in improvement, and cultivation, but also engenders in the Indian a most pernicious feeling of non-responsibility," explained the *Chronicle*. Such arguments overlooked, of course, the fact that most Indians on reservations had been relocated there against their will and that they still lacked basic political protections, including the right to vote, confirmed by the 1884 U.S. Supreme Court case *Elk v. Wilkins*. Secular newspapers did not view allotment as bringing "justice and generosity" to Indians but as a way to strip them of unfair privileges while promoting white settlement.[43]

"Habits of cleanliness": Indian Boarding Schools in California

The Indian boarding school movement also came to California, championed by both Catholics and Protestants as a way to isolate Indian children from pagan ideas and practices. In the *Overland Monthly*, University of California professor Sherman Day explained how, after the influence of boarding schools,

> savage tribal relations, superstitions, barbarous and cruel games, and "medicine" humbugs . . . will vanish spontaneously; and constitutional civil rights, just laws, Christian morality, homesteads in severalty, industrial trades, commonsense medical practice, and the sports and quiet enjoyments of civilized life will take the place of squalor and savagery.

In 1884, the California Presbyterian Synod appointed a missionary to Anaheim who turned his house into a boarding school and church for Indian and Mexican children. Noting that "it seems best to have the Indian pupils some distance from their parents," the synod asked, "Instead of this feeble effort, why can we not have an Indian school equal to that at Carlisle?" After looking into the possibility of establishing a large boarding school in California, the Presbyterian Board of Home Missions decided that the undertaking would be too expensive. However, the state synod retained its hope to one day soon establish a school where Indian children "wholly apart from parental influence, and apart from the scenes and influences of their tribal associations, may be taught the manners and customs of civilized society, [and] be brought under Christian influence." In addition to the makeshift Presbyterian school in Anaheim, several other small church-run Indian schools operated in California during the 1880s, including ones at Chico, San Diego, Yuma, and Banning.[44]

The rise and fall of the boarding school at Round Valley Indian Reservation exemplified the aims of the larger Indian education movement, as well as its pitfalls. Beginning in 1871, Methodist agents Hugh Gibson and then J. L. Burchard had operated one and eventually two day schools on the reservation. Soon after taking control of Round Valley in 1877, however, H. B. Sheldon desired to establish a boarding school where Indian children could be educated away from the "corrupting influences of the camps." Whereas Burchard had relied on tribal networks to promulgate Christianity throughout the entire reservation, Sheldon concentrated his efforts on the young, and he viewed contact with parents, kin, and community as hindrances to civilization. In an 1878 annual report, Sheldon explained that Round Valley's Indian children had made little educational progress in previous years because teachers had made the mistake "(so common) of taking for granted that they are as intelligent and quick to apprehend abstruse ideas as white children." Sheldon's desire for a boarding school was part of his overall dim view of Indians' potential as scholars and Christians. His plan won the approval of a writer for the *California Christian Advocate,* who looked forward to the day when Round Valley children would be taken "out of the filthy holes, and away from the ever-degrading influences of the rancharie."[45]

Church leaders' eagerness to remove Indian children from their parents, with or without their consent, would seem to contradict their usual celebration of the family as the bedrock of American society. They did not, however, recognize Indian families as true families. Partly this was because most Indian parents had not been married in a Christian ceremony. In 1880, Sheldon complained that "some few couples" married by Burchard during the Methodist revival were "still living as husbands and wives, but by far the larger part of them have broken that relation and are now living with others." Instead of nuclear families, with legally married mothers and fathers, Indians seemed to live in sprawling, unstable groups unrecognizable as families to white onlookers. Also, the fact that Indian children were dirty—unsurprisingly, given that they spent most of their time outside—led white observers to assume they were neglected. When she first arrived at Round Valley, Hannah Welch Sheldon, wife of H. B. Sheldon, was horrified to discover the reservation's Indian children "in so filthy a condition that she immediately and continuously applied herself to educate them to habits of cleanliness." The "filth" of their bodies seemed a mark of their supposedly animalistic natures, pagan beliefs, and need to be rescued. Just as proponents of exclusion pointed to the Chinese's lack of "family relations," proponents of allotment and boarding schools portrayed Indians as living in unnatural, un-Christian arrangements that did not need to be respected. Until allotment could create nuclear Christian families, reformers viewed removing Indian children from their parents as a necessary first step toward civilization.[46]

H. B. Sheldon opened his boarding school in August 1881 in Camp Wright, the abandoned Army base near the reservation. The first order of business was giving the children "instructions in the use of soap, combs, shears, and bath tub." In addition to applying the "Gospel of Soap," Hannah Sheldon prioritized teaching the school's forty or so pupils how to perform manual labor, segregated by gender: "the girls to cook, wash, iron, sew, mend, etc.; the boys, to cut wood, milk, care for horses, cows, fowls, etc, whitewash, and other kinds of work." Learning such chores would theoretically prepare them for their future lives as Christian husbands and wives on their own small family farms; in the meantime, the pupils' labor maintained the school.[47]

As with other aspects of H. B. Sheldon's administration at Round Valley, the boarding school became a source of friction between the agent and the reservation's employees and Indians. The school's matron and teachers chafed at Hannah Sheldon's oversight, sending letters to the California Methodist Episcopal Conference accusing her of misappropriating school resources, caring nothing for the pupils' spiritual development, and otherwise hindering "the cause of Christ." Open conflict over the school broke out between H. B. Sheldon and the Methodist missionaries appointed by the Conference to Round Valley. Missionary J. S. Fisher had opposed the building of the boarding school, warning Sheldon, "The Indians will not let their children come. . . . They will burn the buildings before they will let you take the children into there." In 1883, Sheldon banned Fisher's successor, Levi Simmons, from entering the school and asked the Conference to remove him due to his "interference." Simmons earned Sheldon's ire for joining with others opposed to Sheldon's administration, for serving as the Indians' advocate in trying to force Hannah Sheldon out of the school, and for allowing the pupils' parents and friends to take part in church services and other meetings at the school. According to H. B. Sheldon, Simmons also helped teenage Indian boys visit girls sequestered at the school, telling the boys they could "marry any girl out of that school" and that "if they wanted the girls, to go to the school and get them."[48]

Such talk especially upset H. B. Sheldon because he judged one of the boarding school's main purposes to be shielding teenage Indian girls—"especially the young girls from 8 to 15"—from sex until they reached a proper age for marriage. Before the school opened, Sheldon had lamented, like J. L. Burchard had done before him, that he could do little to stop local white men who "seek to debauch" the reservation's teenage Indian girls. After the school began operation, he frequently worried about losing control of the older female pupils, noting that "*our 'Indian way' gives them in marriage as soon as possible.*" Just as the boarding school taught Indian girls how to conduct women's work, it tried to enforce Protestant gender roles by protecting their sexual purity until they reached the proper age for marriage. Levi Simmons's thwarting of this practice was surprising, given the importance placed on policing sex by most missionaries. It is possible that he did so only because he knew many Indians desired access to the school (whether for sexual or other purposes), and he was attempting to win their favor in his struggle against Sheldon.[49]

Officially, children lived at the school "with the consent of parents," but in reality much coercion was necessary, and the Sheldons waged a constant battle to keep students. Some Indian parents refused to allow their children to attend; older students frequently ran away to return to the camps or work on nearby ranches.[50] In one of several petitions sent by Round Valley Indians objecting to H. B. Sheldon in 1882, the Ukies complained especially that the agent "won't allow us to go to church at the Boarding School where our children are." At about the same time, students at the school sent two letters to the Sheldons' district presiding elder demanding that Hannah Sheldon be removed because "when the Scholars are eating she calls them hogs. And we larger Scholars don't want to hear such a word as that. And when the parents come to see their children she drives them away." They also complained that Mrs. Sheldon "said that we was educated for Servants and fit for nothing else and she whip children on hand and feet with raw hide. . . . Mr. Sheldon say to the school, the children ask him to protect them, that not so. We never ask Mr. Sheldon to protect us. We ask our minister Mr. Simmons to protect us against Mrs. Sheldon."[51]

The Indians' petitions presented the boarding school as breaking up Christian families by not allowing parents to visit or worship with their children. The students insisted that Hannah Sheldon was demoralizing, insulting, and physically abusing them instead of raising them up to be educated Christians. In saying that they did not ask for H. B. Sheldon's protection, preferring Simmons, they threw their support behind those on and off the reservation working to depose the agent. Their complaint that Hannah Sheldon treated them as though they were "fit for nothing" but servitude was consistent with her husband's racial attitudes and the larger boarding school movement's emphasis on agricultural and "industrial" training. In an annual report, Sheldon explained that Indians should receive "that education of mind, hand, eye, ear, and habit as shall best fit them for the life that they must live," rather than a training "to the luxurious habits of the white race." It is not surprising that the students bristled at such attitudes.[52]

Long-simmering tensions on the reservation reached their boiling point in the summer of 1883. Seeking to improve his boarding school, H. B. Sheldon traveled east to attend an annual examination at Carlisle Indian Industrial School in Pennsylvania. When he returned, he announced that "changes will be made in July that will make the school more efficient." Inspired by the impressive discipline at Carlisle, Sheldon replaced the boarding school's insubordinate staff and tightened security to allow absolutely no outside visitors. This triggered an immediate and violent response. On the night of July 20, arsonists burned down the school's dining hall and kitchen building. Three nights later, they set fire to the school's main building with the students inside. No one was seriously hurt in either fire, but the school and all its furnishings were destroyed.[53]

Sheldon had so many enemies he was initially unsure who to accuse of the crimes—local settlers still hoping to see the reservation abolished, Levi Simmons and other disgruntled employees or ex-employees, or Indian parents making good on their threat to "burn the buildings." He at first could only blame it on the "spirit of hostility to the school" and the "spirit of insubordination" that had reigned at Round Valley in recent years. Soon after, an official from the Department of the Interior named Robert Belt traveled to Round Valley to make an investigation. Belt identified three full-blooded and two "half-breed" boys, all between the ages of twelve and sixteen, who confessed to the crime "after some skirmishing." Sheldon imprisoned the boys on the reservation, urging the Office of Indian Affairs to send them to an East Coast boarding school to teach them "discipline," insisting that "removing them from home and friends would be a lesson not only to them but to their friends and others." Two weeks later, however, the Commissioner of Indian Affairs instructed Sheldon to release the boys because they "have been sufficiently punished," which Sheldon did with reluctance.[54]

The school burnings were so shocking that they demanded explanation and interpretation, which various parties offered in competing ways. From the perspective of the local press, the burning of the school was the newest example of Sheldon's egregious mismanagement of the reservation.[55] In his letters to the Office of Indian Affairs, Sheldon himself portrayed the burnings as manifestations of male Indian lust and jealousy, a narrative that allowed him to cast himself as a defender of female Indian virtue. He reported that, unbeknownst to him at the time, Indian boys from outside the school had been "clandestinely" visiting girls in the boarding house at night by climbing through an "attic scuttle." He explained that the primary arsonist had lost his girlfriend to another boy and burned the school to say, "I'll make him give her up." "While all this was going on they (the girls) met regularly in class and prayer meeting and were thought by their teachers to be exemplary Christians," Sheldon noted. As in his earlier dismissal of the Methodist revival, Sheldon viewed Indians' professions of Christianity as self-serving deceptions. Sheldon expected Indians to lie, be lascivious, and break rules—it was in their natures. To Sheldon, the burning of the school proved that benevolent white overseers like him needed even greater power to shape all aspects of Indians' lives. As for the boys themselves, one informed Sheldon that "some white man (he don't know who) told him to burn the cook-house," portraying himself as caught up in an intraracial conflict between Sheldon and local white settlers. This explanation shifted the blame off of Indians and, most urgently, off of himself, making the boy only guilty of following a white man's instructions, an idea the reservation was after all based on.[56]

Given the large number of white settlers hostile to Sheldon and the reservation in general, it was hardly unthinkable that a white man might have ordered the arsons. However, the boys had sufficient motive to burn down the school, even without such encouragement. The five arsonists—John Duncan (Yuki), Jack Melendy (Pit River), John Munsell (Concow Maidu), Eben Tillotson (Yuki), and Lieutenant Wilson (Little Lake Pomo)—were all former students in the school who had run away at some point during the year previous to the burnings.[57] All five had signed one or both of the 1882 petitions requesting that Hannah Sheldon be removed. When questioned by investigator Robert Belt, the boys said that they had set the fires because they were "tired of the school" and wanted a break from its constant hard work and harsh discipline. Melendy complained that teachers "made him work too hard and whipped him lots of times." Belt also discovered that the students in the school had been warned about the second fire ahead of time and had accordingly gone to bed "with their clothes on, shoes and aprons buttoned and tied." The fact that the boys told the students about the fire confirmed that the acts of arson were pointedly directed at the school and the Sheldons, rather than being results of a romantic triangle turned violent, as suggested by H. B. Sheldon. Rather, the fires were premeditated acts of rebellion and anger, carried out by individuals who possessed few other ways to effect change on the reservation. Sending petitions to the government and the Methodist conference had not removed the Sheldons from Round Valley; arson was the next step.[58]

The fiery end of the boarding school at Round Valley was a dramatic example of how reformers' best-laid plans could go astray when implemented in the real world. The Sheldons' efforts to enforce Christian ideals of sexuality and to eradicate all signs of Indian identity triggered resistance in various forms. As J. L. Burchard had before him, Levi Simmons recognized that negotiation and accommodation around Indians' desires and traditions were necessary parts of a successful missionary campaign. The Sheldons' pessimistic racial attitudes and righteous inflexibility alienated Indians of all ages. Similar power struggles and processes of mutual accommodation played out in Indian schools and Chinese missions throughout the West.

"Let them become self-supporting and acquiring": Round Valley and the General Allotment Act

The boarding school at Round Valley was a decided failure, but the movement for allotment succeeded at the reservation, as it did nationwide, because it miraculously united all interested parties: the agent, church leaders, local settlers, the Indians, and the government. The fires proved to be a turning point for Sheldon's administration, as his fortunes thereafter turned from bad to horrid. First, three discharged reservation employees accused him of conduct unbefitting a minister at the California Methodist Episcopal annual conference, with a committee finding him guilty of "Falsehood" and "Improper Temper and Words." Soon after, the reservation's physician turned against Sheldon, sending letters to the Commissioner of Indian Affairs and California's Senator John F. Miller urging the agent's removal for gross mismanagement and demoralizing the Indians, reducing "some four or five hundred Christian Indians" into "scarcely . . . a dozen" believers. Sheldon's restrictive vision of Christianity had turned against him, his own statistics now fueling accusations of religious neglect.[59]

The Office of Indian Affairs responded by sending special agent Paris H. Folsom to Round Valley for yet another investigation. After spending six weeks interviewing employees, ex-employees, and Indians, Folsom declared Sheldon guilty of "inexcusable weakness and gross carelessness" in his management. Folsom was especially shocked by the reservation's sanitary conditions; he found an old Indian lying on a mattress that was "sour, filthy, damp, and mildewed from decaying vomit and urine. And this sick man lay within a stone's throw of the agent's house, and so near the agent's Sunday service, that poor man could catch the sound of what must have come to him as a meaningless, soulless, Godless worship." The Round Valley Indians had been the first to reject Sheldon's administration; then reservation employees and the California Methodist Episcopal Conference had turned their backs on him; now, finally, the government denounced him. When Folsom announced his findings to Sheldon, the agent resigned on May 1, 1884. He had managed to last six and a half years as agent. Disturbed by Folsom's report, the U.S. Senate's Committee on Indian Affairs launched its own investigation of Round Valley, conducting hearings in San Francisco and Mendocino County in September 1884 led by Henry Dawes, a Republican from Massachusetts. Sheldon's resignation did not spare him the ignominy of having to testify.[60]

As his fortunes soured, Sheldon blamed many of Round Valley's problems on the reservation system itself, which he said encouraged tribal attachments, laziness, and paganism. Only allotments of land in severalty could generate true civilization and religiosity. Beginning in his 1883 annual report, Sheldon began to attribute the Indians' rejection of Christianity during his tenure to their disappointment at not receiving individual land plots, supposedly promised to them by Burchard:

> In the revival meetings [of the mid-1870s] they were exhorted to become good, and in their minds becoming good became connected with getting lands; and as all wanted lands, they *became good*—i.e., joined the church—and for a time left bad habits. Some were really converted and have lived exemplary lives, considering their knowledge and surroundings. The large part, however, when they saw that their religion did not bring the land they sought, became discouraged and gave up even in the semblance of religion, and relapsed into old habits and customs; nay, became ever worse, and skeptical as to *all* religion.

This explanation of the Methodist revival was an amplification of the one Sheldon had given in 1878, with desire for allotments of land now replacing want of "sugar" as the Indians' reason for joining the church. While shifting blame for his evangelistic failures onto Burchard, Sheldon believed allotment would promote Christianity by allowing the government to fulfill yet another broken promise made to an Indian group. Asked during Dawes's Senate hearing how he would improve Round Valley, Sheldon answered, "I would recommend that the Indians be given land in severalty."[61]

Local white settlers agreed. Many had conspired to break up the reservation for decades, and allotment would mean finally opening Round Valley to commercial development and further white settlement. In 1880, a writer in the Ukiah City *Press* portrayed Round Valley as a potential "terrestrial paradise," waiting to be crisscrossed with new roads and prosperous farms, if only the reservation could be opened. As for the Indians, given that the "benign influences of civilization has diseased them, and that cleanliness kills them," the writer wondered how much longer white settlers would have to wait until the Indians all died off or "lost their individuality by the process of amalgamation"? "If the devil has a grip on them, which the church cannot unloose, why not turn them over to him at once," the writer concluded. Allotment meant no more waiting; Indians would be "amalgamated" immediately, while surplus lands would be sold to capitalist-minded settlers. Sanders Hornbrook, a local farmer who testified before Dawes, urged the government to distribute a third of the reservation's range land to Indian families and to sell the other two-thirds to whites. The Indians "ought to have this swamp land," he said, rather than the much more valuable range land. Reservation head farmer Philo Handy, long favored by many whites in the valley because he was thought to support the "abolishment" of the reservation, similarly told the senators that he would "locate the Indians upon the swamp land" and sell off most of the range land. Asked by Henry Dawes if he thought the Indians were capable of self-sufficient farming, Handy answered, "They are as ready now as they will ever be." Retorted Dawes, "That don't quite answer the question."[62]

California's Methodist leaders largely based their support for allotment on their experiences with Round Valley. Beginning in 1880, Methodists who visited the reservation called for the distribution of its lands in severalty. They believed that private land ownership would solve many of the reservation's problems: it would encourage the Indians to be sedentary, rather than nomadic; it would teach them the "principles of business and practical farming" better than living on the reservation could; it would "put them into possession of a home," the building block of Christian morality and civilization—in short, it would "let them become self-supporting and acquiring." The never-ending controversies arising from Round Valley, together with the Indians' disappointing spiritual recidivism under Sheldon, encouraged Methodists to embrace a plan that would end their involvement with the reservation once and for all.[63]

During the hearing, Handy insisted that the "general desire" of the Round Valley Indians was for private land ownership, a claim that—while furthering his own interests—seems to have been accurate for at least some Indians. As early as 1875, during the height of the Methodist revival, a visitor to the reservation reported the Indians wanted "land in severalty, whereon they could build their own houses, cultivate a few acres, keep some stock, and live in a somewhat independent and assured life like white men." In 1878, when a transfer of the reservation to the Department of War seemed imminent, Sheldon held a meeting with five tribal captains to ascertain their opinions. Beyond opposing the transfer, the captains expressed their desires for land. Charles Munsell, captain of the Concow Maidu and Methodist lay preacher, said, "we want farms, and ranges, so we can make our own living, and schools for our children." James Sherwood, speaking for the Little Lake Pomos, agreed: "we want land, plow, garden, and work. Want to be like white man, and schools for our children, so they grow up like white people children." Peter Hudson of the Redwoods reported, "We want get land, we know we can support ourselves, and we don't want anybody to look down on us. We have been promised land." As with all records of meetings with Indians at Round Valley, the agent's power, presence at the meeting, and control of the transcription makes assuming that these statements reflected the captains' wishes—let alone the wishes of other Indians at Round Valley— problematic. However, as written, they suggest the captains supported breaking up the reservation. Their statements did not make it clear, however, whether the captains wanted land to be distributed to individuals or to entire tribes communally.[64]

In July 1885, 145 Indian men living on the reservation signed a letter to the Commissioner of Indian Affairs demanding allotments of land in severalty. They said they

> have been promised land in severalty for a great many years, year after year, but have been put off from time to time until we have about come to the conclusion that the good time will never come. This is our home, the birth place of many of us, and we do not want to leave our homes, and take refuge in the mountains, or be

> driven from place to place by the white man. . . . Give us all our land and control of the pasture land (or mountains) and we can easily be self-supporting, and will not ask the Government for one cent after we are fairly started.

The letter also requested that reservation lands previously sold to white settlers be returned to the Indians, to give "the head of each family . . . a very small piece of land." Round Valley Indians' previous letters to the government had focused on the dismissal of Sheldon as agent; now, even with Sheldon removed, they desired the end of the reservation altogether. The language and logic of allotment—"severalty," becoming "self-supporting," saving the government money—provided them with a possible path to autonomy and an escape from forced or low-paid wage labor. From their perspective, having experienced firsthand the worst of the reservation system under Sheldon, allotment seemed preferable to remaining perpetual government wards, marginalized, forced to work against their will, and lacking basic political rights. Unlike the Creeks, Choctaws, Cherokees, Senecas, and other Indian groups that opposed allotment in the 1880s, Round Valley Indians had very little to lose. This letter was signed by Charles Munsell, John Brown, and those Indians who had remained on the reservation through thick and thin; their request to break it up was one more piece of damning evidence of the reservation system's utter failure to better the lives of Indians.[65]

Their claim that they had been "promised land in severalty for a great many years," together with similar comments made on other occasions by Peter Hudson and Charlie Brown, gives support to Sheldon's explanation of the earlier Methodist revival. At least some Indians seemed to have understood joining the church and owning their own land as parts of the same process. They joined Christian churches not simply out of calculated self-interest, as reported by Sheldon, but also out of a willingness to adapt to a new way of life necessitated by California's new order. Faced with severely limited options, they embraced cultural change as a survival tool. Throughout the rise and fall of the Methodist revival, Round Valley Indians displayed a preference for autonomy over dependence, for their own Indian preachers over white ministers, and for a fluid mix of religious beliefs over any single static spiritual system, be it traditional beliefs, the Ghost Dance, Catholicism, or Methodism. They embraced allotment in 1885 in a way similar to their embrace of Christianity a decade earlier: it seemed the best option available. If they would have preferred to own the land communally—which many no doubt did prefer, as shown by the "communistic" arrangements created by the Potter Valley and Calpella Indians who left Round Valley in the late 1870s—they recognized that asking for allotment in severalty would be the most persuasive argument in 1885.

They were correct. After the hearing on Round Valley, Dawes and the Committee on Indian Affairs recommended that Congress give the head of each Round Valley Indian family a forty-acre allotment to avoid a "relapse of the Indian into barbarism." At Round Valley, as at reservations throughout the country, allotment seemed a form of simultaneous moral, spiritual, and material uplift. To further prevent a "relapse" into "barbarism," Dawes urged the Women's National Indian Association of Philadelphia to begin a Christian mission at Round Valley because "600 capable and industrious Indians there earnestly ask for a missionary." Claudia White and Anna L. Boorman arrived at Round Valley in April 1886, soon establishing "two Sunday-schools, two sewing schools, women's meetings, Bible readings, house to house visitation, a Saturday evening sociable to displace Indian dances, and general and special instruction in the domestic arts." A new cycle of mission work had begun at Round Valley.[66]

Commissioner of Indian Affairs J. D. C. Atkins accepted the committee's recommendation for allotments at Round Valley but reduced them from forty to thirty acres. To a proposed allotment bill he appended the Round Valley Indians' 1885 letter as proof that sentiment on the reservation was unanimous for allotment in severalty. Dawes introduced the Round Valley bill in the U.S. Senate in January 1886, joining a series of such bills considered by Congress between 1879 and 1887 aimed at introducing allotment at all or specific Indian reservations. Some government officials had favored allotment since the early nineteenth century, and it had been a goal of the Board of Indian Commissioners since its creation in 1869. As allotment's popularity skyrocketed in the 1880s, Congress debated and rejected several plans that were either too "humanitarian" to please western politicians or too stingy to please eastern Indian reformers, an east-west split similar to that on the Chinese question. Debates in Congress over these various allotment plans—like parallel debates over Chinese immigration—turned into referendums on race and religion in the United States.[67]

Opponents of allotment, most prominently Colorado's Republican senator Henry Moore Teller, declared such plans overly optimistic about Indians' ability to rise to civilization under any circumstances. "We insist on treating [the Indian] as if he was a civilized man, when he ought to be treated as a savage, full of the superstitions and weaknesses that belong to savage life," said Teller in 1880, discussing a plan to distribute lands in severalty to the Utes of Colorado. "We ought not to forget that we are dealing with savages—brutal, bloody savages—and we never should deal with savages as we deal with civilized people." Teller was skeptical of reformers' claims that, under allotment, civilization and Christianity for Indians were just around the corner, noting that such promises had been made incessantly by missionaries and agents since the days of "old Jedediah Morse," back in "1818 or 1822—I do not remember which.... Mr. Morse told what progress they were making; he told about the prayer-meetings that the female Indians were holding, and he told about the religious zeal among the Indians all over the country and what strides they were making in civilization. This has been the cry every year since."[68]

These congressmen portrayed the Indians as essentially savage and stubbornly pagan, nowhere near ready for private land ownership. "The men who to-day are endeavoring to impose upon the Indians the theories of civilization that are applicable to white men ... are committing an offense against the race which will result in its extermination," declared Preston B. Plumb from Kansas. "It is a violation of their nature.... We have got to take these Indians as they are; we have got to adapt our legislation to them as they are, not as we would have them." Indians, these critics insisted, were in a primitive stage of human development and could not be rushed into the demands of citizenship or civilization. "You must follow the old rule that is laid down by the Bible," declared Samuel Bell Maxey, a Democrat from Texas. "Let him begin by raising stock; begin by herding. After a while he will be prepared to go to farming; then after a while he will be prepared to go into mechanical pursuits, and so on step by step."[69]

Congressmen who supported allotment agreed with their opponents that Indians were racially and religiously inferior, but they viewed allotment as the best way to manage them. N. P. Hill of Colorado, arguing in favor of allotments for the Utes, declared, "I would much prefer that no Indians should be left in that State," but he did not judge it fair to the white people of New Mexico or Utah to push the Utes—a "worthless set of vagabonds"—there. Further removal was not an option, but neither was allowing Indian reservations to remain obstacles in the path of manifest destiny. "The superior race, under the expansive force of civilization, will push aside the inferior," said George Graham Vest, Democratic senator from Missouri. Given this inevitable extinguishment of Indian societies, Vest believed "the question is between the extermination of the

Indians and the division of their lands in severalty.... [Allotment] is the heroic and proper treatment; and by that treatment civilization will come." Pro-allotment congressmen agreed with their opponents that Indians would inevitably be "push[ed] aside" by whites, but they believed that allotment in severalty might eventually civilize them enough to join white society.[70]

Objecting to being called "dreamers" and Indian "enthusiasts," pro-allotment congressmen usually couched their arguments in terms of how their plans would benefit whites. Allotment, they said, would help white settlers not only by opening reservations for "immediate occupation" but also by ending Indian wars. Other proponents of allotment portrayed Indians as an untapped labor force, if only they could be broken of pagan habits. "Now, sir, the Indian is a physical force; a half million of vigorous, physical, intellectual agents ready for the plastic hand of Christian civilization, living in a country possessing empires of untilled and uninhabited lands," said Blanche Kelso Bruce, an African American senator from Mississippi. "The Indian tribes, viewed from this utilitarian stand-point, are worth preservation, conservation, utilization, and civilization." Taking a different approach, Missouri's Charles O'Neill argued that breaking up reservations would solve the nation's "labor problem" by encouraging "workingmen" to "leave your cities, the hot-beds of vice and corruption, and settle on the public lands, where they can earn a livelihood by their labor." Like halting immigration from China, allotment promised to end the labor strife and urban moral decay that threatened to destroy white Christian America.[71]

A small number of congressmen did offer humanitarian arguments for allotment. They spoke of finally crafting a "true policy of a Christian nation founded on the principles of peace and fraternity and intelligence." Joseph E. Brown, virtually the only Democrat who had opposed Chinese exclusion on religious grounds, favored allotment because it advanced Christianity:

> We will soon find the Indians upon their homesteads advancing in civilization; and under the benign influence of the Christian denominations, we shall see Sunday schools and churches planted among them; and instead of roving bands without fixed habitations, goaded to desperation by injustice and wrong, spreading death and destruction in their pathway, we shall find them in the comfortable homes of civilized man, not

only a Christian people but many of them cultivated
and honorable citizens.

However, such utopian pronouncements, common in reform circles, were
rarely heard in the congressional debates, particularly after the passage of
Chinese exclusion in 1882. Older Radical Republican rhetoric of racial
justice and egalitarianism had been discredited and largely abandoned.[72]

During allotment debates, congressmen on both sides of the issue
directly or indirectly compared Indians with the Chinese and African
Americans. They insisted that Indians were "non-progressive" and "clan-
nish," charges frequently levied against the Chinese. "The savage of a
thousand years ago is the same savage of to-day and of a thousand years
hence," declared Wyoming's S. W. Downey. Proponents of allotment
countered by presenting reservations as a "Chinese wall" that kept Indians stagnant. They claimed that "those who know both the Indian and
the negro [say] that the Indian is the superior. Give, then, to the red man
the black man's chance."[73]

Samuel Bell Maxey used this comparison as grounds to challenge
the idea of giving citizenship to uneducated Indians, given the "failures"
of Reconstruction. "Mr. President, we have had enough, in recent days,
in this country on such matters," he said. Dawes responded by asking why
"the poor and degraded and ignorant African" should be awarded citizenship, but not "an Indian who has left his tribe, turned his back upon the
savage life, has adopted the modes and habits of civilized life, is in all respects like one of us." Not even feigning a defense of congressional Reconstruction, Dawes portrayed civilized Indians as possible allies of whites
in their struggle against dangerously ignorant black voters. Maxey retorted that he agreed with Dawes that the "wild, savage negro" should
not be allowed to naturalize. "Look at your Chinamen," he added, "are
they not specially excepted from the naturalization laws?" This was a re-
suscitation of old Democratic arguments that Indians, African Americans, and the Chinese were equally unfit for citizenship.[74]

Yet Maxey and most Democrats supported the general principle of
allotment—if not all its specifics—and by 1887 Republicans had written
an allotment bill that almost everyone could agree on. Dawes's bill au-
thorized the president to divide reservation lands into 160-acre allotments and award them in severalty to "each head of a family," to be held
in trust by the federal government for twenty-five years. Unmarried and
orphan Indians would receive smaller plots. All Indians who accepted an

allotment, who took up "residence separate and apart from any tribe of Indians," and who "adopted the habits of civilized life" would—at some undefined future point—become U.S. citizens. Leaders of the Cherokees, Creeks, Choctaws, and a handful of other powerful tribes managed to keep themselves exempt for the present. All told, Dawes's General Allotment Act received bipartisan support because it promised to encourage white settlement of the West, promote Christianity and capitalism, and eradicate Indian distinctiveness—to quickly and efficiently make Indians disappear. President Cleveland signed the act on February 8, 1887.[75]

From the perspective of California's Protestant leadership, Chinese exclusion and allotments for Indians provided plans that their various factions could unite around, paths to help them put behind them the conflicts and uncertainties of the late 1870s. Most still supported evangelism to Indians and the Chinese, still hoped to usher in the glorious conversion of the globe, but their optimism had been tempered, and their enthusiasm for a racially diverse, religiously united nation had soured. They had come to blame the slow advances of mission work not on Christianity or their own paternalistic attitudes but on the "intractable" nature of Indians and the Chinese, a journey that paralleled one taken by many white missionaries laboring among freed slaves in the American South during these years. The momentum of Reconstruction that had spurred outreach to Indians and the Chinese in the late 1860s had now reversed, discouraging a focus on racial justice issues nationwide.[76]

Together, Chinese exclusion and the General Allotment Act represented the true end of Reconstruction. A national debate on the place of Indians and the Chinese in American society that had raged since the end of the Civil War had been settled, at least for the moment. As it was in so many arenas, California stood as the vanguard of American racial and religious attitudes. State Republicans had abandoned "sentimental" rhetoric of racial inclusiveness after the disastrous election of 1867, and the national party followed that path in the late 1870s and 1880s. California's political leaders, press, and eventually clergy called for exclusion and allotment long before those measures became federal law. Excluded, impoverished, and targeted for eradication, Indians and the Chinese joined African Americans on the margins of a new kind of Christian nation.

EPILOGUE

In August 1895, a short story entitled "The Ways that Are Dark" by local journalist Adeline Knapp appeared in the San Francisco *Morning Call*. The story described the education of an idealistic minister from New York named Rev. Milton Grober who journeys to San Francisco to "fight for the Chinaman in the very thick of the opposition and cruelty to which he is a victim." Swindled by his Chinese tour guide, Grober nonetheless plans to deliver a "pro-Chinese address" at Metropolitan Temple to the "generous souled but crude and somewhat prejudiced people of California." Before he can give his address, however, Grober discovers that his daughter—"the apple of his eye"—has narrowly been rescued by the San Francisco police department. Charlie, a Chinese man who had been receiving Bible lessons from Grober's daughter, had nearly kidnapped her and forced her to become his "white wife." Grober cancels his speech and takes his daughter home to the East on the next day's train, no longer "so enthusiastic as of old upon the Chinese question."[1]

Playing on longstanding fears of miscegenation and white slavery, Knapp's story was a new expression of an old rhetorical tradition in California that discredited religion-based arguments for racial egalitarianism. By the 1890s, it had become widely accepted in the state that "sentimental" notions of the universal brotherhood of man, easily expressed from the remove of the East, could not withstand the test of California's racial cauldron. In the two decades following the Civil War, California's Protestant ministers had in fact undergone a process of transformation similar to Grober's fictional one. In the late 1860s and early 1870s, state Protestant leaders had offered biblical evidence of the unity of humankind, declaring free immigration from China and the reservation system glorious parts of God's plan to integrate Indians and the Chinese into Christian America while ushering in the conversion of Asia

175

and the world. By the 1880s, virtually no one in California publicly supported either unrestricted immigration or reservations for Indians. A
broad pessimism about the future of a racially heterogeneous society had
taken hold: the Congregationalist *Pacific* now declared itself in opposition to further black migration to California, while the Presbyterian
Occident noted with pride that "the white man"—"these audacious Sons
of Japhet"—had grown to constitute one-third of the world's population.[2]

This shift had occurred for many reasons. Between 1860 and 1890,
California had more than tripled in size, and its population had become
proportionately more native-born and white. As diversity diminished, so
did public support for interracial Protestantism. National developments
—including economic recession, the challenges and setbacks of southern
Reconstruction, the Republican Party's retreat from racial justice issues
after 1877, and calls for sectional reconciliation—reverberated in California, just as trends in the state shaped national debates. As the utopian
post–Civil War moment passed, Protestant reformers failed to sustain
their faith in racial uplift in the face of day-to-day mission work and
mounting public scorn. The paternalistic and inequitable structures of
the missions limited their efficacy, as Chinese and Native American
church members were often unwilling or unable to conform to missionaries' ideals of total personal transformation and Protestant exclusivity.
Facing racial and religious bigotry, Irish Catholics cast themselves as
defenders of white Christian America, broadening and redirecting the
anti-Chinese movement in the late 1870s as the violent rhetoric of the
Workingmen's Party of California made exclusion seem a moderate position. Meanwhile, the rise and fall of Round Valley Indian Reservation as
a model for the Christian assimilation of Indians helped sour Protestants
on the peace policy and the reservation system. As a gulf developed between eastern and western Protestants over racial issues, easterners' dis-
missive rhetoric offended Californians' regional pride and stiffened
their resolve.[3]

Some of these trends would continue in the era now dawning. After
helping to establish the precedent of Chinese exclusion in 1882, Protestant leaders began calling for a widening of the act to protect the nation
from "all undesirable classes of people such as were likely to corrupt the
public mind or the public morals." By guarding the "purity of society here
from foreign contamination," ministers promised to *benefit China and
the other nations of the earth ... by developing here a genuine Christian republic,*" a model for all to follow. Such arguments from Protestant voices
bolstered a broader nativist movement that flourished in California during

the late 1880s and 1890s, resuscitating an anti-Catholicism that had been temporarily submerged by the anti-Chinese consensus. Like earlier anti-Chinese agitators, the new nativists couched their arguments in a mix of Protestantism, free labor ideology, and patriotic zeal. "The idea that the United States is to be the slop-bucket of creation has no foundation in morals, economics or religion," asserted the San Francisco *Daily Evening Bulletin*.[4]

Striking a similar chord, Josiah Strong, a Congregationalist minister in Cincinnati, directed national attention to California and the West in his widely read book *Our Country: Its Possible Future and Its Present Crisis*, published in 1885. "It is the West, not the South or the North, which holds the key to the nation's future," he wrote. Strong warned that an "alien and materialistic civilization" was springing up in the region due to its "foreign" population, a designation he applied to not just immigrants but also Indians and Mexican Americans. The West's "still chaotic" social conditions and ethnic diversity, he insisted, made it especially vulnerable to "Romanism," Mormonism, and other threats he linked to untrammeled immigration.[5] Even more than those from Catholic Europe and Latin America, immigrants from Japan, Korea, and India suffered from this rising tide of nativism as they were branded new heathen menaces.[6]

Yet, a Christian counter-discourse of tolerance and universalism was never totally eradicated in California. After 1882, some of the state's Protestant leaders expressed regret that an important door from China had been shut by exclusion. A. W. Loomis and other missionaries complained that their schools lacked students, "as there are no new Chinese scarcely coming in to keep up the supply." The California Methodist Episcopal Conference blamed "recent anti-Chinese legislation" for its struggling missions, noting, "Many of the Chinese who were friendly toward us are now hostile to us. Questions are asked us which are not easily answered in the light of the religion we profess."[7] As Eureka, Truckee, and almost two hundred other western towns purged Chinese residents from their city limits in the 1880s, church leaders denounced the expulsions as un-Christian. "There is no excuse for this violence," declared the *Pacific*. "It is a shame and a crime." When anti-Chinese agitators in 1886 called for a boycott of any business that continued to employ Chinese labor, Protestant leaders denounced the plan as "petty persecution."[8]

Beginning in 1885, some ministers in California began again to call publicly for free immigration from China. William Pond, who in 1876 had told his white congregation at San Francisco's Bethany Congregational Church that he wanted to "arrest" Chinese immigration, called exclusion in 1885 "in contradiction to the vital principles of our national existence; and either it must be abandoned, or sooner or later this contradiction will develop into conflict irrepressible." Such sentiments triggered a new round of controversy within conferences and congregations, which played out in the religious press. The question of Chinese immigration was once again up for debate.[9]

After virtually abandoning evangelism among San Francisco's Chinese residents in the years leading up to exclusion, the Catholic Church resumed that work in 1883. That year, Gregory Antonucci, an Italian-born former missionary in Canton, opened a Chinese Catholic school and chapel. St. Mary's Cathedral in Chinatown—now called "Old" St. Mary's after the opening of the new Cathedral of Saint Mary of the Assumption in 1891—was turned over to the Missionary Society of Saint Paul the Apostle in 1894, which established a Chinese mission. The passage of exclusion made such work possible; as the anti-Chinese movement lost intensity, Catholics had less to gain from distancing themselves from the Chinese. However, rising anti-Catholicism in California in the 1880s and 1890s provided incentive for some Catholics to keep seeking ways to align themselves with white Christianity. The San Francisco *Monitor* continued to warn of the dangers posed by Chinese "coolies" to white labor, and Peter C. Yorke, San Francisco's most outspoken activist-priest, delivered the final address at the 1901 California Chinese Exclusion Convention. "Now, then, we are face to face with an immigration which is emphatically not Christian," he announced. "Their thoughts are not our thoughts; their blood is not our blood; their outlook is not our outlook." Like the Jesuit James Buchard before him, Yorke demonized the Chinese as a way of championing the Catholic Church's European immigrant membership.[10]

Meanwhile, more and more Chinese Americans were rising to leadership positions in California's Protestant churches. Although Chinese Christians had long served as lay preachers and colporteurs, beginning in 1879 they began to be ordained as full members of the clergy. That year, Ah Ching passed his examination to become an Episcopalian deacon, and other denominations began ordaining Chinese ministers in the 1880s and 1890s.[11] Just as Round Valley Indians had expressed a preference for Native American preachers, so too did Chinese churchgoers say they wanted to be served by Chinese ministers. In 1885, members of the Presbyterian mission in Los Angeles told the Board of Foreign Missions that they wanted Soo Hoo Nam Art as pastor rather than a white missionary named F. H. Robinson. "Robinson only talk English our boys not fond to him," they wrote, "and please hope you send our preacher as soon as you can."[12]

California's first generation of Chinese American clergymen viewed political activism as an integral part of their ministries. Chan Hon Fan, an assistant pastor under Otis Gibson in San Francisco who took charge of the Methodist mission in Portland, Oregon, in the mid-1880s, publicly objected to anti-Chinese comments made by several local white clergymen. "I want you, Rev. E. Trumbull Lee, and you, Rev. Wm. B. Lee, to know that you, being preachers of Christianity, and men that enjoy that 'better civilization' in enlightened America, have, by your unkind words, become great stumbling blocks before a race of benighted souls whom Jesus came to save," he wrote in the *Morning Oregonian*. A veteran of the religious battles waged over Chinese immigration in California, Chan Hon Fan boldly asserted his own vision of Christianity, directly calling out anti-Chinese ministers by name.[13]

Similarly, Presbyterian Ng Poon Chew, the first Chinese graduate of San Francisco Theological Seminary, delivered an address in 1891 portraying immigration to and from China as crucial to saving Asia. "The Christian Chinamen, converted in this country, who go back to China, are among the best, the most faithful, patient, consistent, and energetic Christians to be found anywhere," he said. Ng Poon Chew went on to found *Chung Sai Yat Po,* the first daily Chinese-language newspaper in the United States, leveraging his influence to combat exclusion and other discriminatory laws.[14] Longtime activist Jee Gam, ordained as a full Congregationalist minister in 1895, led efforts against the renewal of the Chinese exclusion act in 1892 and 1902. He called exclusion "un-American, barbarous and inhuman. It is un-Christian, for it is contrary to the teaching of Christ." Along with their counterparts in the East—most prominently Yan Phou Lee, a Presbyterian who graduated from Yale in 1887 —California's Christian Chinese leaders made use of their rising status to fight for political and social justice for Chinese Americans.[15]

In 1885, Chinese Californians won a legal victory, thanks to the activism of two Chinese Presbyterians. Joseph and Mary McGladery Tape, two Chinese immigrants who were married by A. W. Loomis in 1875, sued the San Francisco Board of Education for barring their American-born daughter Mamie from attending public school. The state legislature had not required school districts to educate Chinese children after 1870, and in 1884 the San Francisco Board of Education "absolutely prohibited" the admittance of "any Mongolian child." In their lawsuit, the Tapes were represented by attorney William F. Gibson, Otis Gibson's son, who helped their case proceed to the California Supreme Court. In *Tape v. Hurley*, the court ruled in favor of the Tapes, requiring that Chinese children be granted access to a public education.

Throughout the case, the Tapes presented themselves as assimilated Christians seeking to live out the American dream. In a petition to the Board of Education, Joseph Tape emphasized that he did not wear a queue, that his family dressed in "American costume," and that they lived in "a Christian home, in which the habits and customs peculiar to Americans had been adopted, and the English language spoken by the family." In a letter to the *Daily Alta California*, Mary Tape emphasized that her children "don't dress like the other Chinese" and asked, "Is it a disgrace to be Born a Chinese? Didn't God make us all!!! What right have you to bar my children out of the school because she is a chinese Descend. They is no other worldly reason that you could keep her out, except that. I suppose, you all goes to churches on Sunday!" The Tapes employed their Christianity to challenge racial segregation while reinforcing broader notions of the superiority of Christian marriage, nuclear family, the English language, and American culture.[16]

After *Tape v. Hurley*, San Francisco hurriedly established a separate school for Chinese children rather than permitting them to attend white schools, as the Tapes had sought to do. Nonetheless, Joseph and Mary Tape, Jee Gam, and other Chinese parents elected to send their children to San Francisco's Chinese Primary School, judging it a step forward. Ultimately, however, segregated schools consigned Chinese Californians, with Indians and Mexican Americans, to a perpetual second-class status. California's segregated educational system, though more variegated than the Jim Crow laws passed throughout the South in the 1880s, similarly naturalized and enforced racial difference.

In fact, the U.S. Supreme Court cited California's 1874 decision in *Ward v. Flood*, among other cases, as precedent when establishing the doctrine of "separate but equal" in *Plessy v. Ferguson* in 1896. In his solitary dissent to *Plessy*, Justice John Marshall Harlan, after arguing that "Our constitution is color-blind," used the specter of the Chinese to champion African Americans. "There is a race so different from our own that we do not permit those belonging to it to become citizens of the United States," he wrote, noting that *Plessy* would allow "a Chinaman" to ride with white passengers while prohibiting "citizens of the black race" from doing the same. Almost thirty years after congressional debates over the Fifteenth Amendment had struck a similar chord, proponents of African American civil rights continued to attack the Chinese, a rhetorical move carried to extreme lengths in California's ever-shifting racial hierarchy.[17]

Northern Piute activist Sarah Winnemucca, back in San Francisco on another lecture tour in 1885, employed a similar logic in her defense of Indians. Speaking in Irving Hall, she objected that Indians could not vote while "the man with the lamb's wool on his head and the foreigner" enjoyed the right of suffrage. She said she wished she could put all the Indians of Nevada on a boat and sail it into New York City, to "land them there as immigrants, that they might be received with open arms, blessed with the blessing of universal suffrage." Here, Winnemucca attempted to harness the nation's surging nativist sentiment and retreat from political rights for African Americans on behalf of Indians.[18]

Following the passage of the General Allotment Act, the Indian question was considered solved, but messy realities intervened. A new controversy erupted in California in 1887 over whether Indians in boarding schools should be instructed in English or their native languages. The *Occident* held that "Americans they cannot be in reality or in sympathy so long as they use any other language to the exclusion of our own." When San Francisco minister J. Q. Adams objected, arguing that such a ban would hinder evangelism, the *Occident* insisted that "the Indian," like immigrants, "must give up his foreign or alien distinctions." Because they were American-born, Indians looked to benefit from the rising tide of nativism, but increased concerns over national purity more often encouraged draconian assimilationism.[19]

Allotment did not turn out to be the panacea hoped for by Californians. Nationwide, allotment reduced Indian-held lands by nearly half, from more than 150 million acres in 1881 to less than 78 million acres in 1900. Government agents reported numerous instances of Indians refusing to accept allotments or being unable to establish family farms on land not suited for agriculture.[20] At Round Valley Indian Reservation, Indians received not 160-acre plots, as called for in the General Allotment Act, nor 40-acre plots, as recommended for them by Henry Dawes in 1884, nor even the 30-acre allotments requested by the Commissioner of Indian Affairs in 1886, but 10-acre ones. By the turn of the century, most Round Valley Indians lived on allotments, but their lives had decidedly not improved. "These simple people are still bewildered by their sudden release from the restraints formerly imposed upon them," wrote the reservation agent in 1897, "and, discouraged by constant losses from the [valley's] stock raiders, drugged with the adulterated whisky they are so easily led to swallow, debauched by idleness and dissipation, and defrauded on every hand, they naturally tend to sink into the sloth and vice of their ancient savage state." Unable to support themselves on their small homesteads, Round Valley Indians fell into perpetual debt to local white capitalists, a far cry from the independent Christian farmers envisioned by proponents of allotment.[21]

The same was true for Indians throughout California. In 1906, an agent for the Office of Indian Affairs named C. E. Kelsey investigated the effects of allotment in California. His report indicated that government surveyors from the East, "expecting a soft snap," had found the state's topography "an insolvable enigma." They resorted to creating allotments based on their maps, resulting in more than 300 allotments of "absolute desert" and more than 450 others in the Sierra Nevada mountains that were "absolutely unfit for human habitation." Furthermore, Kelsey noted that "anyone can jump an Indian's allotment, and there seems no practical remedy, or anyone can move the fence over onto the Indian's land, or divert his water, and it is not even a misdemeanor." Ironically, the aspect of the General Allotment Act that benefited California Indians most was its clause granting Indians living on unused federal lands the right to win title to it, allowing the Shasta Indians and other groups to live communally on ancestral homelands.[22]

Agent Kelsey was general secretary of the Northern California Indian Association, an organization of white reformers that formed in 1894 to "help our native race to Christian faith, education, and self-support." The association retained an older model of evangelical uplift, but other organizations that emerged in the early twentieth century—including the Indian Board of Cooperation, the Mission Indian Federation, and the Society of Northern California Indians—focused more on improving the physical conditions of Indians' lives than saving their souls. These new reformers followed in the tradition of lapsed Congregationalist writer Helen Hunt Jackson, whose activism in the early 1880s on behalf of southern California Indians had focused on material rather than spiritual uplift. California Indians themselves played active roles in these Progressive-era organizations, especially the Mission Indian Federation, with its call for "human rights and home rule."[23]

Evangelical-minded reformers also remained active in California. J. L. Burchard, discredited face of the peace policy, stayed involved in Indian mission work long after resigning from Round Valley in 1876. He spent the 1890s working as a missionary to Indians near Ukiah City, preaching the gospel, teaching English, officiating marriages, and promoting temperance. Now in his early seventies, Burchard wrote an article for a Ukiah City newspaper in 1896 arguing that many Indians were well on their way to Christian civilization. "The Indian race has produced some of the greatest intellects on earth," he wrote. He insisted that California Indians were no exception: "I do not hesitate to affirm that no race of people in the same length of time has made greater advancement in civilization." Invoking Acts 17:26, he concluded with a call for Christian sympathy and outreach: "They are our fellow-men, our brothers, made of the one blood of which was made all races of men who dwell upon the face of the earth. We are fortunate; they are unfortunate. They are weak; we are strong. They are ignorant; we are educated. They are poor; we are rich."[24]

Proselytizing and paternalistic, Burchard was a vestige of a vanishing era of racial reform, but the heart of his argument—the idea that beliefs and practices rather than racial stock determined social position—did not die with his generation. By the 1890s, ideas of human universalism and mutability, in opposition to racial determinism, were increasingly voiced by secular thinkers and reformers. The Americanization movement, a nationwide campaign with a strong component in the West, sought to assimilate immigrants through language and civic education. Although most Americanizers were also nativists, and few were able to overcome their racial and ethnic preconceptions, the movement sprang from an optimistic belief that people could change. In its purest form, the Americanization movement insisted that environment—not biology—determined one's path in life.[25]

Meanwhile, a growing faction of social scientists was attacking biological determinism with the concept of "culture." In 1911, Franz Boas published *The Mind of Primitive Man,* a culmination of the more than two decades he had spent refuting racial science. Boas argued that historical and social forces rather than race or heredity shaped human lives. Boas's student Alfred L. Kroeber took the idea of culture a step further in his writings for *American Anthropologist* and other publications in the early twentieth century. Based on his fieldwork among northern California Indians, Kroeber insisted that biology played no role in shaping culture. In the University of California's newly founded anthropology department, Kroeber worked alongside linguist Pliny Earle Goddard, a former Quaker missionary to the Hupa Indians in northwestern California, a demonstration of how much missionaries and social scientists shared in the early twentieth century. The idea of culture advanced by early anthropologists and sociologists helped turn American intellectuals away from hard-line racial science toward cultural relativism. By the 1940s, the tide would turn against scientific racism in the United States.[26]

California's early religious reformers helped lay the groundwork for this transformation of race. During the immediate post–Civil War period, a vocal subset of white, Indian, and Chinese Protestants had fought the idea that biology set a person's fate. They offered an alternate vision of difference based on the assimilation of outsiders that ultimately proved more flexible and better suited to modern America. J. L. Burchard, Otis Gibson, and their generation of church leaders, together with Charles Munsell, Jee Gam, and the hundreds of other Indian and Chinese men and women who joined Christian churches in California during the postbellum era, had tried to demonstrate the fallacy of racial determinism. Those white ministers' turn toward Christian white supremacy in the 1880s reveals the powerful, perhaps indelible, stain of race in American politics and culture.

The rise and fall of their movement also demonstrates Christianity's potential to both fight and justify racism, to erase barriers and to further divide. The terms of the debates would change, but Christian discourse would remain intertwined with American formulations of race throughout the twentieth century and beyond. Today, talk of "heathens" and "pagans" has largely vanished from public political culture, but interwoven notions of religion and race continue to inform battles over immigration, civil rights, "terrorism," war, and the shifting line between citizen and alien.

NOTES

List of Abbreviations

ACALA: Archival Center, Archdiocese of Los Angeles, Mission Hills

AMAR: American Missionary Association Records, California Microfilm, Amistad Research Center, Tulane University, New Orleans

BL: Bancroft Library, University of California, Berkeley

PCUSA-BFMSF: Presbyterian Church U.S.A. Board of Foreign Missions Secretaries' Files, Presbyterian Historical Society, Philadelphia

PSR: Pacific School of Religion, Berkeley

RBIA-NARA-SB: Records of the Bureau of Indian Affairs, Record Group 75, National Archives and Records Administration, San Bruno

RBIA-NARA-W: Records of the Bureau of Indian Affairs, Record Group 75, National Archives and Records Administration, Washington, D.C.

INTRODUCTION

1   Noah Webster, *An American Dictionary of the English Language* (New York: Harper & Brothers, 1848), 484, s.v. "heathen." On the complex meanings of this term, see Sylvester A. Johnson, *The Myth of Ham in Nineteenth-Century American Christianity: Race, Heathens, and the People of God* (New York: Palgrave Macmillan, 2004), 135; and Jennifer C. Snow, *Protestant Missionaries, Asian Immigrants, and Ideologies of Race in America, 1850–1924* (New York: Routledge, 2007), 2–3. Following T. H. Marshall, Judith N. Shklar, and others, I view citizenship as a broad category comprising not just legal and political rights but also civil, social, and economic ones; see T. H. Marshall, *Citizenship and Social Class, and Other Essays* (Cambridge: Cambridge University Press, 1950); and Judith N. Shklar, *American Citizenship: The Quest for Inclusion* (Cambridge, Mass.: Harvard University Press, 1991).

2   Moncure D. Conway, "Wendell Phillips," *Fortnightly Review* 14 (1870): 73.

3   Those in the southwest who were judged to be "Indians" did not receive the benefits of citizenship that those deemed "Mexicans" enjoyed. For overviews of race in the nineteenth-century West, see Richard White, "Race Relations in the

185

American West," *American Quarterly* 38 (1986): 396–416; Sarah Deutsch, "Land of Enclaves: Race Relations in the West, 1865–1990," in *Under an Open Sky: Rethinking America's Western Past,* ed. William Cronon, George Miles, and Jay Gitlin (New York: W. W. Norton, 1992), 110–31; and Elliott West, "Reconstructing Race," *Western Historical Quarterly* 34 (2003): 7–26. For religion, see Gary Topping, "Religion in the West," *Journal of American Culture* 3 (1980): 330–50; *Religion and Society in the American West: Historical Essays,* ed. Carl Guarneri and David Alvarez (Lanham, Md.: University Press of America, 1987); Sandra Sizer Frankiel, "California and the Southwest," in *Encyclopedia of the American Religious Experience,* ed. Charles H. Lippy and Peter W. Williams, 3 vols. (New York: Scribner, 1988), 3:1509–23; D. Michael Quinn, "Religion in the American West," in *Under an Open Sky,* ed. Cronon, Miles, and Gitlin, 145–66; Ferenc Szasz and Margaret Connell Szasz, "Religion and Spirituality," in *The Oxford History of the American West,* ed. Clyde A. Milner II, Carol A. O'Connor, and Martha A. Sandweiss (New York: Oxford University Press, 1994), 359–91; Patricia O'Connell Killen, "Geography, Denominations, and the Human Spirit: A Decade of Studies on Religion in the Western United States," *Religious Studies Review* 21 (1995): 277–84; Laurie F. Maffly-Kipp, "Eastward Ho!: American Religion from the Perspective of the Pacific Rim," in *Retelling U.S. Religious History,* ed. Thomas A. Tweed (Berkeley: University of California Press, 1997), 127–48; Ferenc Morton Szasz, *Religion in the Modern American West* (Tucson: University of Arizona Press, 2000); and Philip Goff, "Religion in the American West," in *A Companion to the American West,* ed. William Deverell (Malden, Mass.: Blackwell, 2004), 286–303.

4   On California in the 1850s, see Leonard Pitt, *The Decline of the Californios: A Social History of the Spanish-Speaking Californians, 1846–1890* (Berkeley: University of California Press, 1966); George Harwood Phillips, *Chiefs and Challengers: Indian Resistance and Cooperation in Southern California* (Berkeley: University of California Press, 1975); Rudolph M. Lapp, *Blacks in Gold Rush California* (New Haven, Conn.: Yale University Press, 1977); Richard H. Peterson, "Anti-Mexican Nativism in California, 1848–1853: A Study of Cultural Conflict," *Southern California Quarterly* 62 (1980): 309–27; Lynwood Carranco and Estle Beard, *Genocide and Vendetta: The Round Valley Wars of Northern California* (Norman: University of Oklahoma Press, 1981); James J. Rawls, *Indians of California: The Changing Image* (Norman: University of Oklahoma Press, 1984); Albert L. Hurtado, *Indian Survival on the California Frontier* (New Haven, Conn.: Yale University Press, 1988); Douglas Monroy, *Thrown among Strangers: The Making of Mexican Culture in Frontier California* (Berkeley: University of California Press, 1990); Tomás Almaguer, *Racial Fault Lines: The Historical Origins of White Supremacy in California* (Berkeley: University of California Press, 1994); Lisbeth Haas, *Conquests and Historical Identities in California, 1769–1936* (Berkeley: University of California Press, 1995); James A. Sandos, "'Because he is a liar and a thief': Conquering the Residents of 'Old' California, 1850–1880," in *Rooted in Barbarous Soil: People, Culture, and Community in Gold Rush California,* ed. Kevin Starr and Richard J. Orsi (Berkeley: University of California Press, 2000), 86–112; William B. Secrest, *When the Great Spirit Died: The Destruction of the California Indians, 1850–1860* (Sanger, Calif.: Word Dancer Press, 2003); Miroslava Chávez-García,

Negotiating Conquest: Gender and Power in California, 1770s to 1880s (Tucson: University of Arizona Press, 2004); Benjamin Madley, "California's Yuki Indians: Defining Genocide in American Indian History," *Western Historical Quarterly* 39 (2008): 303–32; William Deverell, "The 1850s," in *A Companion to California History,* ed. William Deverell and David Igler (Malden, Mass.: Wiley-Blackwell, 2008), 161–74; and William J. Bauer Jr., *We Were All Like Migrant Workers Here: Work, Community, and Memory on California's Round Valley Reservation, 1850–1941* (Chapel Hill: University of North Carolina Press, 2009), 30–57.

5   San Francisco *Daily Evening Bulletin,* 29 June 1857, 2.

6   Stephen Powers, "Aborigines of California: An Indo-Chinese Study," *Atlantic Monthly* 33 (March 1874): 313–23; Nicholas De Genova, "Introduction: Latino and Asian Racial Formations at the Frontiers of U.S. Nationalism," in *Racial Transformations: Latinos and Asians Remaking the United States,* ed. De Genova (Durham, N.C.: Duke University Press, 2006), 8. Although details varied—Powers, for example, believed that only Californian and possibly Latin American Indians were related to the Chinese—this notion was commonplace; see, for example, William Speer, *China and California: Their Relations, Past and Present* (San Francisco: Marvin & Hitchcock, 1853), 3; Arthur B. Stout, *Chinese Immigration and the Physiological Causes of the Decay of a Nation* (San Francisco: Agnew & Deffebach, 1862), 11; Samuel Kneeland, *The Wonders of the Yosemite Valley, and of California,* 3rd ed. (Boston: Alexander Moore, 1872), 53; Stephen Powers, "The California Aborigines," *Proceedings of the California Academy of Sciences* 5 (1873–74): 392–96; and Charles Wolcott Brooks, *Early Migrations: Origin of the Chinese Race* (San Francisco: California Academy of Sciences, 1876).

7   Lai Chun-chuen, *Remarks of the Chinese Merchants of San Francisco, upon Governor Bigler's Message, and Some Common Objections* (San Francisco: Whitton, Towne, 1855), 5; K. Scott Wong, "Cultural Defenders and Brokers: Chinese Responses to the Anti-Chinese Movement," in *Claiming America: Constructing Chinese American Identities during the Exclusion Era,* ed. K. Scott Wong and Sucheng Chan (Philadelphia: Temple University Press, 1998), 16–17.

8   On cultural perceptions of the Chinese, see Stuart Creighton Miller, *The Unwelcome Immigrant: The American Image of the Chinese, 1785–1882* (Berkeley: University of California Press, 1969); Ronald T. Takaki, *Iron Cages: Race and Culture in Nineteenth-Century America* (New York: Knopf, 1979); *The Coming Man: 19th Century American Perceptions of the Chinese,* ed. Philip P. Choy, Lorraine Dong, and Marlon K. Hom (Seattle: University of Washington Press, 1994); Robert G. Lee, *Orientals: Asian Americans in Popular Culture* (Philadelphia: Temple University Press, 1999); John Kuo Wei Tchen, *New York before Chinatown: Orientalism and the Shaping of American Culture, 1776–1882* (Baltimore: Johns Hopkins University Press, 1999); Najia Aarim-Heriot, *Chinese Immigrants, African Americans, and Racial Anxiety in the United States, 1848–82* (Urbana: University of Illinois Press, 2003); and Linda Frost, *Never One Nation: Freaks, Savages, and Whiteness in U.S. Popular Culture, 1850–1877* (Minneapolis: University of Minnesota Press, 2005). On Indians, see Roy Harvey Pearce, *Savagism and Civilization: A Study of the*

Indian and the American Mind (Baltimore: Johns Hopkins Press, 1967); Robert F. Berkhofer, *The White Man's Indian: Images of the American Indian from Columbus to the Present* (New York: Knopf, 1978); Richard Drinnon, *Facing West: The Metaphysics of Indian-Hating and Empire-Building* (Minneapolis: University of Minnesota Press, 1980); Brian W. Dippie, *The Vanishing American: White Attitudes and U.S. Indian Policy* (Middletown, Conn.: Wesleyan University Press, 1982); Helen Carr, *Inventing the American Primitive: Politics, Gender, and the Representation of Native American Literary Traditions, 1789–1936* (New York: New York University Press, 1996); Susan Scheckel, *The Insistence of the Indian: Race and Nationalism in Nineteenth-Century American Culture* (Princeton, N.J.: Princeton University Press, 1998); Philip J. Deloria, *Playing Indian* (New Haven, Conn.: Yale University Press, 1998); Sherry L. Smith, *Reimagining Indians: Native Americans through Anglo Eyes, 1880–1940* (New York: Oxford University Press, 2000); Shari M. Huhndorf, *Going Native: Indians in the American Cultural Imagination* (Ithaca, N.Y.: Cornell University Press, 2001); and Laura M. Stevens, *The Poor Indians: British Missionaries, Native Americans, and Colonial Sensibility* (Philadelphia: University of Pennsylvania Press, 2004).

9   Alexander Saxton, *The Indispensable Enemy: Labor and the Anti-Chinese Movement in California* (Berkeley: University of California Press, 1971); see also Elmer Clarence Sandmeyer, *The Anti-Chinese Movement in California* (Urbana: University of Illinois Press, 1939); Gwendolyn Mink, *Old Labor and New Immigrants in American Political Development: Union, Party, and State, 1875–1920* (Ithaca, N.Y.: Cornell University Press, 1986); and Almaguer, *Racial Fault Lines.* This is not to overlook the work of those scholars who have emphasized cultural elements, listed in note 8.

10   For scholarship on African Americans and/or the South, see note 11. For broader theoretical or comparative perspectives on race and religion, see *Religion and the Creation of Race and Ethnicity,* ed. Craig R. Prentiss (New York: New York University Press, 2003); *Race, Nation, and Religion in the Americas,* ed. Henry Goldschmidt and Elizabeth McAlister (New York: Oxford University Press, 2004); Christine Rosen, *Preaching Eugenics: Religious Leaders and the American Eugenics Movement* (New York: Oxford University Press, 2004); Henry Goldschmidt, *Race and Religion among the Chosen Peoples of Crown Heights* (New Brunswick, N.J.: Rutgers University Press, 2006); Eric L. Goldstein, *The Price of Whiteness: Jews, Race, and American Identity* (Princeton, N.J.: Princeton University Press, 2006); Colin Kidd, *The Forging of Races: Race and Scripture in the Protestant Atlantic World, 1600–2000* (New York: Cambridge University Press, 2006); Snow, *Protestant Missionaries, Asian Immigrants, and Ideologies of Race in America*; Nancy D. Wadsworth, "Reconciling Fractures: The Intersection of Race and Religion in United States Political Development," in *Race and American Political Development,* ed. Joseph E. Lowndes, Julie Novkov, and Dorian T. Warren (New York: Routledge, 2008), 312–36; "Forum: American Religion and 'Whiteness,'" *Religion and American Culture: A Journal of Interpretation* 19 (2009): 1–35; and Derek Chang, *Citizens of a Christian Nation: Evangelical Missions and the Problem of Race in the Nineteenth Century* (Philadelphia: University of Pennsylvania Press, 2010).

11   The overwhelming majority of studies of religion and race in the nineteenth-century United States have focused on either African Americans, the South, or both; see especially H. Shelton Smith, *In His Image, But . . . : Racism in Southern Religion, 1780–1910* (Durham, N.C.: Duke University Press, 1972); Eugene Genovese, *Roll, Jordan, Roll: The World the Slaves Made* (New York: Pantheon Books, 1974); Thomas Virgil Peterson, *Ham and Japheth: The Mythic World of Whites in the Antebellum South* (Metuchen, N.J.: Scarecrow Press, 1978); Albert Raboteau, *Slave Religion: The "Invisible Institution" in the Antebellum South* (New York: Oxford University Press, 1978); *Masters and Slaves in the House of the Lord: Race and Religion in the American South, 1740–1870*, ed. John B. Boles (Lexington: University Press of Kentucky, 1988); Forrest G. Wood, *The Arrogance of Faith: Christianity and Race in America* (New York: Knopf, 1990); Ralph E. Luker, *The Social Gospel in Black and White: American Racial Reform, 1885–1912* (Chapel Hill: University of North Carolina Press, 1991); Mitchell Snay, *Gospel of Disunion: Religion and Separatism in the Antebellum South* (New York: Cambridge University Press, 1993); David B. Chesebrough, *Clergy Dissent in the Old South, 1830–1865* (Carbondale: Southern Illinois University Press, 1996); Christine Leigh Heyrman, *Southern Cross: The Beginnings of the Bible Belt* (New York: Knopf, 1997); Eugene D. Genovese, *A Consuming Fire: The Fall of the Confederacy in the Mind of the White Christian South* (Athens: University of Georgia Press, 1998); Joan L. Bryant, "Race and Religion in Nineteenth-Century America," in *Perspectives on American Religion and Culture,* ed. Peter W. Williams (Malden, Mass.: Blackwell, 1999), 246–58; Eddie S. Glaude Jr., *Exodus!: Religion, Race, and Nation in Early Nineteenth-Century Black America* (Chicago: University of Chicago Press, 2000); John Patrick Daly, *When Slavery Was Called Freedom: Evangelicalism, Proslavery, and the Causes of the Civil War* (Lexington: University Press of Kentucky, 2002); Stephen R. Haynes, *Noah's Curse: The Biblical Justification of American Slavery* (New York: Oxford University Press, 2002); James M. O'Toole, *Passing for White: Race, Religion, and the Healy Family, 1820–1920* (Amherst: University of Massachusetts Press, 2002); Johnson, *The Myth of Ham in Nineteenth-Century American Christianity;* James B. Bennett, *Religion and the Rise of Jim Crow in New Orleans* (Princeton, N.J.: Princeton University Press, 2005); Edward J. Blum, *Reforging the White Republic: Race, Religion, and American Nationalism, 1865–1898* (Baton Rouge: Louisiana State University Press, 2005); Paul Harvey, *Freedom's Coming: Religious Culture and the Shaping of the South from the Civil War through the Civil Rights Era* (Chapel Hill: University of North Carolina Press, 2005); Curtis J. Evans, *The Burden of Black Religion* (New York: Oxford University Press, 2008); John M. Giggie, *After Redemption: Jim Crow and the Transformation of African American Religion in the Delta, 1875–1915* (New York: Oxford University Press, 2008); Charles F. Irons, *The Origins of Proslavery Christianity: White and Black Evangelicals in Colonial and Antebellum Virginia* (Chapel Hill: University of North Carolina Press, 2008); Mark A. Noll, *God and Race in American Politics: A Short History* (Princeton, N.J.: Princeton University Press, 2008); and Laurie F. Maffly-Kipp, *Setting Down the Sacred Past: African-American Race Histories* (Cambridge, Mass.: Harvard University Press, 2010).

12   Although the appearance of *Race, Religion, Region: Landscapes of Encounter in the American West*, ed. Fay Botham and Sara M. Patterson (Tucson: University of Arizona Press, 2006), suggests that western historians' interest in interactions of religion and race may be growing, studies have so far been scant, in part because scholars of nineteenth-century Native American and Asian American history have often de-emphasized religious change or viewed any adoption of Christianity as a straightforward form of assimilation; in Robert F. Berkhofer's classic formulation, "to become truly Christian was to become anti-Indian"; Robert F. Berkhofer, *Salvation and the Savage: An Analysis of Protestant Missions and American Indian Response, 1787–1862* (Lexington: University of Kentucky Press, 1965), 122; for a more recent example, see Willard Hughes Rollings, *Unaffected by the Gospel: Osage Resistance to the Christian Invasion (1673–1906): A Cultural Victory* (Albuquerque: University of New Mexico Press, 2004). Similarly, Gunther Barth wrote that Chinese immigrants in America "clung tenaciously to their culture"; *Bitter Strength: A History of the Chinese in the United States, 1850–1870* (Cambridge, Mass.: Harvard University Press, 1964), 5. More recently, Yong Chen's ambitious *Chinese San Francisco, 1850–1943: A Trans-Pacific Community* (Stanford, Calif.: Stanford University Press, 2000) devotes little attention to Chinese American Christians. For histories that do emphasize nineteenth-century adoptions and adaptations of Christianity, see especially Wesley Stephen Woo, "Protestant Work among the Chinese in the San Francisco Bay Area, 1850–1920" (PhD diss., Graduate Theological Union, 1984); Woo, "Presbyterian Mission: Christianizing and Civilizing the Chinese in Nineteenth Century California," *American Presbyterian* 68 (1990): 167–78; Woo, "Chinese Protestants in the San Francisco Bay Area," in *Entry Denied: Exclusion and the Chinese Community in America, 1882–1943*, ed. Sucheng Chan (Philadelphia: Temple University Press, 1991), 213–45; Timothy Tseng, "Ministry at Arms' Length: Asian Americans in the Racial Ideology of American Mainline Protestants, 1882–1952" (PhD diss., Union Theological Seminary, Columbia University, 1994); Clyde Holler, *Black Elk's Religion: The Sun Dance and Lakota Catholicism* (Syracuse, N.Y.: Syracuse University Press, 1995); Ronald Niezen, *Spirit Wars: Native North American Religions in the Age of Nation Building* (Berkeley: University of California Press, 2000); Bonnie Sue Lewis, *Creating Christian Indians: Native Clergy in the Presbyterian Church* (Norman: University of Oklahoma Press, 2003); Gregory E. Smoak, *Ghost Dances and Identity: Prophetic Religion and American Indian Ethnogenesis in the Nineteenth Century* (Berkeley: University of California Press, 2006); Tisa Wenger, *We Have a Religion: The 1920s Pueblo Indian Dance Controversy and American Religious Freedom* (Chapel Hill: University of North Carolina Press, 2009); Chang, *Citizens of a Christian Nation*; and *Native Americans, Christianity, and the Reshaping of the American Religious Landscape*, ed. Joel W. Martin and Mark A. Nicholas (Chapel Hill: University of North Carolina Press, 2010).

13   Overviews of Reconstruction historiography are plentiful; see Bernard A. Weisberger, "The Dark and Bloody Ground of Reconstruction Historiography," *Journal of Southern History* 25 (1959): 427–47; Richard O. Curry, "The Civil

War and Reconstruction, 1861–1877: A Critical Overview of Recent Trends and Interpretations," *Civil War History* 20 (1974): 215–38; John Hope Franklin, "Mirror for Americans: A Century of Reconstruction History," *American Historical Review* 85 (1980): 1–14; Eric Foner, "Reconstruction Revisited," *Reviews in American History* 10 (1980): 82–100; Michael W. Fitzgerald, "Political Reconstruction, 1865–1877," in *A Companion to the American South*, ed. John B. Boles (Malden, Mass.: Blackwell, 2002), 284–302; Michael Perman, "The Politics of Reconstruction," in *A Companion to the Civil War and Reconstruction*, ed. Lacy K. Ford (Malden, Mass.: Blackwell, 2002), 323–41; *Reconstructions: New Perspectives on the Postbellum United States*, ed. Thomas J. Brown (New York: Oxford University Press, 2006); and Pamela Brandwein, "Reconstruction, Race, and Revolution," in *Race and American Political Development*, ed. Lowndes, Novkov, and Warren, 125–54. Reconstruction historians' lack of attention to Indian Territory is noted in Claudio Saunt, "The Paradox of Freedom: Tribal Sovereignty and Emancipation during the Reconstruction of Indian Territory," *Journal of Southern History* 70 (2004): 63–94.

14   Elliott West, "Reconstructing Race"; Heather Cox Richardson, "North and West of Reconstruction," in *Reconstructions*, ed. Brown, 69; Heather Cox Richardson, *West from Appomattox: The Reconstruction of America after the Civil War* (New Haven, Conn.: Yale University Press, 2007); William Deverell, "Convalescence and California," *Southern California Quarterly* 90 (2008): 1–26; Elliott West, *The Last Indian War: The Nez Perce Story* (New York: Oxford University Press, 2009); David Prior, "Civilization, Republic, Nation: Contested Keywords, Northern Republicans, and the Forgotten Reconstruction of Mormon Utah," *Civil War History* 56 (2010): 283–310. The phrase "Greater Reconstruction" is West's; "Era of Citizenship" is Richardson's. One earlier study on the West is Eugene H. Berwanger, *The West and Reconstruction* (Urbana: University of Illinois Press, 1981). Aside from Prior's article on Mormonism, none of these works focus on religion, nor do three dissertations that examine how Reconstruction politics played out in California: William Penn Moody, "The Civil War and Reconstruction in California Politics" (PhD diss., UCLA, 1950); Donald Michael Bottoms Jr., "'An Aristocracy of Color': Race and Reconstruction in Post-Gold Rush California" (PhD diss., UCLA, 2005); and Stacey Leigh Smith, "California Bound: Unfree Labor, Race, and the Reconstruction of the Far West, 1848–1870" (PhD diss., University of Wisconsin, Madison, 2008). Two studies of the national anti-Chinese movement that make useful comparisons to the treatment of African Americans are Andrew Gyory, *Closing the Gate: Race, Politics, and the Chinese Exclusion Act* (Chapel Hill: University of North Carolina Press, 1998), 17–59; and Aarim-Heriot, *Chinese Immigrants, African Americans, and Racial Anxiety*.

15   Ellen Carol DuBois, *Feminism and Suffrage: The Emergence of an Independent Women's Movement in America, 1848–1869* (Ithaca, N.Y.: Cornell University Press, 1978), 53–78, 262–302; Dale Baum, "Woman Suffrage and the 'Chinese Question': The Limits of Radical Republicanism in Massachusetts, 1865–1876," *New England Quarterly* 56 (1983): 60–77; Suzanne M. Marilley, *Woman Suffrage and the Origins of Liberal Feminism in the United States, 1820–1920* (Cambridge, Mass.: Harvard University Press, 1996), 66–99; Rebecca Edwards,

Angels in the Machinery: Gender in American Party Politics from the Civil War to the Progressive Era (New York: Oxford University Press, 1997); Laura F. Edwards, *Gendered Strife and Confusion: The Political Culture of Reconstruction* (Urbana: University of Illinois Press, 1997); LeeAnn Whites, *Gender Matters: Civil War, Reconstruction, and the Making of the New South* (New York: Palgrave Macmillan, 2005).

16   Eric Foner, *Reconstruction: America's Unfinished Revolution, 1863–1877* (New York: Harper & Row, 1988), 255.

17   Scholarship on the role of religion and race in the colonization of North America is vast. Essential works include Winthrop D. Jordan, *White over Black: American Attitudes toward the Negro, 1550–1812* (Chapel Hill: University of North Carolina Press, 1968); Mechal Sobel, *The World They Made Together: Black and White Values in Eighteenth-Century Virginia* (Princeton, N.J.: Princeton University Press, 1987); David J. Weber, *The Spanish Frontier in North America* (New Haven, Conn.: Yale University Press, 1992); Michael A. Gomez, *Exchanging Our Country Marks: The Transformation of African Identities in the Colonial and Antebellum South* (Chapel Hill: University of North Carolina Press, 1998); Jorge Cañizares-Esguerra, "New Worlds, New Stars: Patriotic Astrology and the Invention of Indian and Creole Bodies in Colonial Spanish America, 1600–1650," *American Historical Review* 104 (1999): 33–68; Karen Ordahl Kupperman, *Indians and English: Facing Off in Early America* (Ithaca, N.Y.: Cornell University Press, 2000); Joyce E. Chaplin, *Subject Matter: Technology, the Body, and Science on the Anglo-American Frontier, 1500–1676* (Cambridge, Mass.: Harvard University Press, 2001); George M. Fredrickson, *Racism: A Short History* (Princeton, N.J.: Princeton University Press, 2002); John Wood Sweet, *Bodies Politic: Negotiating Race in the American North, 1730–1830* (Baltimore: Johns Hopkins University Press, 2003); Stevens, *The Poor Indians*; David J. Silverman, *Faith and Boundaries: Colonists, Christianity, and Community among the Wampanoag Indians of Martha's Vineyard, 1600–1871* (New York: Cambridge University Press, 2005); Rebecca A. Goetz, "From Potential Christians to Hereditary Heathens: Religion and Race in the Early Chesapeake, 1590–1740" (PhD diss., Harvard University, 2006); Kidd, *The Forging of Races*; Nancy Shoemaker, *A Strange Likeness: Becoming Red and White in Eighteenth-Century North America* (New York: Oxford University Press, 2004); Audrey Smedley, *Race in North America: Origin and Evolution of a Worldview*, 3rd ed. (Boulder, Colo.: Westview Press, 2007); Linford D. Fisher, "Traditionary Religion: The Great Awakening and the Shaping of Native Cultures in Southern New England, 1736–1776" (PhD diss., Harvard, 2008); María Elena Martínez, *Genealogical Fictions: Limpieza de Sangre, Religion, and Gender in Colonial Mexico* (Stanford, Calif.: Stanford University Press, 2008); Nicholas Beasley, *Christian Ritual and the Creation of British Slave Societies, 1650–1780* (Athens: University of Georgia Press, 2009); David J. Silverman, "The Curse of God: An Idea and Its Origin among the Indians of New York's Revolutionary Frontier," *William and Mary Quarterly* 66 (2009): 495–534; Katherine Grandjean, "'Our Fellow-Creaturs & our Fellow-Christians': Race and Religion in Eighteenth-Century Narratives of Indian Crime," *American Quarterly* 62 (2010): 925–50; and

David J. Silverman, *Red Brethren: The Brothertown and Stockbridge Indians and the Problem of Race in Early America* (Ithaca, N.Y.: Cornell University Press, 2010).

18   Along with many of the sources cited in note 11, see William Stanton, *The Leopard's Spots: Scientific Attitudes toward Race in America, 1815–59* (Chicago: University of Chicago Press, 1960); Reginald Horsman, *Race and Manifest Destiny: The Origins of Racial Anglo-Saxonism* (Cambridge, Mass.: Harvard University Press, 1981); Michael Banton, "The Classification of Races in Europe and North America, 1700–1850," *International Social Science Journal* 111 (1987): 45–60; Mia Bay, *The White Image in the Black Mind: African-American Ideas about White People, 1830–1925* (New York: Oxford University Press, 2000); Patrick Minges, "Beneath the Underdog: Race, Religion, and the Trail of Tears," *American Indian Quarterly* 25 (2001): 453–79; Bruce Dain, *A Hideous Monster of the Mind: American Race Theory in the Early Republic* (Cambridge, Mass.: Harvard University Press, 2002); and Ariela J. Gross, *What Blood Won't Tell: A History of Race on Trial in America* (Cambridge, Mass.: Harvard University Press, 2008).

19   *Annual Report of the Presbyterian Board of Foreign Missions* (New York: Presbyterian Board of Foreign Missions, 1868), 37.

CHAPTER ONE

1   John S. Hager, *Fifteenth Amendment to Constitution: Speech of Hon. John S. Hager, of San Francisco, in the Senate of California, January 28th, 1870* (Sacramento, Calif., 1870), 7.

2   Ibid., 9–11; Sacramento *Daily Union,* 26 January 1870, 3.

3   Abraham Lincoln, "Meditation on the Divine Will," in *Collected Works,* ed. Roy P. Basler, 9 vols. (New Brunswick, N.J.: Rutgers University Press, 1953–55), 5:403–4.

4   James H. Moorhead, *American Apocalypse: Yankee Protestants and the Civil War, 1860–1869* (New Haven, Conn.: Yale University Press, 1978); Curtis D. Johnson, *Redeeming America: Evangelicals and the Road to Civil War* (Chicago: Ivan R. Dee, 1993); Mitchell Snay, *Gospel of Disunion: Religion and Separatism in the Antebellum South* (Chapel Hill: University of North Carolina Press, 1993); Daniel W. Stowell, *Rebuilding Zion: The Religious Reconstruction of the South, 1863–1877* (New York: Oxford University Press, 1998); *Religion and the American Civil War,* ed. Randall M. Miller, Harry S. Stout, and Charles Reagan Wilson (New York: Oxford University Press, 1998); Terrie Dopp Aamodt, *Righteous Armies, Holy Cause: Apocalyptic Imagery and the Civil War* (Macon, Ga.: Mercer University Press, 2002); Mark A. Noll, *The Civil War as a Theological Crisis* (Chapel Hill: University of North Carolina Press, 2006); George C. Rable, *God's Almost Chosen Peoples: A Religious History of the American Civil War* (Chapel Hill: University of North Carolina Press, 2010).

5   William Penn Moody, "The Civil War and Reconstruction in California Politics" (PhD diss., UCLA, 1950); Barbara McClung MacVicar, "Southern and Northern Methodism in Civil War California," *California Historical Society Quarterly* 40 (1961): 327–42; Gerald Stanley, "Civil War Politics in California," *Southern California Quarterly* 64 (1982): 115–32.

6   C. V. Anthony, *Fifty Years of Methodism: A History of the Methodist Episcopal Church within the Bounds of the California Annual Conference from 1847 to 1897* (San Francisco: Methodist Book Concern, 1901), 231; MacVicar, "Southern and Northern Methodism in Civil War California," 331; Milton S. Latham, *Remarks of Hon. Milton S. Latham, of California, upon Slavery in the States and Territories* (Washington, D.C.: Government Printing Office, 1860), 11.

7   *A Yankee Trader in the Gold Rush: The Letters of Franklin A. Buck,* ed. Katherine A. White (Boston: Houghton Mifflin, 1930), 187; San Francisco *Pacific Appeal,* 1 November 1862, 2.

8   Thomas Starr King to Henry Whitney Bellows, 30 September 1861, Thomas Starr King Letters to Henry Whitney Bellows, 1858–63, BL, copied from Henry Whitney Bellows Collection, Massachusetts Historical Society, Boston; *A Yankee Trader in the Gold Rush,* ed. White, 189; San Francisco *Pacific Appeal,* 24 August 1867, 1; Clifford Merrill Drury, *William Anderson Scott: "No Ordinary Man"* (Glendale, Calif.: Arthur H. Clark, 1967), 250–67.

9   Howard H. Bell, "Negroes in California, 1849–1859," *Phylon* 28 (1967): 151–60; James A. Fisher, "The Struggle for Negro Testimony in California, 1851–1863," *Southern California Quarterly* 51 (1969): 313–24; Gerald Stanley, "Racism and the Early Republican Party: The 1856 Presidential Election in California," *Pacific Historical Review* 43 (1974): 171–87; Larry George Murphy, "The Church and Black Californians: A Mid-Nineteenth-Century Struggle for Civil Justice," *Foundations* 18 (1975): 165–83; Gerald Stanley, "The Politics of the Antebellum Far West: The Impact of the Slavery and Race Issues in California," *Journal of the West* 16 (1977): 19–26; Stanley, "Slavery and the Origins of the Republican Party in California," *Southern California Quarterly* 40 (1978): 1–16; Stanley, "The Slavery Issue and the Election in California, 1860," *Mid-America* 62 (1980): 35–46; Rudolph M. Lapp and Robert J. Chandler, "The Antiracism of Thomas Starr King," *Southern California Quarterly* 82 (2000): 323–42.

10 James C. Zabriskie, *Speech of Col. Jas. C. Zabriskie, on the Subject of Slavery* (Sacramento, Calif.: Democratic State Journal Office, 1856), 9, 10; George C. Bates, *Address of Geo. C. Bates, Esq., which He Was Prevented from Delivering at Sacramento, April 19th, 1856, by a Mob* (San Francisco, 1856), 16; Winfield J. Davis, *History of Political Conventions in California, 1849–1892* (Sacramento, Calif.: California State Library, 1893), 67; Stanley, "Racism and the Early Republican Party"; Edward Stanly, *Speech of the Hon. Edward Stanly, Delivered at Sacramento, July 17th, 1857* (Sacramento, Calif., 1857), 10; Lincoln, "First Inaugural Address," in *Collected Works,* ed. Basler, 4:263.

11 Caleb T. Fay, *Address Delivered before Washington Council No. 1, Union League of America* (San Francisco: Towne & Bacon, 1864), 13; Davis, *History of Political Conventions in California,* 206; Stanley, "Civil War Politics in California."

12   San Francisco *Pacific Appeal*, 6 August 1863, 3; 15 August 1863, 1; Richard R. Wright, *Centennial Encyclopedia of the African Methodist Episcopal Church* (Philadelphia: Book Concern of the A.M.E. Church, 1916), 237.

13   San Francisco *Pacific Appeal*, 13 September 1862, 2; *Journal of Proceedings of the Third Annual Convention of the Ministers and Lay Delegates of the African Methodist Episcopal Church* (San Francisco: B. F. Sterett, 1863), 22.

14   San Francisco *Pacific Appeal*, 15 August 1863, 1.

15   San Francisco *Pacific Appeal*, 27 February 1864, 2; Philip M. Montesano, "San Francisco Black Churches in the Early 1860s: Political Pressure Group," *California Historical Quarterly* 52 (1973): 145–52; Douglas Henry Daniels, *Pioneer Urbanites: A Social and Cultural History of Black San Francisco* (Philadelphia: Temple University Press, 1980); Leigh Dana Johnsen, "Equal Rights and the 'Heathen Chinee': Black Activism in San Francisco, 1865–1875," *Western Historical Quarterly* 11 (1980): 57–68; Robert J. Chandler, "Friends in Time of Need: Republicans and Black Civil Rights in California during the Civil War Era," *Arizona and the West* 24 (1982): 319–40. On the prevalence of Israelitic rhetoric among African Americans, see Albert J. Raboteau, "African-Americans, Exodus, and the American Israel," in *African American Christianity: Essays in History*, ed. Paul E. Johnson (Berkeley: University of California Press, 1994), 1–17; Eddie S. Glaude Jr., *Exodus!: Religion, Race, and Nation in Early Nineteenth-Century Black America* (Chicago: University of Chicago Press, 2000); and Sylvester A. Johnson, *The Myth of Ham in Nineteenth-Century American Christianity: Race, Heathens, and the People of God* (New York: Palgrave Macmillan, 2004).

16   *Proceedings of the California State Convention of Colored Citizens* (San Francisco: The Elevator, 1865), 80–81, 90, 93.

17   Moody, "The Civil War and Reconstruction in California Politics"; Michael Les Benedict, *A Compromise of Principle: Congressional Republicans and Reconstruction, 1863–1869* (New York: Norton, 1974), 272–73; Gerald Stanley, "'The Whim and Caprice of a Majority in a Petty State': The 1867 Election in California," *Pacific Historian* 24 (1980): 443–55; Robert J. Chandler, "'Anti-Coolie Rabies': The Chinese Issue in California Politics in the 1860s," *Pacific Historian* 28 (1984): 29–42.

18   Bret Harte, *San Francisco in 1866; Being Letters to the Springfield Republican*, ed. George R. Stewart and Edwin S. Fussell (San Francisco: Book Club of California, 1951), 24–25. New York later withdrew its ratification; Ohio first rejected then ratified it; Oregon refused to consider it. California eventually ratified, for symbolic reasons, the Fourteenth Amendment in 1959 and the Fifteenth in 1962.

19   *The Statistics of the Population of the United States* (Washington, D.C.: Government Printing Office, 1870), table 1, 3–8. The Indian population was listed as only 7,241 in the census, but Sherburne Cook estimated their population at 25,000 to 30,000; Sherburne F. Cook, *The Population of the California Indians, 1769–1970* (Berkeley: University of California Press, 1976), 199.

20   People v. Hall, 4 Cal. 399 (1854); F. Michael Higginbotham, *Race Law: Cases, Commentary, and Questions*, 2nd ed. (Durham, N.C.: Carolina Academic

Press, 2005), 45–51; Donald Michael Bottoms Jr., "'An Aristocracy of Color,': Race and Reconstruction in Post-Gold Rush California" (PhD diss., UCLA, 2005), 28–49.

21   Davis, *History of Political Conventions in California*, 265; "The Reconstruction Policy of Congress, as Illustrated in California," 1867, BL.

22   Eugene Casserly, *Speech of Hon. Eugene Casserly, on the Fifteenth Amendment, and the Labor Question* (San Francisco, 1869), 3, 11; San Francisco *Daily Examiner*, 30 March 1866, 2.

23   San Francisco *Daily Examiner*, 13 August 1867, 2; Davis, *History of Political Conventions in California*, 260, 293; Eugene H. Berwanger, *The West and Reconstruction* (Urbana: University of Illinois Press, 1981), 139.

24   On the importance of African Americans' military service in their winning of suffrage, see Christian G. Samito, *Becoming American under Fire: Irish Americans, African Americans, and the Politics of Citizenship during the Civil War Era* (Ithaca, N.Y.: Cornell University Press, 2009).

25   William Higby, *Privileges and Immunities of Citizenship* (Washington, D.C.: Government Printing Office, 1866), 6–7; San Francisco *Daily Evening Bulletin*, 15 March 1862, 3.

26   Davis, *History of Political Conventions in California*, 241; San Francisco *Daily Examiner*, 13 August 1867, 2.

27   George C. Gorham, *Speech Delivered by George C. Gorham of San Francisco, Union Nominee for Governor* (San Francisco: Union State Central Committee, 1867), 12; San Francisco *Daily Alta California*, 1 September 1867, 4; Sacramento *Daily Union*, 14 August 1867, 1; San Francisco *Elevator*, 13 September 1867, 2; Alexander Saxton, *The Indispensable Enemy: Labor and the Anti-Chinese Movement in California* (Berkeley: University of California Press, 1971), 83–84; Stanley, "'The Whim and Caprice of a Majority in a Petty State,'" 454–55; Berwanger, *The West and Reconstruction*, 208.

28   See, for example, *Debates and Proceedings of the Constitutional Convention of the State of California*, vol. 2 (Sacramento, Calif.: State Office, 1880), 654.

29   San Francisco *Pacific Appeal*, 31 August 1867, 2; 17 May 1862, 2; 18 April 1863, 3.

30   San Francisco *Elevator*, 15 December 1865, 2; 11 October 1867, 2; David Johns Hellwig, "The Afro-American and the Immigrant, 1880–1930: A Study of Black Social Thought" (PhD diss., Syracuse University, 1973), 99–118; Arnold Shankman, "Black on Yellow: Afro-Americans View Chinese-Americans, 1850–1935," *Phylon* 39 (1978): 1–17; David J. Hellwig, "Black Reactions to Chinese Immigration and the Anti-Chinese Movement, 1850–1910," *Amerasia* 6 (1979): 25–44; Johnsen, "Equal Rights and the 'Heathen Chinee'"; Frank H. Goodyear, "'Beneath the Shadow of Her Flag': Philip A. Bell's *The Elevator* and the Struggle for Enfranchisement, 1865–1870," *California History* 78 (1999): 26–39; Helen H. Jun, "Black Orientalism: Nineteenth-Century Narratives of Race and U.S. Citizenship," *American Quarterly* 58 (2006): 1047–66.

31   *American Missionary*, December 1865, 277; San Francisco *California Christian Advocate*, 1 August 1867, 2; Sacramento *Daily Union*, 14 July 1867, 3; San Francisco *Daily Examiner*, 30 August 1867, 1.

32   Prior to the 1860s, states rather than the federal government exercised the
      most control in defining citizenship; see William J. Novak, "The Legal Trans-
      formation of Citizenship in Nineteenth-Century America," in *The Democratic
      Experiment: New Directions in American Political History*, ed. Meg Jacobs,
      William J. Novak, and Julian E. Zelizer (Princeton, N.J.: Princeton University
      Press, 2003), 85–119; and Samito, *Becoming American under Fire*, 1–4.

33   Cong. Globe, 39th Cong., 1st Sess. 2890, 2892 (30 May 1866); 40th Cong.,
      3rd Sess. 996 (8 February 1869); James M. McPherson, *The Struggle for
      Equality: Abolitionists and the Negro in the Civil War and Reconstruction*
      (Princeton, N.J.: Princeton University Press, 1964); William Gillette, *The Right
      to Vote: Politics and the Passage of the Fifteenth Amendment* (Baltimore:
      Johns Hopkins University Press, 1965); Benedict, *A Compromise of Principle*;
      Eric Foner, *Reconstruction: America's Unfinished Revolution, 1863–1877* (New
      York: Harper & Row, 1988), 228–80; Andrew Gyory, *Closing the Gate: Race,
      Politics, and the Chinese Exclusion Act* (Chapel Hill: University of North
      Carolina Press, 1998), 17–59; Najia Aarim-Heriot, *Chinese Immigrants,
      African Americans, and Racial Anxiety in the United States, 1848–82*
      (Urbana: University of Illinois Press, 2003), 84–102.

34   Cong. Globe, 40th Cong., 3rd Sess. 979, 989, 990 (8 February 1869).

35   Sacramento *Daily Union*, 3 March 1866, 1; Cong. Globe, 41st Cong., 2nd Sess.
      5151, 5152 (4 July 1870).

36   Ellen Carol DuBois, *Feminism and Suffrage: The Emergence of an Independent
      Women's Movement in America, 1848–1869* (Ithaca, N.Y.: Cornell University
      Press, 1978), 53–78, 262–302; Dale Baum, "Woman Suffrage and the 'Chinese
      Question': The Limits of Radical Republicanism in Massachusetts, 1865–1876,"
      New England Quarterly 56 (1983): 60–77; Foner, *Reconstruction*, 255–56,
      447–48, 472–73; Suzanne M. Marilley, *Woman Suffrage and the Origins of
      Liberal Feminism in the United States, 1820–1920* (Cambridge, Mass.: Harvard
      University Press, 1996), 66–99.

37   Stanley, "The Whim and Caprice of a Majority in a Petty State," 451; Robert J.
      Chandler, "In the Van: Spiritualists as Catalysts for the California Women's
      Suffrage Movement," *California History* 73 (1994): 188–201; Philip J. Ethington,
      *The Public City: The Political Construction of Urban Life in San Francisco,
      1850–1900* (New York: Cambridge University Press, 1994), 209–18; Gayle
      Gullett, *Becoming Citizens: The Emergence and Development of the California
      Women's Movement, 1880–1911* (Urbana: University of Illinois Press, 2000),
      13–15; Rebecca J. Mead, *How the Vote Was Won: Woman Suffrage in the
      Western United States, 1868–1914* (New York: New York University Press,
      2004), 18–25; Linda Frost, *Never One Nation: Freaks, Savages, and Whiteness
      in U.S. Popular Culture, 1850–1877* (Minneapolis: University of Minnesota
      Press, 2005), 165–88.

38   Hager, *Fifteenth Amendment to Constitution*, 8.

39   Sacramento *State Capital Reporter*, 7 March 1868, 3; San Francisco *Pioneer*,
      19 March 1870, 1; Sherilyn Cox Bennion, *Equal to the Occasion: Women Editors
      of the Nineteenth-Century West* (Reno: University of Nevada Press, 1990),
      57–62.

40   San Francisco *Daily Alta California*, 13 July 1869, 1; San Francisco *Saturday Evening Mercury*, 4 September 1869, 1.

41   DuBois, *Feminism and Suffrage*, 53–104; Marilley, *Woman Suffrage and the Origins of Liberal Feminism*, 159–86; Louise Michele Newman, *White Women's Rights: The Racial Origins of Feminism in the United States* (New York: Oxford University Press, 1999); Virginia Scharff, *Twenty Thousand Roads: Women, Movement, and the West* (Berkeley: University of California Press, 2003), 68–92; Mead, *How the Vote Was Won*, 35–52.

42   Cong. Globe, 38th Cong., 2nd Sess. 661 (8 February 1865); 41st Cong., 2nd Sess. 1373 (17 February 1870); Moorhead, *American Apocalypse*, 173–235; Jon C. Teaford, "Toward a Christian Nation: Religion, Law and Justice Strong," *Journal of Presbyterian History* 54 (1976): 422–37; Stowell, *Rebuilding Zion*; Gaines M. Foster, *Moral Reconstruction: Christian Lobbyists and the Federal Legislation of Morality, 1865–1920* (Chapel Hill: University of North Carolina Press, 2002), 27–71; Sarah Barringer Gordon, *The Mormon Question: Polygamy and Constitutional Conflict in Nineteenth-Century America* (Chapel Hill: University of North Carolina Press, 2002); Helen Lefkowitz Horowitz, *Rereading Sex: Battles over Sexual Knowledge and Suppression in Nineteenth-Century America* (New York: Vintage Books, 2003), 359–85; David Prior, "Civilization, Republic, Nation: Contested Keywords, Northern Republicans, and the Forgotten Reconstruction of Mormon Utah," *Civil War History* 56 (2010): 283–310.

43   Victor B. Howard, *Religion and the Radical Republican Movement, 1860–1870* (Lexington: University Press of Kentucky, 1990); Mark Wahlgren Summers, "'With a Sublime Faith in God, and in Republican Liberty,'" in *Vale of Tears: New Essays on Religion and Reconstruction*, ed. Edward J. Blum and W. Scott Poole (Macon, Ga.: Mercer University Press, 2005), 112–32; Edward J. Blum, *Reforging the White Republic: Race, Religion, and American Nationalism, 1865–1898* (Baton Rouge: Louisiana State University Press, 2005), 38–49.

44   New York *Times*, 2 January 1869, 1; Cong. Globe, 41st Cong., 2nd Sess. 5155 (4 July 1870).

45   Cong. Globe, 41st Cong., 2nd Sess. 5155, 5162 (4 July 1870).

46   Cong. Globe, 41st Cong., 2nd Sess. 5168–69, 5172 (4 July 1870); *Report . . . on the Effect of the Fourteenth Amendment to the Constitution upon the Indian Tribes of the Country*, 14 December 1870, Congressional Serial Set vol. 1443, 41st Cong., 3rd Sess., report 268 (Washington, D.C.: Government Printing Office, 1870), 1; George Beck, "The Fourteenth Amendment as Related to Tribal Indians: Section I, 'Subject to the Jurisdiction Thereof' and Section II, 'Excluding Indians Not Taxed,'" *American Indian Culture and Research Journal* 28 (2004): 37–68. At the state and local levels, matters were less clear. A very small number of Chinese immigrants, such as the "Siamese twins" Chang and Eng Bunker and the physician Yung Wing, managed to naturalize in the mid-nineteenth century despite their ineligibility under the Naturalization Act of 1790; see Edmund H. Worthy, "Yung Wing in America," *Pacific Historical Review* 34 (1965): 265–87; and John Kuo Wei Tchen, *New York before*

Chinatown: Orientalism and the Shaping of American Culture, 1776–1882 (Baltimore: Johns Hopkins University Press, 1999), 76, 136, 231–32, 247. The confusing and ambiguous political status of Indians during the nineteenth century meant that a small number could at times claim citizenship and, less often, the right to vote; see Jeanette Wolfley, "Jim Crow, Indian Style: The Disenfranchisement of Native Americans," *American Indian Law Review* 16 (1991): 167–202; Ann Marie Plane and Gregory Button, "The Massachusetts Indian Enfranchisement Act: Ethnic Contest in Historical Context, 1849–1869," *Ethnohistory* 40 (1993): 586–618; and Daniel McCool, Susan M. Olson, and Jennifer L. Robinson, *Native Vote: American Indians, the Voting Rights Act, and the Right to Vote* (New York: Cambridge University Press, 2007), 2–6.

47   Sacramento *Daily Union,* 19 January 1870, 3; 29 January 1870, 1; San Francisco *Daily Examiner,* 30 March 1866, 2; "Memorial and Joint Resolution in Relation to Chinese Immigration to the State of California," doc. 26, *Appendix to Journals of Senate and Assembly, of the Seventeenth Session of the Legislature of the State of California,* vol. 2 (Sacramento, Calif., 1868), 3–4.

48   Elmer Clarence Sandmeyer, *The Anti-Chinese Movement in California* (Urbana: University of Illinois Press, 1939); Gunther Barth, *Bitter Strength: A History of the Chinese in the United States, 1850–1870* (Cambridge, Mass.: Harvard University Press, 1964); Saxton, *The Indispensable Enemy*; Dan Caldwell, "The Negroization of the Chinese Stereotype in California," *Southern California Quarterly* 53 (1971): 123–31; Tomás Almaguer, *Racial Fault Lines: The Historical Origins of White Supremacy in California* (Berkeley: University of California Press, 1994), 153–82; Charles J. McClain, *In Search of Equality: The Chinese Struggle against Discrimination in Nineteenth-Century America* (Berkeley: University of California Press, 1994); Judy Yung, *Unbound Feet: A Social History of Chinese Women in San Francisco* (Berkeley: University of California Press, 1995), 15–51; George Anthony Peffer, *If They Don't Bring Their Women Here: Chinese Female Immigration before Exclusion* (Urbana: University of Illinois Press, 1999); Yong Chen, *Chinese San Francisco, 1850–1943: A Trans-Pacific Community* (Stanford, Calif.: Stanford University Press, 2000), 45–141.

49   Presbyterian Church in the U.S.A., Mission to the Chinese in California, "Form of Incorporation of the Chinese Mission for the State of California, under the Charge of the Rev. William Speer," 1852, BL; William Speer, *China and California: Their Relations, Past and Present* (San Francisco: Marvin & Hitchcock, 1853); San Francisco *Oriental,* 1855–56; William Speer, *An Humble Plea, Addressed to the Legislature of California, in Behalf of the Immigrants from the Empire of China to this State* (San Francisco: The Oriental, 1856); William Speer, *Answer to Objections to Chinese Testimony, and Appeal for their Protection by our Laws* (San Francisco, 1857); Earle R. Forrest, "Dr. William Speer, Missionary to the Chinese in China and San Francisco," *Westerners Brand Book* 9 (1953): 99–116.

50   San Francisco *Pacific,* 14 September 1855, 2; William Speer, *The Oldest and the Newest Empire: China and the United States* (Hartford, Conn.: S. S. Scranton, 1870), 591.

51   A. W. Loomis to Walter Lowrie, 3 January 1860, 30 January 1860, folder 3, box 45, PCUSA-BFMSF, 1829–95; San Francisco *Pacific Churchman*, 24 October 1867, 156; John Archbald, *On the Contact of Races: Considered Especially with Relation to the Chinese Question* (San Francisco: Towne & Bacon, 1860); San Francisco *Pacific*, 30 January 1862, 2; 12 December 1865, 2.

52   Arthur B. Stout, *Chinese Immigration and the Physiological Causes of the Decay of a Nation* (San Francisco: Agnew & Deffebach, 1862), 6–9.

53   San Francisco *Daily Alta California*, 22 September 1853, 2.

54   J. Ross Browne, "The Coast Rangers: A Chronicle of Events in California, Part II: The Indian Reservations," *Harper's New Monthly Magazine* 23 (1861): 314; Robert Winston Mardock, *The Reformers and the American Indian* (Columbia: University of Missouri Press, 1971), 85.

55   San Francisco *Daily Alta California*, 26 October 1861, 2; Robert Chandler, "The Failure of Reform: White Attitudes and Indian Response in California during the Civil War Era," *Pacific Historian* 24 (1980): 284–94.

56   Jeremiah Burke Sanderson, untitled speech, n.d. [1870], folder 8, box 2, Jeremiah Burke Sanderson Papers, BL.

57   Sonoma *Democrat*, 23 April 1870, 4.

58   Charles Loring Brace, *The New West: or, California in 1867–1868* (New York: G. P. Putnam & Son, 1869), 213.

CHAPTER   TWO

1   A. W. Loomis to John C. Lowrie, 15 September 1868, folder 3, box 1, PCUSA-BFMSF, 1845–85.

2   *Fifty-Second Annual Report of the Missionary Society of the Methodist Episcopal Church for the Year 1870* (New York: Missionary Society, 1871), 123–28; *American Missionary*, February 1871, 35–36; *The Spirit of Missions* (New York: Board of Missions, Protestant Episcopal Church, 1870), 167–70. Studies of evangelism among the Chinese of California include Sister John Evangelist Hovley, "The Development of the Christian Religion among the Chinese People of San Francisco" (M.A. thesis, Catholic University of America, 1944); Robert Seager II, "Some Denominational Reactions to Chinese Immigration to California," *Pacific Historical Review* 28 (1959): 49–66; Elizabeth Lee Abbott and Kenneth A. Abbott, "Chinese Pilgrims and Presbyterians in the United States, 1851–1977," *Journal of Presbyterian History* 55 (1977): 125–44; Wesley Stephen Woo, "Protestant Work among the Chinese in the San Francisco Bay Area, 1850–1920" (PhD diss., Graduate Theological Union, 1984); Woo, "Presbyterian Mission: Christianizing and Civilizing the Chinese in Nineteenth Century California," *American Presbyterian* 68 (1990): 167–78; Woo, "Chinese Protestants in the San Francisco Bay Area," in *Entry Denied: Exclusion and the Chinese Community in America, 1882–1943*, ed. Sucheng Chan (Philadelphia: Temple University Press, 1991) , 213–45; Timothy Tseng, "Ministry at Arms' Length: Asian Americans in the Racial Ideology of American Mainline Protestants, 1882–1952" (PhD diss., Union Theological Seminary,

Columbia University, 1994); *Keeping Faith: European and Asian Catholic Immigrants,* ed. Jeffrey M. Burns, Ellen Skerrett, and Joseph M. White (Maryknoll, N.Y.: Orbis Books, 2000), 229–46; Yong Chen, *Chinese San Francisco, 1850–1943: A Trans-Pacific Community* (Stanford, Calif.: Stanford University Press, 2000), 130–37; Russell G. Moy, "Resident Aliens of the Diaspora: 1 Peter and Chinese Protestants in San Francisco," *Semeia* 90–91 (2002): 51–67; and Lawrence Jay, "Baptist Work among the Chinese in San Francisco (1848–1888): The Early History of the First Chinese Baptist Church," *American Baptist Quarterly* 21 (2002): 322–36. For evangelism in New York City and Portland, see Daniel Liestman, "'To Win Redeemed Souls from Heathen Darkness': Protestant Response to the Chinese of the Pacific Northwest in the Late Nineteenth Century," *Western Historical Quarterly* 24 (1993): 179–201; Arthur Bonner, *Alas! What Brought Thee Hither?: The Chinese in New York, 1800–1950* (Madison, N.J.: Fairleigh Dickinson University Press, 1997), 112–35; John Kuo Wei Tchen, *New York before Chinatown: Orientalism and the Shaping of American Culture, 1776–1882* (Baltimore: Johns Hopkins University Press, 1999), 242–47; Mary Ting Li Lui, *The Chinatown Trunk Mystery: Murder, Miscegenation, and Other Dangerous Encounters in Turn-of-the-Century New York City* (Princeton, N.J.: Princeton University Press, 2005), 118–21; and Derek Chang, *Citizens of a Christian Nation: Evangelical Missions and the Problem of Race in the Nineteenth Century* (Philadelphia: University of Pennsylvania Press, 2010).

3   Frederick Rudolph, "Chinamen in Yankeedom: Anti-Unionism in Massachusetts in 1870," *American Historical Review* 53 (1947): 1–29; Charles J. McClain, *In Search of Equality: The Chinese Struggle against Discrimination in Nineteenth-Century America* (Berkeley: University of California Press, 1994), 30–31; Andrew Gyory, *Closing the Gate: Race, Politics, and the Chinese Exclusion Act* (Chapel Hill: University of North Carolina Press, 1998), 26–28, 39–59.

4   *American Missionary,* November 1869, 251; October 1870, 234.

5   Joe M. Richardson, *Christian Reconstruction: The American Missionary Association and Southern Blacks, 1861–1890* (Athens: University of Georgia Press, 1986); Karin L. Zipf, "'Among These American Heathens': Congregationalist Missionaries and African American Evangelicals during Reconstruction, 1865–1878," *North Carolina Historical Review* 74 (1997): 111–34; Daniel W. Stowell, *Rebuilding Zion: The Religious Reconstruction of the South, 1863–1877* (New York: Oxford University Press, 1998); Edward J. Blum, *Reforging the White Republic: Race, Religion, and American Nationalism, 1865–1898* (Baton Rouge: Louisiana State University Press, 2005), 51–86; Chang, *Citizens of a Christian Nation.*

6   John Todd, *The Sunset Land; or, The Great Pacific Slope* (Boston: Lee and Shepard, 1870), 257, 261.

7   A. W. Loomis to John C. Lowrie, 10 May 1870, folder 4; 10 November 1871; 26 June 1872, folder 5, box 1, PCUSA-BFMSF, 1845–85; *American Missionary,* November 1875, 249; San Francisco *California Christian Advocate,* 28 October 1869, 508.

8   *American Missionary,* March 1871, 47.

9   Otis Gibson, "Mission to the Chinese of the Pacific Coast: First Annual Report," 25 August 1869, 1869 folder, California Methodist Episcopal Conference Correspondence, 1855–1951, PSR; *Minutes of the California Annual Conference of the Methodist Episcopal Church, Seventeenth Session, Held at Napa City, August 26–31, 1869* (San Francisco, 1869), 18; *American Missionary,* January 1873, 11.

10   *Minutes of the California Annual Conference of the Methodist Episcopal Church,* 1869, 18; *American Missionary,* April 1870, 85.

11   San Francisco *Pacific,* 19 June 1873, 4; *American Missionary,* December 1870, 275.

12   San Francisco *Occident,* 2 April 1870, 105; *Harper's Weekly,* 20 October 1877, 823; San Francisco *California Christian Advocate,* 12 June 1873, 6; Lai Yong, Yank Kay, A Yup, Lai Foon, and Chung Leong, *Chinese Question from a Chinese Standpoint,* trans. O. Gibson (San Francisco: Cubery, 1874); A. W. Loomis to John C. Lowrie, 2 February 1869; 15 February 1870, folder 4, box 1, PCUSA-BFMSF, 1845–85.

13   San Francisco *Daily Alta California,* 26 October 1871, 1; 27 October 1871, 1; 4 March 1872, 2; William R. Locklear, "The Celestials and the Angels: A Study of the Anti-Chinese Movement in Los Angeles to 1882," *Historical Society of Southern California* 42 (1960): 239–56.

14   Michael C. Coleman, *Presbyterian Missionary Attitudes toward American Indians, 1837–1893* (Jackson: University Press of Mississippi, 1985), 139–70; Blum, *Reforging the White Republic,* 38–49; Jennifer C. Snow, *Protestant Missionaries, Asian Immigrants, and Ideologies of Race in America, 1850–1924* (New York: Routledge, 2007), 27–53.

15   H. C. Bennett, *Chinese Labor: A Lecture, Delivered before the San Francisco Mechanics' Institute* (San Francisco, 1870), 13, 11, 39; *American Missionary,* February 1870, 39–40; George Anthony Peffer, *If They Don't Bring Their Women Here: Chinese Female Immigration before Exclusion* (Urbana: University of Illinois Press, 1999), 92; Werner Sollors, *Beyond Ethnicity: Consent and Descent in American Culture* (New York: Oxford University Press, 1986), 59–65; Paul Goodman, *Of One Blood: Abolitionism and the Origins of Racial Equality* (Berkeley: University of California Press, 1998). The use of Acts 17:26 was common; see San Francisco *Pacific,* 25 July 1872, 1; and O. Gibson, *"Chinaman or White Man, Which?": Reply to Father Buchard* (San Francisco: Alta California Printing House, 1873), 17.

16   San Francisco *California Christian Advocate,* 12 February 1874, 4; San Francisco *Occident,* 27 March 1869, 136; *American Missionary,* October 1875, 229.

17   *American Missionary,* December 1869, 280; *Confucius and the Chinese Classics: or, Readings in Chinese Literature,* ed. A. W. Loomis (San Francisco: A. Roman & Company, 1867), 393; *The Nation* 6 (16 January 1868): 53; A. W. Loomis, "What Our Chinamen Read," *Overland Monthly* 1 (1868): 530; Laurie Maffly-Kipp, "Engaging Habits and Besotted Idolatry: Viewing Chinese Religions in the American West," in *Race, Religion, Region: Landscapes of*

Encounter in the American West, ed. Fay Botham and Sara M. Patterson (Tucson: University of Arizona Press, 2006), 60–88.

18   *Annual Report of the Presbyterian Board of Foreign Missions* (New York: Presbyterian Board of Foreign Missions, 1867), 40–41; San Francisco *California Christian Advocate,* 2 December 1869, 570.

19   *Annual Report of the American Baptist Foreign Mission Society* (New York: American Baptist Foreign Mission Society, 1873), 12; *American Missionary,* September 1870, 206; December 1873, 268.

20   *American Missionary,* October 1873, 226; August 1874, 177; September 1874, 203; S. H. Willey to E. M. Cravath, 10 December 1873, AMAR; New York *Christian Advocate,* 8 April 1869, 108. On the origins of "hoodlum," see John T. Krumpelmann, "Hoodlum," *Modern Language Notes* 50 (1935): 93–95.

21   *American Missionary,* October 1870, 233; November 1870, 254; Sacramento *Daily Union,* 16 April 1868, 4.

22   San Francisco *Daily Alta California,* 25 May 1873, 1; 30 May 1873, 1; 12 June 1873, 1; San Francisco *Chronicle,* 29 May 1873, 3; 30 May 1873, 3; San Francisco *Monitor,* 24 May 1873, 4; M. B. Starr, *The Coming Struggle; or, What the People on the Pacific Coast Think of the Coolie Invasion* (San Francisco: Bacon, 1873), 25; *The Chinese Invasion: Revealing the Habits, Manners, and Customs of the Chinese, Political, Social, and Religious, on the Pacific Coast,* ed. H. J. West (San Francisco: Bacon, 1873), 63.

23   William Lobscheid, *The Chinese: What They Are, and What They Are Doing* (San Francisco: A. L. Bancroft, 1873), 8; San Francisco *California Christian Advocate,* 15 May 1873, 4.

24   *American Missionary,* July 1872, 155; San Francisco *Chronicle,* 9 August 1872, 3; William C. Pond, *Gospel Pioneering: Reminiscences of Early Congregationalism in California, 1833–1920* (Oberlin, Ohio: News Printing, 1921), 131–33.

25   George Mooar to Charles H. Howard, 19 September 1873, AMAR. For other rebuttals to Starr, see San Francisco *Occident,* 19 June 1873, 193; San Francisco *California Christian Advocate,* 19 June 1873, 4; and O. Gibson, *The Chinese in America* (Cincinnati: Hitchcock & Walden, 1877), 281.

26   Mendocino *Democrat,* 13 December 1873, 2; Eugene Casserly, *The Chinese Evil—Contracts for Servile Labor—Chinese Immigration the Great Danger* (Washington, D.C.: Government Printing Office, 1870), 5; Winfield J. Davis, *History of Political Conventions in California, 1849–1892* (Sacramento, Calif.: California State Library, 1893), 300, 327, 352.

27   As in the 1860s, the issue of race alone did not decide elections; other important issues in 1871 included subsidies for the railroads, public schools, anti-Catholicism, and charges of corruption against the Democrats.

28   San Francisco *Chronicle,* 29 January 1875, 2.

29   San Francisco *Pacific Appeal,* 19 November 1870, 2. African American activists in San Francisco also fought segregation in theaters during this period; see Lynn M. Hudson, "Entertaining Citizenship: Masculinity and Minstrelsy in Post-Emancipation San Francisco," *Journal of African American History* 93 (2008): 174–97.

30　*The Statutes of California Passed at the Eleventh Session of the Legislature, 1860* (Sacramento, Calif.: Charles T. Botts, 1860), 325; *The Statutes of California Passed at the Eighteenth Session of the Legislature, 1869–1870* (Sacramento, Calif.: D. W. Gelwicks, 1870), 839; San Francisco *Pacific Appeal,* 25 November 1871, 2.

31　Ward v. Flood, 48 Cal. 36 (1874); San Francisco *Daily Examiner,* April 1, 1874, 2; Nicholas Patrick Beck, "The Other Children: Minority Education in California Public Schools from Statehood to 1890" (PhD diss., UCLA, 1975); Charles Wollenberg, *All Deliberate Speed: Segregation and Exclusion in California Schools, 1855–1975* (Berkeley: University of California Press, 1976); Irving G. Hendrick, "Federal Policy Affecting the Education of Indians in California, 1849–1934," *History of Education Quarterly* 16 (1976): 163–85; Irving G. Hendrick, *The Education of Non-Whites in California, 1849–1970* (San Francisco: R & E Research Associates, 1977); Leigh Dana Johnsen, "Equal Rights and the 'Heathen Chinee': Black Activism in San Francisco, 1865–1875," *Western Historical Quarterly* 11 (1980): 57–68; Irving G. Hendrick, "From Indifference to Imperative Duty: Educating Children in Early California," in *Rooted in Barbarous Soil: People, Culture, and Community in Gold Rush California,* ed. Kevin Starr and Richard J. Orsi (Berkeley: University of California Press, 2000), 226–49; Donald Michael Bottoms Jr., "'An Aristocracy of Color': Race and Reconstruction in Post-Gold Rush California" (PhD diss., UCLA, 2005), 128–80; Wendy Rouse Jorae, *The Children of Chinatown: Growing Up Chinese American in San Francisco, 1850–1920* (Chapel Hill: University of North Carolina Press, 2009), 110–39.

32　San Francisco *Elevator,* 8 July 1870, 2; San Francisco *Pacific Appeal,* 5 April 1873, 2; San Francisco *Elevator,* 8 March 1873, 3; James Williams, *Life and Adventures of James Williams, a Fugitive Slave* (San Francisco: Women's Union Print, 1873), 105.

33　San Francisco *Pacific Appeal,* 10 February 1872, 2; 31 May 1873, 2; San Francisco *Elevator,* 19 April 1873, 2; 26 April 1873, 2; 3 May 1873, 3; 24 May 1873, 2; 14 June 1873, 2; 27 September 1873, 2.

34　Beck, "The Other Children," 73; Wollenberg, *All Deliberate Speed,* 33–34.

35　Davis, *History of Political Conventions in California,* 307–8; San Francisco *Chronicle,* 19 February 1873, 3.

36　43 Cong. Rec., 1st Sess. 1463–64 (13 February 1874); San Francisco *Chronicle,* 10 February 1873, 2.

37　On the construction of the "coolie" stereotype, see Sucheng Chan, *This Bittersweet Soil: The Chinese in California Agriculture, 1860–1910* (Berkeley: University of California Press, 1986), 31, 38–41; Gyory, *Closing the Gate,* 32–33, 61–63; Robert G. Lee, *Orientals: Asian Americans in Popular Culture* (Philadelphia: Temple University Press, 1999), 51–82; Tchen, *New York before Chinatown,* 172–75; Moon-Ho Jung, "Outlawing 'Coolies': Race, Nation, and Empire in the Age of Emancipation," *American Quarterly* 57 (2005): 677–701; and Moon-Ho Jung, *Coolies and Cane: Race, Labor, and Sugar in the Age of Emancipation* (Baltimore: Johns Hopkins University Press, 2006).

38   San Francisco *Thistleton's Illustrated Jolly Giant,* August 1873, 2; 5 September 1874, 120; 18 July 1874, 31, 34; New York *Daily Tribune,* 1 May 1869, 2.

39   Joyce Mende Wong, "Prostitution: San Francisco Chinatown, Mid- and Late-Nineteenth Century," *Bridge: An Asian American Perspective* 6 (1978): 23–28; Lucie Cheng Hirata, "Free, Indentured, Enslaved: Chinese Prostitutes in Nineteenth-Century America," *Signs: Journal of Women in Culture and Society* 5 (1979): 3–29; Jacqueline Baker Barnhart, *The Fair but Frail: Prostitution in San Francisco, 1849–1900* (Reno: University of Nevada Press, 1986), 45–50; Benson Tong, *Unsubmissive Women: Chinese Prostitutes in Nineteenth-Century San Francisco* (Norman: University of Oklahoma Press, 1994); Judy Yung, *Unbound Feet: A Social History of Chinese Women in San Francisco* (Berkeley: University of California Press, 1995), 26–37; Lee, *Orientals,* 89–91; Peffer, *If They Don't Bring Their Women Here*; Chen, *Chinese San Francisco, 1850–1943,* 75–87, 289; Clare Sears, "'A Dress Not Belonging to His or Her Sex': Cross-Dressing Law in San Francisco, 1860–1900" (PhD diss., University of California, Santa Cruz, 2005), 108–37; Jorae, *The Children of Chinatown,* 140–75.

40   Albert S. Evans, *Á la California: Sketches of Life in the Golden State* (San Francisco: A. L. Bancroft, 1873), 302; Stuart Creighton Miller, *The Unwelcome Immigrant: The American Image of the Chinese, 1785–1882* (Berkeley: University of California Press, 1969), 160–66; Joan B. Trauner, "The Chinese as Medical Scapegoats in San Francisco, 1870–1905," *California History* 57 (1978): 70–87; Susan Craddock, *City of Plagues: Disease, Poverty, and Deviance in San Francisco* (Minneapolis: University of Minnesota Press, 2000); Nayan Shah, *Contagious Divides: Epidemics and Race in San Francisco's Chinatown* (Berkeley: University of California Press, 2001).

41   *The Statutes of California Passed at the Eighteenth Session of the Legislature,* 330–33; see also Cornelius Cole's comments in San Francisco *Chronicle,* 23 October 1870; 43 Cong. Rec., 2nd Sess. Appendix, 44 (10 February 1875); Peffer, *If They Don't Bring Their Women Here,* 105–13; Kerry Abrams, "Polygamy, Prostitution, and the Federalization of Immigration Law," *Columbia Law Review* 105 (2005): 641–716.

42   A. W. Loomis to John C. Lowrie, 25 April 1867, folder 3, box 1, PCUSA-BFMSF, 1845–85; San Francisco *Occident,* 2 April 1870, 105; *American Missionary,* February 1870, 40.

43   A. W. Loomis, "Chinese Women in California," *Overland Monthly* 2 (1869): 344, 348; San Francisco *Occident,* 16 April 1874, 114; San Francisco *California Christian Advocate,* 29 November 1871, 1; Miller, *The Unwelcome Immigrant,* 62–63; Peggy Pascoe, *Relations of Rescue: The Search for Female Moral Authority in the American West, 1874–1939* (New York: Oxford University Press, 1990); Sarah Refo Mason, "Social Christianity, American Feminism, and Chinese Prostitutes: The History of the Presbyterian Mission Home, San Francisco, 1874–1935," in *Women and Chinese Patriarchy: Submission, Servitude, and Escape,* ed. Maria Jaschok and Suzanne Miers (Hong Kong: Hong Kong University Press, 1994), 198–220; Jeffrey L. Staley, "'Gum Moon': The First Fifty Years of Methodist Women's Work in San Francisco's Chinatown, 1870–1920," *Argonaut* 16 (2005): 4–25.

44   San Francisco *California Christian Advocate*, 19 January 1871, 3; New York *Times*, 17 November 1874, 1; San Francisco *Chronicle*, 28 August 1874, 3; 43 Cong. Rec., 2nd Sess. Appendix, 41 (10 February 1875); Abrams, "Polygamy, Prostitution, and the Federalization of Immigration Law," 677–90.

45   San Francisco *California Christian Advocate*, 19 January 1871, 3; San Francisco *Occident* 26 March 1874, 90.

46   New York *Evangelist*, 24 November 1870, 6.

47   On the complexities of "conversion" as an analytical concept, see Michael D. McNally, "Religion and Culture Change in Native North America," in *Perspectives on American Religion and Culture*, ed. Peter W. Williams (Malden, Mass.: Blackwell, 1999), 270–85; and Linford D. Fisher, "Native Americans, Conversion, and Christian Practice in Colonial New England, 1640–1730," *Harvard Theological Review* 102 (2009): 101–24.

48   *The Missionary Enterprise in China and America*, ed. John K. Fairbank (Cambridge, Mass.: Harvard University Press, 1974); Carl T. Smith, *Chinese Christians: Élites, Middlemen, and the Church in Hong Kong* (New York: Oxford University Press, 1985); Gael Graham, *Gender, Culture, and Christianity: American Protestant Mission Schools in China, 1880–1930* (New York: P. Lang, 1995); Eric Reinders, *Borrowed Gods and Foreign Bodies: Christian Missionaries Imagine Chinese Religion* (Berkeley: University of California Press, 2004).

49   Gibson, *The Chinese in America*, 198; New York *Christian Union*, 6 March 1872, 218.

50   *American Missionary*, July 1875, 164; Huie Kin, *Reminiscences* (Peiping, China: San Yu Press, 1932), 32.

51   Kwan Loy, "Rev. Kwan Loy: Autobiographical," in *Illustrious Chinese Christians*, ed. W. P. Bentley (Cincinnati: Standard Publishing, 1906), 159; A. W. Loomis, "Qwan Loi," folder 3, box 45, PCUSA-BFMSF, 1829–95; A. W. Loomis to John C. Lowrie, 10 November 1871, folder 5, box 1, PCUSA-BFMSF, 1845–85. Jee Gam's $25 monthly salary was insufficient to cover his travel and other mission-related expenses, and by 1874 he had incurred a debt of $200; William C. Pond to E. M. Cravath, 30 May 1874, 29 June 1874, AMAR.

52   Lai Yong, et al., *Chinese Question from a Chinese Standpoint*, 14; Gibson, *The Chinese in America*, 190–91.

53   San Francisco *Daily Alta California*, 22 February 1875, 1.

54   San Francisco *California Christian Advocate*, 20 February 1873, 6.

55   Isaac Mast, *The Gun, Rod, and Saddle; or, Nine Months in California* (Philadelphia: Methodist Episcopal Book and Publishing House, 1875), 53.

CHAPTER   THREE

1   *American Missionary*, May 1874, 112–13.

2   Ulysses S. Grant, "First Inaugural Address," in *A Compilation of the Messages and Papers of the Presidents, 1789–1897*, ed. James D. Richardson, 10 vols.

(Washington, D.C.: Government Printing Office, 1896–99), 7:8; Grant, "First Annual Message," in ibid., 7:38.

3   Robert Lee Whitner, "The Methodist Episcopal Church and Grant's Peace Policy: A Study of the Methodist Agencies, 1870–1882" (PhD diss., University of Minnesota, 1959); Henry E. Fritz, *The Movement for Indian Assimilation, 1860–1890* (Philadelphia: University of Pennsylvania Press, 1963); R. Pierce Beaver, *Church, State, and the American Indians: Two and a Half Centuries of Partnership in Missions between Protestant Churches and Government* (St. Louis, Mo.: Concordia Publishing House, 1966); Robert Winston Mardock, *The Reformers and the American Indian* (Columbia: University of Missouri Press, 1971); Francis Paul Prucha, *American Indian Policy in Crisis: Christian Reformers and the Indian, 1865–1900* (Norman: University of Oklahoma Press, 1976); Brian W. Dippie, *The Vanishing American: White Attitudes and U.S. Indian Policy* (Middletown, Conn.: Wesleyan University Press, 1982), 141–60; Clyde A. Milner II, *With Good Intentions: Quaker Work among the Pawnees, Otos, and Omahas in the 1870s* (Lincoln: University of Nebraska Press, 1982); Robert H. Keller Jr., *American Protestantism and United States Indian Policy, 1869–82* (Lincoln: University of Nebraska Press, 1983); Norman J. Bender, *"New Hope for the Indians": The Grant Peace Policy and the Navajos in the 1870s* (Albuquerque: University of New Mexico Press, 1989); Douglas Firth Anderson, "Protestantism, Progress, and Prosperity: John P. Clum and 'Civilizing' the U.S. Southwest, 1871–1886," *Western Historical Quarterly* 33 (2002): 315–35; Andrew Denson, *Demanding the Cherokee Nation: Indian Autonomy and American Culture, 1830–1900* (Lincoln: University of Nebraska Press, 2004), 89–120; Robert E. Ficken, "After the Treaties: Administering Pacific Northwest Indian Reservations," *Oregon Historical Quarterly* 106 (2005): 442–61; David Sim, "The Peace Policy of Ulysses S. Grant," *American Nineteenth Century History* 9 (2008): 241–68.

4   San Francisco *California Christian Advocate*, 13 February 1873, 4; San Francisco *Pacific*, 16 April 1872, 4.

5   Cong. Globe, 41st Cong., 2nd Sess. 4973 (29 June 1870); 5010 (30 June 1870); Appendix, 437 (4 June 1870); 5009 (30 June 1870); Keller, *American Protestantism and United States Indian Policy*, 104.

6   Keith A. Murray, *The Modocs and Their War* (Norman: University of Oklahoma Press, 1959); Mardock, *The Reformers and the American Indian*, 115–28; Prucha, *American Indian Policy in Crisis*, 85–88; Keller, *American Protestantism and United States Indian Policy*, 127–28; Arthur Quinn, *Hell with the Fire Out: A History of the Modoc War* (Boston: Faber and Faber, 1997).

7   San Francisco *Chronicle*, 13 April 1873, 4; San Francisco *Daily Examiner*, 18 April 1873, 2; San Francisco *Daily Alta California*, 11 May 1873, 2; San Francisco *Chronicle*, 25 May 1873, 2.

8   San Francisco *Daily Alta California*, 15 April 1873, 2; San Francisco *Elevator*, 19 April 1873, 2; San Francisco *Daily Alta California*, 13 April 1873, 2. Other California newspapers responded similarly; see San Francisco *Daily Evening Bulletin*, 14 April 1873, 2; San Francisco *Daily Morning Call*, 13 April 1873, 2; 15 April 1873, 2; San Francisco *Pacific Appeal*, 19 April 1873, 2; Sacramento

Daily Bee, 14 April 1873, 2; 15 April 1873, 2; Sacramento *Daily Record,* 14 April 1873, 2; 15 April 1873, 2; Oakland *Alameda County Gazette,* 19 April 1873, 2; 26 April 1873, 1; 3 May 1873, 2. One dissenting voice of tolerance came from the Sacramento *Daily Union;* see 14 April 1873, 2; 19 April 1873, 4; 21 April 1873, 2.

9   San Francisco *Chronicle,* 14 April 1873, 2; San Francisco *Daily Alta California,* 19 April 1873, 1; Robert Patterson, "Our Indian Policy," *Overland Monthly* 11 (1873): 208, 211.

10 For example, William Lloyd Garrison, "Ferocious Retaliation," New York *Independent,* 1 May 1873, 549–50; *Voice of Peace* 2 (1873): 8–9; Mardock, *The Reformers and the American Indian,* 115–28.

11 San Francisco *Pacific,* 17 April 1873, 4; 24 April 1873, 4; 15 May 1873, 4; San Francisco *Occident,* 17 April 1873, 121; 24 April 1873, 129; 1 May 1873, 137; 22 May 1873, 161; 29 May 1873, 169; San Francisco *California Christian Advocate,* 17 April 1873, 4; 5 June 1873, 4; 3 July 1873, 1; San Francisco *Pacific Churchman,* 17 April 1873, 4.

12 B. C. Whiting to Francis A. Walker, 13 August 1872, roll 44, M234, Letters Received, 1824–81, RBIA-NARA-W; Hugh Gibson to B. C. Whiting, 24 June 1872, letterbook dated 4/1/1871 to 12/11/1875, box 1, Records of the Round Valley Agency, RBIA-NARA-SB.

13 Stephen Powers, "The Northern California Indians: No. V," *Overland Monthly* 9 (1872): 310, 311; Charles Nordhoff, "Northern California," *Harper's New Monthly Magazine* 48 (1873): 42. Nordhoff expanded on these themes in his book *Northern California, Oregon, and the Sandwich Islands* (New York: Harper & Brothers, 1874), 160–67.

14 *Fifty-Fifth Annual Report of the Missionary Society of the Methodist Episcopal Church for the Year 1873* (New York: Missionary Society, 1874), 157. The Methodist Episcopal Church nationwide devoted less money to supporting the peace policy than most denominations; Keller, *American Protestantism and United States Indian Policy,* 54–58.

15 *Annual Report of the Commissioner of Indian Affairs* (Washington, D.C.: Government Printing Office, 1873), 325; Mendocino *Democrat,* 19 September 1872, 3; *Annual Report of the Commissioner of Indian Affairs* (Washington, D.C.: Government Printing Office, 1872), 374.

16 Round Valley Indian Reservation has spawned an historiography of its own; see William Hammond, "History of Round Valley Reservation" (M.A. thesis, Sacramento State College, 1959); Virginia P. Miller, "The 1870 Ghost Dance and the Methodists: An Unexpected Turn of Events in Round Valley," *Journal of California Anthropology* 3 (1976): 66–75; Lynwood Carranco and Estle Beard, *Genocide and Vendetta: The Round Valley Wars of Northern California* (Norman: University of Oklahoma Press, 1981); Virginia P. Miller, "The Changing Role of the Chief on a California Indian Reservation," *American Indian Quarterly* 13 (1989): 447–55; Todd Benson, "The Consequences of Reservation Life: Native Californians on the Round Valley Reservation, 1871–1884," *Pacific Historical Review* 60 (1991): 221–44; Linda Pacini Pitelka, "Mendocino:

Race Relations in a Northern California County, 1850–1949" (PhD diss., University of Massachusetts, 1994); William Bauer, "Working for Identity: Race, Ethnicity, and the Market Economy in Northern California, 1875–1936," in *Native Pathways: American Indian Culture and Economic Development in the Twentieth Century*, ed. Brian Hosmer and Colleen O'Neill (Boulder: University Press of Colorado, 2004), 238–57; Jason Charles Newman, "'There Will Come a Day When White Men Will Not Rule Us': The Round Valley Indian Tribe and Federal Indian Policy, 1856–1934" (PhD diss., University of California, Davis, 2004); Benjamin Madley, "Patterns of Frontier Genocide, 1803–1910: The Aboriginal Tasmanians, the Yuki of California, and the Herero of Namibia," *Journal of Genocide Research* 6 (2004): 167–92; Frank H. Baumgardner III, *Killing for Land in Early California: Indian Blood at Round Valley: Founding the Nome Cult Indian Farm* (New York: Algora Publishing, 2005); William J. Bauer Jr., "'We Were All Migrant Workers Here': Round Valley Indian Labor in Northern California, 1850–1929," *Western Historical Quarterly* 37 (2006): 43–63; Khal Ross Schneider, "Citizen Lives: California Indian Country, 1855–1940" (PhD diss., University of California, Berkeley, 2007); Bauer, *We Were All Like Migrant Workers Here: Work, Community, and Memory on California's Round Valley Reservation, 1850–1941* (Chapel Hill: University of North Carolina Press, 2009); and Khal Schneider, "Making Indian Land in the Allotment Era: Northern California's Indian Rancherias," *Western Historical Quarterly* 41 (2010): 429–50.

17   *California Annual Conference of the Methodist Episcopal Church*, 1902, 64; J. C. Simmons, *The History of Southern Methodism on the Pacific Coast* (Nashville, Tenn.: Southern Methodist Publishing House, 1886), 264; San Francisco *California Christian Advocate*, 2 October 1873, 4; *Annual Report of the Commissioner of Indian Affairs*, 1873, 325–26; J. L. Burchard to B. C. Whiting, 25 November 1872; J. L. Burchard to Edward P. Smith, 31 January 1874, letterbook dated 4/1/1871 to 12/11/1875, box 1, Records of the Round Valley Agency, RBIA-NARA-SB; Mary K. Colburn to E. M. Cravath, February 1874, AMAR.

18   *Annual Report of the Commissioner of Indian Affairs*, 1873, 325; San Francisco *California Christian Advocate*, 20 February 1873, 5; 11 September 1873, 1; 23 October 1873, 4; Mendocino *Democrat*, 29 May 1873, 3; 18 October 1873, 2, 3; Stephen Powers, *Tribes of California* (Washington, D.C.: Department of the Interior, U.S. Geographical and Geological Survey, 1877), 132.

19   J. L. Burchard to J. K. Luttrell, 24 November 1874, roll 46, M234, Letters Received, 1824–81, RBIA-NARA-W; J. L. Burchard to B. C. Whiting, 22 October 1872; 31 March 1873, letterbook dated 4/1/1871 to 12/11/1875, box 1, Records of the Round Valley Agency, RBIA-NARA-SB; *Annual Report of the Commissioner of Indian Affairs*, 1872, 377; *Annual Report of the Commissioner of Indian Affairs*, 1873, 325; *Annual Report of the Commissioner of Indian Affairs* (Washington, D.C.: Government Printing Office, 1874), 313. Mortality was also a factor; according to Burchard, 1875 was the first year that births outnumbered deaths on the reservation; *Annual Report of the Commissioner of Indian Affairs* (Washington, D.C.: Government Printing Office, 1875), 227.

20   San Francisco *California Christian Advocate,* 11 September 1873, 1; 20 February 1873, 5; 19 June 1873, 1; 27 November 1873, 5; 4 December 1873, 1; 22 January 1874, 4; Mendocino *Democrat,* 29 May 1873, 3.

21   San Francisco *Daily Alta California,* 22 January 1874, 2; 23 January 1874, 3; 28 January 1874, 2; 12 February 1874, 2; 21 February 1874, 2; San Francisco *California Christian Advocate,* 19 February 1874, 4; 5 February 1874, 4.

22   San Francisco *Daily Alta California,* 2 March 1874, 2; 4 March 1874, 1, 2; 19 March 1874, 1; 22 April 1874, 2; San Francisco *California Christian Advocate,* 26 February 1874, 4; 5 March 1874, 4; 8 March 1874, 1; 26 March 1874, 4; 2 April 1874, 1; Mendocino *Independent Dispatch,* 24 January 1874, 2; Mendocino *Democrat,* 21 February 1874, 3; San Francisco *Chronicle,* 23 February 1874, 3.

23   San Francisco *California Christian Advocate,* 29 January 1874, 1; 2 April 1874, 5; J. L. Burchard to Edward P. Smith, 28 February 1874; 31 March 1874; 29 December 1874, letterbook dated 4/1/1871 to 12/11/1875, box 1, Records of the Round Valley Agency, RBIA-NARA-SB; *Annual Report of the Commissioner of Indian Affairs,* 1874, 314.

24   *Annual Report of the Commissioner of Indian Affairs,* 1874, 314; San Francisco *California Christian Advocate,* 5 March 1874, 5; 30 July 1874, 1; 22 October 1874, 4; J. L. Burchard to Edward P. Smith, 31 July 1874, letterbook dated 4/1/1871 to 12/11/1875, box 1, Records of the Round Valley Agency, RBIA-NARA-SB; Mendocino *Democrat,* 15 August 1874.

25   San Francisco *California Christian Advocate,* 30 July 1874, 1; 22 October 1874, 4; 29 October 1874, 4.

26   Samuel Breck to J. C. Kelton, 26 June 1874, roll 46, M234, Letters Received, 1824–81; A. G. Tassin, "Extract from Report," 1 January 1875, Special Case 43, RBIA-NARA-W.

27   San Francisco *California Christian Advocate,* 5 March 1874, 4; 24 December 1874, 1.

28   J. L. Burchard to Edward P. Smith, 30 April 1874, letterbook dated 4/1/1871 to 12/11/1875, box 1, Records of the Round Valley Agency, RBIA-NARA-SB; *American Missionary,* May 1874, 112–13; New York *Christian Advocate,* 21 May 1874, 163; 3 December 1874, 389; *Fifty-Sixth Annual Report of the Missionary Society of the Methodist Episcopal Church for the Year 1874* (New York: Missionary Society, 1875), 156; New York *Independent,* 14 January 1875, 8; Isaac Mast, *The Gun, Rod, and Saddle; or, Nine Months in California* (Philadelphia: Methodist Episcopal Book and Publishing House, 1875), 216.

29   San Francisco *Daily Alta California,* 20 April 1874, 2; 11 May 1874, 2; 1 June 1874, 2.

30   San Francisco *California Christian Advocate,* 18 February 1875, 1; J. L. Burchard to Edward P. Smith, 29 December 1874, letterbook dated 4/1/1871 to 12/11/1875, box 1, Records of the Round Valley Agency, RBIA-NARA-SB; 43 Cong. Rec., 2nd Sess. 470–71 (14 January 1875); J. K. Luttrell report on Round Valley Indian Reservation, 16 January 1875, roll 47, M234, Letters Received, 1824–81, RBIA-NARA-W.

31   San Francisco *Monitor and Guardian*, 5 January 1878, 4; Najia Aarim-Heriot,
       *Chinese Immigrants, African Americans, and Racial Anxiety in the United
       States, 1848–82* (Urbana: University of Illinois Press, 2003).

32   George J. Prising to B. R. Cowen, 15 February 1875, Special Case 43, RBIA-
       NARA-W; Citizens of Round Valley to Edward P. Smith, 27 February 1875,
       roll 47, M234, Letters Received, 1824–81, RBIA-NARA-W; Mendocino *Demo-
       crat*, 30 January 1875, 3; 27 February 1875, 3; J. L. Burchard to Edward P.
       Smith, 28 January 1875, letterbook dated 4/1/1871 to 12/11/1875, box 1, Records
       of the Round Valley Agency, RBIA-NARA-SB; J. L. Burchard to Edward P.
       Smith, 30 January 1875, A-1371, ACALA.

33   J. L. Burchard to Edward P. Smith, 30 January 1875, A-1371, ACALA; San
       Francisco *California Christian Advocate*, 18 February 1875, 1; New York
       Christian Advocate, 4 March 1875, 67; 25 March 1875, 89; Edward P. Smith to
       J. L. Burchard, 19 February 1875, 1875 folder, box 15, Records of the Round
       Valley Agency, RBIA-NARA-SB.

34   San Francisco *Daily Alta California*, 2 February 1875, 2; Mendocino *Inde-
       pendent Dispatch*, 6 March 1875, 3.

35   L. H. Patty and A. A. Surgeon to William Vandever, 20 April 1875; statement
       of Mrs. M. A. Lacock, 21 April 1875; statement of William Pollard, 22 April
       1875; statement of J. L. Burchard, 27 April 1875; statement of Indian captains,
       20 April 1875, Special Case 43, RBIA-NARA-W; H. C. Benson to J. M. Reid
       and R. C. Dashiell, 24 April 1875, A-1363, ACALA; Douglas Firth Anderson,
       "'More Conscience Than Force': U.S. Indian Inspector William Vandever,
       Grant's Peace Policy, and Protestant Whiteness," *Journal of the Gilded Age
       and Progressive Era* 9 (2010): 167–96.

36   William Vandever to Office of Indian Affairs, 31 April 1875, Special Case 43,
       RBIA-NARA-W; San Francisco *California Christian Advocate*, 19 August
       1875, 4; 6 May 1875, 4; 12 August 1875, 4; New York *Christian Advocate*,
       2 September 1875, 276.

37   J. L. Burchard to Edward P. Smith, 30 June 1875, letterbook dated 4/1/1871 to
       12/11/1875, box 1, Records of the Round Valley Agency, RBIA-NARA-SB;
       Annual Report of the Commissioner of Indian Affairs, 1873, 325; *California
       Annual Conference of the Methodist Episcopal Church* (San Francisco:
       Methodist Book Depository, 1875), 55, 65; *Annual Report of the Commissioner
       of Indian Affairs*, 1875, 227.

38   A. L. Kroeber, "A Ghost-Dance in California," *Journal of American Folklore* 17
       (1904): 32–35; A. H. Gayton, *The Ghost Dance of 1870 in South-Central Cali-
       fornia* (Berkeley: University of California Press, 1930); Cora Du Bois,
       The 1870 Ghost Dance (Berkeley: University of California Press, 1939);
       Michael Hittman, "The 1870 Ghost Dance at the Walker River Reservation:
       A Reconstruction," *Ethnohistory* 20 (1973): 247–78; Miller, "The 1870 Ghost
       Dance and the Methodists"; Greg Sarris, "Telling Dreams and Keeping Se-
       crets: The Bole Maru as American Indian Religious Resistance," *American
       Indian Culture and Research Journal* 16 (1992): 71–85; Greg Sarris, "Living
       with Miracles: The Politics and Poetics of Writing American Indian Resist-
       ance and Identity," in *Displacement, Diaspora, and Geographies of Identity*,

ed. Smadar Lavie and Ted Swedenburg (Durham, N.C.: Duke University Press, 1996), 27–40; Gregory E. Smoak, *Ghost Dances and Identity: Prophetic Religion and American Indian Ethnogenesis in the Nineteenth Century* (Berkeley: University of California Press, 2006), 113–51; Lee Irwin, *Coming Down from Above: Prophecy, Resistance, and Renewal in Native American Religions* (Norman: University of Oklahoma Press, 2008), 288–99.

39   Mendocino *Democrat*, 9 May 1872, 3; 16 May 1872, 3; Hugh Gibson to Franklin A. Walker, 25 May 1872; 31 May 1872, letterbook dated 4/1/1871 to 12/11/1875, box 1, Records of the Round Valley Agency, RBIA-NARA-SB.

40   Mendocino *Independent Dispatch*, 14 March 1874, 3; New York *Christian Advocate*, 2 September 1875, 276.

41   J. L. Burchard to Edward P. Smith, 30 April 1874; 30 May 1884, letterbook dated 4/1/1871 to 12/11/1875, box 1, Records of the Round Valley Agency, RBIA-NARA-SB; San Francisco *California Christian Advocate*, 30 July 1874, 1.

42   Timothy L. Smith, *Revivalism and Social Reform in Mid-Nineteenth-Century America* (New York: Abingdon Press, 1957); Paul E. Johnson, *A Shopkeeper's Millennium: Society and Revivals in Rochester, New York, 1815–1837* (New York: Hill and Wang, 1978); Sandra S. Sizer, *Gospel Hymns and Social Religion: The Rhetoric of Nineteenth-Century Revivalism* (Philadelphia: Temple University Press, 1978); George M. Thomas, *Revivalism and Cultural Change: Christianity, Nation Building, and the Market in the Nineteenth-Century United States* (Chicago: University of Chicago Press, 1989); Jonathan M. Butler, *Softly and Tenderly Jesus Is Calling: Heaven and Hell in American Revivalism, 1870–1920* (Brooklyn, N.Y.: Carlson, 1991).

43   San Francisco *California Christian Advocate*, 5 March 1874, 4; 19 March 1874, 5; 2 April 1874, 5; *American Missionary*, May 1874, 112.

44   *American Missionary*, May 1874, 112; Miller, "The Changing Role of the Chief on a California Indian Reservation," 448, 451.

45   San Francisco *California Christian Advocate*, 10 February 1876, 6.

46   San Francisco *California Christian Advocate*, 10 February 1876, 6; 13 April 1876, 1.

CHAPTER FOUR

1   San Francisco *Daily Alta California*, 26 February 1873, 1; San Francisco *Catholic Guardian*, 1 March 1873, 302; San Francisco *Daily Morning Call*, 26 February 1873, 3.

2   Pierre-Jean de Smet, *Western Missions and Missionaries: A Series of Letters* (New York: T. W. Strong, 1859), 218–39; John Bernard McGloin, *Eloquent Indian: The Life of James Bouchard, California Jesuit* (Stanford, Calif.: Stanford University Press, 1949); Jay Miller, "The Early Years of Watomika (James Bouchard): Delaware and Jesuit," *American Indian Quarterly* 13 (1989): 165–88.

3   Ray Allen Billington, *The Protestant Crusade, 1800–1860* (New York: Macmillan, 1938); John Higham, *Strangers in the Land: Patterns of American Nativism,*

1860–1925 (New Brunswick, N.J.: Rutgers University Press, 1955); Tyler Gregory Anbinder, *Nativism and Slavery: The Northern Know Nothings and the Politics of the 1850's* (New York: Oxford University Press, 1992); Jenny Franchot, *Roads to Rome: The Antebellum Protestant Encounter with Catholicism* (Berkeley: University of California Press, 1994); Marjule Anne Drury, "Anti-Catholicism in Germany, Britain, and the United States: A Review and Critique of Recent Scholarship," *Church History* 70 (2001): 98–131; John T. McGreevy, *Catholicism and American Freedom: A History* (New York: W. W. Norton, 2003).

4   Peyton Hurt, "The Rise and Fall of the 'Know Nothings' in California," *California Historical Society Quarterly* 9 (1930): 16–49, 98–128; "Los Angeles in 1854–5: The Diary of Rev. James Woods," ed. Lindley Bynum, *Historical Society of Southern California Quarterly* 23 (1941): 83; Leonard Pitt, *The Decline of the Californios: A Social History of the Spanish-Speaking Californians, 1846–1890* (Berkeley: University of California Press, 1966), 215–28; Robert M. Senkewicz, "Religion and Non-Partisan Politics in Gold Rush San Francisco," *Southern California Quarterly* 61 (1979): 351–78; Michael E. Engh, *Frontier Faiths: Church, Temple, and Synagogue in Los Angeles, 1846–1888* (Albuquerque: University of New Mexico Press, 1992), 69–100; Laurie F. Maffly-Kipp, *Religion and Society in Frontier California* (New Haven, Conn.: Yale University Press, 1994), 31–34, 116–18. In 1885, Archbishop Joseph Alemany recalled that Catholics did not face intense prejudice in California during the "early days" of the 1850s; San Francisco *Monitor,* 25 February 1885, 1.

5   Higham, *Strangers in the Land,* 28–30; Robert Michaelsen, "Common School, Common Religion? A Case Study in Church-State Relations, Cincinnati, 1869–70," *Church History* 38 (1969): 201–17; David B. Tyack, "Onward Christian Soldiers: Religion in the American Common School," in *History and Education: The Educational Uses of the Past,* ed. Paul Nash (New York: Random House, 1970), 212–55; Lloyd P. Jorgenson, *The State and the Non-Public School, 1825–1925* (Columbia: University of Missouri Press, 1987), 111–45; Samuel T. McSeveney, "Religious Conflict, Party Politics, and Public Policy in New Jersey, 1874–75," *New Jersey History* 110 (1992): 18–44; Ward M. McAfee, *Religion, Race, and Reconstruction: The Public School in the Politics of the 1870s* (Albany: State University of New York Press, 1998); James W. Fraser, *Between Church and State: Religion and Public Education in a Multicultural America* (New York: St. Martin's Press, 1999), 106–13; Philip Hamburger, *Separation of Church and State* (Cambridge, Mass.: Harvard University Press, 2002), 287–334; Jay P. Dolan, *In Search of an American Catholicism: A History of Religion and Culture in Tension* (New York: Oxford University Press, 2002), 47–70; McGreevy, *Catholicism and American Freedom,* 91–126; George M. Thomas, Lisa R. Peck, and Channin G. De Haan, "Reforming Education, Transforming Religion, 1876–1931," in *The Secular Revolution: Power, Interests, and Conflict in the Secularization of American Public Life,* ed. Christian Smith (Berkeley: University of California Press, 2003), 355–94; Peter R. D'Agostino, *Rome in America: Transnational Catholic Ideology from the Risorgimento to Fascism* (Chapel Hill: University of North Carolina Press, 2004); Benjamin Justice, "Thomas Nast and the Public School Issue of the

1870s," *History of Education Quarterly* 45 (2005): 171–206; Tracy Fessenden, "The Nineteenth-Century Bible Wars and the Separation of Church and State," *Church History* 74 (2005): 784–811.

6   R. A. Burchell, *The San Francisco Irish, 1848–1880* (Berkeley: University of California Press, 1980), 3; William Issel and Robert W. Cherny, *San Francisco, 1865–1932: Politics, Power, and Urban Development* (Berkeley: University of California Press, 1986), 56.

7   San Francisco *Pacific,* 7 November 1867, 2; 6 January 1870, 1; San Francisco *Thistleton's Illustrated Jolly Giant,* 6 June 1874, 2; 5 December 1874, 299; 17 July 1875, 43.

8   *The Statutes of California Passed at the Sixth Session of the Legislature* (Sacramento, Calif.: B. B. Redding, 1855), 237; Mark J. Hurley, *Church-State Relationships in Education in California* (Washington, D.C.: Catholic University of America Press, 1948), 29–77; Miriam Mead Hawley, "Schools for Social Order: Public Education as an Aspect of San Francisco's Urbanization and Industrialization Processes" (M.A. thesis, California State University, San Francisco, 1971); Victor L. Shradar, "Ethnic Politics, Religion, and the Public Schools of San Francisco, 1849–1933" (PhD diss., Stanford University, 1974), 27–37; Catherine Ann Curry, "Shaping Young San Franciscans: Public and Catholic Schools in San Francisco, 1851–1906" (PhD diss., Graduate Theological Union, 1987), 243–45. The California Supreme Court case People v. McCreery, 34 Cal. 432 (1868) ended schools' tax exemption status.

9   Winfield J. Davis, *History of Political Conventions in California, 1849–1892* (Sacramento, Calif.: California State Library, 1893), 307, 337; 43 Cong. Rec., 2nd Sess. 4172 (22 May 1874).

10   John Hemphill, "Our Public Schools: Shall the Lord's Prayer Be Recited in Them?," in *The Pacific Coast Pulpit, Containing Sermons by Prominent Preachers of San Francisco and Vicinity* (San Francisco: Western Reporting and Publishing, 1875), 94.

11   San Francisco *California Christian Advocate*, 18 November 1869, 546; James Buchard, *The Inquisition: A Lecture by Rev. Father Buchard* (San Francisco: San Francisco Monitor, 1873); San Francisco *Occident*, 21 August 1873, 272; San Francisco *American Citizen* 1 no. 2 (February 1874); San Francisco *Thistleton's Jolly Giant*, 7 February 1874, 7; 14 February 1874, 5; 4 April 1874, 11; San Francisco *Thistleton's Illustrated Jolly Giant*, 5 December 1874, 304; 20 February 1875, 129; San Francisco *Chronicle*, 15 February 1875, 3; San Francisco *Occident*, 17 February 1876, 52; McGloin, *Eloquent Indian*, 152–71.

12   San Francisco *Thistleton's Illustrated Jolly Giant*, 5 December 1874, 304; 28 March 1874, 4; 25 December 1875, 414; Hemphill, "Our Public Schools," 95.

13   *A Yankee Trader in the Gold Rush: The Letters of Franklin A. Buck,* ed. Katherine A. White (Boston: Houghton Mifflin, 1930), 229; Franchot, *Roads to Rome*; Jennifer Ting, "Bachelor Society: Deviant Heterosexuality and Asian American Historiography," in *Privileging Positions: The Sites of Asian American Studies*, ed. Gary Y. Okihiro, Marilyn Alquizola, Dorothy Fugita Rony, and K. Scott Wong (Pullman: Washington State University

Press, 1995), 271–80; Robert G. Lee, *Orientals: Asian Americans in Popular Culture* (Philadelphia: Temple University Press, 1999), 83–105; Susan Lee Johnson, *Roaring Camp: The Social World of the California Gold Rush* (New York: W. W. Norton, 2000), 245–46; Karen J. Leong, "'A Distinct and Antagonistic Race': Constructions of Chinese Manhood in the Exclusionist Debates," in *Across the Great Divide: Cultures of Manhood in the American West*, ed. Matthew Basso, Laura McCall, and Dee Garceau (New York: Routledge, 2001), 131–48; Eric Reinders, *Borrowed Gods and Foreign Bodies: Christian Missionaries Imagine Chinese Religion* (Berkeley: University of California Press, 2004), 104–11; Timothy Verhoeven, "Neither Male nor Female: Androgyny, Nativism and International Anti-Catholicism," *Australasian Journal of American Studies* 24 (2005): 5–19; Rosanne Currarino, "'Meat vs. Rice': The Ideal of Manly Labor and Anti-Chinese Hysteria in Nineteenth-century America," *Men and Masculinities* 9 (2007): 476–90.

14   San Francisco *Chronicle*, 19 February 1873, 3. For examples of ape-like Irish Catholics, see San Francisco *Jolly Giant*, 1 January 1874, 4; 28 March 1874, 4; San Francisco *Illustrated Jolly Giant*, 5 September 1874, 109; 12 June 1875, 370; and San Francisco *Wasp*, 26 June 1880, 784. For the national context of anti-Irish hostility, see Billington, *The Protestant Crusade*; Dale T. Knobel, *Paddy and the Republic: Ethnicity and Nationality in Antebellum America* (Middletown, Conn.: Wesleyan University Press, 1986); D. G. Paz, "Anti-Catholicism, Anti-Irish Stereotyping, and Anti-Celtic Racism in Mid-Victorian Working Class Periodicals," *Albion* 18 (1986): 601–16; Noel Ignatiev, *How the Irish Became White* (New York: Routledge, 1995); Lawrence J. McCaffrey, *The Irish Catholic Diaspora in America*, rev. ed. (Washington, D.C.: Catholic University of American Press, 1997), 91–115; L. Perry Curtis Jr., *Apes and Angels: The Irishman in Victorian Caricature*, rev. ed. (Washington, D.C.: Smithsonian Institution Press, 1997); Matthew Frye Jacobson, *Whiteness of a Different Color: European Immigrants and the Alchemy of Race* (Cambridge, Mass.: Harvard University Press, 1998), 48–56; Samuel J. Thomas, "Mugwump Cartoonists, the Papacy, and Tammany Hall in America's Gilded Age," *Religion and American Culture* 14 (2004): 213–50; Kerry Soper, "From Swarthy Ape to Sympathetic Everyman and Subversive Trickster: The Development of Irish Caricature in American Comic Strips Between 1890 and 1920," *Journal of American Studies* 39 (2005): 257–96; and Justice, "Thomas Nast and the Public School Issue of the 1870s." Italian Catholics, though much less numerous than Irish Catholics in San Francisco in the 1870s, encountered similar hostility from Protestants and engaged in comparable forms of anti-Chinese harassment; see Micaela di Leonardo, *The Varieties of Ethnic Experience: Kinship, Class, and Gender among California Italian-Americans* (Ithaca, N.Y.: Cornell University Press, 1984), 56; Robert Orsi, "The Religious Boundaries of an In-between People: Street Feste and the Problem of the Dark-Skinned Other in Italian Harlem, 1920–1990," *American Quarterly* 44 (1992): 313–47; Jacobson, *Whiteness of a Different Color*, 56–62; and David A. J. Richards, *Italian American: The Racializing of an Ethnic Identity* (New York: New York University Press, 1999).

15   San Francisco *Monitor,* 15 November 1873, 4; 25 July 1874, 4; 1 August 1874, 4; San Francisco *Daily Examiner,* 8 July 1873, 2; Hugh Quigley, *The Irish Race in California, and on the Pacific Coast* (San Francisco: A. Roman & Company, 1878), 61; Matthew Frye Jacobson, *Special Sorrows: The Diasporic Imagination of Irish, Polish, and Jewish Immigrants in the United States* (Cambridge, Mass.: Harvard University Press, 1995). The *Monitor* made a special point of responding to the "atrocious calumny and invective" of John Hemphill; see San Francisco *Monitor,* 14 February 1874, 4; 20 February 1875, 4.

16   Steven P. Erie, "Politics, the Public Sector, and Irish Social Mobility: San Francisco, 1870–1900," *Western Political Quarterly* 31 (1978): 279–80; Issel and Cherny, *San Francisco, 1865–1932,* 56; David R. Roediger, *The Wages of Whiteness: Race and the Making of the American Working Class,* rev. ed. (London: Verso, 1991), 133–63; Ignatiev, *How the Irish Became White.*

17   San Francisco *Monitor,* 24 May 1873, 4; 10 May 1873, 4; San Francisco *Catholic Guardian,* 15 March 1873, 10; 12 April 1873, 49; 24 May 1873, 121.

18   *Spirit of Missions* (New York: Board of Missions, Protestant Episcopal Church, 1870), 168; San Francisco *Chinese Record,* 12 February 1877, 4; Joseph Alemany to Aloysius Masnata, 5 August 1874, in Joseph W. Riordan, *The First Half Century of St. Ignatius Church and College* (San Francisco: H. S. Crocker, 1905), 197; John B. McGloin, "Thomas Cian, Pioneer Chinese Priest in California," *California Historical Society Quarterly* 48 (1969): 45–58; Ricky Manalo, "A History of Chinese Catholics in San Francisco and the Bay Area," in *Asian American Christianity Reader,* ed. Viji Nakka-Cammauf and Timothy Tseng (Castro Valley, Calif.: Institute for the Study of Asian American Christianity, 2009), 75–82.

19   San Francisco *Monitor,* 11 February 1873, 4; San Francisco *Daily Evening Bulletin,* 8 November 1872, 2; San Francisco *Daily Alta California,* 26 February 1873, 1; McGloin, *Eloquent Indian,* 110–23; Gerald McKevitt, *Brokers of Culture: Italian Jesuits in the American West, 1848–1919* (Stanford, Calif.: Stanford University Press, 2007).

20   San Francisco *Daily Alta California,* 6 October 1854, 2; Grass Valley *Daily Union,* 11 August 1867, 3; Gunther Barth, *Bitter Strength: A History of the Chinese in the United States, 1850–1870* (Cambridge, Mass.: Harvard University Press, 1964), 145.

21   San Francisco *Occident,* 6 March 1873, 73; O. Gibson, *"Chinaman or White Man, Which?": Reply to Father Buchard* (San Francisco: Alta California Printing House, 1873), 3, 7, 9–10, 17, 19, 27–28.

22   San Francisco *Daily Evening Bulletin,* 15 March 1873, 4; San Francisco *Daily Alta California,* 15 March 1873, 1; 16 March 1873, 2, 5; San Francisco *California Christian Advocate,* 20 March 1873, 4; Gibson, *"Chinaman or White Man, Which?,"* 4; San Francisco *Occident,* 26 March 1870, 120. Ironically, in 1868 the *Pacific* had criticized the Catholic Church for *failing* to target California's Chinese population; San Francisco *Pacific,* 6 November 1868, 4.

23   *Chinese Immigration: The Social, Moral, and Political Effect of Chinese Immigration* (Sacramento, Calif.: State Printing Office, 1876), 29, 138–39, 161–63;

Hiroyuki Matsubara, "Stratified Whiteness and Sexualized Chinese Immigrants in San Francisco: The Report of the California Special Committee on Chinese Immigration in 1876," *American Studies International* 41 (2003): 32–59. Republican state senator George S. Evans and independent Creed Haymond joined Democrats Frank McCoppin, William M. Pierson, M. J. Donovan, George H. Rogers, and Edward J. Lewis.

24 The committee consisted of U.S. senators Oliver Morton (R-Indiana), Aaron A. Sargent (R-California), and Henry Cooper (D-Tennessee) and representatives Edwin Meade (D-New York), William Piper (D-California), and James Wilson (R-Iowa), although Wilson never traveled to California and Meade left halfway though the hearing. Also allowed to question witnesses were Frederick A. Bee (a lawyer hired by San Francisco's Chinese business leaders), Benjamin Sherman Brooks (an independent lawyer), several presidents of anti-Chinese clubs, and A. J. Bryant and Frank M. Pixley, representing the city of San Francisco. The hearing's similarity to a criminal trial was noted by Otis Gibson; see *The Chinese in America* (Cincinnati: Hitchcock & Walden, 1877), 374–75.

25 *Report of the Joint Special Committee to Investigate Chinese Immigration*, 27 February 1877, Congressional Serial Set vol. 1734, 44th Cong., 2nd Sess., report 689 (Washington, D.C.: Government Printing Office, 1877), 55–56, 399, 402, 469–70.

26 *Report of the Joint Special Committee to Investigate Chinese Immigration*, 580; Gibson, *The Chinese in America*, 385–86.

27 S. V. Blakeslee to George Whipple, 13 April 1853; S. V. Blakeslee to George Whipple, 30 July 1854; 29 December 1853, AMAR.

28 *Report of the Joint Special Committee to Investigate Chinese Immigration*, 1035, 1041, 1241, 1243.

29 San Francisco *Chronicle*, 15 November 1876, 2; *Report of the Joint Special Committee to Investigate Chinese Immigration*, 677.

30 San Francisco *Wasp*, 18 November 1876, 138; San Francisco *Thistleton's Illustrated Jolly Giant*, 18 November 1876, 333; *Report of the Joint Special Committee to Investigate Chinese Immigration*, 577; Henry Yu, "Mixing Bodies and Cultures: The Meaning of America's Fascination with Sex between 'Orientals' and 'Whites,'" in *Sex, Love, Race: Crossing Boundaries in North American History*, ed. Martha Hodes (New York: New York University Press, 1999), 444–63.

31 San Francisco *Monitor and Guardian*, 28 October 1876, 4; New York *Catholic World* 26 (1878): 701–2, 704; San Francisco *Thistleton's Illustrated Jolly Giant*, 18 December 1875, 395; 18 November 1876, 333.

32 San Francisco *Daily Alta California*, 16 November 1876, 1; San Francisco *Chronicle*, 16 November 1876, 3; San Francisco *Daily Evening Post*, 16 November 1876, 2; San Francisco *Thistleton's Illustrated Jolly Giant*, 18 November 1876, 333; 2 December 1876, 357; San Francisco *Pacific*, 23 November 1876, 4; San Francisco *California Christian Advocate*, 30 November 1876, 4; Martha Mabie Gardner, "Working on White Womanhood: White Working

Women in the San Francisco Anti-Chinese Movement, 1877–1890," *Journal of Social History* 33 (1999): 73–95.

33   The Burchard-Osuna clash is briefly described in Zephyrin Engelhardt, *The Franciscans in California* (Harbor Springs, Mich.: Holy Childhood Indian School, 1897), 469–70; Peter J. Rahill, *The Catholic Indian Missions and Grant's Peace Policy, 1870–1884* (Washington, D.C.: Catholic University of America Press, 1953), 145–49; John T. Dwyer, *Condemned to the Mines: The Life of Eugene O'Connell, 1815–1891, Pioneer Bishop of Northern California and Nevada* (New York: Vantage Press, 1976), 146–52; Robert H. Keller Jr., *American Protestantism and United States Indian Policy, 1869–82* (Lincoln: University of Nebraska Press, 1983), 178; and Linda Pacini Pitelka, "Mendocino: Race Relations in a Northern California County, 1850–1949" (PhD diss., University of Massachusetts, 1994), 286–88.

34   San Diego *Union,* 7 March 1891; *Encyclopedia of California's Catholic Heritage, 1769–1999,* ed. Francis J. Weber (Mission Hills, Calif.: Saint Francis Historical Society and Arthur H. Clark Co., 2001), 595; Luciano Osuna to Eugene O'Connell, 29 August 1872, A-1140, ACALA.

35   Luciano Osuna to Joseph Alemany, 18 December 1873, A-1206; Luciano Osuna, deposition before John Hamill, 6 June 1874, A-1205, ACALA; J. L. Burchard to Edward P. Smith, 18 April 1874, roll 46; J. L. Burchard to Commissioner of Indian Affairs, 15 June 1875, roll 47, M234, Letters Received, 1824–81, RBIA-NARA-W; Mendocino *Independent Dispatch,* 25 April 1874, 3.

36   J. L. Burchard to Commissioner of Indian Affairs, 15 June 1875, roll 47, M234, Letters Received, 1824–81, RBIA-NARA-W; Thomas J. Pettit to Joseph Alemany, 4 May 1874, A-1309, ACALA; Eugene O'Connell to John Gilmary Shea, 27 August 1874, Diocese of Sacramento Archive, Sacramento; Charles Ewing to Edward P. Smith, 2 May 1874, Special Case 43, RBIA-NARA-W.

37   Luciano Osuna to Eugene O'Connell, 21 December 1872, A-1141; Luciano Osuna to Joseph Alemany, 6 April 1874, A-1306, ACALA.

38   Rahill, *The Catholic Indian Missions and Grant's Peace Policy*; Henry E. Fritz, *The Movement for Indian Assimilation, 1860–1890* (Philadelphia: University of Pennsylvania Press, 1963), 87–108; Francis J. Weber, "Grant's Peace Policy: A Catholic Dissenter," *Montana* 19 (1969): 56–63; Keller, *American Protestantism and United States Indian Policy,* 177–80; Tisa Wenger, *We Have a Religion: The 1920s Pueblo Indian Dance Controversy and American Religious Freedom* (Chapel Hill: University of North Carolina Press, 2009), 29–35.

39   San Francisco *Catholic Guardian,* 11 January 1873, 209; 10 May 1873, 97; 24 May 1873, 123; San Francisco *Monitor,* 20 February 1875, 4; 19 February 1876, 4; San Francisco *Examiner,* 6 January 1874, 2; Santa Clara *Owl,* January 1875, 171.

40   San Francisco *Monitor and Guardian,* 19 February 1876, 4.

41   Santa Clara *Owl,* October 1870, 73, 75; M. Wallrath to J. B. A. Brouillet, 29 September 1875, A-1431, ACALA.

42   People v. de la Guerra, 40 Cal. 311 (1870); Pitt, *The Decline of the Californios*; Albert Camarillo, *Chicanos in a Changing Society: From Mexican Pueblos to*

American Barrios in Santa Barbara and Southern California, 1848–1930 (Cambridge, Mass.: Harvard University Press, 1979); Richard Griswold del Castillo, *The Los Angeles Barrio, 1850–1890: A Social History* (Berkeley: University of California Press, 1979); Douglas Monroy, *Thrown among Strangers: The Making of Mexican Culture in Frontier California* (Berkeley: University of California Press, 1990); Tomás Almaguer, *Racial Fault Lines: The Historical Origins of White Supremacy in California* (Berkeley: University of California Press, 1994), 45–104; James A. Sandos, "'Because he is a liar and a thief': Conquering the Residents of 'Old' California, 1850–1880," in *Rooted in Barbarous Soil: People, Culture, and Community in Gold Rush California,* ed. Kevin Starr and Richard J. Orsi (Berkeley: University of California Press, 2000), 86–112; Miroslava Chávez-García, *Negotiating Conquest: Gender and Power in California, 1770s to 1880s* (Tucson: University of Arizona Press, 2004); F. Michael Higginbotham, *Race Law: Cases, Commentary, and Questions,* 2nd ed. (Durham, N.C.: Carolina Academic Press, 2005), 278–81.

43   *Testimonios: Early California through the Eyes of Women, 1815–1848,* ed. Rose Marie Beebe and Robert M. Senkewicz (Berkeley, Calif.: Heyday Books and Bancroft Library, 2006), 58; Mariano Guadalupe Vallejo, *Recuerdos históricos y personales tocante a la alta California, 1874,* vol. 5, Earl R. Hewitt, trans., BL; Patrick J. Thomas, *Our Centennial Memoir: Founding of the Missions* (San Francisco: P. J. Thomas, 1877), 121; Rosaura Sánchez, *Telling Identities: The Californio Testimonios* (Minneapolis: University of Minnesota Press, 1995), 149–56; Vincent Pérez, *Remembering the Hacienda: History and Memory in the Mexican American Southwest* (College Station: Texas A&M University Press, 2006), 75–92; José Luis Benavides, "'Californios! Whom Do You Support?': *El Clamor Público's* Contradictory Role in the Racial Formation Process in Early California," *California History* 84 (2006–7): 54–66, 73–74.

44   On the label *gente de razón,* see Gloria E. Miranda, "Racial and Cultural Dimensions in *Gente de Razón* Status in Spanish and Mexican California," *Southern California Quarterly* 70 (1988): 265–78; Monroy, *Thrown among Strangers,* 136–37; David G. Gutiérrez, *Walls and Mirrors: Mexican Americans, Mexican Immigrants, and the Politics of Ethnicity* (Berkeley: University of California Press, 1995), 32–33; Douglas Monroy, "Guilty Pleasures: The Satisfactions of Racial Thinking in Early-Nineteenth-Century California," in *Race and Nation: Ethnic Systems in the Modern World,* ed. Paul Spickard (New York: Routledge, 2005), 33–52; and Louise Pubols, *The Father of All: The de la Guerra Family, Power, and Patriarchy in Mexican California* (Berkeley and San Marino, Calif.: University of California Press and Huntington Library, 2009), 23–24.

45   *Ramblings in California: The Adventures of Henry Cerruti,* ed. Margaret Mollins and Virginia E. Thickens (Berkeley, Calif.: Friends of the Bancroft Library, 1954), 44; Vallejo, *Recuerdos históricos y personales tocante a la alta California,* vol. 5; Romualdo Pacheco, *Remarks of Hon. Romualdo Pacheco, of California, in the House of Representatives, Saturday, March 18, 1882* (Washington, D.C.: Thomas McGill, 1882), 5, 9; 47 Cong. Rec., 1st Sess. 2210–11 (23 March 1882); Richard Morefield, *The Mexican Adaptation in American California, 1846–1875* (San Francisco: R and E Research Associates, 1971), 51–52.

46   J. L. Burchard to Commissioner of Indian Affairs, 15 June 1875, roll 47, M234, Letters Received, 1824–81, RBIA-NARA-W; San Francisco *California Christian Advocate*, 10 June 1875, 4.

47   J. L. Burchard to B. C. Whiting, 18 March 1873; J. L. Burchard to Edward P. Smith, 7 October 1873; J. L. Burchard to Edward P. Smith, 30 April 1874; 31 July 1874, letterbook dated 4/1/1871 to 12/11/1875, box 1, Records of the Round Valley Agency, RBIA-NARA-SB; Mendocino *Independent Dispatch*, 6 June 1874, 2.

48   Luciano Osuna to Joseph Alemany, 29 May 1874, A-1309; J. L. Burchard to Edward P. Smith, 9 June 1874, A-1272; Luciano Osuna, deposition to John Hamill, 18 February 1875, A-1415, ACALA.

49   Joseph Alemany and Eugene O'Connell to Commissioner of Indian Affairs, 20 February 1875, A-1326; Charles Ewing to Joseph Alemany, 19 April 1875, A-1380, ACALA; Charles Ewing to Columbus Delano, 5 April 1875, roll 47, M234, Letters Received, 1824–81, RBIA-NARA-W.

50   Columbus Delano to Office of Indian Affairs, 14 May 1875, roll 47, M234, Letters Received, 1824–81, RBIA-NARA-W; William Vandever to J. L. Burchard, 4 June 1875, "Luciano Osana Papers, 1874–1878" folder, box 173, Records of the Round Valley Agency, RBIA-NARA-SB; William Vandever to Commissioner of Indian Affairs, 4 June 1875, A-1427, ACALA.

51   F. E. Kellogg, "Minutes of a Meeting Composed of the Captains and Leaders of the Different Tribes," 12 June 1875, roll 47, M234, Letters Received, 1824–81, RBIA-NARA-W; J. L. Burchard to William Vandever, 16 June 1875, "Luciano Osana Papers, 1874–1878" folder, box 173, Records of the Round Valley Agency, RBIA-NARA-SB.

52   J. L. Burchard to Edward P. Smith, 10 April 1874, roll 46; J. L. Burchard to Commissioner of Indian Affairs, 15 June 1875, roll 47, M234, Letters Received, 1824–81, RBIA-NARA-W; J. L. Burchard to U.S. Marshall, 7 April 1874, "Luciano Osana Papers, 1874–1878" folder, box 173, Records of the Round Valley Agency, RBIA-NARA-SB.

53   J. L. Burchard to William Vandever, 16 June 1875, "Luciano Osana Papers, 1874–1878" folder, box 173, Records of the Round Valley Agency, RBIA-NARA-SB. On the Catholic Church's longstanding but diminishing toleration of folk practices in the southwest, see Michael E. Engh, "From *Frontera* Faith to Roman Rubrics: Altering Hispanic Religious Customs in Los Angeles, 1855–1880," *U.S. Catholic Historian* 12 (1994): 85–105; and Luis D. León, *La Llorona's Children: Religion, Life, and Death in the U.S.-Mexican Borderlands* (Berkeley: University of California Press, 2004), 41–45.

54   William Vandever to Commissioner of Indian Affairs, 2 July 1875, roll 47, M234, Letters Received, 1824–81, RBIA-NARA-W; San Francisco *California Christian Advocate*, 8 July 1875, 4.

55   Columbus Delano to Office of Indian Affairs, 17 July 1875, roll 47, M234, Letters Received, 1824–81, RBIA-NARA-W; William Vandever to J. L. Burchard, 20 July 1875, 1875 folder, box 15, Records of the Round Valley Agency, RBIA-NARA-SB; New York *Catholic World* 26 (1877): 90, 107; Keller, *American Protestantism and United States Indian Policy*, 180.

CHAPTER FIVE

1   *California Annual Conference of the Methodist Episcopal Church* (San Francisco: Methodist Book Depository, 1879), 63, 66; San Francisco *California Christian Advocate,* 24 April 1879, 6; 6 November 1879, 6; New York *Evangelist,* 20 March 1879, 6; Henry B. Sheldon to Commissioner of Indian Affairs, 7 September 1878, letterbook dated 10/1/1877 to 6/10/1879, box 1, Records of the Round Valley Agency, RBIA-NARA-SB.

2   *California Annual Conference of the Methodist Episcopal Church,* 1875, 65.

3   Mendocino *Democrat,* 13 July 1876, 3; San Francisco *California Christian Advocate,* 27 July 1876, 1.

4   *Annual Report of the Commissioner of Indian Affairs* (Washington, D.C.: Government Printing Office, 1876), 16; J. L. Burchard to J. L. Smith, 12 July 1876, roll 48, M234, Letters Received, 1824–81, RBIA-NARA-W.

5   San Francisco *Chronicle,* 25 June 1876, 4; 11 July 1876, 2; Henry E. Fritz, *The Movement for Indian Assimilation, 1860–1890* (Philadelphia: University of Pennsylvania Press, 1963), 176–80.

6   San Francisco *Daily Alta California,* 27 November 1877, 2; San Francisco *Daily Examiner,* 15 July 1878, 2; Mendocino *Beacon,* 12 January 1878, 2; Henry George Waltmann, "The Interior Department, War Department, and Indian Policy, 1871–1930" (PhD diss., University of Nebraska, 1962); Robert Winston Mardock, *The Reformers and the American Indian* (Columbia: University of Missouri Press, 1971), 159–67.

7   San Francisco *California Christian Advocate,* 13 July 1876, 4; 3 August 1876, 4.

8   J. L. Burchard to J. L. Smith, 22 April 1876; 31 July 1876, letterbook dated 12/31/1875 to 10/16/1877, box 1, Records of the Round Valley Agency, RBIA-NARA-SB.

9   W. P. Melendy to A. A. Sargent, 18 January 1875, roll 47, M234, Letters Received, 1824–81, RBIA-NARA-W; J. L. Burchard to J. L. Smith, 31 December 1873; 21 January 1876; 25 February 1876, letterbook dated 12/31/1875 to 10/16/1877, box 1, Records of the Round Valley Agency, RBIA-NARA-SB; Mendocino *Democratic Dispatch,* 11 December 1875, 3; San Francisco *Chronicle,* 24 January 1876, 3. Already having served as missionaries among African Americans in the South, Chinese immigrants in Stockton, and Indians at Round Valley, the two women went next to Peking, China, for the Women's Missionary Union; *Ladies' Repository* 2 (1875): 75.

10 Edward P. Smith to J. L. Burchard, 9 November 1875, 1875 folder, box 15, Records of the Round Valley Agency and Heirship Examiner-At-Large (re. Round Valley), Records of the Bureau of Indian Affairs, Record Group 75, National Archives and Records Administration, San Bruno; *Report on J. L. Burchard,* 28 April 1882, Congressional Serial Set vol. 2068, 47th Cong., 1st Sess., report 1150 (Washington, D.C.: Government Printing Office, 1882), 1–2; Los Angeles *Times,* 25 April 1885, 1.

11   Mendocino *Democratic Dispatch,* 11 December 1875, 3; 20 May 1876, 3; 17 June 1876, 2; 19 August 1876, 2; 30 September 1876, 2; San Francisco *Chronicle,* 24 January 1876, 3; 44 Cong. Rec., 1st Sess. 3563 (3 June 1876).

12   San Francisco *California Christian Advocate,* 27 January 1876, 4; 10 February 1876, 6; 6 April 1876, 6; 24 August 1876, 1; 1 February 1877, 4; 22 February 1877, 4; 1 March 1877, 1; 24 May 1877, 4; San Francisco *Daily Morning Call,* 10 March 1876, 1; Mendocino *Democrat,* 14 October 1876, 3; 24 February 1877, 3; J. L. Burchard to J. L. Smith, 23 June 1876, letterbook dated 12/31/1875 to 10/16/1877, box 1, Records of the Round Valley Agency, RBIA-NARA-SB; San Francisco *Chronicle,* 24 January 1876, 3; Mendocino *Dispatch Democrat,* 7 October 1876, 2; 21 October 1876, 2; San Francisco *Daily Evening Post,* 16 May 1877, 1.

13   J. L. Burchard to J. L. Smith, 16 June 1877; 30 June 1877, letterbook dated 12/31/1875 to 10/16/1877, box 1, Records of the Round Valley Agency, RBIA-NARA-SB.

14   San Francisco *California Christian Advocate,* 28 June 1877, 4; 19 July 1877, 1.

15   H. B. Sheldon to Commissioner of Indian Affairs, 8 January 1878; 24 January 1878; 8 February 1878, 13 February 1878, letterbook dated 10/1/1877 to 6/10/1879, box 1, Records of the Round Valley Agency, RBIA-NARA-SB.

16   *Annual Report of the Commissioner of Indian Affairs* (Washington, D.C.: Government Printing Office, 1878), 12.

17   *Annual Report of the Commissioner of Indian Affairs* (Washington, D.C.: Government Printing Office, 1877), 39; *Annual Report of the Commissioner of Indian Affairs* (Washington, D.C.: Government Printing Office, 1879), 10; *Report (To Accompany Resolution of the Senate of July 4, 1884),* 27 February 1885, Congressional Serial Set vol. 2274, 48th Cong., 2nd Sess., report 1522 (Washington, D.C.: Government Printing Office, 1885), 75, 77, 80–81.

18   Mendocino *Dispatch Democrat,* 19 October 1879, 3; H. B. Sheldon to Commissioner of Indian Affairs, 11 October 1878; 17 October 1878; 26 November 1878; 30 April 1879, letterbook dated 10/1/1877 to 6/10/1879, box 1, Records of the Round Valley Agency, RBIA-NARA-SB; *Annual Report of the Commissioner of Indian Affairs,* 1879, 10; Ukiah City *Press,* 31 October 1881, 3; *Report (To Accompany Resolution of the Senate of July 4, 1884),* 79; Khal Schneider, "Making Indian Land in the Allotment Era: Northern California's Indian Rancherias," *Western Historical Quarterly* 41 (2010): 429–50.

19   San Francisco *California Christian Advocate,* 29 September 1880, 1; H. B. Sheldon to Commissioner of Indian Affairs, 20 March 1879, letterbook dated 10/1/1877 to 6/10/1879, box 1, Records of the Round Valley Agency, RBIA-NARA-SB.

20   Mendocino *Democratic Dispatch,* 26 April 1879, 3; Mendocino *Democrat,* 10 May 1879, 3; John Brown to George Clifford, 27 January 1882, 1882 folder, California Methodist Episcopal Conference Correspondence, 1855–1951, PSR; Pit River Indians to Chester A. Arthur, 24 January 1882; Ukie Indians to Chester A. Arthur, 31 January 1882, roll 24, M732, Interior Department Appointment Papers, RBIA-NARA-W.

21   San Francisco *California Christian Advocate*, 13 April 1876, 1.

22   Mendocino *Democrat*, 19 October 1878, 3; 10 May 1879, 3; San Francisco
       Chronicle, 22 October 1879, 8; Mendocino *Dispatch Democrat*, 19 November
       1880, 3. In 1880 and 1881, several employees and settlers accused Sheldon of
       defrauding the government by trading away a valuable stallion for a worth-
       less "jack" horse; the Office of Indian Affairs sent an investigator, who con-
       cluded that Sheldon had acted unwisely but not for "any personal pecuniary
       benefit"; see roll 24, M732, Interior Department Appointment Papers, RBIA-
       NARA-W.

23   San Francisco *California Christian Advocate*, 25 December 1879, 1; 27 Octo-
       ber 1880, 6; J. P. Thomson, E. B. Bateman, J. K. Chambers, William M. Michel,
       H. Randruss, D. W. Burchard, and J. L. Broaddus to C. P. Berry, May 1880,
       roll 52, M234, Letters Received, 1824–81, RBIA-NARA-W.

24   John C. Lowrie, "Our Indian Affairs," *Presbyterian Quarterly and Princeton
       Review* 3 (1874): 5–22; Francis A. Walker, *The Indian Question* (Boston:
       James R. Osgood, 1874); George Ainslie, "The Indian Question," *Presbyterian
       Quarterly and Princeton Review* 4 (1875): 438–47; J. Elliot Condict, "The In-
       dian Question," *Presbyterian Quarterly and Princeton Review* 5 (1876): 76–93;
       Thomas Williamson, "The Indian Question," *Presbyterian Quarterly and
       Princeton Review* 5 (1876): 608–24; R. H. Milroy, "Our Indian Policy Further
       Considered," *Presbyterian Quarterly and Princeton Review* 5 (1876): 624–28;
       "President Grant's Indian Policy," *Methodist Quarterly Review* 29 (1877):
       409–30; Grindall Reynolds, "Our Bedouins: What Can We Do with Them?,"
       Unitarian Review and Religious Magazine 8 (1877): 139–62; Philadelphia
       Presbyterian, 14 January 1878, 11; 2 February 1878, 8.

25   San Francisco *California Christian Advocate*, 14 December 1876, 4; 10 Janu-
       ary 1878, 4; 6 June 1878, 4; 11 July 1878, 4; 15 August 1878, 4; 10 October 1878,
       4; San Francisco *Pacific*, 20 June 1878, 4; San Francisco *Occident*, 5 February
       1879, 1; 12 February 1879, 1.

26   San Francisco *California Christian Advocate*, 7 February 1878, 4; 15 January
       1880, 4; 11 May 1881, 4; San Francisco *Pacific*, 13 April 1881, 4; J. L. Burchard
       to Carl Schurz, 5 September 1878, roll 50, M234, Letters Received, 1824–81,
       RBIA-NARA-W.

27   Oakland *Herald of Truth*, 1 May 1880, 22.

28   Sarah Winnemucca Hopkins, *Life among the Piutes: Their Wrongs and
       Claims*, ed. Mrs. Horace Mann (Boston: Cupples, Upham, 1883), 267; San
       Francisco *Daily Alta California*, 24 December 1879, 1; Gae Whitney Canfield,
       Sarah Winnemucca of the Northern Paiutes (Norman: University of Oklahoma
       Press, 1983); Sally Zanjani, *Sarah Winnemucca* (Lincoln: University of
       Nebraska Press, 2001).

29   San Francisco *Chronicle*, 14 November 1879, 1; 23 November 1879, 1; 26 No-
       vember 1879, 3; 24 December 1879, 1; San Francisco *Daily Morning Call*,
       22 November 1879, 4; San Francisco *Daily Alta California*, 26 November
       1879, 1; 4 December 1879, 1; 24 December 1879, 1.

30   San Francisco *Daily Alta California*, 1 February 1879, 2; 3 October 1879, 2;
       San Francisco *Chronicle*, 25 June 1876, 4.

31   Fritz, *The Movement for Indian Assimilation*, 198–221; Mardock, *The Reformers and the American Indian*, 150–59, 168–210; Francis Paul Prucha, *American Indian Policy in Crisis: Christian Reformers and the Indian, 1865–1900* (Norman: University of Oklahoma Press, 1976), 128–43; Robert H. Keller Jr., *American Protestantism and United States Indian Policy, 1869–82* (Lincoln: University of Nebraska Press, 1983), 188–204; Frederick E. Hoxie, *A Final Promise: The Campaign to Assimilate the Indians, 1880–1920* (Lincoln: University of Nebraska Press, 1984), 1–43; Valerie Sherer Mathes and Richard Lowitt, *The Standing Bear Controversy: Prelude to Indian Reform* (Urbana: University of Illinois Press, 2003).

32   Report of the Committee of Correspondence on Indian Affairs, 1882, 1882 folder, California Methodist Episcopal Conference Correspondence, 1855–1951, PSR; *California Annual Conference of the Methodist Episcopal Church* (San Francisco: Methodist Book Depository, 1882), 39–40.

33   Nicholas Congiato to John Brouillet, 11 May 1876, A-1465, ACALA.

34   *Chinese Immigration: The Social, Moral, and Political Effect of Chinese Immigration*, 2nd ed. (Sacramento, Calif.: State Printing Office, 1878), 243, 246.

35   "Congregational Association: Fourth Day," unknown newspaper, n.d. [1877], vol. 3, p. 2, scrapbooks on Chinese immigration, 1877–93, BL; *Chinese Immigration*, 2nd ed., 240.

36   San Francisco *Daily Morning Call*, 29 October 1877, 3; San Francisco *California Christian Advocate*, 25 October 1877, 4; *American Missionary*, January 1878, 18.

37   A. A. Sargent, *Chinese Immigration: Speech of Hon. A. A. Sargent, of California, in the Senate of the United States, March 7, 1878* (Washington, D.C.: Government Printing Office, 1878), 23; *Chinese Immigration*, 2nd ed., 240–49; New York *Daily Tribune*, 24 February 1879, 5; San Francisco *Argonaut*, 15 December 1877, 4.

38   San Francisco *Daily Examiner*, 30 August 1867, 1; San Francisco *Daily Alta California*, 6 April 1876, 1; O. C. Wheeler, *The Chinese in America: A National Question* (Oakland, Calif.: Times Publishing, 1880), 11, 35; San Francisco *Daily Evening Bulletin*, 5 July 1879, 1; San Francisco *Pacific*, 19 February 1879, 4; San Francisco *California Christian Advocate*, 23 August 1877, 4; 13 March 1879, 4; San Francisco *Evangel*, 7 February 1879, 4.

39   Winfield J. Davis, *History of Political Conventions in California, 1849–1892* (Sacramento, Calif.: California State Library, 1893), 357–64; Eric Foner, *Reconstruction: America's Unfinished Revolution, 1863–1877* (New York: Harper & Row, 1988), 512–601; Najia Aarim-Heriot, *Chinese Immigrants, African Americans, and Racial Anxiety in the United States, 1848–82* (Urbana: University of Illinois Press, 2003), 180–82.

40   Alexander Saxton, *The Indispensable Enemy: Labor and the Anti-Chinese Movement in California* (Berkeley: University of California Press, 1971), 113–32; William Issel and Robert W. Cherny, *San Francisco 1865–1932: Politics, Power, and Urban Development* (Berkeley: University of California Press, 1986), 125–30; Neil Larry Shumsky, *The Evolution of Political Protest*

and the Workingmen's Party of California (Columbus: Ohio State University Press, 1991); Philip J. Ethington, *The Public City: The Political Construction of Urban Life in San Francisco, 1850–1900* (New York: Cambridge University Press, 1994), 265–82.

41 C. C. O'Donnell, *Address Delivered by Dr. C. C. O'Donnell, the President of the Fourth Ward Anti-Coolie Club* (San Francisco, 1876), 1; *Chinese Immigration,* 2nd ed., 6; G. B. Densmore, *The Chinese in California: Description of Chinese Life in San Francisco* (San Francisco: Pettit & Russ, 1880), 61; "The 'Christian Advocate' on Chinese," unknown newspaper, n.d. [1878], vol. 1, p. 10, scrapbooks on Chinese immigration, 1877–93, BL.

42 San Francisco *Daily Examiner,* 20 February 1879, 2; San Francisco *Daily Morning Call,* 30 October 1877, 2; Edward P. Baker, *Discourse Delivered in the Congregational Church, Fifteenth Street, October 22, 1877* (San Francisco: Mission Local Print, 1878), 10.

43 "Some of the Lies They Circulate," unknown newspaper, n.d. [1878], vol. 3, p. 85; "A Clergyman on the Chinese," unknown newspaper, n.d. [1878], vol. 3, p. 69, scrapbooks on Chinese immigration, 1877–93, BL; Henry Grimm, *The Chinese Must Go: A Farce in Four Acts* (San Francisco: A. L. Bancroft, 1879), 14. See also the Deacon Spud character in Atwell Whitney, *Almond-Eyed: A Story of the Day* (San Francisco: A. L. Bancroft, 1878); and the Serpent-Doves in Iota, *The Raid of the Dragons into Eagle-Land: A Plague(y) Pamphlet* (San Francisco: Mission Mirror Job Printing Office, 1878).

44 San Francisco *Chronicle,* 25 February 1877, 6; New York *Christian Advocate,* 24 January 1878, 53; 24 March 1880, 4.

45 *Debates and Proceedings of the Constitutional Convention of the State of California,* 3 vols. (Sacramento, Calif.: State Office, 1880–81), 1:633, 2:648.

46 Ibid., 3:1238.

47 Ibid., 1:637, 2:650; San Francisco *Argonaut,* 27 October 1877, 4.

48 A. W. Loomis, "Annual Report of the Mission of the Presbyterian Board of Foreign Missions to the Chinese in California," n.d. [1877], folder 4, box 45, PCUSA-BFMSF, 1829–95; Sarah E. Crenshaw, "California Housekeepers and Chinese Servants," *Scribner's Monthly* 12 (1876): 741; Jesse Wood to William Pond, 28 December 1877, AMAR.

49 William Pond to Executive Committee, American Missionary Association, 28 August 1878; M. H. Savage to M. E. Strieby, 13 March 1876, AMAR.

50 San Francisco *Evangel,* 7 December 1876, 1; 16 August 1877, 4; 15 November 1877, 4; 22 November 1877, 4; San Francisco *Daily Morning Call,* 19 November 1877, 1; "Kalloch on the Evangelization of the Chinese," unknown newspaper, n.d. [1877], vol. 3, p. 20, scrapbooks on Chinese immigration, 1877–93, BL; *Annual Report of the American Baptist Home Mission Society* (New York: American Baptist Home Mission Society, 1878), 38; M. M. Marberry, *The Golden Voice: A Biography of Isaac Kalloch* (New York: Farrar, Straus, 1947).

51 San Francisco *Chronicle,* 14 January 1878, 3; San Francisco *Daily Alta California,* 10 July 1878, 1; *Denis Kearney and His Relations to the Workingmen's Party of California* (San Francisco: Faulker & Fish, 1879), 11, 20; Theodore H.

Hittell, *History of California*, vol. 4 (San Francisco: N. J. Stone, 1897), 608; Marberry, *The Golden Voice*, 234–38; Shumsky, *The Evolution of Political Protest*, 202–3.

52   San Francisco *Evangel*, 10 January 1879, 8; 31 January 1879, 8.

53   San Francisco *California Christian Advocate*, 8 November 1877, 4; New York *Christian Advocate*, 11 March 1880, 161.

54   San Francisco *Daily Alta California*, 26 July 1877, 1; 9 April 1878, 1; San Francisco *Daily Examiner*, 12 November 1877, 3; San Francisco *Monitor and Guardian*, 3 November 1877, 4.

55   San Francisco *Daily Alta California*, 26 July 1877, 1; San Francisco *Monitor and Guardian*, 8 April 1876, 4; 4 January 1878, 4; San Francisco *Chronicle*, 8 April 1878, 3; 10 April 1878, 3; 12 April 1878, 3; 28 February 1879, 2.

56   San Francisco *Pacific Appeal*, 1 December 1877, 4; 8 December 1877, 4; 30 November 1878, 4; 15 March 1879, 4; 28 February 1880, 3.

57   David R. Roediger, *The Wages of Whiteness: Race and the Making of the American Working Class*, rev. ed. (London: Verso, 1991); Noel Ignatiev, *How the Irish Became White* (New York: Routledge, 1995).

58   J. H. Shimmons, *The Shame and Scourge of San Francisco, or, An Expose of the Rev. Isaac S. Kalloch* (San Francisco, 1880), 100; San Francisco *Chronicle*, 22 August 1879, 2–3; Irving McKee, "The Shooting of Charles de Young," *Pacific Historical Review* 16 (1947): 271–84; Shumsky, *The Evolution of Political Protest*, 185–92.

59   *Chinatown Declared a Nuisance!* (San Francisco: San Francisco Board of Health, 1880), 11, 14.

60   San Francisco *Chronicle*, 8 September 1879, 2.

61   Boston *Congregationalist*, 26 September 1877, 308; 10 October 1877, 322; 9 October 1878, 324; 30 October 1878, 348; 26 February 1879, 66; 31 March 1880, 100; New York *Christian Advocate*, 27 December 1877, 829; Philadelphia *Presbyterian*, 20 November 1875, 8–9; 29 March 1879, 8; 22 April 1882, 10. An exception to such sentiments was David N. Utter, "'The Chinese Must Go,'" *Unitarian Review and Religious Magazine* 12 (1879): 48–56.

62   New York *California Christian Advocate*, 7 February 1878, 88; San Francisco *Pacific*, 2 July 1879, 4; Boston *Congregationalist*, 10 September 1879, 289; 24 September 1879, 306.

63   Boston *Congregationalist*, 8 January 1879, 10; 24 September 1879, 306; San Francisco *Chronicle*, 10 July 1876, 2; 8 September 1879, 2; San Francisco *Pacific*, 26 March 1879, 4; 9 April 1879, 1.

64   *Investigation by a Select Committee of the House of Representatives Relative to the Causes of the General Depression in Labor and Business; and as to Chinese Immigration*, 10 December 1879, Congressional Serial Set vol. 1928, 46th Cong., 2nd Sess., Mis. Doc. 5 (Washington, D.C.: Government Printing Office, 1879), 264, 270, 354.

65   Ibid., 338, 339, 348, 347.

66   Ibid., 321, 322, 324; see also Healy's later pamphlets opposing immigration restriction: Patrick J. Healy, *Reasons for Non-Exclusion, with Comments on the Exclusion Convention* (San Francisco, 1902); Healy, *Some Reasons Why an Exclusion Act Should Not Be Passed* (San Francisco, 1902); Healy and Ng Poon Chew, *A Statement for Non-Exclusion* (San Francisco, 1905).

67   Augustus Layres, *Facts upon the Other Side of the Chinese Question* (San Francisco, 1876); Layres, *Both Sides of the Chinese Question* (San Francisco: A. F. Woodbridge, 1877); Layres, *Evidence of Public Opinion on the Pacific Coast in Favor of Chinese Immigration* (San Francisco: Friends of Truth, Right, and Justice, 1879); Layres, *The Pro-Chinese Minority of California to the American People, President, and Congress* (San Francisco, 1879); San Francisco *Chinese Record,* 12 February 1877, 4; 12 March 1877, 4; 21 May 1877, 4.

68   New York *Daily Tribune,* 25 February 1879, 1; Joaquin Miller, *Life Amongst the Modocs: Unwritten History* (London: Richard Bentley and Son, 1873), 267–68.

69   *Proceedings at the Organization of the California Chinese Mission, October 7th, 1875* (San Francisco: Cubery, 1875), 13; Wesley Stephen Woo, "Protestant Work among the Chinese in the San Francisco Bay Area, 1850–1920" (PhD diss., Graduate Theological Union, 1984), 227–40; Russell G. Moy, "Resident Aliens of the Diaspora: 1 Peter and Chinese Protestants in San Francisco," *Semeia* 90–91 (2002): 51–67.

70   J. G. Kerr, *The Chinese Question Analyzed* (San Francisco, 1877); "Petition to the Legislature of California," trans. J. G. Kerr, n.d. [1878], BL.

71   J. G. Kerr to John C. Lowrie, 19 October 1877; J. G. Kerr to John C. Lowrie, 10 December 1877, folder 5; J. G. Kerr to John C. Lowrie, 29 May 1878, folder 6, box 45, PCUSA-BFMSF, 1829–95; O. Gibson, *The Chinese in America* (Cincinnati: Hitchcock & Walden, 1877), 192–93; San Francisco *Chronicle,* 4 August 1878, 8.

72   J. C. Nevin to J. G. Kerr, 10 July 1878, folder 6, box 45, PCUSA-BFMSF, 1829–95.

73   Albert Williams to John C. Lowrie, 24 September 1878, folder 2, box 34; Mrs. M. A. Knox to John C. Lowrie, 13 August 1878, folder 6, box 45, PCUSA-BFMSF, 1829–95.

74   Members of the Presbyterian mission in San Francisco to John C. Lowrie, 25 July 1878, folder 6, box 45, PCUSA-BFMSF, 1829–95.

75   A. W. Loomis, "Annual report for San Francisco mission for 1878," 1878; A. W. Loomis to John C. Lowrie, 5 November 1878, folder 6, box 45, PCUSA-BFMSF, 1829–95.

76   San Francisco *Chinese Record,* 30 June 1877, 2; Chicago *Times,* 28 October 1879, 8.

77   Chicago *Daily Tribune,* 6 March 1879, 2; 24 March 1879, 5; Sacramento *Daily Record-Union,* 18 March 1879, 2; 19 March 1979, 3; 24 March 1979, 2; San Francisco *Chronicle,* 19 March 1979, 2; New York *Times,* 19 March 1879, 5; San Francisco *Daily Alta California,* 13 December 1879, 1.

78   *American Missionary,* October 1880, 311; September 1880, 280.

79   San Francisco *California Christian Advocate,* 13 November 1879, 1; San Francisco *News Letter and California Advertiser,* 26 November 1881.

80   *Chinese Immigration,* 2nd ed., 138–39; New York *Times,* 27 February 1879, 5; San Francisco *Daily Alta California,* 28 February 1879, 1.

81   Albert Williams, *A Pioneer Pastorate and Times* (San Francisco: Wallace & Hassett, 1879), 220.

CHAPTER SIX

1   45 Cong. Rec., 3rd Sess. 798–99 (28 January 1879).

2   45 Cong. Rec., 3rd Sess. 1266, 1269 (13 February 1879); 1302 (14 February 1879); Appendix, 60 (28 January 1879).

3   On the Reconstruction context of anti-Mormonism, see Sarah Barringer Gordon, *The Mormon Question: Polygamy and Constitutional Conflict in Nineteenth-Century America* (Chapel Hill: University of North Carolina Press, 2002), 119–25, 144–45; and David Prior, "Civilization, Republic, Nation: Contested Keywords, Northern Republicans, and the Forgotten Reconstruction of Mormon Utah," *Civil War History* 56 (2010): 283–310.

4   *Proceedings of the Republican National Convention* (Concord, N.H.: Republican Press Association, 1876), 57–58; 45 Cong. Rec., 3rd Sess. 1275 (13 February 1879); Shirley Hune, "Politics of Chinese Exclusion: Legislative-Executive Conflict, 1876–1882," *Amerasia* 9 (1982): 5–27; Andrew Gyory, *Closing the Gate: Race, Politics, and the Chinese Exclusion Act* (Chapel Hill: University of North Carolina Press, 1998); Najia Aarim-Heriot, *Chinese Immigrants, African Americans, and Racial Anxiety in the United States, 1848–82* (Urbana: University of Illinois Press, 2003), 196–214.

5   New York *Times,* 18 February 1879, 2; New York *Herald,* 23 February 1879, 13; New York *Independent,* 27 February 1879, 16; Philip Schaff, "Progress of Christianity in the United States of America," *Princeton Review* (July–December 1879): 251; Robert Seager II, "Some Denominational Reactions to Chinese Immigration to California," *Pacific Historical Review* 28 (1959): 60–63; James B. Bennett, *Religion and the Rise of Jim Crow in New Orleans* (Princeton, N.J.: Princeton University Press, 2005), 65–66.

6   Boston *Congregationalist,* 26 March 1879, 98; San Francisco *Chronicle,* 28 February 1879, 2; 8 September 1879, 2; New York *Daily Tribune,* 25 February 1879, 1.

7   45 Cong. Rec., 2nd Sess. 4341 (8 June 1878); 3rd Sess. 1266, 1302 (14 February 1879).

8   45 Cong. Rec., 3rd Sess. 2275–76 (1 March 1879); San Francisco *Chronicle,* 2 March 1879, 8; 4 March 1879, 3; 12 March 1879, 2; Ted C. Hinckley, "The Politics of Sinophobia: Garfield, the Morey Letter, and the Presidential Election of 1880," *Ohio History* 89 (1980): 381–99; Gyory, *Closing the Gate,* 187–211.

9   Augustus Layres, *The Pro-Chinese Minority of California to the American People, President, and Congress* (San Francisco, 1879); Boston *Congregationalist,* 24 March 1880, 89; *American Missionary,* December 1869, 280; "Report on Chinese Missions," 1879 folder, California Methodist Episcopal Conference Correspondence, 1855–1951, PSR.

10   San Francisco *Daily Alta California,* 4 May 1880, 1; 14 May 1880, 1; 17 May 1880, 1; Boston *Congregationalist,* 2 June 1880, 169; Philadelphia *Presbyterian,* 26 June 1880, 5; Oakland *Herald of Truth,* 15 May 1881, 73, 74, 76; 1 June 1881, 84; 15 June 1881, 92; 1 September 1881, 132; San Francisco *Daily Examiner,* 16 May 1881, 3.

11   The school question diminished in importance in the early 1880s, but California's Protestant leaders remained watchful of possible Catholic threats to the public schools; see, for example, San Francisco *California Christian Advocate,* 25 August 1880, 4.

12   George Montgomery to Alphonse Magnien, 23 February 1880, Correspondence of Archbishop Joseph S. Alemany, Archdiocese of San Francisco Archives, St. Patrick's Seminary, Menlo Park; San Francisco *Monitor,* 22 February 1882, 4; 8 March 1882, 4; 29 March 1882, 4; 19 April 1882, 4; 24 May 1882, 4; 19 July 1882, 5.

13   San Francisco *Monitor,* 28 September 1881, 4; San Francisco *Pacific,* 26 April 1882, 5; San Francisco *Daily Alta California,* 18 November 1883, 1; Thomas Denis McSweeney, *Cathedral on California Street: The Story of St. Mary's Cathedral, San Francisco, 1854–1891, and of Old St. Mary's a Paulist Church, 1894–1951* (Fresno, Calif.: Academy of California Church History, 1952).

14   O. Gibson, *"Chinaman or White Man, Which?": Reply to Father Buchard* (San Francisco: Alta California Printing House, 1873), 5; New York *Times,* 17 November 1874, 1; 43 Cong. Rec., 2nd Sess. Appendix, 41 (10 February 1875); O. Gibson, *The Chinese in America* (Cincinnati: Hitchcock & Walden, 1877), 373; *Report of the Joint Special Committee to Investigate Chinese Immigration,* 27 February 1877, Congressional Serial Set vol. 1734, 44th Cong., 2nd Sess., report 689 (Washington, D.C.: Government Printing Office, 1877), 398, 435; *Investigation by a Select Committee of the House of Representatives Relative to the Causes of the General Depression in Labor and Business; and as to Chinese Immigration,* 10 December 1879, Congressional Serial Set vol. 1928, 46th Cong., 2nd Sess., Mis. Doc. 5 (Washington, D.C.: Government Printing Office, 1879), 348.

15   Otis Gibson to Horace Davis, 2 April 1880, Chinese Immigration Pamphlets, vol. 2, no. 15, BL; New York *Christian Advocate,* 19 May 1881, 307.

16   San Francisco *California Christian Advocate,* 12 June 1873, 6.

17   San Francisco *California Christian Advocate,* 8 February 1882, 4; 8 March 1882, 4; Boston *Zion's Herald,* 12 April 1882, 1.

18   San Francisco *Pacific,* 26 April 1882, 4; 3 May 1882, 4; San Francisco *California Christian Advocate,* 8 March 1882, 4; 15 March 1882, 4.

19   San Francisco *California Christian Advocate,* 24 November 1881, 4; Boston *Zion's Herald,* 12 April 1882, 1.

20   San Francisco *Pacific,* 26 April 1882, 4; O. C. Wheeler, *The Chinese in America: A National Question* (Oakland, Calif.: Times Publishing, 1880), 11; San Francisco *Pacific,* 17 March 1880, 1.

21   New York *Christian Union,* 3 March 1880, 198.

22   San Francisco *California Christian Advocate,* 8 June 1881, 1.

23   New York *Christian Advocate,* 23 June 1881, 4; Gyory, *Closing the Gate,* 109–35.

24   *Annual Report of the American Baptist Home Mission Society* (New York: American Baptist Home Mission Society, 1882), 16; Oakland *Herald of Truth,* 15 June 1882, 92.

25   New York *Independent,* 9 March 1882, 16; New York *Christian Advocate,* 23 March 1882, 1; New York *Herald,* 27 March 1882, 8.

26   Philadelphia *Presbyterian,* 22 April 1882, 10; New York *Christian Advocate,* 23 March 1882, 1.

27   San Francisco *California Christian Advocate,* 29 March 1882, 2; San Francisco *Daily Alta California,* 4 March 1882, 2; Luther W. Spoehr, "Sambo and the Heathen Chinese: California's Racial Stereotypes in the Late 1870s," *Pacific Historical Review* 42 (1973): 185–204; Aarim-Heriot, *Chinese Immigrants, African Americans, and Racial Anxiety.*

28   47 Cong. Rec., 1st Sess. 1483 (28 February 1882); 1583 (3 March 1882); 1976 (16 March 1882); Appendix, 39 (16 March 1882).

29   47 Cong. Rec., 1st Sess. 1638 (6 March 1882); 1708 (8 March 1882).

30   47 Cong. Rec., 1st Sess. 1518, 1523 (1 March 1882); 1744 (9 March 1882).

31   47 Cong Rec., 1st Sess. 1546 (2 March 1882); 1981 (16 March 1882); 2134, 2131 (21 March 1882).

32   47 Cong. Rec., 1st Sess. 2042–43 (18 March 1882).

33   47 Cong. Rec., 1st Sess. 1753 (9 March 1882); 2227 (23 March 1882); 2972–74 (17 April 1882); 3412 (28 April 1882).

34   San Francisco *Chronicle,* 5 April 1882, 2; San Francisco *Daily Alta California,* 5 April 1882, 2.

35   San Francisco *Pacific,* 12 April 1882, 4.

36   John Eaton, *Are the Indians Dying Out?: Preliminary Observations Relating to Indian Civilization and Education* (Washington, D.C.: Government Printing Office, 1877).

37   John F. Miller, "Certain Phases of the Chinese Question," *The Californian: A Western Monthly Magazine* 1 (1880): 241.

38   *Supplement to the Codes and Statutes of the State of California,* ed. Theodore H. Hittell, vol. 3 (San Francisco: A. L. Bancroft, 1880), 209; Megumi Dick Osumi, "Asians and California's Anti-Miscegenation Laws," in *Asian and Pacific American Experiences: Women's Perspectives,* ed. Nobuya Tsuchida (Minneapolis: Asian/Pacific American Learning Resource Center and General College, University of Minnesota, 1982), 1–37; David Smits, "'Squaw Men,' 'Half-Breeds,' and Amalgamators: Late Nineteenth-Century

Anglo-American Attitudes Toward Indian-White Race-Mixing," *American Indian Culture and Research Journal* 15 (1991): 29–61; Peggy Pascoe, "Race, Gender, and Intercultural Relations: The Case of Interracial Marriage," *Frontiers: A Journal of Women's Studies* 21 (1991): 5–18; Peggy Pascoe, "Miscegenation Law, Court Cases, and Ideologies of 'Race' in Twentieth-Century America," *Journal of American History* 83 (1996): 44–69; María Raquél Casas, "'In Consideration of His Being Married to a Daughter of the Land': Interethnic Marriages in Alta California, 1825–1875" (PhD diss., Yale University, 1998); Karen Woods, "'A Wicked and Mischievous Connection': The Origins and Development of Indian-White Miscegenation Law," *Legal Studies Forum* 23 (1999): 37–70; Henry Yu, "Mixing Bodies and Cultures: The Meaning of America's Fascination with Sex between 'Orientals' and 'Whites,'" in *Sex, Love, Race: Crossing Boundaries in North American History,* ed. Martha Hodes (New York: New York University Press, 1999), 444–63; Deborah Moreno, "'Here the Society Is United': 'Respectable' Anglos and Intercultural Marriage in Pre-Gold Rush California," *California History* 80 (2001): 2–17; Margaret D. Jacobs, "The Eastmans and the Luhans: Interracial Marriage between White Women and Native American Men, 1875–1935," *Frontiers: A Journal of Women's Studies* 23 (2002): 29–54; Rachel F. Moran, *Interracial Intimacy: The Regulation of Race and Romance* (Chicago: University of Chicago Press, 2003), 17–60; Fay Botham, *Almighty God Created the Races: Christianity, Interracial Marriage, and American Law* (Chapel Hill: University of North Carolina Press, 2009); Peggy Pascoe, *What Comes Naturally: Miscegenation Law and the Making of Race in America* (New York: Oxford University Press, 2009), 84–85.

39   San Francisco *Pacific,* 22 March 1882, 4.

40   *Second Annual Address to the Public of the Lake Mohonk Conference* (Philadelphia: Indian Rights Association, 1884), 3–4; Henry E. Fritz, *The Movement for Indian Assimilation, 1860–1890* (Philadelphia: University of Pennsylvania Press, 1963), 198–221; Robert Winston Mardock, *The Reformers and the American Indian* (Columbia: University of Missouri Press, 1971), 192–228; Francis Paul Prucha, *American Indian Policy in Crisis: Christian Reformers and the Indian, 1865–1900* (Norman: University of Oklahoma Press, 1976), 227–64; Robert H. Keller Jr., *American Protestantism and United States Indian Policy, 1869–82* (Lincoln: University of Nebraska Press, 1983), 205–16; Frederick E. Hoxie, *A Final Promise: The Campaign to Assimilate the Indians, 1880–1920* (Lincoln: University of Nebraska Press, 1984), 1–81.

41   *American Missionary,* December 1885, 371; Prucha, *American Indian Policy in Crisis,* 265–327; Francis Paul Prucha, *The Churches and the Indian Schools, 1888–1912* (Lincoln: University of Nebraska Press, 1979); Robert A. Trennert, "Educating Indian Girls at Nonreservation Boarding Schools, 1878–1920," *Western Historical Quarterly* 13 (1982): 271–90; Frederick J. Stefon, "Richard Henry Pratt and His Indians," *Journal of Ethnic Studies* 15 (1987): 86–112; David Wallace Adams, *Education for Extinction: American Indians and the Boarding School Experience, 1875–1928* (Lawrence: University Press of Kansas, 1995); Clyde Ellis, *To Change Them Forever: Indian Education at the Rainy Mountain Boarding School, 1893–1920* (Norman: University

of Oklahoma Press, 1996); Amelia V. Katanski, *Learning to Write "Indian": The Boarding-School Experience and American Indian Literature* (Norman: University of Oklahoma Press, 2005); *Boarding School Blues: Revisiting American Indian Educational Experiences,* ed. Clifford E. Trafzer, Jean A. Keller, and Lorene Sisquoc (Lincoln: University of Nebraska Press, 2006).

42   San Francisco *Pacific,* 22 December 1886, 4; San Francisco *California Christian Advocate,* 15 January 1880, 4; San Francisco *Occident,* 3 February 1886, 1; 13 April 1887, 1.

43   San Francisco *Daily Alta California,* 8 April 1882, 2; San Francisco *Chronicle,* 7 December 1886, 4; 13 December 1886, 2.

44   Sherman Day, "Civilizing the Indians of California," *Overland Monthly* 2 (1883): 580; San Francisco *Occident,* 6 May 1885, 9; 4 November 1885, 4; Teresa Baksh McNeil, "St. Anthony's Indian School in San Diego, 1886–1907," *Journal of San Diego History* 34 (1988): 187–200; Margaret D. Jacobs, "Resistance to Rescue: The Indians of Bahapki and Mrs. Annie E. K. Bidwell," in *Writing the Range: Race, Class, and Culture in the Women's West,* ed. Elizabeth Jameson and Susan Armitage (Norman: University of Oklahoma Press, 1997), 230–51; R. Bruce Harley, "The Founding of St. Boniface Indian School, 1888–1890," *Southern California Quarterly* 81 (1999): 449–66.

45   H. B. Sheldon to Commissioner of Indian Affairs, 31 December 1877; 18 April 1878; 31 March 1879, letterbook dated 10/1/1877 to 6/10/1879, box 1, Records of the Round Valley Agency, RBIA-NARA-SB; *Annual Report of the Commissioner of Indian Affairs* (Washington, D.C.: Government Printing Office, 1878), 12; San Francisco *California Christian Advocate,* 24 April 1879, 6.

46   *Annual Report of the Commissioner of Indian Affairs* (Washington, D.C.: Government Printing Office, 1880), 10; H. B. Sheldon to Commissioner of Indian Affairs, 10 June 1882, letterbook dated 3/7/1882 to 10/30/1885, box 2, Records of the Round Valley Agency, RBIA-NARA-SB; G. B. Densmore, *The Chinese in California: Description of Chinese Life in San Francisco* (San Francisco: Pettit & Russ, 1880), 117.

47   H. B. Sheldon to Commissioner of Indian Affairs, 31 August 1881; 31 October 1881, letterbook dated 6/11/1879 to 2/28/82, box 1, Records of the Round Valley Agency, RBIA-NARA-SB; San Francisco *California Christian Advocate,* 14 December 1881, 4.

48   Mrs. M. L. Bryant to George Clifford, 21 January 1882; 7 March 1882; Anna S. Reasoner to George Clifford, 9 March 1882, 1882 folder, California Methodist Episcopal Conference Correspondence, 1855–1951, PSR; H. B. Sheldon to Commissioner of Indian Affairs, 10 June 1882, 12 April 1883; 1 May 1883; 16 May 1883; 30 July 1883, letterbook dated 3/7/1882 to 10/30/1885, box 2, Records of the Round Valley Agency, RBIA-NARA-SB; *Annual Report of the Commissioner of Indian Affairs* (Washington, D.C.: Government Printing Office, 1882), 15.

49   H. B. Sheldon to Commissioner of Indian Affairs, 31 March 1879, letterbook dated 10/1/1877 to 6/10/1879; H. B. Sheldon to Commissioner of Indian Affairs, 1 September 1879; 4 February 1881, letterbook dated 6/11/1879 to 2/28/1882, box 1, Records of the Round Valley Agency, RBIA-NARA-SB.

50   Ukiah City *Press*, 4 November 1881, 2; H. B. Sheldon to Commissioner of Indian Affairs, 10 June 1882; 1 August 1882; 28 October 1882, letterbook dated 3/7/1882 to 10/30/1885, box 2, Records of the Round Valley Agency, RBIA-NARA-SB; *Annual Report of the Commissioner of Indian Affairs* (Washington, D.C.: Government Printing Office, 1884), 16.

51   Ukie Indians to Chester A. Arthur, 31 January 1882, roll 24, M732, Interior Department Appointment Papers, RBIA-NARA-W; Round Valley Indian students to George Clifford, 6 January 1882; Round Valley Indian students to George Clifford, 7 February 1882, 1882 folder, California Methodist Episcopal Conference Correspondence, 1855–1951, PSR.

52   *Annual Report of the Commissioner of Indian Affairs* (Washington, D.C.: Government Printing Office, 1883), 18.

53   New York *Times*, 24 May 1883, 8; H. B. Sheldon to Commissioner of Indian Affairs, 1 June 1883; 2 July 1883; 24 July 1883, 21 July 1883; letterbook dated 3/7/1882 to 10/30/1885, box 2, Records of the Round Valley Agency, RBIA-NARA-SB.

54   H. B. Sheldon to Commissioner of Indian Affairs, 25 July 1883; 6 August 1883, letterbook dated 3/7/1882 to 10/30/1885, box 2; E. L. Stevens to H. B. Sheldon, 20 August 1883, "Telegrams from Comm., 1878–1897" folder, box 15, Records of the Round Valley Agency, RBIA-NARA-SB; M. L. Joslyn to R. V. Belt, 26 July 1883, roll 32, M606, Letters Sent by the Indian Division of the Office of the Secretary of the Interior, 1849–1903, RBIA-NARA-W.

55   Ukiah City *Press* undated clipping [ca. November 1883], enclosed in H. B. Sheldon to Commissioner of Indian Affairs, 7 December 1883, letterbook dated 3/7/1882 to 10/30/1885, box 2, Records of the Round Valley Agency, RBIA-NARA-SB.

56   H. B. Sheldon to Commissioner of Indian Affairs, 30 July 1883; 6 August 1883; 31 December 1883, letterbook dated 3/7/1882 to 10/30/1885, box 2, Records of the Round Valley Agency, RBIA-NARA-SB.

57   The tribal affiliations of John Duncan, John Munsell, Lieutenant Wilson, and Jack Melendy appear in a census conducted in April 1881; roll 5, M1791, Schedules of a Special Census of Indians, 1880, RBIA-NARA-W. Eben Tillotson does not appear in the census, but later in his life he served as an informer for anthropologist George M. Foster, who identified him as Yuki; see Walter Goldschmidt, George Foster, and Frank Essene, "The War Stories from Two Enemy Tribes: Yuki and Nomlaki," *Journal of American Folklore* 52 (1939): 141–54.

58   Round Valley Indian students to George Clifford, 6 January 1882; Round Valley Indian students to George Clifford, 7 February 1882, 1882 folder, California Methodist Episcopal Conference Correspondence, 1855–1951, PSR; John Munsell, deposition before R. V. Belt, 3 August 1883; John Duncan, deposition before R. V. Belt, 3 August 1883; Jack Melendy, deposition before R. V. Belt, 3 August 1883; R. V. Belt, "Report on the Burning of the Boarding-School Buildings on the Round Valley Indian Reservation," 20 August 1883, Letters Received, 1881–1907, 1883-#15372, RBIA-NARA-W.

234 Notes to pages 164–169

59 Henry B. Sheldon Trial Transcript and Documents, 1883, PSR; Louis A. Vawter to John F. Miller, 24 November 1883, roll 24, M732, Interior Department Appointment Papers; Louis A. Vawter to Hiram Price, 20 December 1883, item 57, entry 310, Irregularly Shaped Papers, RBIA-NARA-W. Coincidentally, Otis Gibson served as Sheldon's defense counsel in the Conference's trial; what Gibson thought of Sheldon's racial attitudes went unrecorded.

60 Paris H. Folsom to Hiram Price, 2 June 1884, in *Report (To Accompany Resolution of the Senate of July 4, 1884)*, 27 February 1885, Congressional Serial Set vol. 2274, 48th Cong., 2nd Sess., report 1522 (Washington, D.C.: Government Printing Office, 1885), 104, 106; depositions before Paris H. Folsom, 1884, item 57, entry 310, Irregularly Shaped Papers; Paris H. Folsom to Hiram Price, 5 May 1884, roll 24, M732, Interior Department Appointment Papers, RBIA-NARA-W; H. B. Sheldon to Commissioner of Indian Affairs, 1 May 1884, letterbook dated 3/7/1882 to 10/30/1885, box 2, Records of the Round Valley Agency, RBIA-NARA-SB.

61 *Annual Report of the Commissioner of Indian Affairs*, 1878, 12; *Annual Report of the Commissioner of Indian Affairs*, 1883, 18; *Report (To Accompany Resolution of the Senate of July 4, 1884)*, 51; see also *Annual Report of the Commissioner of Indian Affairs*, 1884, 16. As late as 1902, Sheldon continued to insist on this interpretation of the revival; H. B. Sheldon to C. V. Anthony, 4 February 1902, H. B. Sheldon Biographical File, PSR.

62 Ukiah City *Press*, 2 April 1880, 3; *Report (To Accompany Resolution of the Senate of July 4, 1884)*, 55, 58; W. E. Read to John F. Miller, 28 November 1883, roll 24, M732, Interior Department Appointment Papers, RBIA-NARA-W.

63 San Francisco *California Christian Advocate*, 27 October 1880, 6; 10 August 1881, 1.

64 *Report (To Accompany Resolution of the Senate of July 4, 1884)*, 54; Stephen Powers, "Centennial Mission to the Indians of Western Nevada and California," in *Annual Report of the Board of Regents of the Smithsonian Institution, Showing the Operations, Expenditures, and Condition of the Institution for the Year 1876* (Washington, D.C.: Government Printing Office, 1877), 456; H. B. Sheldon to Commissioner of Indian Affairs, 7 September 1878, letterbook dated 10/1/1877 to 6/10/1879, box 1, Records of the Round Valley Agency, RBIA-NARA-SB.

65 Round Valley Indians to Commissioner of Indian Affairs, 19 July 1885, Special Case 43, RBIA-NARA-W; D. S. Otis, *The Dawes Act and the Allotment of Indian Lands*, ed. Francis Paul Prucha (Norman: University of Oklahoma Press, 1973), 40–56.

66 *Report (To Accompany Resolution of the Senate of July 4, 1884)*, 7–8; Amelia S. Quinton, *Missionary Work of the Women's National Indian Association, and Letters of Missionaries* (Philadelphia: Women's National Indian Association, 1885), 17; *Annual Report of the Women's National Indian Association* (Philadelphia: Women's National Indian Association, 1886), 11. On the WNIA, see Valerie Sherer Mathes, "Nineteenth Century Women and Reform: The Women's National Indian Association," *American Indian Quarterly* 14

(1990): 1–18; and Jane E. Simonsen, "'Object Lessons': Domesticity and Display in Native American Assimilation," *American Studies* 43 (2002): 75–99.

67   *Message from the President of the United States, Transmitting a Communication from the Secretary of the Interior, Relative to the Allotment of Lands in Severalty to the Indians on the Round Valley Indian Reservation in California,* 5 January 1886, Congressional Serial Set vol. 2392, 49th Cong., 1st Sess., Ex. Doc. 21 (Washington, D.C.: Government Printing Office, 1886), 6–9; 49 Cong. Rec., 1st Sess. 699 (18 January 1886); Fritz, *The Movement for Indian Assimilation,* 206; Mardock, *The Reformers and the American Indian,* 211–13; Prucha, *American Indian Policy in Crisis,* 228–33.

68   46 Cong. Rec., 2nd Sess. 2060 (2 April 1880); 3rd Sess. 783 (20 January 1881).

69   49 Cong. Rec., 3rd Sess. 941 (26 January 1881); 1st Sess. 1632 (19 February 1886).

70   46 Cong. Rec., 2nd Sess. 2066 (2 April 1880); 2250, 2253 (9 April 1880).

71   46 Cong. Rec., 2nd Sess. 2066 (2 April 1880); 2196 (7 April 1880); 4258 (7 June 1880); 48 Cong. Rec., 2nd Sess. 867 (20 January 1885).

72   46 Cong. Rec., 2nd Sess. Appendix, 237 (9 June 1880); 3rd Sess. 879 (24 January 1881).

73   46 Cong. Rec., 2nd Sess. Appendix, 101 (3 April 1880); Appendix, 233 (1 June 1880); 3rd Sess. 876 (24 January 1881); 49 Cong. Rec., 2nd Sess. 191 (15 December 1886).

74   49 Cong. Rec., 1st Sess. 1632, 1634 (19 February 1886).

75   *The Statutes at Large of the United States of America,* vol. 24 (Washington, D.C.: Government Printing Office, 1887), 388–91.

76   Richard B. Drake, "Freedmen's Aid Societies and Sectional Compromise," *Journal of Southern History* 29 (1963): 175–86; Jacqueline Jones, *Soldiers of Light and Love: Northern Teachers and Georgia Blacks, 1865–1873* (Chapel Hill: University of North Carolina Press, 1980), 111; Joe M. Richardson, *Christian Reconstruction: The American Missionary Association and Southern Blacks, 1861–1890* (Athens: University of Georgia Press, 1986), 252–53; Karin L. Zipf, "'Among These American Heathens': Congregationalist Missionaries and African American Evangelicals during Reconstruction, 1865–1878," *North Carolina Historical Review* 74 (1997): 142–45.

EPILOGUE

1   San Francisco *Morning Call,* 18 August 1895, 16. Knapp borrowed her title from a line in Bret Harte's famous poem "Plain Language from Truthful James," *Overland Monthly* 5 (1870): 287–88; see Gary Scharnhorst, "'Ways that Are Dark': Appropriations of Bret Harte's 'Plain Language from Truthful James,'" *Nineteenth-Century Literature* 51 (1996): 396–98.

2   San Francisco *Pacific,* 28 April 1880, 4; San Francisco *Occident,* 19 August 1885, 9.

3   *Population of the United States in 1860* (Washington, D.C.: Government Printing Office, 1864), 28, 33; *Report on Population of the United States at the Eleventh Census: 1890* (Washington, D.C.: Government Printing Office, 1895), 399, 400.

4   San Francisco *Pacific,* 28 July 1886, 5; 4 November 1885, 4; 14 July 1886, 4; Charles D. Barrows, *The Expulsion of the Chinese: What Is a Reasonable Policy for the Times?* (San Francisco: Samuel Carson, 1886); Priscilla Frances Knuth, "Nativism in California, 1886–1897" (M.A. thesis, University of California, Berkeley, 1947); Brenda D. Frink, "'God Give Us Men!': Manliness, the American Protective Association, and Catholicism in San Francisco, 1893–1896," *Ex Post Facto: Journal of the History Students at San Francisco State University* 11 (2002): 49–64.

5   Josiah Strong, *Our Country: Its Possible Future and Its Present Crisis* (New York: Baker & Taylor, 1885), 149–52; Wendy J. Deichmann Edwards, "Forging an Ideology for American Missions: Josiah Strong and Manifest Destiny," in *North American Foreign Missions, 1810–1914: Theology, Theory, and Policy,* ed. Wilbert R. Shenk (Grand Rapids, Mich.: Eerdmans, 2004), 163–91.

6   Roger Daniels, *The Politics of Prejudice: The Anti-Japanese Movement in California and the Struggle for Japanese Exclusion* (Berkeley: University of California Press, 1962); Tomás Almaguer, *Racial Fault Lines: The Historical Origins of White Supremacy in California* (Berkeley: University of California Press, 1994), 183–204; Erika Lee, *At America's Gates: Chinese Immigration during the Exclusion Era, 1882–1943* (Chapel Hill: University of North Carolina Press, 2003), 32–33.

7   Ira Condit to A. L. Lindsley, 26 December 1884, folder 12; A. W. Loomis to F. F. Ellinwood, 12 October 1883, folder 10; March 1887, folder 16; 22 November 1887, folder 17, box 45, PCUSA-BFMSF, 1829–95; *Sixty-Eighth Annual Report of the Missionary Society of the Methodist Episcopal Church* (New York: Missionary Society, 1886), 299; *Report of the Chinese Mission to the California Conference of the Methodist Episcopal Church, for the Year Ending August 31st, 1890* (San Francisco: Cubery, 1890), 3–4; New York *Independent,* 28 December 1893, 1; *Abstract of Report of the Chinese Mission M. E. Church, California, 1892* (San Francisco: Cubery, 1892), 2.

8   San Francisco *Pacific,* 11 November 1885, 4; 10 February 1886, 4; Jean Pfaelzer, *Driven Out: The Forgotten War against Chinese Americans* (New York: Random House, 2007).

9   William Pond, sermon, 6 May 1876, box 8, William Pond Sermon Collection, United Church of Christ Archives, PSR; *American Missionary,* July 1885, 193; San Francisco *Pacific,* 21 April 1886, 4; 28 April 1886, 4; 5 May 1886, 4; 21 July 1886, 4; 4 August 1886, 4; 11 August 1886, 4; Charles S. Capp, *The Church and Chinese Immigration* (San Francisco, 1890).

10   San Francisco *Monitor,* 21 March 1883, 5; 3 December 1884, 5; 24 February 1886, 4; 24 November 1886, 5; 9 January 1889, 4; San Francisco *Morning Call,* 29 March 1883, 3; *Proceedings and List of Delegates, California Chinese Exclusion Convention* (San Francisco: The Star Press, 1901), 105–6; Thomas Denis McSweeney, *Cathedral on California Street: The Story of St. Mary's*

Cathedral, San Francisco, 1854–1891, and of Old St. Mary's a Paulist Church, 1894–1951 (Fresno, Calif.: Academy of California Church History, 1952); Charles A. Donovan, "The Paulist Mission to the Chinese in San Francisco since 1903," *U.S. Catholic Historian* 18 (2000): 126–42; Ricky Manalo, "A History of Chinese Catholics in San Francisco and the Bay Area," in *Asian American Christianity Reader,* ed. Viji Nakka-Cammauf and Timothy Tseng (Castro Valley, Calif.: Institute for the Study of Asian American Christianity, 2009), 75–82.

11   Ah Ching was also known as Walter C. Young; *Journal of the Twenty-Ninth Annual Convention of the Protestant Episcopal Church in the Diocese of California* (San Francisco: Bacon, 1879), 24–25. Chinese Americans who became ministers in the 1880s and 1890s include Methodists Chan Hon Fan, Fong Sui, Jung Meng, and Lee Chin; Baptist Tong Keet Hing; Presbyterians Huie Kin, Kwan Loy, Ng Poon Chew, and Soo Hoo Nam Art; and Congregationalist Jee Gam. For brief and not entirely reliable biographies of these men, see Frederic J. Masters, "Can a Chinaman Become a Christian?," *Californian Illustrated Magazine* 2 (1892): 622–32; and Ira M. Condit, *The Chinaman as We See Him, and Fifty Years of Work for Him* (Chicago: Fleming H. Revell, 1900), 127–35.

12   E. H. Hyde to A. W. Loomis, 19 January 1885, folder 13, box 45, PCUSA-BFMSF, 1829–95, Presbyterian Historical Society, Philadelphia.

13   Portland *Morning Oregonian,* 25 February 1886, 5.

14   Ng Poon Chew, "The Chinese in San Francisco," in *The Pacific Coast Pulpit,* ed. D. Hanson Irwin (New York: F. H. Revell, 1893), 55; Ng Poon Chew Biographical File, San Francisco Theological Seminary, San Anselmo; Ng Poon Chew Collection, Ethnic Studies Library, University of California, Berkeley; Patrick J. Healy and Ng Poon Chew, *A Statement for Non-Exclusion* (San Francisco, 1905); Ng Poon Chew, *The Treatment of the Exempt Classes of Chinese in the United States: A Statement from the Chinese in America* (San Francisco, 1908).

15   San Francisco *Chronicle,* 20 September 1895, 2; San Francisco *Call,* 20 September 1895, 8; Jee Gam, "The Geary Act: From the Standpoint of a Christian Chinese," 1892, reprinted in *Chinese American Voices: From the Gold Rush to the Present,* ed. Judy Yung, Gordon H. Chang, and Him Mark Lai (Berkeley: University of California Press, 2006), 89; *American Missionary,* February 1902, 99–108; September 1887, 269–73; Yan Phou Lee, "Why I Am Not a Heathen: A Rejoinder to Wong Chin Foo," *North American Review* 143 (1887): 306–12; Yan Phou Lee, "The Chinese Must Stay," *North American Review* 148 (1889): 476–83.

16   *The Statutes of California Passed at the Eighteenth Session of the Legislature, 1869–1870* (Sacramento, Calif.: D. W. Gelwicks, 1870), 839; San Francisco *Daily Evening Bulletin,* 22 October 1884, 1; 15 January 1885, 1; Tape v. Hurley, 66 Cal. 473 (1885); San Francisco *Daily Alta California,* 16 April 1885, 1; Charles J. McClain, *In Search of Equality: The Chinese Struggle against Discrimination in Nineteenth-Century America* (Berkeley: University of California Press, 1994), 136–44; Mae M. Ngai, "History as Law and Life: *Tape v. Hurley* and the

Origins of the Chinese American Middle Class," in *Chinese Americans and the Politics of Race and Culture*, ed. Sucheng Chan and Madeline Y. Hsu (Philadelphia: Temple University Press, 2008), 62–90; Ngai, *The Lucky Ones: One Family and the Extraordinary Invention of Chinese America* (New York: Houghton Mifflin Harcourt, 2010).

17   San Francisco *Occident*, 20 May 1885, 11; Plessy v. Ferguson, 163 U.S. 537 (1896); Gabriel J. Chin, "The Plessy Myth: Justice Harlan and the Chinese Cases," *Iowa Law Review* 82 (1996): 151–82.

18   San Francisco *Morning Call*, 4 February 1885, 3.

19   San Francisco *Occident*, 28 September 1887, 1; 12 October 1887, 8.

20   D. S. Otis, *The Dawes Act and the Allotment of Indian Lands*, ed. Francis Paul Prucha (Norman: University of Oklahoma Press, 1973), 87–155; Frederick E. Hoxie, *A Final Promise: The Campaign to Assimilate the Indians, 1880–1920* (Lincoln: University of Nebraska Press, 1984), 147–87.

21   *Message from the President of the United States, Transmitting a Communication from the Secretary of the Interior, Submitting a Draught of a Bill "to Provide for the Reduction of the Round Valley Indian Reservation in the State of California, and for Other Purposes,"* 20 December 1889, Congressional Serial Set vol. 2741, 51st Cong., 1st Sess., Ex. Doc. No. 72 (Washington, D.C.: Government Printing Office, 1889), 2; *Annual Reports of the Department of the Interior for the Fiscal Year Ended June 30, 1897: Report of the Commissioner of Indian Affairs*, 1897, Congressional Serial Set vol. 3641, 55th Cong., 2nd Sess., doc. 5 (Washington, D.C.: Government Printing Office, 1897), 121; Jason Charles Newman, "'There Will Come a Day When White Men Will Not Rule Us,': The Round Valley Indian Tribe and Federal Indian Policy, 1856–1934" (PhD diss., University of California, Davis, 2004), 276–317; William J. Bauer Jr., *We Were All Like Migrant Workers Here: Work, Community, and Memory on California's Round Valley Reservation, 1850–1941* (Chapel Hill: University of North Carolina Press, 2009), 115–29.

22   C. E. Kelsey, *Report of the Special Agent for California Indians to the Commissioner of Indian Affairs* (Carlisle, Penn.: Indian School Print, 1906), 12–15; Brian Daniels, "'Finding a Home Place': The Dawes Act and the Landless Shasta Indians in Northern California" (paper presented at the American Society for Ethnohistory Annual Conference, Riverside, California, 2003); Khal Schneider, "Making Indian Land in the Allotment Era: Northern California's Indian Rancherias," *Western Historical Quarterly* 41 (2010): 429–50.

23   Cornelia Taber, *California and Her Indian Children* (San Jose, Calif.: Northern California Indian Association, 1911), 26; Warren K. Moorehead, *The American Indian in the United States: Period 1850–1914* (Andover, Mass.: Andover Press, 1914), 335–39; Mission Indian Federation constitution, ca. 1922, San Diego A-2-M Exhibits 73–116, Equity Case Files, Records of District Courts of the United States, Record Group 21, National Archives and Records Administration, Washington, D.C.; Valerie Sherer Mathes, *Helen Hunt Jackson and Her Indian Reform Legacy* (Austin: University of Texas Press, 1990); Cathleen D. Cahill, "Reassessing the Role of the 'Native Helper': Christian Indians and the Woman's National Indian Association" (paper presented at

the Women and American Religion: Reimagining the Past Conference, Martin Marty Center, University of Chicago, 2003); Timothy M. Wright, "'We Cast Our Lot with the Indians from that Day On': The California Indian Welfare Work of the Reverends Frederick G. Collett and Beryl Bishop-Collett, 1910 to 1914" (M.A. thesis, California State University, Sacramento, 2004); Heather Ponchetti Daly, "Fractured Relations at Home: The 1953 Termination Act's Effect on Tribal Relations Throughout Southern California Indian Country," *American Indian Quarterly* 33 (2009): 427–39.

24   New York *Christian Advocate*, 14 September 1893, 599; 27 September 1894, 630; 12 September 1895, 594; Boston *Zion's Herald*, 10 August 1898, 1021; Ukiah City *Republican Press*, 10 April 1896, 5.

25   James R. Barrett, "Americanization from the Bottom Up: Immigration and the Remaking of the Working Class in the United States, 1880–1930," *Journal of American History* 79 (1992): 996–1020; Gayle Gullett, "Women Progressives and the Politics of Americanization in California, 1915–1920," *Pacific Historical Review* 64 (1995): 71–94; Matt García, *A World of its Own: Race, Labor and Citrus in the Making of Greater Los Angeles, 1900–1970* (Chapel Hill: University of North Carolina Press, 2001), 65–69, 109–12; Frank Van Nuys, *Americanizing the West: Race, Immigrants, and Citizenship, 1890–1930* (Lawrence: University Press of Kansas, 2002); William Deverell, *Whitewashed Adobe: The Rise of Los Angeles and the Remaking of its Mexican Past* (Berkeley: University of California Press, 2004), 42–46; James R. Barrett and David R. Roediger, "The Irish and the 'Americanization' of the 'New Immigrants' in the Streets and in the Churches of the Urban United States, 1900–1930," *Journal of American Ethnic History* 24 (2005): 3–33; Andrew Theodore Urban, "Rooted in the Americanization Zeal: The San Francisco International Institute, Race, and Settlement Work, 1918–1939," *Chinese America: History and Perspectives* 21 (2007): 95–101.

26   Franz Boas, *The Mind of Primitive Man* (New York: Macmillan, 1911); George W. Stocking Jr., *Race, Culture, and Evolution: Essays in the History of Anthropology* (New York: Free Press, 1968); Carl N. Degler, *In Search of Human Nature: The Decline and Revival of Darwinism in American Social Thought* (New York: Oxford University Press, 1991); Lee D. Baker, *From Savage to Negro: Anthropology and the Construction of Race, 1896–1954* (Berkeley: University of California Press, 1998). Similarities between sociologists and Protestant missionaries are noted in Henry Yu, *Thinking Orientals: Migration, Contact, and Exoticism in Modern America* (New York: Oxford University Press, 2001), 19–30.

BIBLIOGRAPHY OF PRIMARY SOURCES

Manuscript Sources

Amistad Research Center, Tulane University, New Orleans
    American Missionary Association Records

Archdiocese of Los Angeles Archives, San Fernando Mission, Mission Hills
    Correspondence Files

Archdiocese of San Francisco Archives, St. Patrick's Seminary, Menlo Park
    Joseph S. Alemany Correspondence

The Bancroft Library, University of California, Berkeley
    Chinese Immigration Pamphlets
    Jeremiah Burke Sanderson Papers
    J. G. Kerr, trans. "Petition to the Legislature of California," n.d. [1878]
    Presbyterian Church in the U.S.A., Mission to the Chinese in California.
    "Form of Incorporation of the Chinese Mission for the State of California,
    under the Charge of the Rev. William Speer," 1852
    "The Reconstruction Policy of Congress, As Illustrated in California," 1867
    Scrapbooks on Chinese immigration, 1877–93
    Thomas Starr King Letters to Henry Whitney Bellows, 1858–63
    Mariano Guadalupe Vallejo. *Recuerdos históricos y personales tocante a la alta California*, 1874

Diocese of Sacramento Archive, Sacramento
    Correspondence Files

Ethnic Studies Library, University of California, Berkeley
    Ng Poon Chew Collection

Presbyterian Historical Society, Philadelphia
  Presbyterian Church U.S.A. Board of Foreign Missions Secretaries' Files, 1829–95
  Presbyterian Church U.S.A. Board of Foreign Missions Secretaries' Files, 1845–85

San Francisco Theological Seminary, San Anselmo
  Ng Poon Chew Biographical File

United Church of Christ Archives, Pacific School of Religion, Berkeley
  William C. Pond Sermon Collection

United Methodist Conference Archives, Pacific School of Religion, Berkeley
  Biographical Files
  California Annual Conference of the Methodist Episcopal Church. 1873–1923
  California Methodist Episcopal Conference Correspondence, 1855–1951
  Henry B. Sheldon Trial Transcript and Documents, 1883

United States National Archives and Records Administration, San Bruno
  Bureau of Indian Affairs, Record Group 75, Records of the Round Valley Agency and Heirship Examiner-At-Large (re. Round Valley)

United States National Archives and Records Administration, Washington, D.C.
  Bureau of Indian Affairs. Record Group 75, Interior Department Appointment Papers, California, 1849–1907, M732
  Bureau of Indian Affairs. Record Group 75, Irregularly Shaped Papers
  Bureau of Indian Affairs. Record Group 75, Letters Received, 1824–81, M234
  Bureau of Indian Affairs. Record Group 75, Letters Received, 1881–1907
  Bureau of Indian Affairs. Record Group 75, Letters Sent by the Indian Division of the Office of the Secretary of the Interior, 1849–1903, M606
  Bureau of Indian Affairs. Record Group 75, Special Case 43
  Bureau of Indian Affairs. Record Group 75, Schedules of a Special Census of Indians, 1880, M1791
  District Courts of the United States, Record Group 21, Equity Case Files

Periodicals

American Missionary (New York)
Annual Report of the American Baptist Home Mission Society (New York)
Annual Report of the Commissioner of Indian Affairs (Washington)
Annual Report of the Missionary Society of the Methodist Episcopal Church (New York)
Annual Report of the Presbyterian Board of Foreign Missions (New York)
Annual Report of the Women's National Indian Association (Philadelphia)
Atlantic Monthly (New York)

Boston *Congregationalist*
Boston *Zion's Herald*
California Annual Conference of the Methodist Episcopal Church (San Francisco)
The Californian: A Western Monthly Magazine (San Francisco)
Californian Illustrated Magazine (San Francisco)
Chicago *Daily Tribune*
Chicago *Times*
Congressional Globe (Washington)
Congressional Record (Washington)
Congressional Serial Set (Washington)
Grass Valley *Daily Union*
Harper's New Monthly Magazine (New York)
Harper's Weekly (New York)
Ladies' Repository (Cincinnati)
Mendocino *Beacon*
Mendocino *Democrat*
Mendocino *Dispatch Democrat*
Mendocino *Independent Dispatch*
Methodist Quarterly Review (New York)
The Nation (New York)
New York *Catholic World*
New York *Christian Advocate*
New York *Christian Union*
New York *Daily Tribune*
New York *Evangelist*
New York *Herald*
New York *Independent*
New York *Times*
North American Review (Boston)
Oakland *Alameda County Gazette*
Oakland *Herald of Truth*
Overland Monthly (San Francisco)
Philadelphia *Presbyterian*
Portland *Morning Oregonian*
Presbyterian Quarterly and Princeton Review (New York)
Sacramento *Daily Bee*
Sacramento *Daily Record-Union*
Sacramento *Daily Union*
Sacramento *State Capital Reporter*
San Diego *Union*
San Francisco *American Citizen*
San Francisco *Argonaut*
San Francisco *California Christian Advocate*
San Francisco *Catholic Guardian*
San Francisco *Chinese Record*
San Francisco *Daily Alta California*
San Francisco *Daily Evening Bulletin*

San Francisco *Daily Evening Post*
San Francisco *Daily Examiner*
San Francisco *Daily Morning Call*
San Francisco *Elevator*
San Francisco *Evangel*
San Francisco *Monitor*
San Francisco *Monitor and Guardian*
San Francisco *News Letter and California Advertiser*
San Francisco *Occident*
San Francisco *Oriental*
San Francisco *Pacific*
San Francisco *Pacific Appeal*
San Francisco *Pacific Churchman*
San Francisco *Pioneer*
San Francisco *Saturday Evening Mercury*
San Francisco *Thistleton's Illustrated Jolly Giant*
San Francisco *Wasp*
Santa Clara *Owl*
Scribner's Monthly (New York)
Sonoma *Democrat*
The Statutes of California (Sacramento)
Ukiah City *Press*
Ukiah City *Republican Press*
Unitarian Review and Religious Magazine (Boston)
Voice of Peace (San Francisco)

Pamphlets and Books

Abstract of Report of the Chinese Mission M. E. Church, California, 1892. San Francisco: Cubery, 1892.

Anthony, C. V. *Fifty Years of Methodism: A History of the Methodist Episcopal Church within the Bounds of the California Annual Conference from 1847 to 1897.* San Francisco: Methodist Book Concern, 1901.

Appendix to Journals of Senate and Assembly, of the Seventeenth Session of the Legislature of the State of California. Vol. 2. Sacramento, Calif., 1868.

Archbald, John. *On the Contact of Races: Considered Especially with Relation to the Chinese Question.* San Francisco: Towne & Bacon, 1860.

Baker, Edward P., Rev. *Discourse Delivered in the Congregational Church, Fifteenth Street, October 22, 1877.* San Francisco: Mission Local Print, 1878.

Barrows, Charles D. *The Expulsion of the Chinese: What Is a Reasonable Policy for the Times?* San Francisco: Samuel Carson, 1886.

Bates, George C. *Address of Geo. C. Bates, Esq., which He Was Prevented from Delivering at Sacramento, April 19th, 1856, by a Mob.* San Francisco, 1856.

Bennett, H. C. *Chinese Labor: A Lecture, Delivered before the San Francisco Mechanics' Institute.* San Francisco, 1870.

Boas, Franz. *The Mind of Primitive Man.* New York: Macmillan, 1911.

Brace, Charles Loring. *The New West: or, California in 1867–1868.* New York:
G. P. Putnam & Son; London: N. Trubner, 1869.

Brooks, Charles Wolcott. *Early Migrations: Origin of the Chinese Race.*
San Francisco: California Academy of Sciences, 1876.

Buchard, James. *The Inquisition: A Lecture by Rev. Father Buchard.* San Francisco:
San Francisco Monitor, 1873.

Bynum, Lindley, ed. "Los Angeles in 1854–5: The Diary of Rev. James Woods."
Historical Society of Southern California Quarterly 23 (1941): 65–86.

Capp, Charles S. *The Church and Chinese Immigration.* San Francisco, 1890.

Casserly, Eugene. *The Chinese Evil—Contracts for Servile Labor—Chinese
Immigration the Great Danger.* Washington, D.C.: Government Printing
Office, 1870.

———. *Speech of Hon. Eugene Casserly, on the Fifteenth Amendment, and the Labor
Question.* San Francisco, 1869.

Chinatown Declared a Nuisance! San Francisco: San Francisco Board of Health,
1880.

*Chinese Immigration: The Social, Moral, and Political Effect of Chinese
Immigration.* Sacramento, Calif.: State Printing Office, 1876. 2nd ed., 1878.

Condit, Ira M. *The Chinaman as We See Him, and Fifty Years of Work for Him.*
Chicago: Fleming H. Revell, 1900.

Conway, Moncure D. "Wendell Phillips." *Fortnightly Review* 14 (1870): 59–73.

Davis, Winfield J. *History of Political Conventions in California, 1849–1892.*
Sacramento, Calif.: California State Library, 1893.

Debates and Proceedings of the Constitutional Convention of the State of California.
3 vols. Sacramento: State Office, 1880–81.

Densmore, G. B. *The Chinese in California: Description of Chinese Life in San
Francisco.* San Francisco: Pettit & Russ, 1880.

Denis Kearney and His Relations to the Workingmen's Party of California. San
Francisco: Faulker & Fish, 1879.

Eaton, John. *Are the Indians Dying Out?: Preliminary Observations Relating to
Indian Civilization and Education.* Washington, D.C.: Government Printing
Office, 1877.

Evans, Albert S. *Á la California: Sketches of Life in the Golden State.* San Francisco:
A. L. Bancroft, 1873.

Fay, Caleb T. *Address Delivered Before Washington Council No. 1, Union League of
America.* San Francisco: Towne & Bacon, 1864.

Gibson, O. *"Chinaman or White Man, Which?": Reply to Father Buchard.*
San Francisco: Alta California Printing House, 1873.

———. *The Chinese in America.* Cincinnati, Ohio: Hitchcock & Walden, 1877.

Gorham, George C. *Speech Delivered by George C. Gorham of San Francisco, Union Nominee for Governor.* San Francisco: Union State Central Committee, 1867.

Grimm, Henry. *The Chinese Must Go: A Farce in Four Acts.* San Francisco: A. L. Bancroft, 1879.

Hager, John S. *Fifteenth Amendment to Constitution: Speech of Hon. John S. Hager, of San Francisco, in the Senate of California, January 28th, 1870.* Sacramento, Calif., 1870.

Harte, Bret. *San Francisco in 1866; Being Letters to the Springfield Republican.* George R. Stewart and Edwin S. Fussell, eds. San Francisco: Book Club of California, 1951.

Healy, Patrick J. *Reasons for Non-Exclusion, with Comments on the Exclusion Convention.* San Francisco: Printed for the Author, 1902.

————. *Some Reasons Why an Exclusion Act Should Not Be Passed.* San Francisco, 1902.

Healy, Patrick J., and Ng Poon Chew. *A Statement for Non-Exclusion.* San Francisco, 1905.

Higby, William. *Privileges and Immunities of Citizenship.* Washington, D.C.: Government Printing Office, 1866.

Hittell, Theodore H., ed. *Supplement to the Codes and Statutes of the State of California.* Vol. 3. San Francisco: A. L. Bancroft, 1880.

Hittell, Theodore H. *History of California.* Vol. 4. San Francisco: N. J. Stone, 1897.

Hopkins, Sarah Winnemucca. *Life Among the Piutes: Their Wrongs and Claims.* Mrs. Horace Mann, ed. Boston: Cupples, Upham, 1883.

Huie Kin. *Reminiscences.* Peiping, China: San Yu Press, 1932.

Iota. *The Raid of the Dragons into Eagle-Land: A Plague(y) Pamphlet.* San Francisco: Mission Mirror Job Printing Office, 1878.

Jee Gam. "The Geary Act: From the Standpoint of a Christian Chinese." In Judy Yung, Gordon H. Chang, and Him Mark Lai, eds., *Chinese American Voices: From the Gold Rush to the Present,* 86–90. Berkeley: University of California Press, 2006.

Journal of Proceedings of the Third Annual Convention of the Ministers and Lay Delegates of the African Methodist Episcopal Church. San Francisco: B. F. Sterett, 1863.

Journal of the Twenty-Ninth Annual Convention of the Protestant Episcopal Church in the Diocese of California. San Francisco: Bacon, 1879.

Kelsey, C. E. *Report of the Special Agent for California Indians to the Commissioner of Indian Affairs.* Carlisle, Penn.: Indian School Print, 1906.

Kerr, J. G. *The Chinese Question Analyzed.* San Francisco, 1877.

Kneeland, Samuel. *The Wonders of the Yosemite Valley, and of California.* 3rd ed. Boston: Alexander Moore, 1872.

Kwan Loy. "Rev. Kwan Loy: Autobiographical." In W. P. Bentley, ed., *Illustrious Chinese Christians*, 154–62. Cincinnati, Ohio: Standard Publishing, 1906.

Lai Chun-chuen. *Remarks of the Chinese Merchants of San Francisco, upon Governor Bigler's Message, and Some Common Objections.* San Francisco: Whitton, Towne, 1855.

Lai Yong, Yank Kay, A Yup, Lai Foon, and Chung Leong. *Chinese Question from a Chinese Standpoint.* Rev. O. Gibson, trans. San Francisco: Cubery, 1874.

Latham, Milton S. *Remarks of Hon. Milton S. Latham, of California, upon Slavery in the States and Territories.* Washington, D.C.: Government Printing Office, 1860.

Layres, Augustus. *Both Sides of the Chinese Question.* San Francisco: A. F. Woodbridge, 1877.

———. *Evidence of Public Opinion on the Pacific Coast in Favor of Chinese Immigration.* San Francisco: Friends of Truth, Right, and Justice, 1879.

———. *Facts upon the Other Side of the Chinese Question.* San Francisco, 1876.

———. *The Pro-Chinese Minority of California: To the American People, President, and Congress.* San Francisco, 1879.

Lincoln, Abraham. *Collected Works.* Roy P. Basler, ed. 9 vols. New Brunswick, N.J.: Rutgers University Press, 1953–55.

Lobscheid, W. *The Chinese: What They Are, and What They Are Doing.* San Francisco: A. L. Bancroft, 1873.

Loomis, A. W., ed. *Confucius and the Chinese Classics: or, Readings in Chinese Literature.* San Francisco: A. Roman & Company, 1867.

Mast, Isaac. *The Gun, Rod, and Saddle; or, Nine Months in California.* Philadelphia: Methodist Episcopal Book and Publishing House, 1875.

Miller, Joaquin. *Life amongst the Modocs: Unwritten History.* London: Richard Bentley and Son, 1873.

Moorehead, Warren K. *The American Indian in the United States: Period 1850–1914.* Andover, Mass.: Andover Press, 1914.

Ng Poon Chew. "The Chinese in San Francisco." In D. Hanson Irwin, ed., *The Pacific Coast Pulpit,* 49–56. New York: F. H. Revell, 1893.

———. *The Treatment of the Exempt Classes of Chinese in the United States: A Statement from the Chinese in America.* San Francisco, 1908.

Nordhoff, Charles. *Northern California, Oregon, and the Sandwich Islands.* New York: Harper & Brothers, 1874.

Pacheco, Romualdo. *Remarks of Hon. Romualdo Pacheco, of California, in the House of Representatives, Saturday, March 18, 1882.* Washington, D.C.: Thomas McGill, 1882.

The Pacific Coast Pulpit, Containing Sermons by Prominent Preachers of San Francisco and Vicinity. San Francisco: Western Reporting and Publishing, 1875.

Pond, William C. *Gospel Pioneering: Reminiscences of Early Congregationalism in California, 1833–1920*. Oberlin, Ohio: News Printing, 1921.

Population of the United States in 1860. Washington, D.C.: Government Printing Office, 1864.

Powers, Stephen. "The California Aborigines." *Proceedings of the California Academy of Sciences* 5 (1873–74): 392–96.

———. "Centennial Mission to the Indians of Western Nevada and California." In *Annual Report of the Board of Regents of the Smithsonian Institution, Showing the Operations, Expenditures, and Condition of the Institution for the Year 1876*, 449–60. Washington, D.C.: Government Printing Office, 1877.

———. *Tribes of California*. Washington, D.C.: Department of the Interior, United States Geographical and Geological Survey, 1877.

Proceedings and List of Delegates, California Chinese Exclusion Convention. San Francisco: The Star Press, 1901.

Proceedings at the Organization of the California Chinese Mission, October 7th, 1875. San Francisco: Cubery, 1875.

Proceedings of the California State Convention of Colored Citizens. San Francisco: The Elevator, 1865.

Proceedings of the Republican National Convention. Concord, N.H.: Republican Press Association, 1876.

Report on Population of the United States at the Eleventh Census: 1890. Washington, D.C.: Government Printing Office, 1895.

O'Donnell, C. C. *Address Delivered by Dr. C. C. O'Donnell, the President of the Fourth Ward Anti-Coolie Club*. San Francisco, 1876.

Quigley, Hugh. *The Irish Race in California and on the Pacific Coast*. San Francisco: A. Roman & Company, 1878.

Quinton, Amelia S. *Missionary Work of the Women's National Indian Association, and Letters of Missionaries*. Philadelphia: Women's National Indian Association, 1885.

Report of the Chinese Mission to the California Conference of the Methodist Episcopal Church, for the Year Ending August 31st, 1890. San Francisco: Cubery, 1890.

Richardson, James D., ed. *A Compilation of the Messages and Papers of the Presidents, 1789–1897*. Washington, D.C.: Government Printing Office, 1896–99.

Riordan, Joseph W. *The First Half Century of St. Ignatius Church and College*. San Francisco: H. S. Crocker, 1905.

Sargent, Aaron A. *Chinese Immigration: Speech of Hon. A. A. Sargent, of California, in the Senate of the United States, March 7, 1878*. Washington, D.C.: Government Printing Office, 1878.

Second Annual Address to the Public of the Lake Mohonk Conference. Philadelphia: Indian Rights Association, 1884.

Shimmons, J. H. *The Shame and Scourge of San Francisco, or, An Expose of the Rev. Isaac S. Kalloch.* San Francisco, 1880.

Simmons, J. C. *The History of Southern Methodism on the Pacific Coast.* Nashville, Tenn.: Southern Methodist Publishing House, 1886.

Smet, Pierre-Jean de. *Western Missions and Missionaries: A Series of Letters.* New York: T. W. Strong, 1859.

Speer, William. *Answer to Objections to Chinese Testimony, and Appeal for their Protection by our Laws.* San Francisco: n.d.

———. *China and California: Their Relations, Past and Present.* San Francisco: Marvin & Hitchcock, 1853.

———. *An Humble Plea, Addressed to the Legislature of California, in Behalf of the Immigrants from the Empire of China to this State.* San Francisco: The Oriental, 1856.

———. *The Oldest and the Newest Empire: China and the United States.* Hartford, Conn.: S. S. Scranton; San Francisco: H. H. Bancroft, 1870.

The Spirit of Missions. New York: Board of Missions, Protestant Episcopal Church, 1870.

Stanly, Edward. *Speech of the Hon. Edward Stanly, Delivered at Sacramento, July 17th, 1857.* Sacramento, Calif., 1857.

Starr, M. B. *The Coming Struggle: or, What the People on the Pacific Coast Think of the Coolie Invasion.* San Francisco: Bacon, 1873.

The Statistics of the Population of the United States. Washington, D.C.: Government Printing Office, 1870.

The Statutes at Large of the United States of America. Vol. 24. Washington, D.C.: Government Printing Office, 1887.

Stout, Arthur B. *Chinese Immigration and the Physiological Causes of the Decay of a Nation.* San Francisco: Agnew & Deffebach, 1862.

Strong, Josiah. *Our Country: Its Possible Future and Its Present Crisis.* New York: Baker & Taylor, 1885.

Taber, Cornelia. *California and Her Indian Children.* San Jose, Calif.: Northern California Indian Association, 1911.

Thomas, Patrick J. *Our Centennial Memoir: Founding of the Missions.* San Francisco: P. J. Thomas, 1877.

Todd, John. *The Sunset Land; or, The Great Pacific Slope.* Boston: Lee and Shepard, 1870.

Walker, Francis A. *The Indian Question.* Boston: James R. Osgood, 1874.

Webster, Noah. *An American Dictionary of the English Language.* New York: Harper & Brothers, 1848.

West, H. J., ed. *The Chinese Invasion; Revealing the Habits, Manners, and Customs of the Chinese, Political, Social, and Religious, on the Pacific Coast.* San Francisco: Bacon, 1873.

Wheeler, O. C. *The Chinese in America: A National Question.* Oakland, Calif.: Times Publishing, 1880.

White, Katherine A., ed. *A Yankee Trader in the Gold Rush: The Letters of Franklin A. Buck.* Boston: Houghton Mifflin, 1930.

Whitney, Atwell. *Almond-Eyed: A Story of the Day.* San Francisco: A. L. Bancroft, 1878.

Williams, Albert. *A Pioneer Pastorate and Times.* San Francisco: Wallace & Hassett, 1879.

Williams, James. *Life and Adventures of James Williams, a Fugitive Slave.* San Francisco: Women's Union Print, 1873.

Wright, Richard R. *Centennial Encyclopaedia of the African Methodist Episcopal Church.* Philadelphia: Book Concern of the A.M.E. Church, 1916.

Zabriskie, James C. *Speech of Col. Jas. C. Zabriskie, on the Subject of Slavery.* Sacramento, Calif.: Democratic State Journal Office, 1856.

Acknowledgments

M
y interest in California history began inadvertently. I was a recent college grad with little direction and fewer job prospects
when I moved from Oregon to the San Francisco Bay Area in
1997 and somehow landed a position as a researcher for Heyday Books
in Berkeley. I spent almost every day of the next six months in the Bancroft Library at UC Berkeley reading firsthand accounts of the California
gold rush. It was a crash course in nineteenth-century California (and
United States and world) history that cultivated a fascination with the
subject that propelled me back to school, first to an M.A. program at San
Francisco State University and then to UCLA for a Ph.D. I thank Malcolm
Margolin for taking a chance on me back in 1997 and for all his encouragement in the years since. I also had the good fortune to work for
Richard J. Orsi and Marlene Smith-Baranzini on *California History* journal in the late 1990s, and I thank them for their friendship and editorial
training. My time at SFSU was personally and intellectually transforma-
tive due to the preparation and nurturing I received from Bill Bonds, Lynn
Bonfield, Scot Brown, Robert W. Cherny, Lee Davis, William Issel, Barbara Loomis, Susan Sherwood, Mark Sigmon, and the late Jules Tygiel.

At UCLA, my advisor Stephen Aron guided the dissertation that became this book through its twists and turns with patience and good humor.
His suggestions, comments, and corrections have improved every aspect
of this project. Thank you for everything, Steve! Henry Yu gave me much
of his time during the early formation of my research agenda, and I thank
him for his continuing support and advice. I'm grateful also for the help
and inspiration I received from committee members Joel Martin, Rudy
Busto, and Robin Derby. I have learned much about history and how to be
a historian from my cohort at UCLA—Rob Baker, Miguel Chavez, Matt
Goldsmith, Michael Hawkins, Natalie Joy, Deirdre Cooper Owens, Jeremy

Salfen, Jesse Schreier, Rebecca Sheehan, Citlali Sosa-Riddell, and Jakobi Williams—and I feel lucky to count them as friends and colleagues.

My two years teaching for the American Cultures Studies program at Loyola Marymount University provided an ideal climate to undertake book revisions and reimagining. Edward Park and Deena González served as wonderful mentors during that process, dispensing advice and good cheer in equal measure. In addition, I thank Karen Mary Davalos, Liz Faulkner, Brian Foster, Lisa Justine Hernandez, Joseph Jewell, Juan Mah y Busch, Victor Polanco, Nicolas Rosenthal, Ulli Ryder, and Jane Yamashiro for their help and example.

I made final revisions while at Indiana University, Bloomington, under the auspices of a New Faculty Fellowship from the American Council of Learned Societies. Numerous people at IU—especially Brandon Bayne, David Brakke, Joe Dodson, Constance Furey, Matthew Guterl, David Haberman, Sarah Imhoff, Sylvester Johnson, Michael McGerr, Eva Mroczek, John Nieto-Phillips, Eugene Park, Rich Phillips, Stephen Selka, Will Smith, Aaron Stalnaker, and Matthew Suriano—helped make Bloomington a friendly and productive place for me.

A great many librarians and archivists provided indispensable help. In particular, I thank Jeffrey Burns at St. Patrick's Seminary for telling me about Luciano Osuna and directing me toward Round Valley Indian Reservation. My thanks go also to Stephen Yale, United Methodist Archives, Pacific School of Religion; Kay Schellhase, United Church of Christ Archives, Pacific School of Religion; Francis J. Weber, Archdiocese of Los Angeles Archives; Michael Peterson, San Francisco Theological Seminary; John Hedger, National Archives and Records Administration in San Bruno; Mary Frances Morrow, National Archives and Records Administration in Washington, D.C.; Peter Blodgett, Huntington Library; Lucinda Glenn, Graduate Theological Union; Gary Kurutz, California History Room, California State Library; Betty Layton, American Baptist Historical Society; Marva Felchlin and Kim Walters, Autry National Center; William Breault, Diocese of Sacramento Archives; Kevin Newburg for his assistance photocopying materials at United Methodist Archives Center, Drew University; and the staffs of the Presbyterian Historical Society; Department of Special Collections, UCLA; San Francisco History Room, San Francisco Public Library; Bancroft Library, UC Berkeley; Ethnic Studies Library, UC Berkeley; Special Collections and University Archives, Marquette University; Department of Special Collections, Stanford University; Amistad Research Center, Tulane University; San Diego Historical Society; Southern Baptist Historical Library and Archives;

Division of Rare and Manuscript Collections, Cornell University; American Philosophical Society; and Mendocino County Historical Society.

The generous fellowships and grants that I received from the UCLA Department of History, UCLA Library, Autry National Center, Huntington Library, Presbyterian Historical Society, UCLA Institute of American Cultures, John and LaRee Caughey Foundation, Loyola Marymount University Center for the Study of Race and Ethnicity, and especially the American Council of Learned Societies truly made the completion of this book possible.

Numerous scholars gave me advice, comments on various chapters, or help finding primary sources. Besides many of the people already mentioned, my thanks go to Adam Arenson, Eric Avila, Edward J. Blum, Matthew Bokovoy, Robert Borneman, Anne S. Butler, Rogelio Casas, Lawrence Culver, Brian Daniels, Ellen DuBois, Michael Engh, John Mack Faragher, Janet Fireman, Brenda Frink, Joseph Genetin-Pilawa, Philip Goff, Erik Greenberg, Laurie Maffly-Kipp, Glenna Matthews, Ward McAfee, Gerald McKevitt, the late Melissa Meyer, Paul Reeve, Jan Reiff, Heather Cox Richardson, Virginia Scharff, Josh Sides, Stacey Smith, Jeff Staley, Josh Stein, Manu Vimalassery, Richard White, Tim Wright, and fellow participants in Western Historians Eating and Talking (WHEAT) at UCLA, the 2007 Autry National Center-Huntington Library-USC-Stanford University western history dissertation workshop, and the 2010–12 Young Scholars of American Religion program at IUPUI's Center for the Study of American Religion and Culture. Special thanks goes to Rose Marie Beebe for her timely translation of an important letter.

Thank you also to Western Histories series editor Bill Deverell for his support and advice, to editors Susan Green and Jean Patterson for all of their work, to the anonymous readers who provided detailed suggestions for the manuscript, and to everyone at the Huntington Library and the University of California Press who helped produce this book. A portion of this book was published in earlier form as "Anti-Catholicism and Race in Post-Civil-War San Francisco" in the *Pacific Historical Review* and is reprinted here by permission of University of California Press. I appreciate the insights provided by editors David A. Johnson, Carl Abbott, Susan Wladaver-Morgan, and their anonymous reviewers.

I'm so grateful for the love and support I've always received from my families: Dean, Jo, Paula, Bob, Emily, Leni, Wade, Judy, Jacob, and Joan. I wish my mom and stepfather were alive to read these words.

Finally, I'm happy to declare that this book simply wouldn't exist without my wife, Geneva. To her, and to Dorothy and Roy, I send my love.

Index

Page numbers in italic type refer to illustrated material.

A

Abbott, Granville, 150
abolitionism, 24–26, 124, 150–51
  in California, 13–14, 25
  in the Northeast, 1, 7, 13
  rhetoric of, 45, 70, 151
  See also slavery
Acts of the Apostles, 42, 122, 183, 202n15
Adams, J. Q., 181
adultery, 109, 124
African Americans, 3–4, 6, 69, 85, 137
  attempts to evangelize, 7, 44–45, 57
  attitudes toward Chinese, 20–21, 37,
    47–48, 126–27
  attitudes toward Indians, 20–21, 37, 48,
    171
  caricatures of, *83*, *140*
  in Chinese exclusion debates, 152–53
  Christianity of, 1, 3, 12–13, 15–16, 21, 153
  compared to Indians, 139, 172
  and "heathens," 12, 21, 25, 36, 49, 181
  marginalization of, 9, 12, 82, 173
  migration to California, 176
  and miscegenation, 129
  political rights of, 12, 14, 16, 42, 44, 58,
    150–51
  racism toward, 2, 17–19, 25, 27, 30, 46, 156
  segregation of, 47–48, 81, 180
  winning of male suffrage, 1–2, 7, 11–12,
    22–23, 25–26, 152
  and Workingmen's Party of California,
    126–27
  See also slavery

African Methodist Episcopal Church, 15,
  47–48
agriculture, 29, 64, 122, 166–67, 170, 181–82
  on individual Indian homesteads, 115, 157,
    160, 167, 181–82
  and support for Chinese immigration, 90
  training Indians for, 160, 162
  See also General Allotment Act of 1887;
    land ownership; Round Valley Indian
    Reservation
Ah Ching, 178, 237n11
alcohol, 16, 71, 83, 128–29
  and Indians, 67, 115, 181–82
Alemany, Joseph, 93, 94, 213n4
  attempts to evangelize the Chinese,
    85–86
  petition to evangelize at Round Valley,
    98–101
  portrait of, *145*
  relocation of San Francisco cathedral, 144
  support for Chinese exclusion, 126
  and Workingmen's Party of California,
    126
allotment. *See* General Allotment Act of
  1887
American Baptist Foreign Mission Society,
  44
American Baptist Home Mission Society,
  150
American Missionary Association, x, 44, 46,
  157
  attempts to evangelize the Chinese,
    35–36, 89, 119, 124
  and Round Valley Indian Reservation, 57,
    64, 68
American Party (Know Nothing Party), 79,
  126

post–Round Valley mission work of, 182–83
reforms at Round Valley by, 64–66
reliance on tribal networks, 159
resignation of, 110
Round Valley Indians' views of, 74–75, 99, 114
support for allotment, 116
use of corporal punishment by, 65, 69–71, 98
burial rites, 49, 62, 79, 110
Burlingame, Anson, 36
Burlingame Treaty, 36, 40, 45, 119, 128, 143, 146
Burnett, Mary A., 57, 64, 66, 109, 221n9
Burnett, Peter, 79

C
California
    Board of Land Commissioners, 2
    boarding schools, 158–64
    Constitution of 1879, 120, 122–23, 126
    in federal Reconstruction debates, 3, 6–7, 22–24
    and Fifteenth Amendment, 11–12, 16–17, 19, 22–23, 27, 30
    foreign miners tax, 28, 42
    gold rush, 15, 19, 45
    as mission field, 7–8, 31, 35–39, 57–58
    post-1870 racial politics in, 46–49, 59–60, 81, 120–22, 125, 141–43
    public school controversies in, 47–48, 78–82, 83, 84, 86, 144, 179–80
    racial oppression in, 2–3, 14, 28–30, 42, 177
    woman suffrage movement in, 24–25
California Workingmen's Party. See Workingmen's Party of California
Californios. See Mexican Americans
Call, Wilkinson, 152
Calpellas, 112–14, 169
Camp Wright, 64, 67, 72, 160
Canby, Edward, 60–63, 61
Canton (China), 131, 178
Cantonese, 39, 85
Captain Jack (Modoc), 60–61
Captain Jack (Pomo), 113
Carlisle Indian Industrial School, 157–58, 162
Casserly, Eugene, 19, 46, 59
Cathedral of Saint Mary of the Assumption (San Francisco), 144–45, 178

Catholics, 8, 24–25, 75, 79–80, 84–88, 98, 101, 146
    attitudes toward Indians, 93–96, 158
    burial rites of, 79
    Chinese evangelism by, 29, 78, 85–86, 144, 178
    compared to the Chinese, 82–84, 84, 89–90, 123, 129–30
    labor competition with the Chinese, 85–86
    opposition to Chinese immigration, 77–78, 85–87, 96–97, 126, 142–45, 178
    and peace policy, 93–102
    response to 1876 federal hearing, 91–92
    and Workingmen's Party of California, 120, 126–27
    See also anti-Catholicism; Franciscans; Irish Catholics; Jesuits; Mexican Americans
celebrations, 39, 55, 134, 136, 149
    Fourth of July, 16, 67, 107, 110–11
Chan Hon Fan, 149, 179, 237n11
Chan Pak Kwai, 55, 105–6
    anti-Catholicism of, 136
    lecture tour of Midwest, 105, 134
Che-Na-Ta-Da-La (Modoc), 60–61
Cheng Game, 55–56
Cherokees, 7, 168, 173
Chicago, 79, 134
Chico (California), 159
children
    African American, 47–48, 81, 127
    Chinese, 47–48, 82, 179–80
    Chinese imagined as, 37–39, 173, 176, 178
    Christian education of, 80–81
    Indian, 47–48, 82
    Indians imagined as, 68, 71, 97–98, 109, 173, 176
    Mexican, 158
    mixed-race, 91, 91
    at Round Valley Indian Reservation, 64, 67, 106–7, 114, 158–64, 167
    white, 49, 90, 167
China, 51–55, 87, 125, 130–33, 136, 146–49, 176
    allegiance to, 4, 83
    Catholic mission work in, 82, 85
    commerce with, 38
    customs of, 49, 146–47, 149
    Protestant mission work in, 31, 35, 39–40, 45, 82, 132–33, 148–49
    See also Burlingame Treaty; Chinese Americans; immigration

Praise for *American Heathens*

"A fresh analysis of something that we have never properly understood: California's critical place in the national struggle to define citizenship during the Reconstruction era. Paddison resurrects the forgotten campaigns of Protestant reformers to bring Indians and Chinese into the tent of American citizenship, campaigns which boldly asserted the value of human universalism over the doctrine of Christian white male supremacy. California was the worse for their failure, and so—Paddison suggests—was the nation. A superbly researched and wonderfully written study."

—Josh Sides, Whitsett Professor of California History,
California State University, Northridge

"Joshua Paddison 'went West' and struck gold. *American Heathens* is a must read not just for historians of race, religion, and Reconstruction, but also for anyone interested in the religious politics of multiculturalism. Widely and meticulously researched, Paddison's study helps demolish the assumption that Reconstruction was solely an East Coast, white-black affair. *American Heathens* is a triumph of insight."

—Edward J. Blum, San Diego State University;
author of *Jesus in Red, White, and Black:
The Son of God and the Saga of Race in America*

"Joshua Paddison's *American Heathens* tells us much about race and religion in California. More significantly, it places California and religion at the center of the national histories of Reconstruction and citizenship in the United States. It illustrates how competing visions of Christianity shaped formulations of race, and how religion influenced federal Indian policy. Its exploration of Chinese Christians and clergy is especially significant to Asian American history. Ultimately, *American Heathens* demonstrates American Christianity's 'potential to both fight and justify racism.'"

—Lawrence Culver, Utah State University;
author of *The Frontier of Leisure:
Southern California and the Shaping of Modern America*

"*American Heathens* is a groundbreaking book. Comfortably using the new methodological synthesis of social, cultural, and political history, Paddison sets out to reframe the standard narrative of Reconstruction, focusing our attention on California. The solutions forged in local public policy were, he contends, powerfully revealing of an emerging national consensus on immigration, citizenship, and race; they were also deeply structured by religion. In stressing these two contributions—the centrality of religion, and the need to re-read Reconstruction through the West—*American Heathens* is a powerful, impactful, re-orienting book. But beyond these major contributions, it is also just a great local history, consistently ribboned with quirky California details, and brought to life by a series of fascinating preachers, sojourners, and rabble-rousers."

—Matthew Pratt Guterl,
Rudy Professor of American Studies and History and
Chair, American Studies, Indiana University